General Finance Series

通用财经类系列

电子商务案例分析

(双语)

⊙ 王丹萍 编著

线上学习资料

復旦大學 出版社

内容提要

电子商务兴起于二十世纪九十年代中期，经过二十多年的发展已经形成了比较成熟的框架体系。近年来大数据、云计算、人工智能等新技术的问世和普及更是给电子商务的发展注入了新的活力。技术的成熟和经济的发展不仅促进了电子商务行业创新频现，也催生了一批极具代表性的电子商务企业。这些企业在经营过程中的经验和教训，未来发展中将面临的问题都值得深入分析和探讨。同时，这些企业来自不同的国家，用中英文双语研读它们的发展故事，不仅有利于归纳和总结电子商务企业经营和发展的规律，而且可以从中了解不同经济、文化和政治背景对电子商务发展的影响。

鉴于此，本书精选了三十个中外经典的电子商务案例，并以权威期刊、书籍、研究报告及网络资源为基础进行案例编写。通过对案例的介绍和分析，帮助读者理解电子商务的基本概念、原理、模式及发展趋势，了解当前电子商务领域最新的技术应用和管理理念。全书共分十章，覆盖了电子商务的商业模式、电子商务的基础架构、网络营销、电商监管与未来等四个主题。每章包括理论介绍、全英文案例及中文解析、案例分析方法指导。每个案例均附有单词解释和难点翻译，以帮助读者扫除语言障碍，更好地理解案例内容。除此之外，每章结尾均附有要点归纳和练习与思考，供读者复习巩固使用。本书旨在通过案例介绍和分析，帮助读者了解电子商务的基本理论，掌握案例分析的基本方法，并能将其应用于今后实际问题的分析与解决，从而促进读者专业知识、外语水平及能力素质的全面发展。

由于时间仓促，编者水平有限，书中难免存在不足之处，恳请广大读者批评指正，以帮助我们后续修正和完善。

目录
Contents

电·子·商·务·案·例·分·析

Part I E-Commerce Models
第一部分 电子商务模式

Chapter 1 Online Retailing 002
第一章 网上零售

Section 1 Online Retailing 003
第一节 网上零售

Section 2 Amazon—King of Online Retailing 005
第二节 亚马逊——网上零售之王

Section 3 Walmart—Retailing Giant Goes Online 015
第三节 沃尔玛——零售巨头迈向线上

Section 4 Taobao—Chinese C2C E-Commerce Leader 023
第四节 淘宝——中国C2C电商的领头羊

Section 5 Case & Case Analysis 032
第五节 案例与案例分析

Chapter 2 B2B E-Commerce 035
第二章 B2B电子商务

Section 1 B2B E-Commerce 036
第一节 B2B电子商务

Section 2 Alibaba—B2B from China to the World 038
第二节 阿里巴巴——从中国迈向世界的B2B

Section 3   IndiaMART—Working for SMEs   048
第三节   印度市场网——为中小企业工作

Section 4   Target Corporation—Retailer-Supplier Collaboration   054
第四节   塔吉特公司——零售商与供应商之间的协同

Section 5   Types of Case Analysis   061
第五节   案例分析的种类

Chapter 3 Emergences of New Models   064
第三章 新电商模式的兴起

Section 1   New E-Commerce Models   065
第一节   新电商模式

Section 2   Groupon—Integration of Online and Offline   066
第二节   团宝网——线上线下的整合

Section 3   Ctrip—Making Low-Cost Travel Possible   075
第三节   携程——让低成本旅游成为可能

Section 4   eBay—Offering the Affordable Auctions   084
第四节   易贝——提供老百姓用得起的拍卖

Section 5   Case Analysis Preparation   090
第五节   案例分析前的准备

Part II E-Commerce Infrastructures
第二部分 电子商务的基础架构

Chapter 4 Supply Chain and Logistics   094
第四章 供应链与物流

Section 1   Supply Chain and Logistics   095
第一节   供应链与物流

Section 2   Apple—Winner of "Best Supply Chain Management"   097
第二节   苹果——"最佳供应链管理"获得者

Section 3   Jingdong—Leading Logistics, Winning E-Market   106
第三节   京东商城——引领物流,赢得市场

Section 4   Yihaodian—Winning by Supply Chain   115
第四节   1号店——供应链致胜

Section 5   Case Analysis Methods   125
第五节   案例分析方法

Chapter 5   New Technologies Changing E-Commerce   128
第五章   改变电子商务的新技术

Section 1   New Technologies Changing E-Commerce   129
第一节   改变电子商务的新技术

Section 2   Cloud Computing—New Profit Engine of Amazon   132
第二节   云计算——亚马逊的利润新引擎

Section 3   Big Data—Power Source of Netflix   141
第三节   大数据——Netflix 的力量来源

Section 4   Autonavi—Building a New Portal of Mobile Life   148
第四节   高德——打造移动生活新门户

Section 5   Case Analysis Methodology—SWOT Analysis   154
第五节   案例分析方法解析——SWOT 分析法

Part III   Online Marketing
第三部分   网络营销

Chapter 6   Personalization & Customization   160
第六章   个性化与定制化

Section 1   Personalization and Customization   161
第一节   个性化与定制化

Section 2   LightInTheBox—Personalized Wedding Gown Services from China   163
第二节   兰亭集势——来自中国的定制婚纱服务

Section 3　Mogujie—Personalization Based on Online Community　　173
第三节　蘑菇街——基于网上社区的个性化

Section 4　NIKEiD—Customized Services　　179
第四节　NIKEiD——定制化服务

Section 5　Case Analysis Process　　188
第五节　案例分析流程

Chapter 7　Online Advertising　　191
第七章　网络广告

Section 1　Online Advertising　　192
第一节　网络广告

Section 2　Google Adwords—a Profit Source of Google　　194
第二节　竞价排名广告——谷歌的利润源泉

Section 3　The Vancl Style—Vancl's Online Advertising　　203
第三节　凡客体——凡客的在线广告

Section 4　Microblog Advertising—Xiaomi's Miracle　　213
第四节　微博广告——小米的奇迹

Section 5　Case Discussion　　221
第五节　案例讨论

Chapter 8　Interactions Between E-Commerce and Social Media　　224
第八章　电子商务与社交媒体的相互作用

Section 1　Interactions Between E-Commerce and Social Media　　225
第一节　电子商务与社交媒体的相互作用

Section 2　Facebook—From Social Media to Social Commerce　　228
第二节　脸谱网——从社交媒体到社交商务

Section 3　Tudou—Everyone Can Be a Director of Life　　238
第三节　土豆网——每个人都是生活的导演

Section 4 WeChat—Digging the Value of SNS 247
第四节 微信——挖掘社交网络服务的价值

Section 5 Case Presentation 258
第五节 案例分析演示

Part IV　Supervision and Future
第四部分　监管与未来

Chapter 9　Roles Government Should Play in E-Commerce 264
第九章　政府在电子商务中应该扮演的角色

Section 1 Government's Roles in E-Commerce 265
第一节 电子商务中政府的角色

Section 2 Battles Between Qihoo and Tencent 269
第二节 奇虎与腾讯之争

Section 3 What Does Price War Bring to Jingdong and Suning? 277
第三节 价格战为京东和苏宁带来了什么？

Section 4 Baidu's Copyright Dilemma 285
第四节 百度的版权困境

Section 5 Case Reports 292
第五节 如何写案例分析报告

Chapter 10　Where Is E-Commerce Going? 296
第十章　电子商务去向何方？

Section 1 Future of E-Commerce 297
第一节 电子商务的未来

Section 2 AliPay vs. WeChat Pay—Mobile Payment Influencing Financial Services 300
第二节 支付宝与微信支付——影响金融服务的移动支付

Section 3 Lvmama—Seizing the Long Tail of Online Travel Services 308
第三节 驴妈妈——抓住网上旅游服务的长尾

Section 4　The Uber Effect—Impacts of Mobile Apps　　　　　　　　315
　第四节　优步效应——移动应用的影响

Section 5　Case Analysis Methodology—Comparative Analysis　　324
　第五节　案例分析方法解析——比较分析法

Part I E-Commerce Models

第一部分 电子商务模式

Chapter 1 第一章   Online Retailing 网上零售

 Learning Objectives（学习目标）

After finishing this chapter, you should be able to:
1. Define online retailing (e-tailing) and describe its characteristics;
2. Differentiate e-tailing business models;
3. Identify the critical success factors of Amazon;
4. List the strengths and weaknesses of Walmart when it moved online;
5. Describe Taobao's strategies of market-entry and customer keeping;
6. Understand case and case analysis.

 Introduction（内容简介）

Online retailing, or e-tailing, is a pervasive e-commerce model. It is so close to the real life that many people begin their online shopping toddling with e-tailing. Along with the development of information technology and economy, consumers require more on the quality, efficiency and security of e-tailing. What kind of e-tailing model should be chosen? How to survive the fierce competition of e-tailing? The questions will be answered in this chapter.

Chapter 1 is composed of 5 sections. The brief introduction to e-tailing is made in section 1. Three e-tailing cases are explained respectively in section 2, 3, and 4. Section 5 focuses on the basic theories of case studies—cases and case method.

Section 1
Online Retailing
第一节 网上零售

▶ **Key Words**

1. retailing *n.* 零售
2. online retailing (e-tailing) *n.* 电子零售/网上零售
3. consumer *n.* 消费者

▶ **Definition of Online Retailing**

Online retailing, also called as electronic retailing or e-tailing, refers to the retailing wholly or partially conducted over the Internet. Generally, it includes B2C, C2C and other consumer-oriented business models.

▶ **Online Retailing Business Models**

Online retailing can be classified based on different criteria:

1. Classification by revenue model

Online retailing is categorized into four models based on its revenue source (Table 1-1). Classification by revenue model focuses on the primary revenue source of an e-tailer. For example, sales of goods is the Amazon's primary rather than the unique revenue source because it also gains revenues from other businesses such as cloud services.

Table 1-1　E-tailing Classification by Revenue Model

Variations	Description	Revenue Sources	Examples
Product/Services sales	Charge consumers directly for products or services offered	Sales of goods	Amazon.com
Content provider	Charge the monthly or annual fees for content or information offered	Subscription fees	WSJ.com
Transaction brokers	Make money by charging commission for enabling the transactions between sellers and buyers	Transaction fees (commission)	eBay.com

2. Classification by Distribution Channel[①]

---

① 埃弗瑞姆·特伯恩(Efraim Turban),戴维·金(David King)著,王健改编,《电子商务导论》,中国人民大学出版社,2006年。

1) Direct sale retailers. Manufacturers sell directly from company sites to individual customers, e. g. Dell.

2) Pure-play e-tailers. The retailer has no physical stores but an online sales presence by which the products or services are offered to consumers, e. g. Amazon.

3) Click-and-mortar retailers. Retailers own both the physical stores and the online offering channels.

▶ Characteristics of Successful E-tailing

1. High brand recognition. Brand recognition refers to the extent to which a brand is recognized for stated brand attributes or communications. The successful e-tailers usually have the high brand recognition like DangDang—the successful online bookstore in China. Particularly, in the fierce e-tailing competition, the high brand recognition enables the high consumers' stickiness since people always think of the brand name in decision-making.

2. Cooperating with the highly reliable or well-known vendors. Because e-tailers usually procure rather than produce the commodities, it is very important to ensure the quality of procurement. Cooperating with highly reliable vendors ensures not only the quality of the products but also the trust from the consumers. Particularly, for the new-entry e-tailers, cooperating with the vendors owning the good business reputation is an effective way to establish their own brand strengths in the short term.

3. Focusing on the offline services. As differentiation can hardly be implemented for the comprehensive e-tailers (e. g. online supermarket), the quality of offline services is a critical factor to improve customers' satisfaction. For example, Jingdong, a famous online supermarket in China, has been well-known due to its quick, professional and consistent quality delivery.

4. Furthermore, the successful click-and-mortar retailers can be characterized as:

1) Keeping the consistency between online and offline channels. A retailer should keep the consistency between online and offline. The product/service quality should also be kept consistent. The seamless integration of the two channels (online and offline) enables more conveniences and higher loyalty.

2) Offering powers to consumers. Empowering consumers is the core philosophy of online business models or self-services. The Internet enables consumers to complete most of the online shopping process such as browsing products, making the decision, paying for the products. A click-and-mortar retailer should design a friendly interface and provides the necessary supports such as payment system and after-sale system for the consumers so that they can shop comfortably each time.

3) Leveraging the channels. The successful click-and-mortar retailers are found to

own the capability of creating the optimized and value-added services for their customers by leveraging the two channels. Usually, these services are flexible and customer-oriented. For example, customers are allowed to freely return the items purchased online at the nearest physical store as well as order via the web at the physical store items unavailable there.

Section 2
Amazon—King of Online Retailing
第二节 亚马逊——网上零售之王

I Key Words

1. lamaster *n.* 逃兵
2. exotic *adj.* 异国的
3. reincorporate *vt.* 再合并
4. skeptics *n.* 怀疑论者
5. virtual *adj.* 虚拟的
6. affiliate *vt.* 使……加入
7. backlash *n./vt.* 抵制

II Case

About Jeff Bezos

Jeff Bezos (Figure 1-1), the CEO of the largest online bookstore—Amazon, was born in Albuquerque, New Mexico, U.S.A. He grew up in his grandparents' farm in Texas and showed his intense interests in science at an early age. After he graduated from Princeton University with a degree in computer science and electrical engineering, Jeff Bezos went to Wall Street and worked as an IT engineer. Due to the excellent performance in working, Jeff Bezos was promoted quickly and became a senior vice president. When his career looked bright, Jeff Bezos made a decision that changed his life as well as an industry—quitting from the highly-paid job and moved to Seattle in 1994 to found his own business. Seattle, a beautiful city

Figure 1-1　Jeff Bezos[①]

---

① http://www.Forbes.com

located in Washington State which was called "The High Tech Paradise" because some famous IT companies such as Microsoft headquartered there and provided the rich personnel.

After reading a report about the future of the Internet which projected annual web commerce growth at 2,300%, Bezos created a list of 20 products which could be marketed online. He narrowed the list to what he felt were the five most promising products: compact discs, computer hardware, computer software, videos, and books. Bezos finally decided that his new business would sell books online, due to the large world-wide demand for literature, the low price points for books, along with the huge number of titles available in print①. At this time, Seattle provided another benefit for Bezos' business—the famous book seller—Znhram located in the city and it could supply the resources needed by Bezos.

Foundation of Amazon

In July 1994, Jeff Bezos and his partners founded Amazon in his garage in Bellevue, Washington State. The initial team was composed of not only the IT experts (e.g. Jeff Bezos, lamaster of Microsoft) but also the Rock & Roll musicians. The small team looks unusual. However, it is the informal team that created a miracle of online retailing later.

When naming the website, Bezos decided to use a word beginning with "A" so that it would appear early in alphabetic order. Besides, Bezos thought that Amazon, a long-history river, is an "exotic and different" place just as he planned his store to be. Actually, Amazon originates from a warlike women tribe who lived in Asia Minor in Greek mythology. As time goes by, "Amazon" symbolizes courage and ambition. Naming this website as Amazon to some extent indicates Jeffrey Bezos's ambition to establish the kingdom of online retailing. Since 2000, Amazon's logotype has featured a curved arrow leading from A to Z, representing that they carry every product from A to Z, with the arrow shaped like a smile (Figure 1-2)②.

Figure 1-2　Amazon's Logo③

译 在为网站命名的时候,贝佐斯决定使用"A"字母开头的单词,只为能让企业信息排在电话黄页的前面,便于用户查找。最后采用"amazon"这个名字除了它能让人联想起古老而充满异国情调的亚马逊河之外,还因为它本身所代表的勇气和野心。

In July 1995, Amazon began service and sold its first book—Douglas Hofstadter's *Fluid Concepts and Creative Analogies: Computer Models of the Fundamental Mechanisms*

---

① http://en.wikipedia.org/wiki/Amazon.com
② http://en.wikipedia.org/wiki/Amazon.com
③ http://www.google.com

of Thought. In October 1995, Amazon announced itself to the public. In 1996, it was reincorporated in Delaware.

Business Models

Amazon employs a multi-level e-commerce strategy. Amazon started off by focusing on Business-to-Consumer relationships between itself and its customers, and Business-to-Business relationships between itself and its suppliers but it then moved to incorporate Customer-to-Business transactions as it realized the value of customer reviews as part of the product descriptions. It also facilitates customer to customer with the provision of the Amazon marketplace which act as an intermediary to facilitate consumer to consumer transactions. The company lets almost anyone sell almost anything using its platform. In addition to affiliate program that lets anybody post Amazon links and earn a commission on click through sales, there is a program which lets those affiliates build entire websites based on Amazon's platform.

Some other large e-commerce sellers use Amazon to sell their products in addition to selling them through their own websites. The sales are processed through Amazon and end up at individual sellers for processing and order fulfillment and Amazon leases space for these retailers. Small sellers of used and new goods go to Amazon Marketplace to offer goods at a fixed price. Amazon also employs the use of drop shippers or meta sellers. These are members or entities that advertise goods on Amazon who order these goods direct from other competing websites but usually from other Amazon members. These meta sellers may have millions of products listed, have large transaction numbers and are grouped alongside other less prolific members giving them credibility as just someone who has been in business for a long time. Markup is anywhere from 50% to 100% and sometimes more, these sellers maintain that items in stock when the opposite is true. As Amazon increases their dominance in the marketplace these drop shippers have become more and more commonplace in recent years. On November 3, 2015, this online retail giant opened the doors of its first brick and mortar store—Amazon Books, at University Village in Seattle[①]. This store benefits the residents who are unable to take advantage of Amazon's delivery service.

Financial Performance

Initially, Amazon chose a "slow growth" model which means there would be no profiting for four or five years. The business model was so unusual in the late 1990s that many stockholders complained about the company not reaching profitability fast enough to

---

① Alexandra Gibbs, Amazon's next chapter? Opening a physical bookstore, CNBC. com, 2015-11-03.

justify investing in or to even survive in the long term. When the Internet bubble burst at the start of the 21st Century, destroying many e-companies in the process, Amazon survived, and grew on past the bubble burst to become a huge player in online retailing. In the fourth quarter of 2001, Amazon announced its first profit— $5 million, on revenues of more than $1 billion. This profit margin, though extremely modest, proved to skeptics that Amazon's unconventional business model could succeed.

Compared to the physical bookstores and mail order catalogs, a remarkable strength of an online bookstore is the unlimited virtual warehouse. While the largest physical bookstores and mail order catalogs might offer 200,000 titles, an online bookstore could "carry" several times more. Amazon has been taking good advantage of the strength to provide the customers the high quality products with the low cost. The result is amazing:

Amazon's annual sales increased from $15.7 million in 1996 to $48 billion in 2011. And its forth quarterly sales increased from $12.95 billion in 2010 to $17.43 billion in 2011. Amazon issued its initial public offering of stock on May 15, 1997, trading under the NASDAQ stock exchange symbol AMZN, at a price of $18.00 per share. In July 2015, Amazon announced better-than-expected net income— $92 million—for the second quarter. That news boosted the stock considerably and made CEO Bezos the biggest gainer of the year. His fortune jumped $16.5 billion, pushing him into the top five of The Forbes 400.

Twenty years after its foundation, Amazon has become the largest online bookstore as well as the 3rd largest bookstore all over the whole world. What enables Amazon to outstand from the e-retailing industry with the fierce competition?

Critical Success Factors for Amazon

1. Easy browsing and searching Webpage. Amazon's website offers a variety of functionalities such as browsing and searching by which a customer can easily find the products needed. Amazon's web-design was so good that it became a good example of e-commerce web designing. The company also invested heavily in a massive amount of server capacity for its website, especially to handle the excessive traffic during the December Christmas holiday season.

2. Useful product information. When visiting Amazon.com, a customer can not only get access to the product information such as author and price quickly but also learn about the inventory and delivery time. Besides, Amazon allows users to submit reviews to the web page of each product. Reviewers may rate the product on a rating scale from one to five stars. Amazon provides a badging option for reviewers which indicates the real name of the reviewer (based on confirmation of a credit card account) or which indicates that the reviewer is one of the top reviewers by popularity. Customers may comment or vote on the

reviews, indicating whether or not they found it helpful to them. If a review is given enough "helpful" hits, it appears on the front page of the product. In 2010, Amazon was reported as being the largest single source of Internet consumer reviews. "Search Inside the Book" is another feature offering product information. It allows customers to search for keywords in the full text of many books in the catalog. The feature started with 120,000 titles (or 33 million pages of text) on October 23, 2003. There have been currently about 300,000 books in the program. Amazon has cooperated with around 130 publishers to allow users to perform these searches.

3. Low price. Low price is one of the obvious advantages of e-tailing. The low price should be attributed to two reasons: one is that e-tailing cuts off the intermediaries, which leads to the relatively lower price compared the traditional offline sales; the other is that the tax free policy exempts the sales taxes charging the consumers. A notable thing is how Amazon outstands from the fierce competition since low price is a universal strategy adopted by most e-tailers. Actually, the value-added products and services contribute much to Amazon's success.

4. Various marketplace services. After realizing the threats from the competitors like eBay, Amazon employed some new services such as online auction. Online auction is a useful experiment to satisfy different customers' need though it ended in failure. In addition, Amazon imported C2C by affiliating third-party sellers who are called associates. In 2008, about 40% of its sales derived from third-party sellers who sell products on Amazon. Associates are not only allowed to display and sell their products on Amazon but also receive a commission for referring customers to Amazon by placing links on their websites to Amazon, if the referral results in a sale. Worldwide, Amazon has over 900,000 members in its affiliate programs. According to W3Techs, the Amazon Affiliate Program is used by 1.2% of all websites, and it is the second most popular advertising network after Google Ads[①]. Unlike eBay, Amazon sellers do not have to maintain separate payment accounts since all payments are handled by Amazon. Associates can get access to the Amazon catalog directly on their websites by using Amazon Web Services (AWS) or XML service. A new affiliate product, aStore, allows associates to embed a subset of Amazon products within another website, or linked to another website. In June 2010, Amazon Seller Product Suggestions was launched to provide more transparency to sellers by recommending specific products to third-party sellers to sell on Amazon. Products suggested are based on customers' browsing history. The diversity of market services not only satisfies customers' demands but also enables the new profiting sources.

5. Outstanding Customer Relationship Management (CRM). "Earth's Most

---

① Usage of advertising networks for websites, W3Techs.com, 2014-07-22.

Customer-centric Company" has become the slogan of Amazon. Amazon has been emphasizing CRM. That is why Amazon's customers doubled during only nine month from 1998 to 1999 and its returning visitors contributed 72% to the quarterly sales in 1999. Amazon implements its CRM by the following measures:

1) Amazon Sales Rank (ASR) enables consumers to reach the most popular products quickly. ASR is a relative indicator of popularity that is updated hourly. Effectively, it is a "best sellers list" for the millions of products stocked by Amazon. Products that appear in the list enjoy additional exposure on the Amazon website, and this may lead to an increase in sales. In particular, products that experience large jumps (up or down) in their sales ranks may be included within Amazon's lists of "movers and shakers," and this also provides additional exposure that may lead to an increase in sales.

2) Highly automated and efficient back-end support. Amazon differentiates itself from the competitors by the high efficient delivery in the United States—Three Days Delivery. Moreover, it launched a new delivery program—One Hour Delivery. It even acquired a famous express mail company to hit the goal. Fulfillment centers are located in North America, Europe and Asia, often near airports. These centers also provide warehousing and order-fulfillment for third-party sellers. With this innovative program, a third-party seller can send inventory to an Amazon fulfillment center; when customers place orders, Amazon takes care of packing and shipping the products to their buyers. The customers can combine third-party seller products with Amazon items and receive Super Saving Shipping and other benefits, such as customer service and returns support directly from Amazon[1]. Warehouses are large and each has hundreds of employees. The employees are responsible for the basic tasks such as unpacking and inspecting incoming goods; placing goods in storage and recording their location; picking goods from their computer recorded locations to make up an individual shipment; and shipping. A central computer which records the location of goods and maps out routes for pickers plays a central role; the employees carry hand-held computers which communicate with the central computer and monitor their rate of progress. A picker with their cart may walk 10 or more miles a day[2]. To improve the working efficiency, Amazon began to adopt robot in its warehousing and order-fulfillment since July 2015.

3) Personalized services. Amazon has been utilizing cookie, a small piece of data sent from a website and stored in the user's web browser, to capture consumers' need. By virtue of cookie, Amazon records data on customers' behavior which enables it to offer or

---

[1] Amazon.com Warehousing and Delivery systems, https://ritalogisticsblog.wordpress.com/2010/05/14/amazon-com-warehousing-and-delivery-systems/, 2010-05-14.

[2] Amazon.com, https://en.wikipedia.org/wiki/Amazon.com

recommend an individual specific item, or bundles of items based upon preferences demonstrated through purchases or items visited. Though cookie has been proven an effective tool of personalization, the problems such as privacy intrusion cause the controversy.

6. The effective information management. The Linux-based technical infrastructure keeps Amazon running. As of 2005, Amazon had the world's three largest Linux databases. The central data warehouse of Amazon is made of 28 HP servers with four CPUs per node running Oracle database software. Amazon's technology architecture handles millions of back-end operations every day, as well as queries from more than half a million third-party sellers. Concerning the security due to hundreds of thousands of credit card numbers sent to Amazon's servers everyday, Amazon employs Netscape Secure Commerce Server using the Secure Socket Layer protocol which stores all credit card details in a separate database. The technical infrastructure with high efficiency and security helps Amazon to keep the high website visiting[①].

7. Expansion through business alliances. Amazon began the business alliances since 2001.

1) From 2001 to August 2011, Amazon operates retail websites for Target, Sears Canada, bebe Stores, Marks & Spencer, Mothercare and Lacoste. For a growing number of enterprise clients, Amazon provides a unified multichannel platform where a customer can interact with some people they call the retail website, standalone in-store terminals, or phone-based customer service agents. On October 18, 2011, Amazon announced a partnership with DC Comics for the exclusive digital rights to many popular comics, including Superman, Batman, Green Lantern, The Sandman, and Watchmen. The partnership caused well-known bookstores like Barnes & Noble to remove these titles from their shelves.

2) In November 2013, Amazon announced a partnership with the United States Postal Service to begin delivering orders on Sundays. The service, included with Amazon's standard shipping rates, initiated in metropolitan areas of Los Angeles and New York due to the high-volume and inability to deliver timely, with plans to expand into Dallas, Houston, New Orleans, and Phoenix by 2014.

3) In addition, Amazon owned some companies which operate on their own brand. Audible. com is a seller and producer of spoken audio entertainment, information, and educational programming on the Internet. Audible sells digital audiobooks, radio, and TV programs, and audio versions of magazines and newspapers. Through its production arm, Audible Studios, Audible has also become the world's largest producer of downloadable

---

① Julia Layton, How Amazon Works, https://money.howstuffworks.com/amazon1.htm.

audiobooks. On January 31, 2008 Amazon announced it would buy Audible for about $300 million. The deal closed in March 2008, and Audible became a subsidiary of Amazon.

8. Continuous innovations. Innovation is the source of sustainable development of an enterprise. Amazon has never halted innovation since it was founded.

1) One-Click order technology (One-Click Shopping). As long as you shop on Amazon once, all your order-related information such as your name, address and telephone number is stored by Amazon. Next time when you shop again, Amazon fills in your information above automatically and what you have to do is choosing the products you need. So many e-tailers simulated the technology that consumers today can easily benefit from it on almost all the retailing websites. However, in the late 1990s when the online retailing field was still "a desert of innovation", Amazon can be awarded as "The Pioneer" of online innovation due to the technology.

2) After realizing the huge potential of e-books, Amazon released its first e-book reader Kindle I in 2007 and released other Kindle products such as Kindle Fire. Amazon Kindle devices enable users to download, browse, and read e-books, newspapers, magazines, blogs, and other digital media via wireless networking. The hardware platform, developed by Amazon subsidiary Lab126, began as a single device and now comprises a range of devices, including dedicated e-readers with E-ink electronic paper displays, and Android-based tablets with color LCD screens. In 2013, Kindle announced its entry to Chinese market (Figure 1-3).

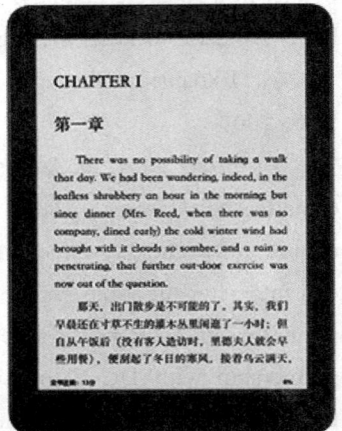

Figure 1-3　Kindle Sold in China[①]

3) Obviously, Amazon has never been satisfied with being only an e-tailer. It has been seeking a new role in the market. Today, it is a leading cloud computing service provider. Amazon Elastic Compute Cloud (EC2) is a central part of Amazon's cloud computing platform, Amazon Web Services (AWS). EC2 allows users to rent virtual computers on which to run their own computer applications. A user can create, launch, and terminate server instances as needed, paying by the hour for active servers, hence the term "elastic". Many businesses have benefited from EC2. For example, *The New York Times*, an influential newspaper chose EC2 when it planned to transform all the TIF data into PDF data. Compared to the traditional method estimated to cost a few months, it only spent 36 hours to achieve the goals. The powerful computing ability of cloud computing

---

① http://www.amazon.com.cn

enables the sharply reduced data transformation cost. Another similar example is from Eli Lilly & Co., a big medical company. Using EC2, Eli Lilly & Co., decreased the cost of data analysis to 89 U.S. dollar, which usually spent more than one million dollars before.

Challenges Encountered by Amazon[①]

Since its foundation, the company has attracted not only attention and praise but criticism and controversy from multiple sources over its actions. These include: luring customers away from the site's brick and mortar competitors, poor warehouse conditions for workers, anti-competitive actions, price discrimination, and so on.

In December 2011, Amazon faced backlash from businesses for running a one-day deal to promote its new Price Check app. Shoppers who used the app to check prices in a brick-and-mortar store were offered a 5% discount to purchase the same item from Amazon. The company also faced accusations of putting undue pressure on suppliers to maintain and extend its profitability. One effort to squeeze the most vulnerable book publishers was known within the company as the Gazelle Project, as Bezos suggested, "that Amazon should approach these small publishers the way a cheetah would pursue a sickly gazelle." In July 2014, the Federal Trade Commission launched a lawsuit against the company alleging it was promoting in-app purchases to children, which were being transacted without parental consent.

Barnes & Noble sued Amazon on May 12, 1997, alleging that Amazon's claim to be "the world's largest bookstore" was false. Barnes and Noble asserted, Amazon.com "isn't a bookstore at all. It's a book broker." The suit was later settled out of court, and Amazon continued to make the same claim. Walmart sued Amazon on October 16, 1998, alleging that Amazon stole their trade secrets by hiring former Walmart executives. Although this suit was also settled out of court, it caused Amazon to implement internal restrictions and the reassignment of the former Walmart executives.

Amazon also attracted widespread criticism by both current and former employees, as well as the media and politicians for poor working conditions. In 2011, it was publicized that at the Breinigsville, Pennsylvania warehouse, workers had to carry out work in 100°F (38℃) heat, resulting in employees becoming extremely uncomfortable and suffering from dehydration and collapse. Loading-bay doors were not opened to allow in fresh air as "managers were worried about theft". Amazon's initial response was to pay for an ambulance to sit outside on call to cart away overheated employees. *The New York Times* published a scathing story detailing the high-pressure, long-hour work environment inside the retailer. In a letter to employees in response, the *Washington Post* owner wrote that he

---

[①] http://en.wikipedia.org/wiki/Amazon.com

didn't recognize the company described but said that anyone working in the company like that "would be crazy to stay". In late July the company proposed a plan for high-speed-drone airspace that would enable flying robots to carry packages to consumers. Some workers, "pickers", who travel the building with a trolley and a handheld scanner "picking" customer orders can walk up to 15 miles a day back and forward, and if they fall behind on their targets, they can be reprimanded. The handheld scanners feed back to the employee real time information on how fast or slowly they are going, and also serve to allow Team Leads and Area Managers to track the specific locations of employees and how much "idle time" they gain when not working.

According to Sina, Amazon's net sales for the third fiscal quarter of 2014 was 20.579 billion dollars which increased by 20% compared to the same period in 2013. Its net deficit is 43.7 million dollars which is more than that of the same period last year[①].

Has Amazon succeeded? Some people say "Yes" while the others think its success has not been assured. Undoubtedly, Amazon has become the most recognized e-tailer worldwide after the 20 years of operation.

Case Analysis

作为全球知名的网上零售商,亚马逊因其快速的增长、杰出的业绩表现以及它与众不同的创立者——杰夫·贝佐斯(以下简称贝佐斯)而广受瞩目,贝佐斯本人也荣登2018年福布斯亿万富豪排行榜第一名[②]。尽管案例中介绍了贝佐斯本人的经历,但本案例的分析重点仍然应该放在亚马逊成功的关键因素,也就是"为什么"。

到底是什么导致了亚马逊的成功?这是一个甚至对贝佐斯本人而言也不易回答的问题。亚马逊设计良好,能帮助用户快速搜索及浏览信息的网站是第一原因。那么什么是设计得好的网站呢?其实并没有统一的标准,界面友好、信息详细都是考虑的因素。然而对于消费者而言,标准仅有一个:好用!在当年大多数人对于上网还很陌生的时候,亚马逊设计了关键词搜索、消费者评价以及作者信息链接等功能。这些精心设计的细节在今天看来已经司空见惯,然而却给当时初次体验网上购物的消费者留下深刻印象:在亚马逊购物与线下购物一样简单!消费者如何能拒绝这样轻松便利的购物方式呢?除此之外,亚马逊有效的客户关系管理也是促成它成功的重要原因之一:销量排名(ASR)不仅帮助顾客快速发现畅销商品,而且增加了商品的曝光度,反过来进一步提升销量;自动化高效的后台支持实现了快速准确的配送,令亚马逊在电商尚在萌芽的年代就抢先赢得了"电子商务的最后一公里";借助cookie为消费者推荐心仪的商品,尽管因为涉及顾客隐私而引起争议,但亚马逊基于对客户需求的精准捕捉实现个性化营销的理念却在今天的电子零售中备受推崇。第三个需要特别强调的原因是创新。亚

---

① 亚马逊公布第三季度财报同比亏损扩大,新浪科技,2014-10-24。
② https://www.forbes.com/profile/jeff-bezos/

马逊为什么能在竞争如此激烈的网上零售中保持旺盛的生命力？答案就是持续不断的创新。首先，亚马逊在电子商务技术尚不成熟的年代就模仿线下购物流程，推出了"一键式"技术，让顾客可以通过鼠标点击轻松实现从商品挑选到结账付款的流程，消除了上网新手的顾虑。其次，尽管卖纸质书起家，亚马逊却挑战自我，推出了电子图书阅读器——Kindle，让人们可以随时随地轻松享受阅读乐趣的同时也掀起了电子书的潮流。再次，亚马逊之所以成为全球知名的企业，是因为它从不满足于仅仅做一个网上零售商，而是积极向其他领域拓展。早在人们对云计算还仅仅停留在理论设想阶段的时候，亚马逊就已经开始了实践探索，并推出了 EC2 这一具有代表性的云服务，不仅大大提升了数据处理的效率，而且令亚马逊跻身全球顶尖云服务商之列。现在，亚马逊已经发展成为集零售、云计算、人工智能服务为一体的大型互联网企业。亚马逊成功的原因很多，归纳起来就是——以顾客为中心。自成立以来，亚马逊一直贯彻这一管理理念：无论是友好的网站设计和高效的后台支持，还是多样化的产品和服务以及持续不断的创新，永远将顾客放在首位。正因为如此，亚马逊赢得了客户，也赢得了市场。在亚马逊的成功因素中，低价并非最重要的因素，因为它在很大程度上是由电子商务本身的特性所决定的，是几乎所有网上零售的共性而非亚马逊独有的特性。这也从侧面说明，经营电子商务一味地追求低价并非长久之计。

最后需要强调的是，除了上述原因，机遇也是亚马逊的成功必不可少的一个因素。亚马逊成立之时电子商务正处于萌芽时期，线上零售几乎空白，而投资者们也青睐这种新的商业模式，这为它顺利进入市场奠定了基础。企业把握市场机遇的能力及其进入市场的时机非常重要，在变化快速且竞争激烈的电子商务行业尤其如此。而电商企业的领导者更是应该像"猎人紧盯猎物"一样随时关注市场动态，找准时机切入，并做好失败的准备。正如贝佐斯所说："失败是创新的一部分……与其追随潮流，不如投身于自己热爱的事业等潮流来追随你。"这是亚马逊提供的宝贵经验。

Section 3
Walmart—Retailing Giant Goes Online
第三节　沃尔玛——零售巨头迈向线上

Key Words

1. merchandise *vi.* 经商/*n.* 商品
2. affluent *adj.* 丰富的，富裕的
3. lead time 交付周期（订货至交货的时间）

Case

About Walmart[①]

In 1945, a businessman and former J. C. Penney employee, Sam Walton, purchased a branch of the Ben Franklin Stores from the Butler Brothers. His focus was on selling products at low prices to get higher-volume sales at a lower profit margin, portraying it as a crusade for the consumer. He was able to find lower-cost suppliers than the ones used by other stores and passed on the savings in the product pricing. Within the fifth year, the store made $250,000 in revenue. On July 2, 1962, Walton opened the first Walmart Discount City store at 719 W. Walnut Street in Rogers, Arkansas. Within its first 5 years, the company expanded to 24 stores across Arkansas and reached $12.6 million in sales. In 1968, it opened its first stores outside Arkansas, in Sikeston, Missouri and Claremore, Oklahoma.

The company was publicly listed on the New York Stock Exchange in 1972. In late 1980s and early 1990s, the company rose from a regional to national giant. By its 25th anniversary in 1987, there had been 1,198 stores with sales of $15.9 billion and 200,000 associates. This year also marked the completion of the company's satellite network, a $24 million investment linking all operating units of the company with its Bentonville office via two-way voice and data transmission and one-way video communication. At that time, it was the largest private satellite network, allowing the corporate office to track inventory and sales and to instantly communicate to stores.

In 1988, the first Walmart Supercenter was opened in Washington, Missouri. By 1988, Walmart had become the most profitable retailer in the U. S. and by October 1989 it had become the largest in terms of revenue. In July and October of 1990, it opened its first stores in California and Pennsylvania respectively. By mid-1990s, it had been far and away the most powerful retailer in the United States and expanded into Mexico in 1991 and Canada in 1994. It spreaded to other states like New England, Maryland, and Delaware, Vermont being the last state to get a store in 1995. In the same year, its online store was opened.

In 1998, Walmart introduced the "Neighborhood Market" concept with three stores in Arkansas, which is a chain of grocery stores that average about 38,000 square feet. They are used to fill the gap between discount store and supercenters, offering a variety of products, including full lines of groceries, pharmaceuticals, health and beauty aids, photo developing services, and a limited selection of general merchandise.

---

① https://en.wikipedia.org/wiki/Walmart

In 2002, Walmart was listed for the first time as America's largest corporation on the Fortune 500 list, with revenues of $219.8 billion and profits of $6.7 billion. Since then, it has remained on the list every year, except for 2006 and 2009. In 2005, Walmart had $312.4 billionin sales, more than 6,200 facilities around the world—including 3,800 stores in the United States and 2,800 elsewhere, employing more than 1.6 million associates worldwide.

Walmart has been the world's largest company by revenue, according to the Fortune Global 500 list in 2014, the biggest private employer in the world with over two million employees, and the largest retailer in the world. As one of the U.S. top retailers, Walmart was ranked 1st on the Fortune 500 in 2013. About 100 million Americans shop at its more than 2,000 U.S. stores each week. It has over 11,000 stores in 27 countries.

Why did Walmart move online?

For some time, this world's largest retail chain did't seem to worry much about the world's largest online mall—Amazon. After all, only about a quarter of Walmart customers shopped at Amazon, according to data. However, with the fast development of network technologies and online transactions, Walmart could not neglect some trends any longer:

Firstly, Walmart's traditional customers and bargain hunters were making less than $50,000 a year[①]. Along with the popularization of the Internet, consumers spreaded out their purchase across channels, forcing Walmart to expand the online marketing budgets.

Secondly, the youth who were tech savvy and the less-strapped shoppers who frequented Walmart during the recession were rediscovered by Amazon. As what an Analyst said, "Amazon has moved from being this unusual niche competitor for Walmart to a force that can reinvent the industry... The affluent shopper is trading back out of Walmart and Amazon is a bigger part of their life than before." Walmart's customers' trolling for deals at Amazon put pressure on Walmart to fix its operation.

The changing habits of Walmart's customers and Amazon's growing clout forced Walmart to pay more attention to the online market as never before. In 1995, Walmart established its own online store.

What Are Its Strengths and Weaknesses When Walmart Goes online?

For Walmart, a well-know retailer with the successful offline experiences, going online is not an easy decision. Analyzing its strengths and weaknesses can help us to understand the supports and obstacles encountered by a traditional retailer when it chooses the strategy of "click and brick".

---

① David Welch, Wal-Mart Losing out to online Retailers, *Bloomberg News*, 2012-03-20.

Strengths

1. Cost leadership strategy. This strategy has helped Walmart to become the low cost leader in the retail market. This strategy requires selling products at low price and providing a no frill services to achieve higher economies of scale and attract masses of consumers. It is exactly what the company has been doing. It sells products at much lower prices than competitors do, builds warehouse style superstores that contain extensive range of products without offering much additional benefits or services. Due to the large scale of its operations, Walmart can exercise strong buyer power on suppliers to reduce the prices. Higher economies of scale results in lower prices that are passed to consumers. All of these result in cost reductions and lower prices for consumers.

2. Wide range of products. Walmart can offer wider range of products than any other retailer. It sells grocery, entertainment, health and wellness, apparel and home related products among many other categories and offers both branded and its own label goods. Wide range of products attract more customers to Walmart stores.

3. The established brand name and a loyal customer base that is increasingly going online to purchase. With the high brand recognition, it is not hard to appeal the customers to Walmart's website. It can also save the cost of propagation.

4. Strategic vendor partnership. Walmart embarks on strategic sourcing to find products at the best price from suppliers who are in a position to ensure they can meet demand. The company establishes strategic partnership with most of their vendors, offering them the potential for long-term and high volume purchases in exchange for the lowest possible prices. Furthermore, Walmart streamlines supply chain management by constructing communication and relationship networks with suppliers to improve material flow with lower inventories. The network of global suppliers, warehouses, and retail stores have been described as behaving almost like a single firm.

5. The efficient inventory control and fulfillment systems. Inventory and fulfillment management are the two crucial tasks for e-commerce services. Under a Walmart's supply chain initiative called Vendor Managed Inventory (VMI), manufacturers become responsible for managing their products in Walmart's warehouses. As a result, Walmart is able to expect close to 100% order fulfilment on merchandise. When replenishing inventory, Walmart employs the cross docking tactic which means the direct transfer of products from inbound or outbound truck trailers without extra storage, by unloading items from an incoming semi-trailer truck or railroad car and loading these materials directly into outbound trucks, trailers, or rail cars (and vice versa), with no storage in between. Cross docking keeps inventory and transportation costs down, reduces transportation time, and eliminates inefficiencies. Walmart's distribution costs was estimated at a mere 1.7% of its

cost of sales—far superior to competitors like Kmart (3.5%) and Sears (5%)①. The established inventory and fulfillment systems offer Walmart the experience of order fulfillment and balance inventory and cost.

 高效的库存控制和订单履行系统。存货和订单管理是电子商务的两个关键环节。在沃尔玛发起的供应商管理库存(VMI)的模式下,供应商负责对沃尔玛仓库中的存货进行管理,使订单履行率接近100%。在补货过程中,沃尔玛采用了交叉配货法,借助拖车和卡车,在收货地和发货地之间直接运送商品,取消了商品储存,降低了库存和运输成本,减少了运输时间,提高了效率。沃尔玛的分销成本仅为销售成本的1.7%,远远优于竞争对手Kmart和Sears。已有的库存和订单履行系统使沃尔玛获取了平衡订单履行和存货成本的经验。

6. The efficient distribution network. Walmart owns highly-automated distribution centers, which operate 24 hours a day and are served by Walmart's truck fleet. In the United States alone, the company has more than 40 regional distribution centers for import flow and more than 140 distribution centers for domestic flow. When entering a new geographic arena, the company first determines if the area will be able to contain enough stores to support a distribution center. Each distribution center supports between 75 to 100 retail stores within a 250-mile area. Once a center is built, stores are gradually built around it to saturate the area and the distribution network is realigned to maximize efficiencies through a process termed "reoptimization". The effect is obvious: trucks do not have to travel as far to retail stores to make deliveries, shorter distances reduce transportation costs and lead time, and shorter lead time means holding less safety inventory. If shortages do occur, replenishment can be made more quickly because stores receive daily deliveries from distribution centers②. The distribution network supports about 11,000 chain stores, which enable Walmart to allocate products flexibly and support after-sale services such as returning.

 高效的分销网络。沃尔玛拥有24小时车队服务的高度自动化分销中心。仅仅在美国,该公司就有40多个负责进口物流的地区分销中心和140多个负责国内物流的分销中心。当事业版图拓展到一个新的地区时,沃尔玛首先考虑的是该地区能否容纳分销中心周围足够多的门店。每个分销中心能支持250英里内的75至100家门店。一旦建成一个分销中心,新的门店就会围绕它逐渐遍布周边地区,分销网络也会通过"再优化"流程实现分销网络的再整合。这样做的效果很明显:卡车不用长途奔波将商品配送至远距离的门店,运输距离的缩短减少了成本,缩短了交货提前期,而更短的交货提前期也意味着安全库存下降。即使发生缺货,由于分销中心每天都向各门店配送商品,补货能快速实施。分销网络支持沃尔玛在全球11 000多家门店,也使其能灵活地分配产品,支持退货等售后服务。

---

① Clara Lu, Walmart's successful supply chain management, https://www.tradegecko.com/blog/incredibly-successful-supply-chain-management-walmart, 2014-05-07.

② Jimmy Alyea, Analyzing Wal-Mart's Distribution and Logistics System, http://jimmyalyea.blogspot.com/2012/02/analyzing-wal-marts-distribution-and.html, 2012.

7. Competence in information management. Walmart has the largest information technology infrastructure of any private company in the world. Its state-of-the-art technology and network design allow it to accurately forecast demand, track and predict inventory levels, create highly efficient transportation routes, and manage customer relationships and service response logistics. For example, Walmart implements the first companywide use of Universal Product Code bar codes, in which store level information is immediately collected and analysed, and the company then devises Retail Link, a mammoth Bentonville database. Through a global satellite system, Retail Link is connected to analysts who forecast supplier demands to the supplier network, which displays real-time sales data from cash registers and to Walmart's distribution centers. In addition, Walmart also networks its suppliers through computers. It entered into collaboration with P&G for maintaining the inventory in its stores and built an automated re-ordering system, which links all computers between P&G factory through a satellite communication system. P&G then delivered the item either to Walmart distribution centre or directly to the concerned stores[①].

Weaknesses[②]

1. More than one focuses. Compared to the pure online players like eBay, Walmart has to be distracted by an enormous brick and mortar business. The dual channels may lead to the internal competition day-in day-out, which hurts Walmart's operation. Meanwhile, Walmart lacks e-commerce experience. Despite its brand strength in traditional retailing, Walmart is still a rookie of online operation. Unlike amazon who has developed all the expertise in full support of e-commerce, Walmart has to start over, which is a big challenge for it.

2. Logistics and delivery. Logistics is what makes Walmart great. But delivery is a different matter. Walmart dabbles in same-day delivery and even goes a step further than Amazon by using stores as fulfillment centers, turning 4,000 stores into bases for same day delivery. Two-thirds of the U.S. population lives within 5 miles of a Walmart, and trucks crisscrossing the country arrive daily to replenish the stores, which can greatly reduce shipping costs. However, the process comes with serious limitations, particularly since it diverts workers' attention away from ensuring stores are clean and properly stocked. Walmart also creates a vast new logistics system that includes building new warehouses for Web orders. As Walmart's online orders grow, it has turned to makeshift spaces carved out of store-serving distribution centers and third-party warehouse operators to help handle the

---

① Clara Lu, Walmart's Successful Supply Chain Management, https://www.tradegecko.com/blog/incredibly-successful-supply-chain-management-walmart, 2014-05-07.

② Mike Schoultz, Why the Wal-Mart E-commerce Strategy Won't Beat Amazon, http://www.digitalsparkmarketing.com/general-business/Wal-Mart-E-commerce-strategy/, 2015-04-05.

load, which causes the rising costs. The statistics implies that Walmart's online shipping can cost $5 to $7 per parcel, while Amazon averages $3 to $4 per parcel.

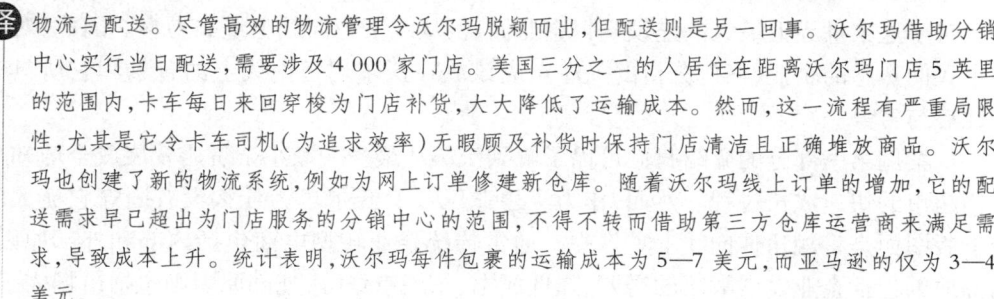

物流与配送。尽管高效的物流管理令沃尔玛脱颖而出,但配送则是另一回事。沃尔玛借助分销中心实行当日配送,需要涉及4 000家门店。美国三分之二的人居住在距离沃尔玛门店5英里的范围内,卡车每日来回穿梭为门店补货,大大降低了运输成本。然而,这一流程有严重局限性,尤其是它令卡车司机(为追求效率)无暇顾及补货时保持门店清洁且正确堆放商品。沃尔玛也创建了新的物流系统,例如为网上订单修建新仓库。随着沃尔玛线上订单的增加,它的配送需求早已超出为门店服务的分销中心的范围,不得不转而借助第三方仓库运营商来满足需求,导致成本上升。统计表明,沃尔玛每件包裹的运输成本为5—7美元,而亚马逊的仅为3—4美元。

3. Existing in-store strategies. Walmart has an enormous and growing network of brick and mortar outlets—4,000 in the U.S. and counting. Those stores generate an equally enormous product offering. There is a long way for Walmart on being able to put all the products online where they can be easily found. At some stage these stores and product offering may be an advantage for Walmart. But those are technology constrained goals that are, for now, out of reach. And that is not even considering how Walmart might solve its internal competition problems.

4. The slow innovation. Walmart Labs develop Pangaea, a global technology platform with scan and go apps that let shoppers buy in store via a smart phone, and online operations in growing markets outside the U.S. such as Brazil and China. Walmart tries doing more new things, but it is slowed down by the legacy business and its mindset since it is hard for such a giant retailer to make changes.

5. Customer set differences. Walmart demographics, a quarter of whom reportedly do not use debit or credit cards or even have a bank account, represent a big difference with its key e-commerce competitor like Amazon whose big advantage is not only in consumer disposable income, but also in ability to operate and shop online and take advantage of frequent new technology features.

6. High employee turnover. The business suffers from high employee turnover that increases firm's costs, as it has to train new employees more often. The main reason for high employee turnover is low skilled, poorly paid jobs. Additionally, Walmart has been criticized for poor work conditions, low wages, unpaid overtime work and female discrimination, which causes fewer skilled workers to work for it.

Walmart's rise to online dominance really just revolves around turning an otherwise complicated shopping experience into one that feels quaint and easy. It can accomplish this by setting up a strong behind-the-scenes infrastructure that puts the customer experience at the forefront. And isn't that what their new strategy is all about—giving the customer what they want where and when they want it? It seems much easier said than done.

Case Analysis

作为全球著名的连锁超市,沃尔玛在1995年开设网上超市以后吸引了大量的目光。对于这家世界上最大的连锁零售企业而言,从线下迈向线上绝非易事。因此,对于这个我们熟悉的企业,案例分析的关注点应该放在沃尔玛迈向线上的背景和它所具有的优势与劣势。

从案例第一部分的介绍我们可以了解到沃玛从最初一家小杂货店发展成全球知名连锁超市的快速成长过程。然而,作为零售业巨头的沃尔玛为什么没有固守它庞大的线下版图而是将触角伸向线上零售呢?通常传统企业转型电商包括内部和外部原因。内部原因包括企业发展战略的需要、降低成本、拓展市场等;外部原因则包括市场需求、竞争压力、技术成熟等。显然,沃尔玛发展线上零售的主要原因是遭遇了来自最大的网上书店亚马逊的竞争威胁。亚马逊以其低价和便利迅速赢得了消费者的青睐,尤其是偏好线上购物的年轻人的追捧。从并不起眼的图书市场开始,亚马逊逐步蚕食零售业的各个领域,甚至开始改变人们的购物习惯和整个零售产业链,意识到这一点的沃尔玛在1995年开设网站,进军网上零售。应该说作为一家体量庞大的传统零售商,沃尔玛无论在对行业发展前景的预测还是在反应速度上都表现出色,这使它避免了巴诺书店①的悲剧。然而,采用"鼠标+水泥"这样的重大决策要求企业对自身的优势与劣势必须有一个清醒的评估——这也是本案例分析的第二个重点。

说到沃尔玛,你能想到什么?低价?商品种类繁多?规模效应?……的确,这些都是沃尔玛的优势,但也是传统大型零售商的共同优势,并非沃尔玛独有。这里的优势分析应侧重于沃尔玛独有的优势及其对线上零售带来的益处,这就需要思考:线上零售需要哪些基本要素?沃尔玛是否具备?首先,沃尔玛高效的供应链管理是它迈向线上时的一大优势。作为拥有11 000家门店、市场遍及27个国家的零售巨头,沃尔玛高效的供应链管理有口皆碑。它曾连续5年被Gartner列为"全球25家最佳供应链管理企业"之一②。沃尔玛的低价商品是它的一大优势,而低价的背后离不开高效的供应链管理:砍掉部分上游批发商,转而直接向制造商采购,和上游供应商建立战略合作伙伴关系,以长期大批量采购换取低价,这些措施可以帮助沃尔玛在供应链管理的第一个环节——采购中赢得优势;对于零售商最头痛的库存问题,它提出了供应商管理库存(VMI)模式,将传统的零售商独自管理商品库存改为共同协议下的供应商管理库存,打破了传统的各自为政的库存管理模式,降低了库存成本并使订单履行率接近100%,这个优势在线上运营中仍然可以发挥;沃尔玛建立了24小时作业的自动化分销中心,它不仅可以保证门店的及时供货并降低运输成本,还可以为线上订单的配送以及退货提供支持。其次,电子商务要求企业必须有出色的信息管理,而沃尔玛在过去的线下运营中早已积累了丰富的经验和扎实的技术基础。沃尔玛拥有全球民营企业中最庞大的信息技术架构,同时最新的信息技术(如产品条码技术、射频技术)能帮助它有效管理从采购、库

---

① 美国著名的线下连锁书店,因为受到线上书店的冲击,经营陷入困境。
② https://www.gartner.com

存、发货、配送到售后的所有环节,完全能适应线上零售高效精准服务的要求。

尽管沃尔玛成功的线下运营为其迈向线上奠定了基础,然而与亚马逊等线上零售商相比,它的劣势也十分明显:首先是它引以为傲的库存管理。沃尔玛在库存补货中创造性地采用了"跨库作业",将货物从工厂直接运达门店(或附近的分销中心),大大缩短了补货周期,降低了库存和运输成本。然而,线上零售的最后一站并不是门店,而是每个顾客——配送地点更加分散,对配送质量和速度的要求也更高。以前用大卡车在分销中心和门店之间来回穿梭的方式显然不再适用。沃尔玛尝试外包的方式,但结果并不尽如人意,其线上订单的运输成本高于亚马逊,沃尔玛的低成本优势在这一环节消失殆尽。其次,尽管沃尔玛对于技术创新一直持积极的态度,然而相比同行亚马逊,它仍然显得有些力不从心。例如,亚马逊在仓储物流管理中已经成功运用人工智能技术,不仅提高了订单履行效率,而且大大降低了人力成本,这一方面沃尔玛稍显逊色。同时,沃尔玛曾经的成功容易使其管理理念固化,其庞大的商业架构和悠久的企业文化可能反而成为创新的阻力。再次,沃尔玛还必须面对双渠道运营中常见的渠道资源冲突、顾客年龄层相对老化、网购动力不足以及线上运营人才匮乏的问题。

当沃尔玛涉足网上零售时,优势与劣势兼而有之,并可能相互转化。面对虎视眈眈的竞争对手,沃尔玛的使命从原来的"让普通人以低价享受与富人同样的产品和服务"转变为"让顾客随时随地以低价享受高质量的产品和服务"——这才是它迈向线上的真正目标。

Section 4
Taobao—Chinese C2C E-Commerce Leader
第四节 淘宝——中国 C2C 电商的领头羊

I Key Words

1. platform *n.* 平台
2. marketplace *n.* 市场,集市
3. mainstream *n.* 主流
4. boutique *n.* 精品店
5. SMEs(Small and Medium Enterprises)中小企业
6. circulation *n.* 流通
7. fraud *n.* 欺骗
8. click farm *n.* 刷单
9. unscrupulous *adj.* 肆无忌惮的

II Case

About Taobao

As a subsidiary of Alibaba Group, Taobao was founded on May 10, 2003. It provides a platform for businesses and individual entrepreneurs to open online retail stores that cater to consumers in China (including Hong Kong, Macau, Taiwan) and other countries (Figure 1-4). By now, it has become the largest C2C platform in China.

Country	Percent of Visitors	Rank in Country
China	92.8%	3
South Korea	1.7%	13
Japan	1.2%	63
United States	0.9%	402

Figure 1-4　Taobao's Visitors by Country[①]

With around 760 million product listings as of March 2013, Taobao Marketplace was one of the world's top 10 most visited websites[②]. It provides the most comprehensive product offering ranging from collectibles and hard-to-find items to mainstream retail categories such as consumer electronics, clothing and accessories, sporting goods and household products. In March 2013, the combined gross merchandise volume (GMV) of Taobao Marketplace and Tmall.com exceeded 1 trillion yuan[③].

Sellers are able to post new and used goods for sale or resale on the Taobao Marketplace either through a fixed price or by auction. The overwhelming majority of the products on Taobao Marketplace are brand new merchandise sold at a fixed price, while auctions merely make up a very small percentage of transactions. Buyers can assess seller backgrounds by information available on the site, including ratings, comments and complaints.

Taobao's Market Entry Strategies

When Jack Ma, CEO of Alibaba, launched Taobao in 2003, Yiqu has been acquired by eBay which promised to increase the investment in Chinese market and accounted for more than 80% of C2C market share in China. Few people forecasted Taobao's growth in the future. However, only after two years, Taobao accounted for more than 60% of C2C market share in China. At this time, Taobao became one of the top three C2C platforms (the other two were eBay and 1Pai) in China. In October 2005, Alibaba Group took over the operation of China Yahoo! as part of its strategic partnership with Yahoo! Inc. As a result, 1Pai was incorporated into Taobao in January 2006 and its original customers were also imported into Taobao. By virtue of mergers and acquisitions (M&A), Taobao eliminated one of its competitors.

---

① http://www.alexa.com/siteinfo/taobao.com#trafficstats
② Alexa.com Taobao Statistics, Alexa.com, 2013-10-21.
③ Taobao, Wikipedia, https://en.wikipedia.org/wiki/Taobao

As a latecomer of Chinese C2C market, how does Taobao grow rapidly and defeat its competitors? Five market entry strategies can explain it.

1. Low price. Taobao is famous for its low-price. The low price products attract lots of consumers. An interesting phenomenon is some boutiques even become consumers' "fitting rooms". "Trying on the clothes and finding them on Taobao" also becomes a trend. According to Pan (2009)[①], pricing has a significant influence on selling goods but with negative coefficient and absolute value. Because buyers can not identify the goods visually, the high price goods are harder to sell online. Majority of young people can not afford the high price products which are sold in the physical stores. For this reason, they prefer to shop at Taobao. The numerous small and medium enterprises (SMEs) in China are the sources of the low price. Under the traditional circulation model, it is very hard for the SMEs to develop a marketing channel due to the limited personnel, money and social networks. For a long time, product sales have been a big problem with the SMEs though the quality of their products is good. By virtue of Taobao, the products can be displayed and sold online with low cost and unlimited market. Particularly, the products can be sold to the consumers directly, cutting off the intermediaries existing in the traditional circulation. As a result, a new marketing channel and the brand recognition are built. On the other hand, consumers are able to get access to the tremendous product information, make the purchase decision easily and acquire the preferred commodities with lower price. Who can reject it? Besides, it also implements activities of in-store marketing like discounts, coupons, tie-in package and full sent grasp. The promotion catches the consumer psychology of buying the cheaper things. For example, the "Singles' Day" launched since 2011 is well known as the great discount. The "Singles' Day" in 2013 brought Taobao the daily revenue of 35 billion yuan.

2. The "It is Free" strategy. Differing from eBay which charges sellers the insertion fees and final value fees, Taobao offers the C2C sellers platform for free initially. In October 2005, Alibaba announced that "Taobao is going to keep the free strategy for another three years."[②] Undoubtedly, the free strategy requires the huge investment which probably causes the high risk. However, it enables Taobao to quickly enter C2C market dominated by eBay and acquired more than 60% market share in the short term. The free strategy works as a powerful weapon of Taobao in the battle with eBay. In fact, Taobao has become the most successful C2C platform, greatly surpassing eBay as well as people's

---

[①] Pan Y. Improving the "Cyber Lemons" Problem with the Counteracting Mechanism in Chinese E-commerce Market: Based on the Data from Taobao.com (China)[C]//Proceedings of the 53rd Annual Meeting of the ISSS-2009, Brisbane, Australia. 2009, 1(1).

[②] eBay Lectures Taobao That Free Is Not a Business Model, http://www.scmp.com/node/521384, 2005-10-21.

expectation.

3. Web design based on customers' demand. Taobao's friendly interface impresses the visitors (Figure 1-5). The helpful functionalities such as searching and browsing as well

Figure 1-5　Taobao's Interface[①]

as the colorful page enable the customers to navigate on the website easily and joyfully. The secret behind the successfully designed web is the data collecting and analyzing scientifically. The classification of commodities, the display of products, color matching and their influences on a customer's online shopping behavior are analyzed carefully so as to work out the best plan of web designing. It turns out that all these efforts are worthwhile—users get used to Taobao's web designing so fast that they are not willing to transfer to another website easily since it will take some time to learn to use. The well-designed web also contributes to Taobao's high users' stickiness. Compared to Taobao, eBay-Yiqu's web designing is not so satisfying since it just simply copies the original model in America.

4. Establishing the secure online payment system. To much extent, Taobao's success should be attributed to Alipay. Alipay is an escrow service provided by Alibaba. Its strength lies in its security and the mechanism that the funds are only released once the customer is satisfied, which solves the problem of credit. For all intents and purposes, Alipay is the Chinese equivalent of Paypal, and can be used to pay for products for different Chinese businesses, including popular online shopping sites such as Taobao,

---

① www.taobao.com

Jingdong and Tmall. With 450 million users, Alipay owns the biggest market share in China by far①. It has partnered with over 100 financial institutions (including Visa and Mastercard) and support transactions in 12 major foreign currencies. The longer you live in China, the more advantageous it becomes to have an Alipay account and the knowledge of how to use it. For regular Alipay users, there are Alipay mobile apps available for free for Android and iOS, allowing them to make payments on the move.

> **译** 建立安全的网上支付系统。从某种程度上说,淘宝的成功应该归功于支付宝。支付宝是阿里巴巴提供的现金担保服务,其优势在于安全性和买家满意后才支付的机制,解决了电商中的信用问题。就开发动机而言,支付宝可以说是中国的"贝宝",它能用于包括淘宝、京东和天猫等在内的知名网站的购物支付。迄今为止,拥有4.5亿用户的支付宝在中国第三方支付市场占有最大份额。它已经同100多家金融机构建立合作关系,支持12种货币的交易。在中国生活越久,你就越能感受支付宝的优势,对手机用户而言,支付宝能同时支持安卓和iOS系统。

5. The periodical propagation strategies. Propagandizing and advertising are the crucial marketing strategies for all the e-tailers. However, due to the exclusive agreement between eBay-Yiqu and the famous portals, Taobao initially could not take advantage of the traditional propagation channels. It had to depend on the word-of-mouth (WOM) marketing which refers to the passing of information between a non-commercial communicator and a receiver concerning a brand, a product, or a service②. Fortunately, the strategy has proven successful due to Taobao's strong WOM foundation (e.g. sufficient levels of satisfaction, trust and commitment). At the second stage, Taobao focused on the propagation specified to the SMEs who were anxious to expand the market but was unable to find the appropriate channels. Taobao offers the C2C platform where the SMEs can display, propagate, and sell their products directly to the end consumers without the geographic limits. The strategy focusing on SMEs enables Taobao to not only affiliate tremendous SMEs members but also establish the brand strength, which prepares for the next stage well. At the third stage, Taobao began its strategic alliances with the well-known web medias such as Sohu and MSN. Thanks to the solid bases built at the first stage, Taobao had the capability to cooperate with the well-known enterprises. MSN, in particular, chose Taobao to align with, which changed the routine of cooperating with eBay in other countries③. The strategic alliances with the famous enterprises indicates that Taobao has eliminated the barriers due to the exclusive agreement between eBay-Yiqu and the famous portals and built the new marketing channels.

---

① 2017支付宝用户数量达4.5亿,南方财富网,http://www.southmoney.com/yinhang/zhifubao/201708/1504324.html, 2017-08-04.

② http://en.wikipedia.org/wiki/Word_of_mouth

③ 王静一,从淘宝网的竞争策略看C2C市场发展,《商业时代》,2006.

Taobao's Customer Keeping Strategies[①]

1. Instant communication. The virtuality makes the instant communication between the transaction parties necessary. Taobao launched AliWangWang, a free Instant Message (IM) software, to enable the easy communication between buyers and sellers prior to the purchase. With AliWangWang, buyers and sellers can make a "talk" about product information, delivery and negotiation. It has become a habit among Chinese online shoppers to interact with the sellers through AliWangWang to inquire about products and to bargain prior to purchasing products. Realizing the huge potential of SNS, Taobao launched Taojianghu, a SNS platform, which enables the users to make the instant communication with the people in their social network. The distinct feature of Taojianghu is the combination of SNS and online shopping platform. By virtue of Taojianghu, a Taobao user is able to not only contact his or her families, friends, colleagues and the people in the social network and view the user profile but also share the shopping experience and implement business negotiation. Converting the social network communication into the real online shopping activities, Taojianghu realized the "Behavior Marketing".

2. Quality. Quality is the critical factor ensuring the sustainable development. It is not easy for a C2C platform to supervise the product or service quality since it is the individual sellers rather than the platform that offer the product or service to the end consumers. Taobao adopts some effective measure to ensure the product and service quality.

1) Real-name authentication system. Taobao imported the real-name authentication system not long after it was founded. The system authenticates both a buyer and a seller. The former is required to supply ID information and the latter is required to submit business licenses in addition to ID. The system benefits quality supervision on the one hand and enables the easy data collection on the other hand.

2) Customers' review. There are three classes of customers' review: Good, Moderate and Bad. Each class of review corresponds to a seller's points (Good: 1 point; Moderate: 0 point; Bad: -1 point). The accumulation of a seller's points decides its creditability level. Customers' review can not only normalize sellers' activities (e.g. product quality, after-sale services) but also provide the useful references for the succeeding buyers.

3) Quality guarantee. Quality guarantee is achieved by several methods:

- Faithful description. A seller makes a commitment that the description of the commodities is faithful. It helps to avoid the inconsistency between the description and the goods;

---

① https://en.wikipedia.org/wiki/Taobao

• 7 days non-reason returning. This means the products can be returned without any reason in 7 days after purchase;

• Quality products. A seller make a commitment that the commodities sold are certified;

• 30 days maintenance services. It is specified to the electronic instruments. The free maintenance services are provided by the sellers in 30 days after purchase. These measures alleviate the buyers' concerns about product quality.

3. Sellers' unions. Taobao encourages the sellers to establish their own unions to realize self-management. There are two types of unions: industrial unions and regional unions. Sellers' unions can benefit each member by improving the capability of negotiation, decreasing the delivery and procurement costs and normalizing the members' activity. The unions particularly supply the credit guarantee for the members, which improves the buyers' confidence in online transactions.

4. Security. The security of online shopping has been one of the concerns of users. Lack of sense of security prevents some potential customers to purchase online. Alipay, the third-party payment system launched by Alibaba, decreases the risk of information reveal and avoids the possible losses.

Possible problems with Taobao

Though Taobao has become undoubtedly the top C2C platform in China, there are still some problems obsessing the famous e-tailer, some of which, if can not be solved well, will probably become a serious obstacle:

1. Click farm. Click farm is a form of click fraud, where a large group of low-paid workers are hired to click on paid advertising links for the click fraudster (click farm master or click farmer). The workers click the links, surf the target website for a period of time, and possibly sign up for newsletters prior to clicking another link[①]. Research suggests that over a third of consumers regularly check ratings and reviews before they choose to buy something online. With the rising brand recognition of Taobao, more and more sellers enter the C2C platform to develop their online businesses, which leads to the even fiercer competition. The growing significance of this virtual seal of approval for enhancing sales and the competition pressure has unleashed a rather unscrupulous business activity. Rather than wait for users to register their approval of your products and services, why not simply buy a whole shed-load of "likes" and instantly demonstrate your popularity? As a result, some sellers employ the services of a click farm. The situation is so serious that it has even formed "an underground industrial chain of click farming".

---

① https://en.wikipedia.org/wiki/Click_farm

Hundreds of companies have sprung up in the last couple of years specializing in click farming, delivering bundles of online approval to businesses requiring a quick and dirty way to boost their popularity. Click farming has seriously hurt Taobao's brand image. Though Taobao has adopted some solutions such as seeking the click farms by virtue of big data or closing the online stores that are suspected of click farming, the benefits have been limited.

2. Counterfeits crisis. According to a survey from China's State Administration for Industry and Commerce (SAIC) in 2015, more than 40% of online purchases made by Chinese consumers are fake. This highly pointed to Taobao and Tmall, because nearly 60% of their products are counterfeit[①]. For nearly 10 years, Taobao has been struggling against counterfeit products on its platform. Obviously, Taobao has not completed its battle with counterfeit goods. With the transaction volume of 3 trillion yuan on its site, it is difficult for Taobao to always check the authenticity of selling products. It even affects a lot the popularity and credibility of Taobao.

3. Poor delivery quality. For a long time, Taobao has not built its own logistics system. To save the cost, the sellers on Taobao usually outsource the delivery to the logistics companies. Since the sellers can not supervise the whole process of delivery, the delivery problems such as loss of goods or damage to them often occur. As a result, buyers usually complain of the poor quality of delivery and blame it on Taobao. In 2011, Taobao launched its "Big Logistics Plan" which focuses on the self-constructed logistics system. As long as the system is built, all the products can be delivered through Taobao's logistics system and the quality of services can be improved.

If Taobao wants to keep itself in the position of C2C leader, it has to make an effort to solve the problems.

Case Analysis

中国人大多熟悉淘宝,这有利于我们对这个案例的理解和分析。尽管淘宝和亚马逊均是知名的电子商务企业,但它们的成长环境和发展路径都大相径庭。因此,在分析这一案例时,重点应该放在这些不同之处。我们可以通过回答以下三个问题来全面深入地分析这一案例。

1. 淘宝是如何在竞争激烈的环境中发展起来的? 与亚马逊进入一个几乎空白的市场不同,淘宝在2003年成立的时候,不得不面对那些中国网上零售市场中极具竞争力的对手。例如:易趣,这家后来被美国eBay收购的企业当时已拥有超过80%的C2C市场份额。淘宝采取了一些策略来争取自己的生存空间;第一个策略就是低价——淘

---

① Counterfeits Crisis on Taobao, Chinese Largest E-commerce site, http://ecommercechinaagency.com/counterfeits-crisis-on-taobao-chinese-largest-E-commerce-site, 2015-03-18.

宝的商品价格明显比线下同类产品低。既然消费者能够在淘宝上轻松获取商品信息，快速做出购买决策，并以更低的价格获取心仪的商品，他们有什么理由拒绝这样的购物模式呢？低价策略能迅速捕捉消费者"贪便宜"的心理，刺激短期消费需求。而淘宝正是通过这一策略迅速占领市场，建立了知名度。这里又涉及一个拓展问题：低价策略是否有效呢？一般而言，短期内实施低价策略的确成效显著，它能有效刺激销售，帮助企业占领市场。但是，低价策略可能引发竞争对手的博弈行为，从而导致价格战。由于网上信息透明，企业的反应会更加迅速，价格战也会更快更激烈。因此，实施低价策略必须谨慎，不能跟风盲从。第二个策略是为交易双方提供免费的交易平台①。这种以补贴吸引人气的策略是基于双边市场的重要特性——网络外部性（网络效应），即一种产品的价值取决于它对交易另一方的价值。现实中，它通常表现为一种产品的价值取决于使用该产品另一方用户的数量。淘宝一开始通过免费策略吸引卖家入驻，它吸引的卖家越多，对于买家而言价值越高，就能相应地吸引更多的买家使用淘宝进行交易，反之亦然。尽管买卖双方并非为了提升产品对对方的价值而进入平台，但淘宝这种策略的确发挥了双边市场网络效应的优势。第三个策略是提供安全的网上支付系统。交易双方的信任问题是横亘在不少电商网站发展道路上的一道难题，也因此支付成为影响网上交易的关键因素。美国最大的C2C网站eBay正是收购了第三方支付系统贝宝（paypal），解决了网上支付安全问题，才得以迅速发展。同样地，淘宝推出的第三方支付平台——支付宝在其发展历程中扮演了重要的角色。除了安全支付外，支付宝在网上交易中提供了现金担保的功能，通过设定7天的支付期解决了交易双方不信任的问题，对淘宝的迅速发展起到了至关重要的作用。

2. 网上零售商应该如何留住客户？由于网上交易的虚拟性，缺少线下购物带给人们的全方位感官体验，因此对电商企业而言，留住客户的难度甚至大于线下。要提高客户粘性，提高产品和服务的质量是一个有效的方法。作为C2C平台，淘宝并不向消费者直接出售商品，这就加大了质量监管的难度。商家实名制认证、客户评价、质量担保这些措施尽管仍有局限，但在一定程度上保证了产品和服务的质量。作为双边平台，除了留住消费者，淘宝也必须持续吸引优质商家。免费入驻、卖家联盟、店铺推广优惠等措施有效地提高了卖家的粘性，也相应地吸引了更多的买家。

3. 成功的网上零售商应如何实现可持续发展？"创业难，守业更难"。没有人会否认淘宝的成功，但它面临的问题同样不能忽视。长期以来，淘宝最为大众所诟病的就是它的产品和服务质量问题：假冒伪劣商品、售后难以尽如人意、虚假信用评价等不仅被频频曝光，而且已经在一定程度上影响了淘宝的品牌形象。尽管实名认证、假货识别机制、假货曝光平台等措施相继推出，但收效不甚理想。虽然作为一家拥有近千万卖家的大型电商交易平台质量问题并不能完全消除，但面对消费者投诉和受到损害的企业信誉，淘宝必须采取更有效的措施来保护品牌形象，实现长期的可持续发展。

---

① 淘宝一开始为吸引卖家入驻采取了免费策略，后来才逐渐对其收费。

Section 5
Case & Case Analysis
第五节　案例与案例分析

1. What is a case?

A case is a description of an actual situation, commonly involving a decision, a challenge, an opportunity, a problem or an issue faced by a person (or persons) in an organization[1]. It is usually a real situation that happened just as described though part of information is hidden due to the business intelligence. Cases are provided in such a way that you can replace the manager in a specific situation to make decisions to solve the problems.

2. What is a case analysis?

As a methodology used in social science, a case analysis involves an in-depth investigation of a phenomenon within its real-life context. It analyzes persons, groups, events, decisions, periods, policies, institutions or other systems that are studied holistically by one or more methods. A case analysis involves single or multiple cases, includes quantitative evidence, relies on multiple sources of evidence, and benefits from the prior development of theoritical propositions[2].

3. Why case analysis?

Not only can case analysis broaden your insights by reading different cases, but also it enables you to develop the following skills:

1) Understanding skills. By reading cases carefully, you can increase your understanding of what managers should do and why they should do it in a specific scenario.

2) Analytical skills. During the process of case analysis, you can develop qualitative and quantitative frameworks to analyze business situations, including problem identification skills, data handling skills, strengths and weaknesses evaluation skills and critical thinking skills.

3) Decision-making skills. A case analysis usually requires you to place yourself in the position of a manager and make a decision. That means you have to identify the possible alternatives, establish the evaluation criteria, evaluate alternatives and make the best choice in a specific situation.

---

[1] Louise A. Mauffette-leenders, James A. Erskine, Michiel R. Leenders, *Learning with Cases*, Ivey Publishing (Fourth Edition), 2008.

[2] http://www.pressacademia.org/case-studies/definition-of-case-study

4) Application skills. For the applied discipline such as e-commerce, knowing "what" and "why" is not enough. You have to know "how", which requires your application skills. By virtue of a case analysis, you can apply the tools, techniques and theories you have learned to an organization in a similar situation so as to improve your practice skills.

5) Oral and written communication skills. Discussion, presentation and writing reports are necessary for a case analysis. When you make a discussion or presentation, you not only listen to your peers but also express your points and convince them of your views. Besides, you have to learn to express your points by writing a case analysis report. As a result, a set of speaking, listening, writing and debating skills are developed.

6) Social and cooperation skills. When participating in a discussion, preparing the team presentation or case report, you have to socialize and cooperate with your peers. It helps you to practice the conflict resolution skills and the art of compromise, which will benefit your future career.

Summary（本章小结）

Online Retailing, also called as electronic retailing or e-tailing, refers to the retailing wholly or partially conducted over the Internet. E-tailing can be classified by revenue model or distribution channel. The successful e-tailers usually cooperate with highly reliable or well-known vendors and establish the high brand recognition.

Amazon's success can be attributed to its well-designed website which provides browsing aids, low prices, various marketplace services, diversification through business alliances and outstanding customer relationship management. Particularly, the continuous innovations such as e-book readers and cloud services enable its sustainable development. Amazon still encounters some challenges such as the criticisms. Probably, its success has not been assured. Undoubtedly, Amazon is the most recognized e-tailer worldwide after the 20 years of operation.

After viewing the great success of the e-tailers such as Amazon, the retailing giant, Walmart established its own online store in 1995 because it planned to cut a piece from the e-tailing cake. Exploiting a new channel online means not only to build a website but also to adjust the existing managerial models and processes. As a traditional retailer with more than 30-year history, Walmart has its strengths, as well as weaknesses and encounters opportunities and threats.

Taobao was founded in 2003. It provides a platform for businesses and individual entrepreneurs to open online retail stores. By now, it has become the largest C2C platform in China. When Taobao entered the C2C market initially, few people forecasted Taobao's growth in the future. However, only two years after its foundation, Taobao had accounted for more than 60% of C2C market share in China. Taobao's rapid growth should be attributed to its market-entry timing, the platform based business model and customer keeping strategies.

A case is a description of an actual situation, commonly involving a decision, a challenge, and opportunity, a problem or an issue faced by a person or persons in an organization. A case analysis enables you to develop the comprehensive skills such as analytical skills and communication skills. That is why we emphasize case analysis so much.

 Exercises & Tasks（练习与任务）

▶ *Exercises*

1. What are the differences between e-tailing and traditional retailing?
2. Can you illustrate the examples of e-tailing models based on distribution channel?
3. What can you learn from Amazon if you plan to build your own e-tailing business?
4. What are the possible problems with the brick-and-mortar e-tailer such as Walmart?
5. What advices can you provide to Taobao based on your shopping experiences on the website?

▶ *Tasks*

Choose an e-tailer and prepare a 20-minute presentation which includes:
1. Background introduction to the e-tailer;
2. Analysis of its success or failure;
3. Conclusion which may be summarization, comments or advices.

Chapter 2 第二章

B2B E-Commerce
B2B 电子商务

 Learning Objectives（学习目标）

After finishing this chapter, you should be able to:
1. Define and categorize B2B e-commerce;
2. Define collaborative commerce and describe its three forms;
3. Identify the critical success factors and expansion of Alibaba;
4. List the reasons for IndiaMART's achievements;
5. Explain the strengths and weaknesses of Target's c-commerce;
6. Describe the types of case analysis.

 Introduction（内容简介）

    B2B business is an important category of e-commerce, which is also the primary revenue source of e-commerce. People are not familiar with B2B because it focuses on the transactions among enterprises. It plays a significant role in e-commerce industry since it not only enables the lower transaction costs for small and medium sized enterprises (SMEs) but also restructures the traditional industrial chains.

    Chapter 2 is composed of 5 sections. The brief introduction to B2B e-commerce is made in section 1. Three B2B cases are offered respectively in section 2, 3, and 4. Section 5 focuses on the types of case analysis.

Section 1
B2B E-Commerce
第一节　B2B 电子商务

▶ Key Words

1. collaborative *adj.* 协调的　　2. collaborative commerce（c-commerce）协同商务
3. replenishment *n.* 补充

▶ B2B (Business-to-Business)

B2B, one of the e-commerce models, refers to the transactions between businesses conducted electronically over the Internet, extranets, intranets, or private networks①.

Due to the large volume and amount, B2B has been dominating e-commerce volume even though most of the public attention focuses on B2C. According to the statistics, Chinese B2B e-commerce sales reached $1.6 trillion in China in 2014②.

▶ B2B Categories

B2B e-commerce can be classified based on different criteria—revenue model or the number of transaction parties. It is categorized into four categories based on the former criteria (Table 2-1):

Table 2-1　B2B Categories Based on Revenue Model③

Business Model	Examples	Description	Revenue Source
Marketplace	Alibaba.com	Help bring buyers and sellers together to reduce procurement costs for a specific industry	Transaction fees
E-distributor	Grainger.com	Offer products to other businesses directly like distributors, reducing sales cycles and mark-up	Sales of goods
B2B Services Provider	Salesforce.com	Rent Internet-based software applications to businesses	Rental fees

---

①　埃弗瑞姆·特伯恩(Efraim Turban),戴维·金(David King)著,王健改编,《电子商务导论》,中国人民大学出版社,2006年,第203页.

②　Frank Tong, B2B E-commerce sales reach $1.6 trillion in China in 2014, https://www.internetretailer.com/2015/04/13/b2b-E-commerce-sales-reach-16-trillion-china-2014, 2015-04-13.

③　Kenneth C. Laudon, Carol Guercio Traver, *E-commerce Business*, *Technology*, *Society*, Addison-Wesley Publishing, 2002, p.78.

When the focus is on the number of transaction parties, B2B e-commerce can be categorized into four types①:

1. Sell side B2B. One seller to many buyers. The seller usually dominates the negotiation with buyers since the latter have barely choices.

2. Buy side B2B. One buyer from many sellers. The buyer usually dominates the negotiation with sellers since there are many procurement choices in the marketplace. This business model accounts for a large percentage.

3. Exchanges B2B. Many sellers to many buyers. The amount of sellers and buyers are almost equal and all the parties can make the exchange in the e-marketplace freely.

4. Collaborative commerce. The collaborative planning, designing, developing, managing and researching products through their life cycle among the supply chain participants by virtue of inter-organization information system.

A special category of B2B—Collaborative Commerce

Collaborative commerce (c-commerce) was firstly defined by Gartner—the largest IT consulting company in the U. S. A. It emerged in late 1990s and aims at the cross-regions and cross-industries cooperation among business partners and the thorough improvement of effectiveness. Collaborative commerce is so closely interrelated to e-commerce that it is called as "A New Face of e-commerce" or "The Next Stage of e-commerce". In practice, c-commerce can be embodied in three forms②:

The first form is industry-wide collaborative resource planning, forecasting, and replenishment (CPFR). It involves working with partners to forecast demand, developing production plans, coordinated shipping, warehousing, and stocking activities to ensure retail and wholesale shelf space is replenished with just the right amount of goods.

The second form of collaboration is demand chain visibility. It emphasizes the collaboration between manufacturers and retailers to reduce inventory levels and costs across the entire value chain. It can be realized by increasing the total volume of information transmitted between retailers and manufacturers, with daily transmission of information on all products indicating retail warehouse shipments to each store, warehouse inventory levels, orders in transit (shipped but not yet received) and product

---

① 埃弗瑞姆·特伯恩(Efraim Turban),戴维·金(David King)著,王健改编,《电子商务导论》,中国人民大学出版社,2006年,第205页。

② Kenneth C. Laudon, Carol Guercio Traver, *E-commerce Business, Technology, Society*, Addison-Wesley Publishing, 2002, p. 707.

shortages①.

The third form of collaboration is manufacturing and marketing coordination. Manufacturers use private industrial networks to coordinate both their internal design and marketing activities, as well as relate activities of their supply and distribution chain partners. iPhone, for instance, the well-known smart phone brand developed by Apple, is the result of collaborative manufacturing. Apple designs iPhone and its operating system platform; manufacturers respectively from Japan, Korea, Germany are in charge of critical parts such as CPU and memory; manufacturers from Taiwan produce the substitutable parts; all the components are assembled in the production lines in mainland of China (Figure 2-1).

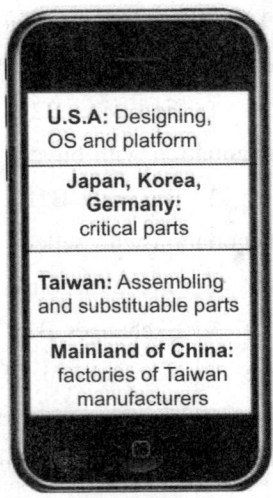

Figure 2-1 C-commerce Behind an iPhone

Section 2
Alibaba②—B2B from China to the World
第二节 阿里巴巴——从中国迈向世界的 B2B

Key Words

1. covet *vt.* 觊觎
2. position *vt.* 为……定位
3. on par with 与……同等水平
4. opaque *adj.* 不透明的

Case

About Jack(Yun) Ma

Jack (Yun) Ma was born in Hangzhou, Zhejiang Province, China. After graduating from Hangzhou Teacher's Institute in 1988, he worked in Hangzhou Dianzi University as a lecturer in English and International Trade. Obviously, Jack Ma was not satisfied with being a teacher. He quit his stable job and decided to begin his own business.

During the visit to the U.S. for a Government undertaking project related to the

---

① Seung Chang Lee, Bo Young Pak, Ho Geun Lee, Business value of B2B electronic commerce—The critical role of inter-firm collaboration, *Electronic Commerce Research and Applications*, 2 (2003) pp. 350-361.
② Alibaba here refers to Alibaba.com—the primary B2B website of Alibaba Group.

building of highways in 1995, Jack Ma was first told about the Internet and computers. Computers were pretty rare in China then, as they were associated with high cost and the Internet or E-mails were non-existent. When Jack Ma searched the first word—"Beer" on the Mosaic browser, it popped out the information from different countries, but signs of China nowhere. He then searched the word "China" and not a single information popped out. From that moment on, Jack Ma decided to build his entrepreneur related to the Internet[①].

In 1995, Jack Ma founded China Yellowpages, which is widely believed to be China's first Internet-based company. At that time, few Chinese people learned about the Internet. To persuade customers to accept their services, Jack Ma had to show them how to get connected to the Web in front of them so as to prove that the Internet did exist. From 1998 to 1999, Ma headed an information technology company established by China International Electronic Commerce Center, a department of the Ministry of Foreign Trade and Economic Cooperation.

Foundation of Alibaba

In 1999, after persuading 17 of his other friends to invest and join him in his new e-commerce startup, Jack Ma with his partners began a B2B company in his apartment. It took Jack Ma some time to choose an appropriate name since he positioned the company as a global enterprise. It is said that when Jack Ma had a lunch in an American restaurant one day, the word "Alibaba" popped up from his brain. Alibaba is a character from Arabic folk tale—"Ali Baba and the Forty Thieves". He asked the people around and found they all knew the name well. Finally, Jack Ma decided to name his company after the famous folk tale character—Alibaba.

At the beginning, the businesses developed not very smoothly. Alibaba didn't have a single penny in investment from outside investors though they later raised $20 million from SoftBank and another $5 million from Goldman Sachs in 1999. Trudy Dai, one of the first dozen employees of Alibaba, used to spend all night sending e-mails, trying to answer queries from American customers without letting on that she was Chinese. Gradually, it had some success in connecting small Chinese manufacturers to potential customers, including the overseas ones Dai was reassuring over e-mail. But the friends and students who made up the workforce were earning just 550 yuan (then $66) a month. Facing the difficulties, Jack Ma said, "Americans are strong at hardware and systems, but regarding information and software, all of our brains are just as good... Yahoo's stock will fall and

---

① Srikanth AN, Jack Ma—The Inspirational Story of Alibaba Founder, http://www.shoutmeloud.com/jack-ma-alibaba-founder.html, 2015-06-25.

eBay's stock will rise. And maybe after eBay's stock rises, Alibaba's stock will rise." [1] It looked like a joke at that time. However, the joke did come true after fifteen years.

Today, Alibaba.com is the world's largest online business-to-business (B2B) trading platform for businesses which currently serves more than 79 million members from more than 240 countries and territories. In September 2014, Alibaba Group listed on NYSE and became one of the most valuable technical companies in the world after raising $25 billion from its U.S. IPO. Since its successful IPO, Alibaba has been called as a combination of eBay, Amazon and PayPal.

Alibaba's Expansion

Though owning more than half B2B market in China, Alibaba is obviously not satisfied its achievements. It has been expanding its business kingdom to a broader market.

1. From China to the world

Alibaba has been working hard on internationalization by what it can do in a cross-border B2B business. Initially, it focused on exporting from China so as to take advantage of the rich resources. Now, it expands the businesses to other countries. Alibaba has three main services: the company's English language portal Alibaba.com handles sales between importers and exporters from more than 240 countries and regions; the Chinese portal 1688.com is developed for domestic business-to-business trade in China; In addition, Alibaba offers a transaction-based retail website, AliExpress.com, which allows smaller buyers to buy small quantities of goods at wholesale prices.

There are two extra opportunities for Alibaba's international expansion. First, there are millions of overseas Chinese in North America, Europe and Australia. They all want to make businesses with the domestic merchants, which makes them the potential customers of Alibaba. Besides, there's no language problem with them. But it forces Alibaba to work on payment and logistics. Second, hundreds of millions Chinese have a huge potential of consumption overseas. This is what foreign merchants get excited about. With AliPay, Alibaba enables the transactions between foreign merchants and Chinese SMEs, pay in RMB, and Alibaba makes sure the transaction parties to get the currency of their choice and handle logistics.

2. From cities to countryside

In October 2014, Alibaba planned to invest 10 billion yuan ($1.6 billion) within

---

[1] Alyson Shontell, In 1999, Alibaba's CEO Told Employees 2 Things They Needed to Do to Be Successful: Beat Americans and Work Longer Hours, http://www.businessinsider.com/jack-mas-early-1999-speech-to-alibaba-employees-2014-9, 2014-09-22.

three to five years to build thousands of facilities in rural China to tap rising demand in these areas.

The facilities include 1,000 "county operational centers" and 100,000 "village service stations". People will see Alibaba's network extend to one third of China's counties and one sixth of its rural areas. The centers focus on improving logistics services and cultivating more buyers and sellers in rural areas so that they can enjoy the low cost and high efficient online transactions without leaving home. According to the statistics, the amount of rural netizens has reached 178 million, accounting for 28.2% of the total. Alibaba's rural facilities plan implies its ambition of expanding the existing market to the broad rural market[①].

3. From PC end to mobile ends

By June 2014, the amount of Chinese cellphone netizens had rose up to 527 million, almost half of Chinese total population[②]. After viewing the potentials of mobile commerce, Alibaba began to expand its businesses from personal computer to mobile ends such as mobile phone and tablet. Alibaba made key investments in the field like Sina Weibo, AutoNavi. Meanwhile, its competitors also coveted this "Huge Cake". For example, Tencent attempted to cut a slice from the huge cake by virtue of its popular social media—WeChat. E-commerce is one segment that's perhaps the most complex when it comes to mobile. Alibaba not only has to deal with browsing and selection but logistics and payment, which implies issues of reliability and security.

Fortunately, Alibaba has Alipay, the online payment escrow service unit. It plays a significant role in maintaining Alibaba's huge amount of customers and directing them to the mobile ends. Alibaba uses Alipay for overseas operations in a way similar to those at home. The strategy is aimed at luring overseas companies to Alibaba's e-commerce sites.

4. From B2B platform to online ecosystem

Alibaba's ambition obviously is not limited to B2B e-commerce. In the past decades, it has been devoting to building a business ecosystem (Figure 2-2). Buyers and sellers are at the heart of Alibaba ecosystem. Enabling buyers and sellers to discover, select and transact with each other on Alibaba platforms has been Alibaba's primary goal. Originating from a single B2B platform, Alibaba has been making efforts to consolidate and expand its platform. As a result, an integration of different functional platforms is established—Alibaba Group. The system is composed of three layers:

 阿里巴巴的野心显然不限于B2B电商,在过去将近20年的时间里,它一直致力于打造一个商业生态系统[图2-2]。买卖双方位于阿里巴巴商业生态系统的核心。帮助双方发现、选择以

---

① Xinhua, Alibaba Targets Rural Expansion, Shenzhen Daily, 2014-10-15.
② The 34th Report of Chinese Internet Development, CNNIC, 2014-06.

及相互交易一直是阿里巴巴的首要目标。源于 B2B 平台，阿里巴巴一直努力巩固和扩展其平台，并建成了集多平台于一体的阿里集团。这一体系包括三个层次：

1）Customers-oriented layer. This layer includes the e-commerce platforms specified to individual consumers such as Taobao, Tmall, Juhuasuan and Aliexpress.

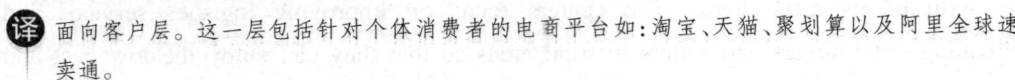面向客户层。这一层包括针对个体消费者的电商平台如：淘宝、天猫、聚划算以及阿里全球速卖通。

• Taobao is the online shopping destination for Chinese consumers looking for wide selection, value and convenience.

• Tmall is dedicated to providing a premium shopping experience for increasingly sophisticated Chinese consumers in search of top-quality branded merchandise.

• Juhuasuan is a platform offering qualified products at discounted prices by aggregating the demand from numerous consumers. It mainly does this through flash sales which make products available at discounted prices for a limited period of time.

• Aliexpress is a global retail marketplace targeting at consumers worldwide, many of whom located in Russia, Brazil and the United States.

2）Businesses-oriented layer. This layer is composed of the e-commerce platforms targeting at SMEs such as Alibaba.com, 1688.com and Alimama.

面向企业层。这一层由瞄准中小企业的电商平台组成，包括阿里巴巴全球电商网站、阿里巴巴国内电商网站以及阿里妈妈。

• Alibaba.com and 1688.com are the B2B platforms. The former focuses on the global wholesale trade while the latter targets at domestic wholesale in China.

• Alimama is an online marketing technology platform that offers sellers on Alibaba Group's marketplaces online marketing services for both personal computers and mobile devices. Through the Taobao Affiliate Network, Alimama also provides those sellers with such marketing services on third-party websites.

3）Supporting layer. This layer consists of the service platforms like Alipay, Cainiao and Aliyun which provide the supportive infrastructures like logistics.

支持层。这一层主要包括支付宝、菜鸟物流以及阿里云等后台基础支持平台。

• Launched in December 2004, Alipay provides a secure, trustworthy and convenient way for individuals and businesses to make and receive payments online and on mobile phones.

• Established in September 2009, Aliyun develops highly scalable platforms for cloud computing and data management. It provides a comprehensive suite of cloud computing services to support the participants of Alibaba Group's online and mobile commerce ecosystem, including sellers, and other third-party customers and businesses.

• Cainiao operates a logistics information platform which provides real-time access to information for both buyers and sellers, as well as information that allows delivery service providers to improve the efficiency and effectiveness of their services.

The three layers interconnect, interact and interdepend effectively, which enables a complete and efficient ecosystem. During the past 16 years, Alibaba has grown up to an integrated online ecosystem from a single B2B platform (Figure 2-2). So many changes occurred but one thing—serving the sellers and buyers affiliated by Alibaba. In the future, where is Alibaba going? Just as what Jack Ma said, "Alibaba is going to build three systems—Platform, Finance and Data."①

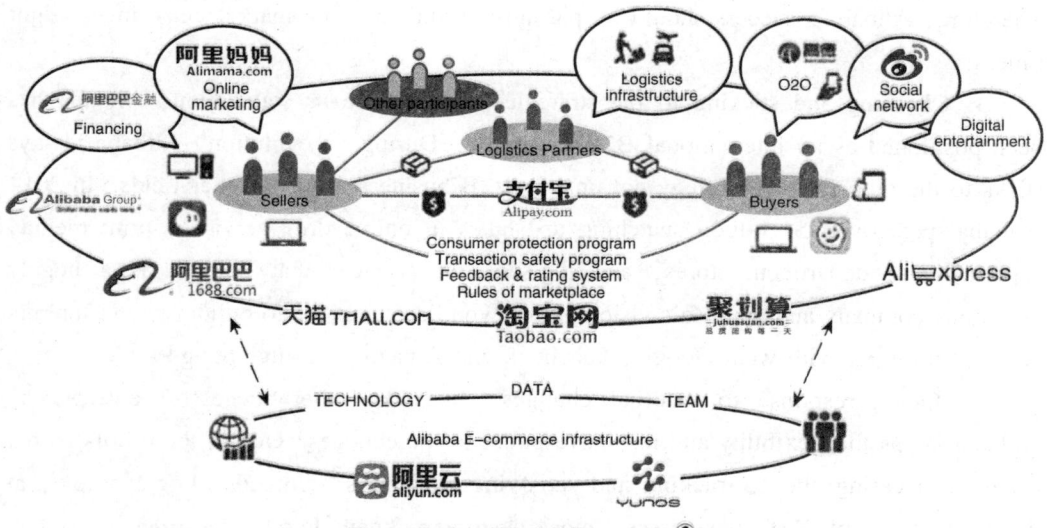

Figure 2-2   Alibaba Ecosystem②

Critical Success Factors for Alibaba

1. Right business positioning. One of the contributions of Jack Ma is he accurately positioned Alibaba—serving small and medium enterprises (SMEs). The number of SMEs accounts for more than 90% of Chinese enterprises and the huge volume builds the solid base for Alibaba's online businesses on the one hand. On the other hand, SMEs are more anxious for business information due to the limited information access. Therefore, Alibaba's B2B services are naturally attractive for them.

2. Market entry in the right time. Jack Ma and his partners founded Alibaba in 1999

---

① 马云绘阿里"蓝图":平台、金融和数据, 中国企业家(北京), http://money.163.com/12/0911/08/8B3VLBPN00253G87.html, 2012-09-11。
② www.chinainternetwatch.com

when China was experiencing the transition from planned economy to market economy. The state-owned trading companies in turn were forced to convert into private companies and be responsible for profiting on their own. As a result, the trading companies, especially the small and medium enterprises (SMEs), had to decide what to sell, where to sell the products and whom to make the deals with. Due to the limited resources, it was very hard for them to find the necessary information especially when the potential trading partners located overseas. Alibaba just plays the role of trading matching which connects the sellers and the buyers together and helps them to find the matched partners with high efficiency and low trading cost. Actually, there were some similar platforms entering the B2B market before or after Alibaba. Unfortunately, most of them failed. Therefore, Alibaba's success should be partially attributed to its market entry in the right time.

3. Choosing and sticking to the strategic focus. Since its foundation, Alibaba has been positioned as an international B2B enterprise. During its evolution, Alibaba always sticks to the globalization strategy not only in B2B businesses but in other fields. In 2014 Alibaba spent over $4 billion snatching up stakes in online drug services, print media, supermarkets, department stores, and logistics. It is clear that Alibaba is a hugely ambitious company and that Ma's vision goes beyond e-commerce to build a whole Internet ecosystem on par with what Google, Facebook and Amazon are attempting[1].

4. Quick response to external changes. Just like other successful enterprises, Alibaba keeps the flexibility and instant response to the changes. One of the proofs is that it has been caring about, tracking and satisfying customers' demands. For example, at the early stage of B2B businesses, most customers knew barely the rules of online transactions. Alibaba provided the necessary supports including how to do cross-border trade online, how to make international payment, how to describe products and introduce company, how to build trustful relationship with trading partners, and how to avoid the Internet fraudulence[2]. The quick response to external changes can, to some extent, explain why Alibaba survived the "Internet bubble bursting" in 2000 and the global financial crisis in 2008.

5. Well-designed platform. A well-designed platform should be helpful and easy to use for the customers especially for the new customers. Alibaba implements this by offering product list, product search, inquiry basket and trade managers. These functionalities enable users to post sales offer, search information, make inquiry through Buyer Leads and

---

[1] Drew Bernstein, Betting on Jack Ma: Three Keys to Alibaba's Success, *Forbes*, 2014-09-18.
[2] Jingzhi Guo, Iok Ham Lam, Ieong Lei, Xin Guan, Pei Hin Iong and Meng Chao Ieong, Alibaba International—Building A Global Electronic Marketplace, The Proceedings of IEEE International Conference on E-Business Engineering, 2006-10-24.

Inquiry Basket and make negotiation with partners. The well-designed platform facilitates the network effect which means that one user of a good or service has on the value of that product to other people. When a network effect is present, the value of a product or service is dependent on the number of others using it. The more users on the one side (e.g. sellers) choose the platform, the more users on the other side (e.g. buyers) would like to use the platform.

6. Credit system. Credit is a critical element for an e-commerce platform. Unfortunately, China's credit system had not been established when Alibaba was founded. Due to lack of trust between the transaction parties, users were reluctant to make the deals online. To eliminate the obstacle, Alibaba launched Trustpass which requires the sellers to supply the credit documents to the buyers on the exchange website. Trustpass alleviates users' concerns on online frauds and facilitates B2B transactions. After viewing the effectiveness of Trustpass, Alibaba launched another important creditability tool—Alipay in 2003, which has grown up to be China's top third-party payment system of online transactions.

7. Effective communication with stakeholders. As a Chinese company, every step Alibaba takes is potentially subject to misunderstanding. China has a more opaque and volatile business environment compared with the West. Short-sellers will seize on any inconsistencies to try to knock the company down. Alibaba provides extremely clear explanations and very detailed data that answer investors' concerns before they arise. It also keeps the communication with investors to show how transactions with private entities within Alibaba are truly at arms-length and beneficial to public investors.

8. Government's supports. Chinese government officials are eager for a local company to break into the ranks of tech's global elite, and the huge payoff for Alibaba will highlight just how valuable official Chinese support can be. Alibaba's rise has been propelled by government policies and government provides local champions such as Alibaba with the space they need to become viable players globally. For example, Alibaba was relatively slow to move into social networks, but the company has been playing catch-up. In 2013, it became a major shareholder in Sina Weibo, a microblogging service that would compete with Twitter and Facebook which are banned to operate in China. As a result, Alibaba had an unimpeded entry into the world's largest Internet market, even though it was a relative latecomer, and it would continue to grow without challenge from American competition. Another example is online video. Chinese government has banned Google's online video service for years. Alibaba owns 5.5% of Huayi Brothers Media, a film and TV production company in Beijing, and on April 29, Alibaba and Yunfeng Capital, a private-equity firm co-founded by Ma, agreed to pay $1.22 billion for a stake in Beijing-based Internet television company Youku Tudou. As with social networking, Chinese

government has kept the world's biggest competitor out of Alibaba's way[1].

Challenges Encountered by Alibaba

As the most successful B2B website, Alibaba is still encountering some challenges:

1. Keeping the advantage of intermediary agent. A manufacturer needs a steady supply of raw material and needs to maintain large and expensive inventories to ensure that it does not run out of raw material. With the rising production cost (e. g. salary), many manufacturers, especially the SEMs, are eager to find a way to decrease the procurement cost. As an international B2B brand, Alibaba should keep the ability to electronically connect the sellers and the buyers with the best prices.

2. Order fulfillment. Since Alibaba is a B2B platform supplying a space of online transaction, all the users have to conduct the logistics on their own or by virtue of third party logistics. If a user chooses the former, the delivery quality can be controlled while the cost is relatively high. If a user picks third party logistics provider which does not provide a platform to place orders and monitor delivery, the user would lose control over the logistics. The dissatisfaction with delivery quality may cause the loss of platform users. As customers demand faster and more accurate delivery cycles, Alibaba's ability to manage logistics can be a key differentiator and competitive advantage. Hence B2B systems that enable and monitor order fulfillment are indispensable. Taobao's "Big Logistics Plan" launched in 2011 is a big step to logistics services.

3. The threats from the competitors in online finance field such as Tencent. Payment is the most attractive slice of the online finance cake. For Alibaba and Tencent, "who will win the payment fight" might very well be a life-or-death question. The reason is simple: e-commerce marketers fight for lower and lower margins. In such a commoditized market, payment is the one part of the business where margins get (less) compressed and a major path for growth and there is still much room for expansion. But China doesn't have a monopolistic payment system such as PayPal. It has two Internet champions fighting for the market—Alibaba and Tencent[2]. In March 2013, Alibaba announced its plan to integrate its payment and micro-payment businesses to set up a micro-finance service group. The move helps strengthen Alibaba in the mobile Internet and social media sectors.

4. Quality and integrity problems. Alibaba offers a Gold Supplier membership to try to ensure that each seller is genuine. To qualify for a Gold Supplier membership, a supplier must complete an authentication and verification process by a reputable third-party security

---

[1] Bruce Einhorn, How China's Government Set up Alibaba's Success, *Bloomberg Businessweek*, 2014-05-07.
[2] WeChat payment: 5 Reasons Tencent Might Kill Alipay, https://walkthechat.com/wechat-payment-5-reasons-tencent-might-kill-alipay/

service provider appointed by Alibaba.com. While the majority of suppliers are reported to be genuine, there have been cases of sellers seeking to defraud unsuspecting buyers. In February 2011, Alibaba's corporate office admitted that it granted the mark of integrity of its "China Gold Supplier" program to more than 2,000 dealers that had subsequently defrauded buyers. The announcement caused the controversy and the decline of its share price. Though adopting some corrective actions, Alibaba's commitment to quality and integrity, versus a damage control view suggests that the subscription-driven, third-party verified "China Gold Supplier" program is endangered by diminished trust in its endorsement system, removing the incentive for global buyers to choosing Alibaba as their Business-to-Business service, thus more broadly endangering Alibaba through impact on its brand and capabilities.

5. The global brand image needed to be strengthened. Alibaba has not been well-known yet overseas due to its international services being limited to e-commerce services for Chinese living abroad. Following the expected NYSE listing, global attention increased sharply for Alibaba and there is great interest in whether the company will suddenly expand overseas operations to take advantage of the publicity. Increasing overseas business is essential for Alibaba to maintain its strong domestic business base. In China, 255 million people use Alibaba's websites to buy goods and services offered by an estimated 8 million companies[①]. The company says that overseas operations are key in keeping its huge number of customers satisfied.

After almost twenty years evolvement, as the largest B2B platform in China, Alibaba has built its brand strength and position in B2B field. Though encountering some challenges, Alibaba is predicted an optimistic future. However, to become a company that lasts at least 102 years, Alibaba has a long way to go.

Case Analysis

对于成功的企业，人们往往将注意力放在它取得的成绩和领导人的传奇上。实际上，企业成功的原因才是案例分析应该关注的焦点，对于本案例亦是如此。阿里巴巴从中国的一个 B2B 电商网站成长为一个综合性的大型集团，构建出一个复杂而全面的商业生态系统，它成功的秘诀是什么？如果我们从天时地利人和的角度去分析原因，那么必须承认阿里巴巴（以下简称阿里）成功的第一个关键因素就是时间点——它选择了一个恰当的时机进入市场。阿里 1999 年成立的时候，中国的电子商务才刚刚起步，电商市场尤其是 B2B 市场里几乎没有强有力的竞争对手，这为阿里提供了宝贵的成长时间和空间。但在另一方面，这个新兴市场意味着人们对电子商务尚不熟悉，甚至没有听说过，这给阿里开拓市场造成了很大的难度，当时它面临的主要问题就是：如何说服人

---

① Jo Ling Kent, Alibaba IPO: 5 Things to Know, http://www.investopedia.com/articles/investing/081214/5-things-know-about-alibaba-ipo.asp, 2015-12-16.

们相信并接受 B2B 这种新模式。幸运的是，阿里自始至终都将目标客户锁定在中国有贸易需求的中小企业，这种明确的市场定位是其成功的第二个关键原因。与传统的思维不同，阿里并未瞄准知名大企业，而是专注于为中小企业服务。由于它的平台模式解决了长期以来困扰国内中小企业的交易信息不对称的问题，因此迅速吸引了不少客户并建立了自己在中国 B2B 电商行业的品牌知名度。阿里的市场定位采用的是典型的"蓝海策略"，专注于比较小众且竞争相对较小的"蓝海市场"。正是它坚持自己的市场定位，把握住机会迅速成长，等别的竞争对手意识到这一市场机遇的时候，阿里巴巴已经在中国 B2B 电商行业遥遥领先，成为市场的领导者。阿里成功的第三个原因是它善于在灵活性与坚持之间巧妙平衡。一方面，自它成立之日起，阿里一直瞄准 B2B 电商市场不放松，并成为行业翘楚；另一方面，阿里又从不囿于 B2B 电商，而是根据市场需求迅速进行业务调整，例如不断增加和更新服务功能。事实上，企业要在灵活性与坚持之间进行权衡并不容易，但阿里却做到了。不同于一般电商企业仅仅关注用户流量，阿里总是专注于为客户解决问题从而实现双赢——用户的问题得到解决，阿里从中获益（如：服务费、品牌知名度）。建立 B2B 交易诚信系统就是一个典型的例子：阿里成立的时候，中国还没有健全的诚信体系，用户的诚信观念也比较淡薄，网上欺诈等纠纷屡见不鲜，这也令不少用户对于双方不见面的网上交易望而却步。鉴于此，阿里先后推出了诚信通和支付宝，企业认证和 7 天付款的机制有效地解决了交易双方的信任问题，吸引了更多的用户，支付宝更是发展成为中国最大的第三方支付系统。在中国这样一个人际距离较近，看重社会关系的市场环境中，企业的成功往往离不开政府的支持，阿里巴巴也是如此。政府给予的政策支持和促成的项目成为阿里成功的保障。

成功企业的一个共同特点就是：永不满足于现状，持续创新。与亚马逊一样，阿里自成立以来从未停止创新的脚步，并在此过程中成功实现了企业扩张。在地理位置层面，阿里从中国走向世界，从中国城市拓展至农村；在技术层面，阿里从电脑端拓展至移动端；在商业模式层面，阿里从双边市场拓展至多边市场。很显然，阿里巴巴的野心远远超出人们的想象——建立一个覆盖线上线下，融电商、金融、数据、娱乐等为一体的完整的商业生态圈。

Section 3
IndiaMART—Working for SMEs
第三节 印度市场网——为中小企业工作

Key Words

1. crore *n.* 一千万卢比
2. lakh *n.* 十万卢比
3. increment *n.* 增量
4. enquiry *n.* 询盘

 *Case*

About InidaMART

As the world's second largest B2B website after Alibaba and the largest online marketplace in India, InidaMART is an e-commerce company that provides B2B sales and also B2C and C2C via its portal. It was founded by Dinesh Agarwal and Brijesh Agrawal in 1996, headquartered in Noida, India. InidaMART initially aimed at the customers in India and no one would have thought to see it as the big beast it has become today. As of end 2017, it owned more than 58 million buyers, 4.6 million suppliers and supplied 65 million products[1].

In early 2009, the firm received 50 crore Series A round funding from Intel Capital, a part of which was invested in IndiaMART, One97 Communications and Global Talent Track. In March 2016, it raised Series C Funding from Amadeus Capital Partners and Quona Capital. It was claimed that these funds would be used to scale up the activities of IndiaMART[2].

InidaMART's Revenue Model

Basically, IndiaMART gains its revenue from three sources[3]:

1. Online directories. IndiaMARToffers business & companies directory with free business listings of Indian companies, exporter, importer and detailed information on the website. IndiaMART encourages those listed under different sections to have a web presence of their own and offers its expertise on site building for which it charges its merchants a fee. Besides, it also makes money from registration fee. Although most firms are listed free of cost, those who are provided some exclusive services are not entitled to. Only in the financial year 2000-2001, the website gained revenue from the two catalogues was Rs 205.61 lakhs which was also the major share of revenue earned by IndiaMART.

2. B2B auctions. The business was launched in December 2000, which gave IndiaMART an opportunity to cash the high visibility it had earned for the past few years. On the Auction platform, suppliers are allowed to register online and list their inventory for auction on an annual basis. The sellers decide the reserve price, minimum bid price and bid increment amount and buyers can bid on the items listed free of cost after going through the product information online. When the auction times out the sellers are introduced to the

---

[1] https://corporate.indiamart.com/about-us/
[2] https://en.wikipedia.org/wiki/IndiaMART
[3] Ashok. K. Roy, Case Study—Indiamart Makes Money While Others Flounde, https://corporate.indiamart.com/2001/06/01/case-study-indiamart-makes-money-while-other-flounder/, 2001-06-01.

winner to complete the transaction.

3. Web advertising. IndiaMART offers online advertising for the businesses on the platform. By virtue of the advertisements, the products, services and promotion information can reach the potential customers efficiently and facilitate the trading between sellers and buyers. As a result, IndiaMART can make money for charging advertising service fees.

IndiaMART's strategy of network expansion to reach larger SMEs markets and offering multiple business services and solutions thereby generates multiple revenue streams.

InidaMART's B2B Services

As a B2B platform aiming at international trade, IndiaMART offers services to both sellers and buyers:

1. Buyers can proactively seek sellers on IndiaMART by:

1) Keyword input box—The most common and effective way to search. Typing relevant terms and keywords into this box, a buyer is able to find what he or she is looking for.

2) Browsing brands—Browse the brands posted by IndiaMART and find the preferred suppliers.

3) Browsing products—Latest products uploaded onto IndiaMART can be viewed on the Products Tab. To browse the favorite products, a customer just click on relevant product categories indexed along the left-side margin of the home page.

4) Contact suppliers. Once a buyer finds what he or she is looking for, he or she can send an inquiry immediately by offering the email ID and name.

Besides, IndiaMART provides three tools which help sellers to make deals and succeed efficiently: Quick Learn which helps sellers to understand the basics of online transactions and get advanced tips to generate more business; Emerging Business Forum which stays updated with business topics from India's biggest SME discussion forums; Leaders of Tomorrow which helps sellers to get to know how leaders have successfully driver their business.

2. Sellers can sell on IndiaMART by virtue of 4 steps:

1) Provide their basic details like name, email ID and mobile number by which IndiaMART's representatives can contact;

2) Update business profile, including contact address, business details and company name;

3) Add products. Each seller is able to add up to 400 products;

4) Get business enquiries. After completing the first three steps, sellers can wait for

the enquiries from the potential buyers via email, call or buy leads.

Additionally, IndiaMART offers payment protection for buyers by virtue of IndiaMART PayX which brings buyers a secure and trusted way of buying. Buyers can negotiate their business deal with sellers directly and then use IndiaMART PayX for a reliable and secure transaction. By using IndiaMART PayX, buyers know that they will receive exactly the goods or services they expect before the payment is made to the seller. It is simple to use by three steps:

1) Deposit with IndiaMART PayX. Buyers deposit money to IndiaMART PayX after they finalize deal with sellers;

2) Receive the product. Buyers wait for the delivery of goods and confirm the delivery;

3) IndiaMART PayX pays sellers. Once buyers confirm the delivery and feel satisfied with it, IndiaMART PayX releases payment to sellers.

Reasons for IndiaMART's Achievements

IndiaMART's achievements should be attributed to the following reasons:

1. Focusing on the core business. Connecting with suppliers and buyers is the core business of IndiaMART. The company has been focusing on how to scale the marketplace by augmenting their listing services by getting more buyers and SMEs and maximizing business growth for them. In addition, it launched an initiative to target on bigger brands for both buying and selling requirements. Its "Big Brands" program is a major growth area since it focused on small and medium enterprises. This program features connecting large manufacturing corporations with suppliers across the country and the world[①].

2. Appropriate positioning. IndiaMART positions itself as a powerful marketing tool, targeting specifically on sellers and buyers. The Internet is a powerful marketing tool to introduce merchants' products to new customers and connect with potential buyers and suppliers. Thousands of international manufacturers, suppliers, wholesalers and trade agents go to IndiaMART everyday, to list their products and find buyers. Additionally, IndiaMART adds Quick Learn feature which enables sellers to find the potential buyers efficiently.

3. Powerful search functionality which provides relevant and helpful information. IndiaMART ranks the professionals and the active businesses in the search results. All companies listed in the directory are according to their membership status, international business certification, and the frequency of their online activity. The community enables

---

① Vishal Krishna, Indiamart Is Aiming for Rs 2,000 cr Revenue by 2020. Here Is How It Wants to Get There, https://yourstory.com/2016/06/indiamart-dinesh-agarwal/, 2016-06-03.

buyers to shop over the world from their office or home with unbelievable savings. Besides, IndiaMART integrates location and auto-suggested features and introduces phonetic algorithms which works even when there are minor spelling mistakes in keywords of search.

4. Offering a wide range of products. These products include genuine brand names, OEM and non-branded goods, wholesale bulk lots, unique (as well as) hard to find items, surplus & liquidation clearance products and more. The wide range of products enables buyers to have enough options to make the final purchase decision. As a result, the buyers are willing to visit IndiaMART's website, which in turn attracts more sellers to make deals on the website.

5. Maintaining the quality of online trading community by valuing trust, foremost, and working diligently. Thousands of companies and traders are banned, restricted or just not listed. It has been devoted to protecting the customers, helping them to deal only with companies guided by professional business practices. It also offers a trust program through a distinguished and independent third party service which has proven itself both credible and reliable in the past.

6. Trust program. Developing a reputation for trust among customers is important for SMEs, particularly in the e-commerce environment where perceived risk is more pronounced than in traditional commerce. Once trust is established, a firm learns that coordinated efforts will lead to outcomes that exceed what the firm would achieve if it acts solely. As a result, it will facilitate more firms to join in the trading on a platform. To establish a trusted online B2B community for international trade, IndiaMART developes a business verification system called TrustSEAL, which checks the credibility and trustworthiness of SMEs. IndiaMART awards TrustSEAL package to the companies that have proven themselves via sophisticated online identity validation processes. All the suppliers issued TrustSEAL package can own TrustSEAL logo, TrustSEAL stamp in IndiaMART listing, TrustSEAL certificate and Trust report, which helps them to attract genuine buyers, get distinct visibility and higher listing across IndiaMART network.

7. Continuous innovation in technology. It is very hard to survive the B2B e-commerce. For IndiaMART, it has been innovating to increase its revenues and profitability. For example, the company introduced "buy leads" product that enables SMEs to work an "open tendering" process. It also has been devoting to wiping out inefficiencies in the marketplace. For example, there is a virtual phone service, which helps buyers connect smoothly with suppliers and ensures that the buyer's call is never missed by a supplier. Besides, users' logging history helps IndiaMART to provide a high degree of personalisation and recommendations for users, which results in increasing repeat usage and higher conversion.

Where Is IndiaMART Going?

IndiaMART offers inclusive corporate perseverance to the worldwide trade community. Its online gateway is for traders to work together efficiently, resourcefully, and profitably. The company allows SEMs to proliferate their trades by simplifying the trading process and facilitating the interactions between the genuine firms. For the companies who attempts to sell the products or look for the resources over the world, IndiaMART is a premium option to explore. As the top B2B platform over the world, IndiaMart is obviously not satisfied with its current territory. It has been offering more valued-added services: In June 2016, IndiaMART claimed to become a Rs 2,000- crore entity, with three revenue streams and investment in data science technology and automation tools to support its customers. Furthermore, it planned to increase the exposure in online retailing via Tolexo.com, facilitating a B2C-like experience for the B2B retail world[1]. In March 2017, IndiaMart announced its entry in the payments space to enable over three million sellers on its platform by launching the buyer and seller protection program[2]. In May 2018, IndiaMART launched its digital campaign focusing on various benefits of Payment Gateway—Pay with IndiaMART, which allows merchants to receive payment instantly in their account even on a bank holiday and accept advance payments[3].

In the future, how to expand its market and compete with the existing players such as Alibaba while keeping its core competences is the primary task for IndiaMART.

Case Analysis

对于本案例中的企业——印度市场网(IndiaMART),大家并不熟悉。虽然知名度和规模尚不及阿里巴巴,但这家成立于1996年,现已成长为全球排名第二的B2B电商平台仍然有其独到之处。我们的分析重点也放在其商业模式和成功原因上。

与阿里巴巴类似,印度市场网仍然采取了平台商业模式,即将供求双方吸引到平台上来进行自由的贸易交换,并从中获益。印度市场网的收入主要来自三个方面:一是B2B竞拍服务,通过促成双方的竞拍交易,该网站从中获取佣金;二是向平台用户收取注册和商品目录展示费;三是广告服务费,即为企业提供广告服务,

---

[1] Vishal Krishna, Indiamart Is Aiming for Rs 2,000 cr Revenue by 2020. Here Is How It Wants to Get There, https://yourstory.com/2016/06/indiamart-dinesh-agarwal/, 2016-06-03.

[2] Ani, IndiaMART Forays into Fintech, Plans to Enable 3 Million Sellers with A Suite of Products, https://retail.economictimes.indiatimes.com/news/E-commerce/e-tailing/indiamart-forays-into-fintech-plans-to-enable-3-million-sellers-with-a-suite-of-products/57534236, 2017-03-08.

[3] Indiatelevision Team, IndiaMART Promotes Payment Gateway for SMEs, http://www.indiantelevision.com/mam/marketing/brands/indiamart-promotes-payment-gateway-for-smes-180521, 2018-05-21.

在平台上为其展示商品,并从中获取广告服务费。可以看出,印度市场网的收入来源与阿里巴巴等平台大同小异,都是通过为交易各方提供有附加价值的服务来获取收入。

作为一开始立足于印度本国市场的电商网站,印度市场网能在成立后的20多年里发展成为全球B2B电商领域的翘楚,其背后的原因值得深入剖析。首先是明确的定位和坚持主业。印度市场网成立的初衷就是"让企业做生意更容易",而它多年来也一直坚持宗旨,为全球企业尤其是中小企业提供沟通和交易的渠道,并通过Quick learn等高附加值的服务降低企业的交易成本,提高交易效率。与阿里巴巴不同,印度市场网并没有大规模进行平台从双边到多边的拓展,除了通过Tolexo.com增加B2C业务曝光度以外,它仍然坚持将业务重点放在B2B电子商务领域,致力于以高附加值的服务吸引和留住客户。这种策略能让它将优势资源集中在一个领域,深挖其中的价值,但也可能因为业务单一而受到后来者的竞争威胁。其次,印度市场网围绕用户需求,提供全方位的服务,以提高客户黏性。搜索是电商网站的必备功能,印度市场网除了为买卖双方提供快速、准确的搜索服务以外,还自行开发了集定位、搜索自动建议以及语音搜索功能为一体的服务,以提升用户的搜索体验;另外,该网站坚持为用户提供多样化的商品选择,以6 500多万种商品满足不同客户的需求。为了保证商品的质量,印度市场网还进行供应商筛选,并推出商家诚信项目对供应商的资质和商业信誉进行审查,既降低了客户交易风险,又提升了网站本身的品牌形象。与很多成功的电子商务企业一样,印度市场网的成功还归因于它持续不断的创新。它先后推出采购信息、虚拟在线电话等技术创新帮助用户降低交易成本,提升交易效果。

在过去几年中,印度市场网通过不断推出高附加值的服务成功地吸引和留住客户,也巩固了它在B2B电商市场的领先地位。但是面对阿里巴巴等强大的竞争对手,这家创办已经20多年的网站仍然有很长的路要走。

Section 4
Target Corporation—Retailer-Supplier Collaboration
第四节 塔吉特公司——零售商与供应商之间的协同

Key Words

1. emergence *n.* 出现
2. EDI 电子数据交换
3. legions of 大批的
4. resistance *n.* 排斥
5. perseverance *n.* 坚持不懈
6. proliferate *vt.* 使扩大

Case

Target and Collaborative Commerce

Target Corporation (Target) is an American retailing company, founded in 1902 and headquartered in Minneapolis, Minnesota. It is the second-largest discount retailer in the United States, Walmart being the largest. The company was ranked the 36th on the Fortune 500 as of 2013 and was a component of the Standard & Poor's 500 index. In early 2013, Target expanded into Canada and now operates over 100 locations through its Canadian subsidiary.

As a retailer, Target has to conduct e-commerce activities with about 20,000 trading partners, which involves collaborative commerce (C-commerce) among different supply chain participant. As mentioned above, collaborative commerce refers to the collaborative planning, designing, developing, building and managing products through their life cycle among the supply chain participants by virtue of inter-organization information system. Collaborative commerce involves not only the collaboration of resources, businesses and goals within an organization (e. g. inventory, production, sales and accounting) but the collaboration between internal and external resources, that is, the coloration of the whole supply chain (e. g. demand, supply, production, procurement and transactions).

EDI—The Tool Aiding Target's C-commerce

How does Target handle the collaboration with its thousands of suppliers? Target established a VAN-based EDI system which gets its partners connected. EDI, or Electronic Data Interchange, is an electronic communication system that enables the communication, sharing of information, designing and planning between an enterprise and its partners.

EDI began in early 1970s when the transportation industry (i. e. ocean, trucking and rail) formed the Transportation Data Coordinating Committee (TDCC). The technology has been adopted by many businesses worldwide as a vehicle to eliminate paper works associated with business transactions, thereby eliminating errors caused by entering data manually. However, computer technology was very different at that time, and the majority of computers were mainframe computers running proprietary operating systems. There was few standard for communicating between computers built by different manufacturers and even computers manufactured by the same company had difficulty in exchanging information. Many of the early EDI standards were oriented to solving these problems, though many of them seem trivial in today's PC and Internet-enabled world.

1. EDI and Target's C-commerce[①]

EDI has been widely used for decades and have accumulated experience on critical business factors necessary for successful collaborative commerce. If the economic principles governing c-commerce remain unchanged regardless of the network infrastructure, experience in traditional EDI practices can provide Target with useful insights for Internet-based c-commerce as well. When organizations develop EDI just to replace traditional communications means (such as postal mail or fax), the impacts of the system on organizational performance would be limited. However, if companies establish EDI to create "collaborative commerce" with partner firms, EDI would offer much more significant productivity gains.

For Target, EDI not just as a new communication means, but also as a vehicle which enables new collaboration with trading partners. Target and its business partners that were once vertically integrated and manufactured product to stock evolved into virtual collaborations with legions of specialists producing products and services for current demand. Demand and supply chains also evolved into flexible, technology-enabled partnership that can produce custom products. Besides, EDI also facilitates the traditional manufacturers' collaboration with Target to move closer to project and flow-based manufacturing across multiple partners. Likewise, service organizations are able to coordinate with channel partners more easily to present a unified front to the customer. This trend represents the "collaborative B2B commerce" with trading firms.

2. How does EDI work for Target?

The key part of EDI system is a translator which is a program enabling the encryption and decryption during the course of data transmission so as to ensure the security and efficiency of data transmission among Target and its partners. The work process of EDI is composed of 4 steps:

1) A sender takes out the data with the readable format like word document. Translator is in charge of interpreting the data into message—a machine language, which is actually the data encryption. For example, an upstream vendor takes out an e-invoice and prepares for data transmission by virtue of the translator.

2) Message is sent to a partner's data center by virtue of telecommunication infrastructure. By virtue of the extranet connecting Target and its partners, the vendor sends the e-invoice encrypted to Target's data center over EDI.

3) A receiver fetches the message from the data center. Target takes out the e-invoice right after it arrives in the data center.

[①] S. C. Lee, B. Y. Pak, H. G. Lee Elsevier, Business Value of B2B Electronic Commerce: The Critical Role of Inter-firm Collaboration, *Electronic Commerce Research and Applications*, Vol. 2(4), 2003, pp. 350–361.

4) Translator re-interprets the message into the readable format which is ready for the future usage. Leveraging the translator, Target reinterprets the e-invoice into the original format so that it can be used in the future.

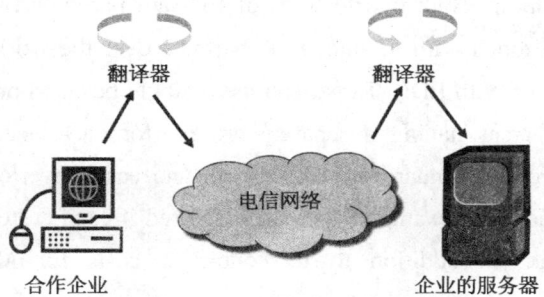

Figure 2-3 Working Process of EDI

3. How does EDI benefit Target? [1][2]

1) Reduced labor cost of mailing and data entry. In a paper-based world, one computer typically prints a document that is then sent (i.e. via mail, fax) to a trading partner where a person reenters the information into a second computer system. The process is time consuming and high cost. EDI reduces the cost of mailing and receiving documents because there is no longer an envelope to route or a fax machine to load. As a result, the low cost and high accuracy of data transmission between Target and its partners can be ensured. According to the statistics, switching to EDI transactions can lower the transaction cost by at least 35%.

2) Higher quality information. Typographic errors can have significantly great consequences than just the labor costs of reviewing and re-typing the data. Some of these costs are easy to quantify while others are less simple. For example, shipping the wrong item to a customer can incur additional shipping and labor cost from customer support required to research and correct the problem. These costs can be easily quantified from bills and timesheets. However, this problem may also lead to dissatisfied customers, who then either take their business elsewhere or become more price-sensitive in future negotiations. Quantifying such costs is clearly difficult, nevertheless they are important to recognize. Fortunately, the quick and accurate information transmission ensure the high quality of information in EDI system since it eliminates the manual input. It is calculated that EDI solution cuts down document errors by 30% to 40%.

3) Better communications, improved business processes. The use of standards known by both sender and receiver ensures correct interpretation of the information, regardless of

---

[1] http://www.mkat.com/cab/sagehtm.htm
[2] https://www.edibasics.com/benefits-of-edi

their nationalities or activity sectors. EDI also creates feedback systems to ensure that documents are actually delivered and received by the correct party. This can eliminate the need for follow-up phone calls and emergency retransmission of documents, which saves the cost of communication. Both two features of EDI are particularly important for Target since it has to keep in touch with its numerous partners over the world.

4) Standardization. With EDI, Target can use a single business process to communicate with each customer, versus having a separate process for each one. While the costs of individual variations from a standard are often small and easily overlooked, the cumulative effects can be substantial. For example, the costs incurred if each customer requires a unique printed invoice format. In addition to the one-time costs for MIS (Management of Information Systems) to create the new format, there are additional ongoing costs such as the additional time it takes to add a new customer and the amount of additional education and training required for support personnel. The standardized data pattern, document formats and communication tools of EDI system can help to avoid the problems.

EDI's adaptability streamlines the flow of communication and helps Target to enhance business relationships with its trading partner.

SWOT Analysis of Target's Collaborative Commerce

Is c-commerce suitable for Target? It is necessary to make a thorough evaluation when choosing the business model. A SWOT analysis enables the evaluation.

Strengths

1. Long-term cooperation experiences. As a retailer with long-history, Target has the necessary experience of cooperating with its suppliers. This benefits Target's c-commerce in two ways: first, the long-term cooperation with suppliers enables Target the capabilities of procurement, inventory and logistics which are required by c-commerce; second, c-commerce usually gets the partners connected to the EDI-based extranet, which requires the smooth communications. The stable cooperation built previously makes it possible to persuade the partners to join the c-commerce network.

2. Powerful technical infrastructure. Target builds two technical systems to implement its collaborations with partners. One is a Van-based network which involves part of suppliers to share information, communication and other activities related to collaboration; the other is EDI system which enables the suppliers who were not connected to Target by the network. Both systems establish a solid base for the collaboration that Target and its numerous suppliers to share information, design products, make production plan and so on.

3. Brand strength. Due to the established brand strength, Target has owned a good

business reputation not only for consumers but also for suppliers. As a result, the suppliers are willing to participate in the c-commerce network so as to implement the collaboration in different aspects such as R&D, sales.

4. Sufficient investment in c-commerce system. A network-based c-commerce usually requires high investment. SMEs hardly afford the system. The long-term good performance makes it possible for Target to provide the sufficient financial supports for c-commerce building, maintaining and operating. For example, in 2013, the company returned $2.5 billion to shareholders through dividends and share repurchase, representing more than 125% of net earnings; Target's full-year 2013 adjusted earnings per share of $4.38 reflect disciplined inventory and expense management despite softer-than-expected U.S. sales; in early 2014, Target corporation reported the fourth quarter net earnings of $520 million, or $0.81 per share, and full-year net earnings of $1,971 million, or $3.07 per share.

Weaknesses

1. The complexity of c-commerce systems may cause the technical and managerial problems. C-commerce system is complicated since it involves the coordinations among different partners. Particularly, Target's c-commerce system has to conduct its coordinations with about 20,000 suppliers, which even makes the implementation of c-commerce more complicated. The technical and managerial problems probably occur in practice.

2. Lack of c-commerce experience. Since the implementation of c-commerce is complex as mentioned above, it even requires even more on the capabilities and experience of c-commerce implementation. Though owning rich experience in cooperating with partners, Target barely has c-commerce experience which may lead to the problems with collaborations.

Opportunities

1. The rapid development of the Internet technologies. The emergences of new technologies such as ERP possibly add more value to c-commerce system. As a result, the collaboration between Target and its partners is getting more efficient and effective.

2. Customers' higher requirements of the products and services. In the buyer-side market, customers are even more powerful, which enables them to require more on products and services. That means, Target has to strengthen its collaboration with the partners so as to generate high value-added and innovative products and services. C-commerce platform provides e-mail, message boards, chat rooms, and online corporate data access globally, despite of the time zone. This is beneficial to satisfy Target's customers better.

Threats

1. External resistance from partners. C-commerce involves the information sharing among partners which means the participants have to partially open its database. This may cause the resistance from participants because opening database involves information security, which may lead potential threats.

2. Internal resistance to new models and approaches. C-commerce means the internal members in Target have to learn extra skills which may cause heavy workload. Therefore, the internal resistance to c-commerce possibly becomes to another threat to Target's c-commerce implementation.

3. The attacks from competitors. In essence, c-commerce system is a computer network. There is a risk of being attacked by competitors. As long as the system is accessed by hackers, the critical data may be revealed.

Target has the obvious strengths and opportunities to implement c-commerce despite the possible weaknesses and threats. The practice of the company also proves it, which means c-commerce benefits its success.

Case Analysis

本案例的主题是协同商务,因此,案例分析的重点也应该放在与之相关的两个问题:一是塔吉特是如何实现它与全球超过 20 000 家合作伙伴之间的有效协同的?二是该公司实行协同商务有何优劣势?前者可以通过 EDI 在塔吉特协同商务中的作用来回答;后者则可以利用 SWOT 分析来完成。

首先必须明确,EDI 问世的时间早于电子商务,它是企业之间进行安全快速沟通的一种数据交换标准(协议)。最初的 EDI 是基于企业的私有网络进行的,成本很高,中小企业无法承受。随着网络技术的成熟,EDI 的成本降低,开始被普遍应用,并在协同商务中发挥作用。对塔吉特而言,EDI 不仅是沟通工具,而且是实现企业间协同的重要通道,具体而言,它的作用表现在 4 个方面:首先是降低成本。EDI 最大的贡献在于它改变了原来企业间基于纸质作业的沟通模式,缩短了作业周期,降低了数据传输的成本;其次保证高质量的数据传输。传统的人工操作模式需要反复录入数据,不仅效率低下,而且数据安全性较差。在 EDI 系统中,塔吉特可以利用加密技术实现它与合作方之间高效安全的数据传输,也避免了手工誊写可能导致的错误;再次是更好的沟通模式帮助改善商业流程。一方面 EDI 在信息收发双方都采用相同的语言和数据格式,避免了因为语言文化的差异导致沟通不良;另一方面,EDI 设置了专门的信息反馈机制,以确保信息准确地传送至接收方。这两点对于需要与全球众多合作伙伴进行频繁沟通的塔吉特而言尤为重要;最后是标准化操作。借助 EDI,塔吉特可以用一套标准化程序与众多合作伙伴进行有效沟通,避免了多程序模式下沟通模式更改(如文件格式更新)导致的信息成本上升。可以看出,EDI 技术在成本、数据质量、沟通流程等方面的优势使它在塔吉特与其合作方的协同中发挥了重要作用。

　　协同商务的优点不言而喻,但它也意味着较高的成本投入,它是否真的适合塔吉特公司? SWOT 分析可以帮助我们客观评估:就优势而言,雄厚的资金实力是塔吉特的第一个优势。要构建一个实现该企业与全球 2 万多家合作商之间协同的系统,大量的资金投入是必不可少的。塔吉特历年来稳定的财务表现为此项投入奠定了基础;而该企业所拥有的 EDI 系统和增值网络(VAN)为商务协同提供了良好的技术支持。构建这样一个复杂的协同商务系统,仅有资金和技术是不够的,还需要劝说遍布全球的众多合作商加入该网络,这对于塔吉特的沟通能力是一项很大的挑战。庆幸的是,多年以来的供应链管理经验和自身的品牌号召力让塔吉特能够胜任这项复杂的任务;其次,缺少处理协同商务的经验以及庞大而复杂的协同系统是塔吉特在迈向协同之路上面临的障碍,这意味着该企业必须从系统设计到实施维护步步谨慎,否则可能造成严重的后果;当然,快速发展的计算机网络技术和顾客日益提升的对产品和服务的要求也使塔吉特实施协同商务成为必然。与此同时,塔吉特也必须面对来自公司内部和外部对协同商务的排斥以及可能的安全隐患。作为一家老牌零售商,保持与上游供应商有效的沟通,建立高效的协同商务系统,实现塔吉特与供应商在资源规划、预测、库存、营销等方面的高效协同是这家历史悠久的企业的必经之路。

Section 5
Types of Case Analysis
第五节　案例分析的种类[①]

　　There are many cases for analysis. If we dig deeper, we can find there are four subdivisions of case analysis, each of which is selected to use depending upon the investigator's goals and/or objectives. These types of case analysis include the following:

　　1. Illustrative case analysis. It is the primarily descriptive analysis. It typically utilizes one or two instances of an event to show the existing situation. Illustrative case analysis serves primarily to make the unfamiliar things familiar and to give readers a common language about the topic in question.

　　2. Exploratory (or pilot) case analysis. It is the condensed case analysis performed before implementing a large scale investigation. Its basic function is to help identify questions and select types of measurement prior to the main investigation. The primary

---

　　① https://en.wikipedia.org/wiki/Case_study#Types_of_case_studies

pitfall of this type of study is that initial findings may seem convincing enough to be released prematurely as conclusions.

3. Cumulative case analysis. It serves to aggregate information from several sites collected at different times. The idea behind the analysis is that the collection of past studies will allow for greater generalization without additional cost or time being expended on new, possibly repetitive studies.

4. Critical instance case analysis. It examines one or more sites either for the purpose of examining a situation of unique interest with little to no interest in generalization, or to call into question a highly generalized or universal assertion. This method is useful for answering cause and effect questions.

In practice, you can choose the appropriate case analysis type based on your goals and try different types if it is possible so as to improve your case analysis skills.

 Summary（本章小结）

B2B refers to the transactions between firms conducted electronically over the Internet, extranets, intranets, or private networks. It has been dominating e-commerce revenue since the volume of a B2B transaction is much bigger than B2C. As one of the e-commerce models, B2B can be further classified into different varieties based on revenue model or the amount of transaction parties.

Alibaba is a B2B website in China founded in 1999. At that time, nobody anticipated it would become the largest B2B website as well as the well-known e-commerce group in China. When founding Alibaba, Jack Ma positioned it as an international enterprise, which helps to explain Alibaba's expansion from China to world, from cities to countryside, from PC end to mobile ends and from B2B platform to online ecosystem. If we explore what causes Alibaba's success, we can find the factors such as appropriate business positioning, right time of market entry, choosing and sticking to the strategic focus, quick response to external changes, well-designed platform, creditability system, effective communication with stakeholders, government's supports. Even though Alibaba has achieved such a great success, it still encounters some challenges such as keeping the advantage of intermediary agent, the threats from the competitors, quality and integrity problems and lack of international brand strength. As one of the most successful e-commerce enterprise, Alibaba still has a long way to go.

Established in 1996, IndiaMART is one of the leading online B2B directory aiming to aid and encourage international trade community for doing trusted trade globally. By virtue of the all-around services, the B2B services offered by IndiaMART attract and keep the customers successfully. The causes that IndiaMART can survive the fierce competition should be attributed to its powerful search functionality, appropriate positioning, offering a wide range of products, working diligently to maintain the quality of online trading community, providing industry-leading resources and the tools to help the customers to efficiently exchange products online and launching trust program. In order to keep the sustainable development, IndiaMART should continue innovation and find new strategies for the future growth.

Target is an American retailing company, founded in 1902. As the second-largest discount retailer in the United States, Target has to conduct e-commerce activities with about 20,000 trading partners, which involves c-commerce among different supply chain participant. C-commerce involves not only the collaboration of resources, businesses and goals within an organization (e.g. inventory, production, sales and accounting) but also the collaboration between internal and external resources, that is, the coloration of the whole supply chain (e.g. demand, supply, production, procurement and transactions). To handle the collaboration with its thousands of suppliers, Target established a VAN-based EDI system to get its partners connected. EDI is an electronic communication system that enables the communication, sharing of information, designing and planning between an enterprise and its partners. EDI helps Target to realize the reduced labor cost of mailing and data entry, timeliness of information, higher quality information, better communications, improved business processes and standardization. Not each firm has the capability of implementing c-commerce. SWOT analysis enables us to identify the strengths, weaknesses, opportunities and threats for Target to implement c-commerce.

There are four subdivisions of case analysis, each of which is selected to use depending upon the goals and/or objectives of the investigator. Understanding the types of case analysis helps us to adopt an appropriate method for a specific case.

 Exercises & Tasks (练习与任务)

▶ *Exercises*

1. What are the critical success factors for a B2B enterprise's operation?
2. Describe the roles of EDI in c-commerce.
3. How to realize the efficient c-commerce?
4. What are the types of case analysis?

▶ *Tasks*

Choose a B2B firm and prepare a 20-minute presentation which includes:

1. Background introduction to the B2B firm;
2. Analysis of its success or failure;
3. Conclusion which may be summarization, comments and advices.

Chapter 3 Emergences of New Models
第三章 新电商模式的兴起

 Learning Objectives（学习目标）

After finishing this chapter, you should be able to:
1. Understand the definition of O2O and its difference from B2C;
2. Identify the reasons behind Groupon's success;
3. Grasp the basic value chain in online travel services and differentiate the roles that a travel website plays in the services;
4. Explain how Ctrip realizes the low-cost travel;
5. Describe what causes eBay's success;
6. Identify the four steps of case analysis preparation.

 Introduction（内容简介）

With the changes of demand, consumers have not been satisfied with the initial e-commerce services such as B2C, C2C and B2B. On the other hand, the rapidly developed technology and economy also make it possible for the emergences of new e-commerce business models.

Chapter 3 is composed of 5 sections. The brief introduction to e-commerce new models is made in section 1. Three new models cases are explained respectively in section 2, 3, and 4. Section 5 focuses on the process of case analysis preparation.

Section 1
New E-Commerce Models
第一节 新电商模式

▶ **Key Words**

1. emergence *n.* 出现,兴起   2. influx *n.* 流入,注入

O2O (Online to Offline) is a new business model combining the online shopping and the offline transactions. O2O model usually provides information, services, booking discount and pushes the messages to Internet users, who in return will be converted into the customers of the particular offline business partners. The business model is particularly suitable to consumer goods and services, such as food and beverage, fitness, movies and beauty salon①. Though both of them are e-tailing, O2O and B2C are different: the former emphasize "pay online, consume offline" while the latter emphasize "pay online, deliver offline".

Internet is becoming the most common channel used to search travel and book reservations. A travel website, or OTA (Online Travel Agent), is dedicated to travel services. The site may be focused on travel reviews, the booking of travel and some other related services. The emergence of OTA shortens the travel service value chain and decreases the service cost.

An online auction is an auction which is held over the internet. Online auctions come in many different formats, but most popularly they are ascending English auctions, descending Dutch auctions, first-price sealed-bid, Vickrey auctions, or sometimes even a combination of multiple auctions, taking elements of one and forging them with another. The scope and reach of these auctions have been propelled by the Internet to a level beyond what the initial purveyors had anticipated. This is mainly because online auctions break down and remove the physical limitations of traditional auctions such as geography, presence, time, space, and a small target audience. This influx in availability has also made it easier to commit unlawful actions within an auction②.

---

① Ricky, What is O2O stand for? What are the differences between O2O, B2C and C2C?, https://www.chinaabout.net/o2o-stand-for-differences-o2o-b2c-c2c/, 2013-04-17.

② https://en.wikipedia.org/wiki/Online_auction

Section 2
Groupon—Integration of Online and Offline
第二节 团宝网——线上线下的整合

▎ Key Words

1. blend *n./vi./vt.* 混合
2. breakeven *n.* 盈亏平衡
3. redemption *n.* 拯救
4. upfront *adj./adv.* 预付的,在前面的
5. swamp *n./vt/vi* 沼泽、使……陷入困境

▎ Case

Groupon's Foundation[①]

Groupon, founded in November 2008, is a deal-of-the-day website that features discounted gift certificates usable at local or national companies. Its name blends "group" and "coupon". Its first deal was a half-price offer for pizzas for the restaurant on the first floor of its building in Chicago. Not only did Groupon launch daily local deals, but also it established multiple channels including: Groupon Goods, launched in September 2011, which focuses on discounted merchandise; Groupon Getaways, which offers vacation packages and travel deals; and Groupon Live, where consumers can find discounts on ticketed events—concerts, sporting events, theater, etc.

The idea for Groupon was created by Andrew Mason. The idea subsequently gained the attention of his former employer, Eric Lefkofsky, who provided $1 million in "seed money" to develop the idea. In April 2010, the company was valued at $1.35 billion. According to a report conducted by Groupon's marketing association and reported in Forbes Magazine and the Wall Street Journal, Groupon was "projecting that the company is on pace to make $1 billion in sales faster than any other business, ever".

Since its foundation, Groupon has achieved the goals in the short term which includes:

1. Realizing breakeven only in 7 months after its foundation;
2. From January 2010 through January 2011, Groupon's monthly revenues in America grew from $11 million to $89 million[②];
3. Serving more than 150 markets in North America and 100 markets in Europe, Asia

---

① https://en.wikipedia.org/wiki/Groupon
② https://techcrunch.com/2011/03/23/groupon-u-s-revenues/

and South America and owning 35 million registered users only in 2 years. Currently, Groupon is active in 15 countries and more than 500 markets around the world;

4. Groupon has worked with more than one million merchants to date and 49.5 million global active customers.

Groupon's Business Model[①]

Groupon works as an assurance contract using ThePoint's platform: If a certain number of people sign up for the offer, then the deal becomes available to all; if the predetermined minimum is not met, no one gets the deal that day. This reduces risks for retailers, who can treat the coupons as quantity discounts as well as sales promotion tools. Besides, Groupon's business model satisfies consumers' curiosity and willingness to get larger discount. It cooperated with the businesses and launched a daily timed buy spree of service product through a simple interface for network sales promotion. It spurs demand with the help of the marketing of localized target groups. To some extent, such "online purchasing, offline consumption" model drives service industry surroundings' linkage effects[②].

 团宝网采用了 Thepoints. com 网站的(销售)确保合同模式:如果参加团购的消费者达到一定数量,那么优惠商品或服务即可成交;如果事先设定的最低参团数量没有达到,那么该项优惠即取消。这种模式降低了零售商的风险,使其可以将优惠券作为打折或者促销手段。除此之外,团宝网的这种模式也满足了消费者的好奇心和消费欲,使其可以获得力度更高的折扣。团宝网与商家合作,借助简单的网络界面推出每日购物狂欢,实施网络促销。从某种程度上说,这种"线上购买,线下消费"使服务行业实现了连锁效应。

Groupon makes money by keeping approximately half the money the customer pays for the coupon while the retailers get the rest. For example, if a $240 worth of home painting service is purchased by the consumer for $50 through Groupon, then the business gets $25 and Groupon keeps $25. Owing to Groupon's market being primarily composed of female customers, the deals are often focused on the health, fitness and beauty markets. Though Groupon has been attempting more services, there are certain businesses to which Groupon initially did not offer, including shooting ranges and strip clubs. Later, the businesses were featured on Groupon.

Unlike classified advertising, the merchant does not pay any upfront cost to participate. Groupon collects personal information from willing consumers and then contacts only those consumers, primarily by daily email, who may possibly be interested in a particular product or service.

---

① http://en.wikipedia.org/wiki/Groupon#Business_model
② Zuo Peng, Wu Yin, Business model research of Chinese Groupon Development, The Proceedings of International Conference on Management and Service Science (MASS), pp.1-4, 2011.

Groupon employs a large number of copywriters who draft descriptions for the deals featured by email and on the website. Groupon's promotional text for the "deals" has been seen as a contributing factor to the popularity of the site, featuring a distinctive mix of thorough fact-checking and witty humor.

The site also launched a mobile application available on different operation systems such as Android and iOS. It allows users to buy deals on their smart phones and retrieve them using the screen as a coupon. Groupon is also a part of several Daily Deal Aggregators, which helps it expand its target audience, gain traffic and increase sales and revenue.

What Causes Groupon's Fast Growth?

If we analyze carefully, we can find the causes of Groupon's fast growth:

1. Entering the market in the right time. Groupon was founded in late 2008 when the economy depression led to the shrink of market. Particularly, the financial crisis occurring at the end of 2008 severely hit the economy. American people especially the housewives had to make a plan of cutting down the life expenses. The deal-of-the-day model satisfied the need so well that it attracted the housewives to find good deals from Groupon on the one hand and helped the merchants expand a new promotion channel on the other hand.

2. Being adaptable to consumers' shopping habits. Americans are prone to use coupon when shopping. According to CreditCards.com, 85% of Americans use coupons[1]. Over the years, offering coupons has become an increasingly important promotional method in America. In 2010, redemption of coupons going through clearinghouses surged 23% to 3.2 billion coupons (and up 30% to $3.5 billion in value) in America[2]. Due to the economy recession, people who were short of money became more interest in the marketing tool. Groupon sells coupons by which a customer can save 50%-90% of the product value. The business model not only suits consumers' shopping habits but also help merchants attract more customers. That is why it popularized rapidly.

3. Focusing on one thing. Unlike some e-commerce websites which preferring business models diversification, Groupon has been focusing on one model—offering discounted products and services based on group buying. This makes it devote to one thing on the one hand and establish a clear brand image on the other hand. As what Groupon's chief operation officer pointed out, Groupon's success should be attributed to its innovative

---

[1] Brandon Carter, Coupon Statistics: The Ultimate Collection, https://blog.accessdevelopment.com/ultimate-collection-coupon-statistics, November 15, 2017

[2] Li kim Goh, Discount Coupon Usage Continues To Grow, $2.5 Billion Through September, Should Easily Top 2009's $3.2 Billion, http://tommytoy.typepad.com/tommy-toy-pbt-consultin/2010/11/discount-coupon-usage-continues-to-grow-25-billion-through-september-should-easily-top-2009s-32-bill.html, 2010-11-01.

business model and its concentration.

4. Business model which is attractive to local merchants. Groupon establishes a platform which connects local merchants with consumers. The merchants post the information of promotion to attract the potential customers. Consumers browse and choose their favorite deals, pay for them and enjoy the services like restaurants, spas, manicures, training classes offline. Groupon provides local merchants an effective channel by which they can reach the customers efficiently, increase sales and improve brand awareness. Advertising on Groupon is much cheaper than advertising on the traditional media like TV or newspaper. Therefore, Groupon is especially attractive for the small and medium sized merchants. In addition to the low-cost advertising, Groupon keeps its attractiveness for local merchant by virtue of valuable customers, profit-driven marketing strategies and new ways to grow. Groupon's demographic data shows: 97% of its subscribers are between 18 and 54 years old, over 82% of them have a bachelor or higher degree[1]. The customers who are well-educated and employed become the important revenue source of the local businesses. According to Groupon's internal data of Q3 2015, more than 900 million units were sold on the website, which means the platform is good at setting the merchants' business up for success. In fact, more than 80% of Groupon's campaigns are immediately profitable. Besides, local merchants are allowed to boost their online presence and connect with customers on the Groupon Page, drive revenue through full-priced offerings, and manage demand via online booking.

5. Easy access to the Internet and guaranteed service. With the development of information technology and the popularization of smart devices, it is even easier for people to get access to the Internet. Groupon launched its mobile application which is compatible with different operating system like Android and iOS. By virtue of mobile app, subscribers can search or browse the products or services they prefer and make deals easily. In addition, Groupon's guaranteed service and safe payment system improve its reliability.

6. Appropriate marketing strategies. Starting its business in Chicago, Groupon quickly expands its businesses to other cities and countries. The enterprise did not frequently use the traditional marketing methods like advertising to build its brand image. Instead, it chose word-of-mouth marketing. Groupon encouraged subscribers to do the propagation by email, social network and launched rebate activities in return for it. Meanwhile, it cooperated with the well-known businesses such as Gap, Sears to improve its business reputation. As a result, Groupon soon drew the attention from the nationwide

---

[1] Feng Xu, A Comparative Study of Online Group-Coupon Sale in USA and China, A comparative study of online group-coupon sale in USA and China, The Proceedings of International Conference on Artificial Intelligence, Management Science and Electronic Commerce (AIMSEC), Page(s). 1806-1809, 2011

media such as CNN, ABC, the Washington Post, New York Times, Wall Street Journal and so on. The news reports further improved its brand awareness. Besides, the excellent copywriting is another critical part of its marketing strategies. Groupon collected personal information with consumers' approval and delivered advertisements via email. Groupon always made the copywriting interesting, humorous and attractive to absorb people's attention.

Possible Problems with Groupon[1][2]

Despite Groupon's success, there are some problems which can not be ignored:

1. The low margin of retailers. According to Groupon's business model, retailers post their deals (e. g. 50% off) on Groupon to attract the consumers and get only part of the revenue since the site takes up to 50% of what a consumer pays. The discount and the commission squeeze the margin of retailers. Why do they still cooperate with Groupon? Because they expect Groupon to bring in new customers who wouldn't have purchased something otherwise. However, the margins are too low even though new customers are acquired. Besides, the retailers often have to suffer losses in the first transaction to ensure the customers' repurchase. However, the customers who are price-sensitive will transfer to a new retailer as long as it offers more attractive deals.

2. Customer service issues. Small businesses who participate in a deal site frequently get overwhelmed by the response and they can't support all of the customer inquiries that come through all at once. A successful deal could temporarily swamp a business with too many customers, risking a possibility that customers will be dissatisfied, or that there won't be enough product to meet the demand. Gap, a large clothing retailer, was able to handle 445,000 coupons in a national deal (although it experienced server problems at one point), but a smaller business could become suddenly flooded with customers. One coffee shop in Portland, Oregon struggled with an increase of customers for three months, when it sold close to 1,000 Groupons on one day it was offered, according to one report[3]. Besides, a frustrating thing for customers comes from the price difference between Groupon site and the company's official website. This happened with FTD, a florist. It offered a Groupon for Valentine's day flowers which offered $20 off from $40 worth of stuff. However, FTD's website offered lower price than the site which users were able to access through the Groupon link. These types of situations have occurred several times — whereby the prices through Groupon were increased by the retailer to make up for the

---

[1] Evan Britton. Five Key Problems Currently Facing Groupon. http://www.businessinsider.com/five-key-problems-currently-facing-groupon-2011-2, Feb. 16, 2011.
[2] https://en.wikipedia.org/wiki/Groupon#Competitors
[3] https://en.wikipedia.org/wiki/Groupon

coupon sold. It will cause customers' dissatisfaction and even damage the retailers' business reputation.

3. The lack of customer loyalty. Many merchants have believed that their Groupon deals would help them build a loyal customer base which shops directly with the merchant, without Groupon in the middle. However, in many cases a Groupon deal merely attracts one-time bargain hunters who are often put off by the full retail price (which would be at least double the price of a coupon that is discounted by at least 50%) and do not return until they encounter another Groupon deal that suits them. Of the merchants featured in North America in Q4 2012, 84% of them continued to run deals in Deal Bank as of the end of February 2013 while only 50% of deals were with merchants refeaturing with Groupon.

4. The threats from competitors. Since viewing Groupon's success, there have been over 500 sites similar to Groupon, including over 100 in the United States. Though most of them are not regarded as the powerful rivals, some emergent market incomers such as LivingSocial, which used the same business model and received an investment from Amazon of $175 million have been described as a serious competitor. A more critical problem faced by Groupon is that some Internet giants such as Google and Facebook have been attempting to enter the market. In 2011, Google launched a competing product, called Google Offers, following its failure to purchase Groupon for $6 billion. In April 2011, Facebook began testing a social-buying program. These moves were speculated to be a competitive threat to Groupon, though Facebook ended the project by August 2011. In addition to the direct competitions, the indirect threats can't be ignored either. For example, as Groupon looked to expand beyond daily deals to become a marketplace for local commerce, the company came into competition with many large players. Groupon Goods competes with Amazon. Facebook planned to launch "Local Market", a buying and selling community powered by Facebook groups, that also indirectly competes with Groupon. All of the competition will ultimately force Groupon to continue to innovate and stay on its toes if it is going to remain the market leader. So far Groupon has been able to do so — but the low barriers to entry in this space will make it difficult for Groupon to maintain its current market share.

Where Is Groupon's Future?[①]

As a platform based on the two-sided market, the primary task of Groupon is to satisfy and keep the two sides of exchanges—retailers and consumers. However, Groupon has a

---

① William Hsu, Groupon Is Hitting the Wall. Does It Have A Future Beyond Daily Deals?, *MuckerBits*, 2011-12-14.

tough job to make something that is valuable to merchants and consumers to keep them loyal. Where should Groupon go in the future? The following are some of the major opportunities that Groupon should consider:

1. Local search (online + offline)

This is worth $10 Billion a year in the U.S. Money is bleeding out of the print Yellow Pages industry and virtually disappearing into thin air—at the rate of $1 Billion a year. The Internet players in local search—Yelp, YP (AT&T Interactive), Google, Bing and Foursquare—are not close to growing collectively anywhere near $1B a year. As a result, there is a sizable opportunity left as SMBs (small and medium business) continue to look for new customer acquisition channels to replace old ones.

Because Groupon has very little idea of what a consumer might want, it must offer generic deals at a huge discount to get buyers over the hump for purchasing. Search is the opposite. The intent is clear—as a result, discounts can be significantly lower than 50% off to generate a conversion. In turn, the lower discount enables higher ROI for the advertisers and a more sustainable business model for Groupon.

2. Expand product portfolio into retention, viral marketing

Word-of-mouth remains the cheapest and most effective marketing channel for SMBs. The key to generating word-of-mouth is to focus on the satisfaction and retention of existing customers. Only 10% of SMBs should really be doing a daily deal promotion and only another 20% should consider a search marketing campaign—but 100% of all SMBs should have a retention strategy to help generate word-of-mouth and increase customer lifetime value. There are lots of small and large startups in the "SMB CRM" space. Most are struggling with scaling SMB acquisition. Groupon's immense sales platform can be the channel with which to achieve market penetration in this category. Startups founded more recently are focused on leveraging social platforms like Facebook and Twitter to manage relationships with customers.

Groupon can inexpensively acquire companies like Hootsuite or Sprout Social, given the saturation in this space. If Groupon has ambitions of acquiring revenue faster with more proven products, the established companies like ZocDoc, DemandForce, or even Constant Contact are expensive but less risky bets. Combining its email marketing expertise and database with a SMB CRM platform should be a strategic imperative for Groupon.

3. Become a local mobile advertising network

It's been said a thousand times before: "mobile is local". What makes mobile application users unique is that they are looking to engage with their local surroundings. Yet there still isn't a mobile ad network of scale that has truly taken advantage of location as its main competitive strategy.

The proliferation of local mobile apps combined with lack of local mobile monetization options creates a huge opportunity in mobile local advertising for Groupon to exploit. As with email marketing, display advertising also lives and dies on the ability to discern user intent. By turning offers into targeted advertising, Groupon can quickly create a mobile local ad network. It can enter the space easily by acquiring technology from the multitude of sub-scale startups in this space or partner with a horizontal mobile ad network to build a local specific mobile ad network.

4. Get into the mobile payment business

This is perhaps the riskiest market for Groupon to enter, but also the largest of Groupon's various opportunities. It's no secret that companies like Google, MasterCard and ISIS are betting on offers/deals as the killer application to drive adoption for their technologies. Square is also betting a significant portion of its long-term business model around offers.

Groupon has the option of simply being an offer provider for these companies or become a mobile payments company itself. Working with issuing banks, acquiring banks, networks, merchant acquiring partners and carriers requires a completely different competency—but no one in the current competitive space, not even Google, has the sales platform to acquire the hundreds and thousands of local offers needed to create value to the end consumer and the sales force to enable the tedious task of selling and installing new payment terminals. Actually, Groupon made its first move in 2012 when it announced its jumping into the mobile payment business going to the direct competition with America Express, Square, Google and Paypal.

Groupon is an ambitious company shouldering unrealistic expectations of continued growth. With hundreds of millions of dollars in the bank, it is most likely actively pursuing all of the options mentioned above. It has taken Google almost 10 years to move beyond search (i.e., display, video, Android). That Groupon would need to find a second act within five years of starting its original business is a testament to its impressive historical growth, as well as the fragility of its core business model.

Case Analysis

团购就其本身而言，并非一种新的商业模式，它实际上早在电子商务诞生以前就作为一种营销手段被普遍采用。其实质是当购买人数达到一定数量时，可以获得谈判优势，从而以较低的价格获得产品或服务。团宝网采取的商业模式本质上就是团购，但它无论从规模还是影响力上都远远超过了传统的团购。那么，团宝网的团购与传统的线下团购有何区别呢？又是什么因素导致了它的成功呢？这是本案例分析的两个侧重点。

团宝网尽管是从网上团购开始的，但它显然不是仅仅将线下的团购搬到线上这么简单。首先,团宝网自己并不是团购交易中的卖方或买方,它扮演的是交易中介的角色:将有团购促销的商家和有购买需求的消费者吸引到网站上来,让双方进行自由的交易匹配,并从中抽取中介费。很明显,这就是前面章节所提及的双边市场模式。团宝网作为一个基于双边市场的交易平台,积极吸引交易双方,从而充分发挥双边市场的网络效应(网络外部性):越多的卖家在平台上打折促销,就会吸引越多的买家到此进行消费;反之,越多的买家到平台上购物,就会吸引越多的卖家入驻平台。正是借助网络效应,使得以团购起家的团宝网远远超越了个体卖家打折促销的范畴,发展成一个双边交易平台;其次,因特网没有时空限制的特点也令团宝网突破了传统卖家或交易平台的时间及空间界限,吸引来自全球各地的买卖双方来此进行交易;再次,团宝网"线上支付,线下消费"的O2O模式将线上线下的资源有机整合在一起,消费者能够轻松在线挑选产品和服务,并完成支付,然后到线下商家进行消费。这种模式一方面为消费者提供了更多的选择;另一方面,通过促销优惠将其引导至特定商家,降低了双方的交易成本,解决了传统团购中交易双方信息搜索和匹配的问题。因此,可以看出,团宝网始于团购,但突破了团购的局限,借助因特网快速发展为一个成功的双边交易平台。

从案例中的数据可以看出,团宝网不仅成功,而且发展速度极快,仅在7个月内就实现了收支平衡,这在"烧钱"的电商行业极为少见。因此,剖析它快速成长的原因成为本案例分析的第二个重点。团宝网的成功首先得益于它的商业模式。如上所述,尽管团宝网始于团购,但它并未局限于这种直接面向消费者的零售模式,而是将团购的供求双方吸引过来,引导他们进行自由的交易匹配,自己则转而化身为双方的交易中介,从而构建起基于双边市场的交易平台。双边平台的网络效应等优势在淘宝、亚马逊等案例分析中均有详细说明,此处不再赘述。其次,团宝网在恰当的时点进入市场,对自己的定位有明确目标,并将此目标贯彻始终。我们已经反复强调时点对于电商企业的重要性,对亚马逊是如此,对阿里巴巴是如此,对团宝网也是如此。与前两者不同,团宝网诞生时整个电子商务经历十几年的发展无论在技术还是在商业模式方面都已经相对成熟,它似乎没有赶上前辈们所经历的"电子商务淘金时代"。幸运的是,它所面对的O2O市场才刚刚萌芽,市场空间足够大。更重要的是,2008年的金融危机所引发的全球经济危机令人们不得不寻求减少开支,压缩生活成本的途径,而以团购打折为初衷的团宝网在此时进入市场正好满足了这种需求。自此开始,团宝网一直瞄准两大群体:需要进行产品推广的零售商(尤其是中小零售商)和以"价廉物美"为目标的消费者,为他们提供交易平台和相关服务。与其他电商企业不同,该网站并未将业务向其他领域大肆拓展,而是采取了比较保守的扩张策略,侧重于"网上优惠券"服务,力求在该领域精益求精[①]。团宝网这种"专精"策略收到了成效,使它快速成长为网上团购行业的翘楚,也成功吸引了更多人的关注。敏锐地觉察到这种关注后,团宝网充分利用它开展口碑营销,不仅降低了营销成本,而且让相关信息通过社交网站、新闻媒体快速散播,进一步吸引了

---

① 2012年,团宝网首次涉足移动支付领域,但影响不大。

网站流量。当然,团宝网的快速发展也得益于互联网技术尤其是移动互联技术的快速普及。越来越多的年轻人愿意使用手机、平板电脑等设备快速上网,轻松挑选价廉物美的商品满足需求,团宝网开发的 APP 程序很好地满足了这种需求。可以看出,团宝网的成功并非一蹴而就,而是在商业模式的选择,营销策路的制定,市场的准确定位以及进入市场的时点等方面谨慎决策,加上技术的成熟和人们消费习惯的改变将这个网站送上了成功之路。

Section 3
Ctrip—Making Low-Cost Travel Possible
第三节 携程——让低成本旅游成为可能

Key Words

1. definitive *adj.* 最终的
2. China Lodging Group 汉庭集团
3. pursuant to 依据……
4. proponent *n.* 支持者

Case

Background Introduction

Ctrip is a platform, founded in 1999, for hotel accommodations, airline tickets and pre-packaged-tours in China. Ctrip targets its services primarily at business and leisure travelers who do not travel in groups. In all transactions it acts as the sole agent. Ctrip aggregates information on hotels and flights and enables its customers to make hotel and flight bookings. The company also sells packaged tours that include transportation and accommodations, as well as guided tours in some instances.

Investment and Financial Performance[①]

Ctrip publicly listed on Nasdaq in 2003 and the company is currently listed on the NASDAQ with a market cap of roughly $20 billion, which makes it one of the world's largest online travel agents.

In March 2010, Ctrip entered into definitive agreements with China Lodging Group. Ctrip subscribed for ordinary shares to be issued by China Lodging and purchased ordinary

---

① http://ir.Ctrip.com/phoenix.zhtml? c = 148903&p = irol-news&nyo = 0

shares from certain existing shareholders of China Lodging. The aggregate number of ordinary shares that Ctrip purchased from China Lodging and the selling shareholders pursuant to the agreements was equal to approximately 8% of China Lodging's total ordinary shares outstanding immediately after the closing of this investment.

In September 2013, Ctrip officially launched a new version of the mobile application—Ctrip Travel 5.0. Following the launch, the company announced that Ctrip's mobile platform contributed to over 40% of total hotel booking transactions at its peak level, which exceeded the respective booking percentages from its websites and call centers. Mobile has become the key booking platform for Ctrip since then.

In August 2014, The Priceline Group and Ctrip announced that the two companies expanded an existing commercial agreement established in 2012 to strengthen their global partnership. In addition, The Priceline Group agreed to invest $500 million through a convertible bond and Ctrip granted The Priceline Group permission to acquire Ctrip shares in the open market. The Priceline Group may hold up to 10% of Ctrip's outstanding shares.

In October 2015, Ctrip announced that the company completed a share exchange transaction with Baidu. As a result of the transaction, Baidu owned ordinary shares of Ctrip representing approximately 25% of Ctrip's aggregate voting interest, and Ctrip owned ordinary shares of Qunar representing approximately 45% of Qunar's aggregate voting interest.

In December 2016, Ctrip reported the fourth quarter and full year 2016 financial results, which shows Ctrip achieved strong financial results: for the full year ended December 31, 2016, net revenues were 19.2 billion yuan ($2.8 billion), representing a 76% increase from 2015; accommodation reservation revenues were 7.3 billion yuan ($1.1 billion), representing a 58% increase from 2015.

How Does Ctrip Make Low-Cost Travel Possible?

One of the attractive traits of Ctrip is the low-cost travel services compared to the offline services. The low cost includes not only the low price of online travel services but also the lowered searching cost for the customers. How does Ctrip realize the low-cost travel?

Firstly, it adopts the business model which shortens the value chain. In the traditional travel service value chain, there are usually 4 nodes—services suppliers (e.g. airlines), global distributors, retail travel agents and end customers including business travelers and leisure travelers (Figure 3-1). Travel services such as ticket booking are provided originally by the suppliers. By virtue of distributors and retail travel agents, they are supplied to the end customers. Obviously, the process adds value at each node. The more nodes the value chain contains, the higher prices the end customers get. In traditional value chain, merchants and GDS (global distribution systems) have far higher profit margin up to 50%. Travel agencies receive fees and commission that rarely rise above 10% to 15% of the amount of the travel booked[①]. Suppliers such as airlines and hotels would like to eliminate middlemen such as GDS and develop a direct relationship with customers. The emergence of OTA (online travel agencies) enables them to achieve the objective. Successful online travel agencies attempt to turn into merchants by purchasing large blocks of travel inventory and then reselling it to the public, eliminating the global distributor and earning much higher returns, which is called as re-intermediation. Ctrip's business model shortens the traditional travel services value chain which is composed of three nodes: services suppliers, Ctrip and end customers. Actually, Ctrip plays the role of online travel agent in the value chain. Travel services are provided directly to the end customers by Ctrip rather than the process from distributors to retail travel agents. The less nodes in the value chain decrease the travel service price and improve the service efficiency (Figure 3-2).

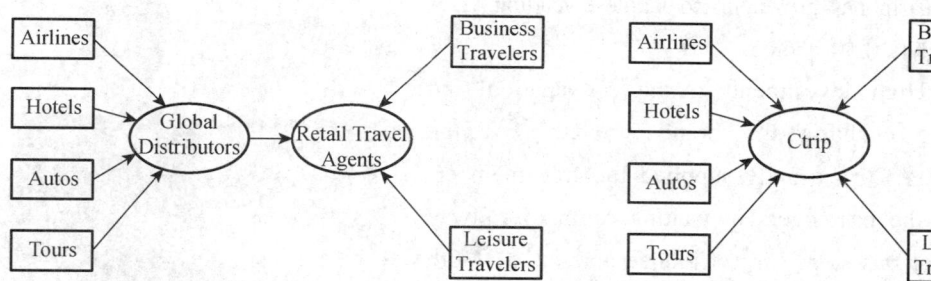

Figure 3-1 Traditional Travel Services Value Chain

Figure 3-2 Online Travel Services Value Chain

Secondly, Ctrip establishes a successful travel information platform. Under the traditional travel service model, travelers have to spend much time searching information (e.g. call the offline agents one by one), which increases the searching cost. By virtue of Ctrip, they can get access to the information easily: the end customers are able to search the services they need anytime, everywhere. Consequently, Ctrip allows the customers to get access to the travel services information easily, which decreases the searching cost.

Finally, Ctrip enables the suppliers to lower the marketing cost. The seasonal trait of travel services makes the unbalanced revenues of the suppliers. Generally, they don't worry about the revenues in season while the unoccupied hotel rooms and flight seats cause the dropping revenue off season. Ctrip allows the suppliers to post the promotion information off season, which enables the information to reach the potential customers efficiently.

---

① Kenneth C. Laudon, Carol Guercio Traver, *E-commerce Business*, *Technology*, *Society*, Addison-Wesley Publishing, 2002, pp. 620-621.

SWOT Analysis

With the rapid development of Internet technology and economy, online travel services are popularizing. In addition to Ctrip, many online travel agents are trying to cut a slide from the huge cake. How can Ctrip survive from the competition? SWOT analysis helps us to understand it clearly.

Strengths

1. The "first-entry" advantage. Ctrip was founded in 1999 when Chinese online travel market was still at its infancy. The market with few competitors provided a valuable opportunity by which Ctrip was able to occupy the market and grow rapidly. Ctrip seized the opportunity and realized the quick growth. When other entrants like Lvmama tried to move into the market, Ctrip has grown up to Chinese leading OTA and travelers' first choice.

2. High investment in the propagation and marketing enabling the brand strength. At the beginning, Ctrip usually supplied the free member-card for the passengers in waiting room of railway stations or bus stop, airport lounge and so on. With the card, people are allowed to log in Ctrip.com and try its online services while getting the credits in their account or discount. Though the method seems simple and low-efficient, many people gradually remember the brand name—XieCheng (Ctrip) and some of them become Ctrip's

Figure 3-3　Ctrip's Advertisement[①]

customers. After establishing its brand in China, Ctrip turned to more efficient as well as expensive propagation media such as TV. It hired Deng Chao—a famous actor in China to film a short video advertisement in 2013 (Figure 3-3). The slogan of the advertisement is so impressive that the brand name of Ctrip has been spreaded quickly.

3. High service quality online and offline, during transactions and after-sale services. One of the important factors enabling Ctrip to outstand the fierce competition lies in that it has been keeping the high quality of services. For example, its well-designed web pages enable users to find the information as soon as possible; it allows users to make the price comparison among different services and make the most suitable decisions; it supplies not

---

① www.ctrip.com

only the online assistance (e. g. Q&A) but also the phone call so that users can get the necessary helps; users can request the document such as invoice after travelling.

4. Large customer group which builds the solid base for the customer acquisition. Compared to other competitors, Ctrip has established its solid customer base by virtue of marketing propagation at early stage, which is beneficial for customer acquisition. According to the statistics, Ctrip had accounted for 48.9% of market share by 2014, ranking No. 1 of OTA[①].

5. Partnership with famous suppliers. One of the reasons why Ctrip attracts the customers is its partnership with famous travel services suppliers. As an OTA, Ctrip connects upstream suppliers and customers. Ctrip realized that as long as there were quality problems customers would blame them on Ctrip rather than the upstream suppliers because they get the services through Ctrip. Therefore, Ctrip adopts a strict system by which it can select the qualified suppliers so as to keep the high quality services. The partnership system proves effective because it helps Ctrip to improve customers' trust in the brand. Besides, Ctrip also develops its partnership through shareholding. For example, Ctrip is one of the stockholders of some upstream suppliers (e. g. Rujia Hotel), which is beneficial for the quality control.

6. Scientific management. Ctrip is known as a proponent of scientific management in using rigorous data analysis in managerial decision-making. For example, Ctrip used to rigorously evaluate the impact of telecommuting on the company's profits. It conducted an experiment on 242 employees involving professors at Stanford and Beijing University. The experiment found that employees randomly assigned to work at home for 9 months increased their output by 13.5% versus the office-based control group, and their quit rates fell by almost 50%. So Ctrip decided to cut the office space by adding telecommuting and roll the practice out across the firm.

Weaknesses

1. Single B2C model encountering the fierce competition. Since its foundation, Ctrip has been adopting B2C business model, that is, Ctrip provides the travel services to end users as an OTA. This model is good for service quality control. However, the single B2C model is unable to satisfy customers' personalized need well and it is encountering the challenges from the competitors such as Qunaer, which is a travel information service platform(although the two emerged in 2015). For example, the customers who are looking for cheaper services would prefer Qunaer since it offers more choices.

2. Security breach with the website. Like many e-commerce websites, Ctrip is also

---

① 老大携程市场份额落后 艺龙坐困"千年老二", 投资潮, 2014年9月2日

faced with security risks. The risks lie in: 1) online payment. Unlike physical goods retailing, online travel service usually involves large amount of payment. As long as the payment security problems such as hacking occur, it may lead to huge losses due to the high prices of travel services; 2) privacy intrusion. As a famous OTA, Ctrip stores a large number of customers' information such as telephone number and mailing address. If the information is not managed well, it probably causes privacy problems. In March 2014, Ctrip was reported of the security flaws with its platform. Though Ctrip announced the problem solved instantly, it still caused the skepticism for its information security.

3. Low brand awareness out of China. Ctrip has built its brand strength successfully in China in the past few years. Unfortunately, its brand name has not popularized all over the world. Though the domestic market is large enough, it will reach saturation one day, especially when more competitors are entering the market. Expanding its oversea market will be an important task for Ctrip. Fortunately, Ctrip has realized and attempted to establish partnership with foreign peers.

Opportunities

1. Rapid development of Chinese travel market. The significant growth of residents' income facilitates the development of tourism industry. The increase of disposable income enables residents to afford travel services. As a result, the travel service demand grows rapidly. According to a report, Chinese gross domestic travel consumption reached 262.7 billion yuan in 2013, ranking No.1 of the global domestic travel market. The country is the largest source of tourists in the world as Chinese travelers made 100 million outbound trips in 2014①.

2. Significant rising of netizens and mobile phone users. According to CNNIC, Chinese netizens volume had reached 649 million, 85.8% of which was mobile phone users by the end of 2014②. Corresponding to the rapid growth of netizens, the online travel transaction volume in 2014 was 5 times as large as that in 2008③.

3. Business partnership with Qunar. In October 2015, Ctrip and Qunar, the second largest OTA in China, agreed to a share swap and partnership. The deal was made about five months after Qunar rejected a buyout offer from Ctrip amid fierce competition for online bookings in China. According to the agreement, Baidu, which controls Qunar, owned 25% of Ctrip, and the companies combined products and services. Ctrip owned a

---

① Lulu Yilun Chen and Tim Culpan, Ctrip, Qunar Agree to Share Swap, Form Business Partnership, https://www.bloomberg.com/news/articles/2015-10-26/Ctrip-qunar-said-to-plan-merger-creating-chinese-travel-giant, October 26, 2015.
② 第35次CNNIC报告:中国互联网络发展状况统计,《中国互联网络信息中心》,2015-02-03。
③ 2014中国旅游业发展报告:中国是最大的国内旅游市场国,《人民网》,2014-12-15。

45% voting interest in Qunar. The merging not only creates China's biggest online travel service but also alleviates travel price war[1].

Threats

1. New competitors are entering the online travel market. Just as what mentioned above, China has a huge online tourism market which is attracting many players to enter. For example, e-long and lvmama built their own online travel websites. In addition, other e-commerce websites such as Taobao also established its own online travel service channel. The competitors' entries probably cause market share distraction.

2. Restrictions from macro-policies. Government's policies sometimes probably become the constraints for an enterprise's development. For example, in April 2014, Chinese Ministry of Railways announced www.12306.cn, the unique authorized website for online train tickets booking.

Future of Ctrip

As an important Chinese OTA, Ctrip's development in the future will be unavoidably impacted by the trends:

1. Competition will be even fiercer since price can be compared online easily. Therefore, competition among sites tends to focus on scope of offerings, ease of use, payment options and personalization.

2. It's very hard for pure online travel sites to profit. While being successful in attracting a large Internet audience share and influencing significant offline travel purchases, competitive forces on the Internet have restricted the ability of online travel services to show strong profits. Though Ctrip gained net profit of 5.4 billion yuan in 2013, which makes it the unique OTA achieving profitability in China[2], the rising operation cost like the personnel salary, propagation cost will make it very hard for the largest OTA to keep profiting.

3. Some segments should be captured. According to Ctrip's financial report in 2016, the segments including hotel reservation, transportation, packaged tours and corporate travel may contribute the most to its growth. The transportation segment was expected to contribute the maximum share to Ctrip's revenue, driven by volume growth across all travel streams, because the segment's revenue was expected to rise by 90%-95% YoY (Year over Year) for the 3rd Quarter of 2016; the second segment was hotel researvation since its revenue was expected to rise by 50%-55% YoY, and the packaged tour was the third

---

① 第35次CNNIC报告:中国互联网络发展状况统计,《中国互联网络信息中心》,2015-02-03。
② 李碧雯,携程被收购传闻:或为百度流量抢占市场份额,《理财周报》,2014-04-14。

segments as its revenue was expected to rise by 35%–40% YoY[①].

4. Offering personalized services. With the popularization of online travel services and the increase of mobile phone users, travelers are not satisfied with the standard package any longer, instead, they desire personalized services. Ctrip has made the first step of it: making lots of effort in artificial intelligence, big data and cloud computing, Ctrip attempts to capture its customers' purchasing power, hobbies and travel preferences accurately so as to provide tailor-made offerings.

Case Analysis

作为中国知名的旅游服务网站,携程以其低价优质的服务在网上旅游市场站稳了脚跟。低价意味着利润空间的压缩,长期以来中国旅游网站大面积亏损的现象也证明了这一点。然而,携程却能在2013年成为中国唯一一家实现盈利的旅游网站,同时还能保证亲民的价格。它是如何做到的? 回答这个问题意味着本案例分析的重点在于:1) 携程如何让低成本旅游成为可能? 2) 它有何独特的优势,又面临哪些问题?

携程的低价可以归因于两个要素:其一是商业模式。传统的旅游服务价值链中,至少有4个节点:旅游服务供应商、全球分销商、旅游零售代理商(旅行社)以及终端客户,为了获取利润,每个节点上的企业层层加价,客户最终获取的旅游服务价格较高也就不可避免。而在携程的商业模式下,节点被缩减为3个:旅游服务供应商、携程网以及终端客户,携程网直接向上游采购旅游服务并将其转售给下游客户。价值链的缩短不仅意味着信息传递周期缩短,而且由于中间商的减少使得旅游服务的最终价格得以降低。因此,携程扮演了类似网上零售商的角色,只不过在旅游行业中它有一个特定的名称:线上旅游服务代理商(OTA);其二是信息平台。携程成功地建立了一个连接上游服务商和下游客户的高效的旅游信息平台。传统的旅游服务模式下,下游客户所支付的高成本不仅源自服务本身的高价格,也包括较高的信息搜索成本。那时由于通讯条件的限制,信息传递不畅,消费者要旅游需要挨家拨打旅行社电话,获取信息,并进行比价,最终做出购买决策。这个过程费时费力,导致用户的搜索成本居高不下。携程的旅游服务平台提供大量机票、酒店等信息,用户只需输入关键词,设定出游条件即可在短短几分钟内进行信息浏览、比较,并做出购买决策,大大降低了搜索成本。不仅如此,携程的信息平台也降低了旅游供应商的营销成本。旅游行业的季节性明显,淡旺季的收入差异较大,对于酒店、航空公司等供应商而言,如何在淡季将闲置的资源(如:空置的酒店房间)以低价推销出去需要花费大量的营销成本,而且由于时空限制,效果也比较有限。借助携程的平台,供应商可以以相对低廉的成本,发布促销信息,并利用因特网没有时空限制的优势,将其快速传达给潜在的

---

① Ally Schmidt, These Segments Will Contribute the Most to Ctrip's Future Growth, https://marketrealist.com/2016/09/what-ctrip-coms-increasing-leverage-means-for-investors, 2016-09-03.

客户(在移动互联时代尤其如此),不仅缩短了信息传递的时间,也节约了宣传推广的成本。

通过SWOT分析可以看出,携程拥有明显的先发优势。作为中国第一批网上旅游服务商(OTA)之一,成立于1999年的携程进入当时几乎空白的中国网上旅游市场,精心耕耘,快速成长为行业翘楚。作为市场先行者,携程的确遇到了很好的发展机会,但在市场开发方面也遭遇了很大困难:当时中国互联网才刚刚兴起,上网的人都很少,更遑论上网预订旅游服务。如何进行有效的宣传推广,让人们迅速熟悉携程这个品牌是当时该网站面临的巨大挑战。携程采用了最原始的推广办法:人对人宣传网站品牌。这就是为什么在最初几年里,人们总可以在机场候机大厅、车站候车室等地方见到携程的推广人员逐个地向过往旅客发放会员卡,介绍携程的服务。这个办法在今天看来稍显笨拙,而且成本较高,但正是这种不计成本的推广方法,让消费者逐渐熟悉了携程。携程极有远见地意识到营销推广在电子商务中的重要性,并为此投入了大量资源,这也是携程的第二个优势。质量永远是企业的立足之本,携程自成立以来一直贯彻这一宗旨:携程坚持和商业信誉良好的上游供应商合作,不仅保证了服务质量,而且也借此塑造了良好的品牌形象,提高了消费者对品牌的满意度和信赖度。与实体产品不同,服务的质量贯穿于整个服务过程中,携程无法通过事前采购进行检验,因此寻找具有品牌知名度、服务质量有保证的供应商显得尤为重要。消费者一旦对服务质量有所不满,将直接针对作为旅游服务中间商的携程而非上游供应商,并且通过网络将这种不满进行传播,这将对携程的品牌造成负面影响。也是因为意识到这一点,携程不仅在选择合作方时非常谨慎,而且还通过设计良好的网站和手机APP,比价服务,线上线下客服沟通以及售后服务等全方位多渠道的措施来保证服务质量。就价格本身而言,携程并非行业最低,但它却因为高质量的服务获得了溢价优势。除此之外,携程经过多年积累的庞大客户群及其借助数据技术实现的科学管理也是它的优势。而近年来中国旅游市场的快速增长,互联网尤其是移动互联网的迅速普及和携程近年来的一系列战略合作(如:2015年与去哪儿的合并)不仅为其进一步发展提供了机遇,也在一定程度上强化了上述优势。与此同时,携程自身的劣势与面临的威胁也不容忽视:首先是商业模式过于单一的问题。自成立以来,携程一直采用B2C模式,尽管该模式有利于控制服务质量,但标准化的流程不利于实现个性化服务。幸运的是,2015年携程与去哪儿成功合并,后者旅游搜索引擎的模式可以在一定程度上弥补这一不足。其次,2014年爆发的携程客户信息泄露事件暴露了该网站在信息管理和保护消费者隐私等方面仍然有改进的空间。另外,尽管携程近年来作出了包括与加勒比皇家游轮合作等海外拓展的决策,但它的国际知名度仍有待加强。近年来,互联网"跨界"现象频出,阿里旗下的"飞猪"旅游迅速崛起,驴妈妈等个性化旅游服务网站后来居上,这些来自相同或不同行业的竞争者以及政府的行业政策是携程在未来决策时必须考虑的因素。

Section 4
eBay—Offering the Affordable Auctions
第四节 易贝——提供老百姓用得起的拍卖

I Key Words

1. fabricated *adj.* 组合的
2. phenomenal *adj.* 显著的
3. acquisition *n.* 收购
4. hefty *adj.* 强有力的
5. vanquish *vt.* 征服
6. in a nutshell 一言以蔽之
7. liquidation *n.* 清算,偿还
8. galvanized *adj.* 激活的
9. paramount *adj.* 最重要的
10. invincible *adj.* 无敌的

II Case

eBay's Foundation[①]

eBay is an American multinational corporation and e-commerce company, providing C2C and B2C services via Internet. It is headquartered in San Jose, California, United States. eBay was founded by Pierre Omidyar in 1995, and became a notable success story of the dot-com bubble. It is a multi-billion dollar business with operations localized in over thirty countries.

eBay is famous for an online auction and shopping website on which people and businesses buy and sell a broad variety of goods and services worldwide. In addition to its auction-style sales, the website also provides "Buy It Now" shopping. It is not a free website, instead it charges users an invoice seller fee if they have sold or listed any items.

One of the first items sold on AuctionWeb was a broken laser pointer for $14.83. The frequently repeated story that eBay was founded to help Omidyar's fiancée trade Pez candy dispensers was fabricated by a public relations manager in 1997 to interest the media, which was not interested in the company's previous explanation about wanting to create a "perfect market".

eBay's Growth

In January 1997 the site hosted 2,000,000 auctions, compared with 250,000 during the whole of 1996. In 1997, the company received $6.7 million in funding from the venture

---

① https://en.wikipedia.org/wiki/EBay

capital firm Benchmark Capital.

eBay went public on September 21, 1998. eBay's target share price of $18 was all but ignored as the price went to $53.50 on the first day of trading.

By early 2008, the company had expanded worldwide, counted hundreds of millions of registered users, more than 15,000 employees and revenues of almost $7.7 billion.

eBay's Expansion

eBay realized its expansion by virtue of a series of acquisition:

In February 2002, eBay acquired iBazar, a similar European auction web site founded in 1998 and then bought PayPal, a third party payment system on October 14, 2002.

In 2005, eBay acquired Skype and significantly expanded its customer base to more than 480 million registered users worldwide. To focus on its core e-commerce and payments businesses, eBay completed the sale of Skype for $2.75 billion by owning 30% equity in the company in late 2009.

In September 2014, eBay announced it would split into two independent public companies—eBay and PayPal—by the end of 2015.

Business Model

eBay offers online auction service that allows users to sell merchandise and prospective buyers to place bids on a wide variety of items. The time of the auction can last anywhere from a few days to a few weeks. Throughout the duration of the auction, bids are accumulated. At the end of the auction, the bidder with the highest bid is then awarded the item. Although eBay started its business in the United States, the online auction has expanded its service to over thirty countries around the world. The items up for bid range from trading cards to automobiles. eBay actually plays the role of a broker which connects sellers and buyers[①].

1. Selling. In order to sell merchandise membership to the eBay site is required. The user must create a seller profile. The membership is free of charge and can be completed on the eBay's site. Sellers then pick a category that suits the item that they will be selling and then upload pictures of the item. The first picture is free, however additional pictures require a small fee. Listing an item costs about two dollars, which is the minimum fee. Extra listing options such as "Bold", "Print", "Extra large photos" and the "Buy now" option will add onto the base fee. The seller sets how high the bid will start, the duration of the auction and determines the shipping costs and rates. The seller is responsible for all aspects concerning the auction and it is his or her responsibility to answer all questions that

---

① Lan Moore, How Does eBay Work?, www.eHow.com

the potential buyers may have. At the conclusion of the auction, the seller must send an invoice with the cost and shipping information to the buyer. When the item has been paid for and shipped, the seller must leave feedback for the buyer.

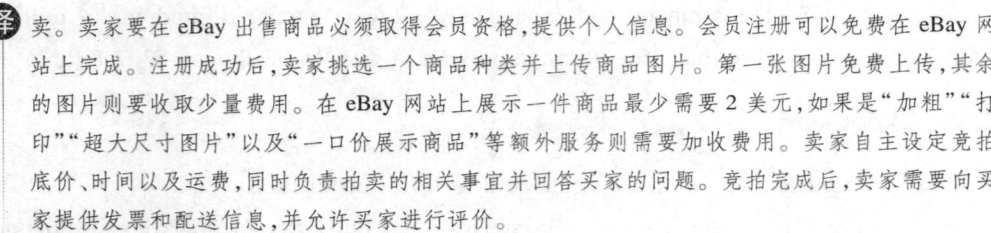
卖。卖家要在 eBay 出售商品必须取得会员资格,提供个人信息。会员注册可以免费在 eBay 网站上完成。注册成功后,卖家挑选一个商品种类并上传商品图片。第一张图片免费上传,其余的图片则要收取少量费用。在 eBay 网站上展示一件商品最少需要 2 美元,如果是"加粗""打印""超大尺寸图片"以及"一口价展示商品"等额外服务则需要加收费用。卖家自主设定竞拍底价、时间以及运费,同时负责拍卖的相关事宜并回答买家的问题。竞拍完成后,卖家需要向买家提供发票和配送信息,并允许买家进行评价。

2. Buying. To be able to bid on and buy auctioned users must have a member profile. This can be the same profile that is used to sell items. The buyer is allowed to bid as many times as possible. There are programs available to download which make it possible to bid at the last second. These are called "sniping" programs and are widely used during an auction. If the buyer has the highest bid, he or she will be notified that the item has been won. The buyer must now wait for the item to be shipped then pay the seller preferably through PayPal. When the transactions have been completed, the buyer must leave feedback for the seller. Buyers and sellers who receive positive feedback are awarded points. The higher the point total, the more experienced and trustworthy the buyer or seller is.

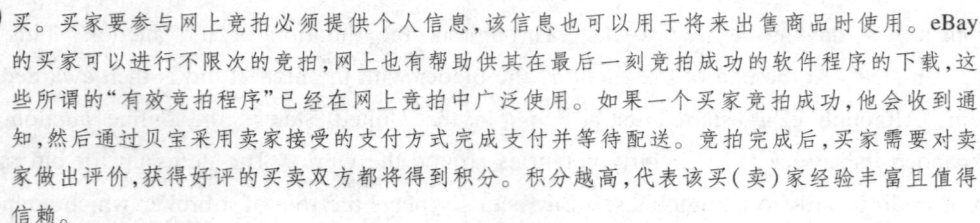
买。买家要参与网上竞拍必须提供个人信息,该信息也可以用于将来出售商品时使用。eBay 的买家可以进行不限次的竞拍,网上也有帮助供其在最后一刻竞拍成功的软件程序的下载,这些所谓的"有效竞拍程序"已经在网上竞拍中广泛使用。如果一个买家竞拍成功,他会收到通知,然后通过贝宝采用卖家接受的支付方式完成支付并等待配送。竞拍完成后,买家需要对卖家做出评价,获得好评的买卖双方都将得到积分。积分越高,代表该买(卖)家经验丰富且值得信赖。

eBay generates revenue by a complex system of fees for services, listing product features, and a Final Value Fee for sales proceeds by sellers. Since November 2012, the U.S.-based eBay has charged $0.10 to $2, based on the opening or reserve price, as an insertion fee for a basic auction-style listing without any adornments. The Final Value Fee amounts to 10% of the total amount of the sale, which is the price of the item plus shipping charges. Fixed-price listings have an insertion fee of $0.30, and the Final Value Fee varies based on category and total amount of the sale (e.g. 13% for DVDs & Movies up to $50). In addition, eBay owns the PayPal payment system that has fees of its own①.

---

① https://en.wikipedia.org/wiki/EBay

> **译** eBay 通过一套复杂的收费体系获取收入,包括展示产品以及向卖家收取销售提成。自 2012 年 11 月起,美国 eBay 向卖家收取 0.1—2 美元不等的产品登录费;10% 的销售提成(销售提成基于产品售价加运费进行计算);一口价商品收取 0.3 美元的产品登录费以及基于产品种类和销量而变化的销售提成。例如,对于销售收入满 50 元的 DVDs 和电影,其提成比例为 13%。除此之外,eBay 的支付系统贝宝还要向卖家另外收费。

What Makes eBay A Successful Online Auction Site?[①]

eBay's business model has proven its worth and continues to thrive even as eBay's management explores new avenues. What are the building blocks of the auction giant's extraordinary and persistent success?

1. Reaching critical mass. In business practices, critical mass refers to the revenue level at which fundamental changes can occur in a firm, and can make it largely self-sufficient in resources for continued viability, vitality, and growth. Thanks to the two factors, critical mass was realized by eBay. One is the first-mover advantage which enables eBay to dominate the online auction space and grow rapidly in a less mature market. The other is network effect. As a two-sided exchange platform, eBay affiliates sellers and buyers to make exchanges on its website. The more sellers post their commodities on eBay, the more buyers would like to visit the website and vice versa, which is the so-called cross-sides network effect.

2. Vanquished competition. At any rate, whether through first-mover momentum or superior service, eBay has capitalized on the network effect to a greater extent than any other e-commerce company. In a nutshell, eBay's critical mass of customers creates an ever-expanding sphere of influence resembling a magnetic field. Large and small merchants gravitate to eBay because that is where buyers are clustered. Consumers flock there because of the great product selection. The result is a juggernaut that has vanquished latecomers, such as Yahoo! Auctions and Amazon Auctions. Both of those operations are still in business, but they have reduced expectations and make relatively small contributions to their parent companies' balance sheets.

3. Lack of inventory. The company's core auction business has no inventory, since its customers supply the product. This is another key to eBay's success since it simplifies eBay's role—the company merely provides virtual space and software tools—widens its operating margins, leaving its balance sheet unencumbered by warehousing and fulfillment costs. With no inventory headaches, the company is free to focus on site operation and software management. The tools supplied to eBay's merchants enhance this value proposition.

---

① Brad Hill, What Makes eBay Invincible, E-commerce Times, 2003.

4. The attractive business channel. A crucial point that is often overlooked is eBay's value as a customer acquisition tool for small merchants, which is thought a key contributor to eBay's value. Small merchants are willing to sell at a loss on eBay in order to capture new customers. Although this phenomenon is primarily a small-business dynamic, even large businesses get into the act when disposing of excess inventory. Using eBay as a liquidation channel can be far less expensive than using a traditional liquidator. Such corporate leveraging of eBay's platform adds value to the customer experience as well, as increasingly brand-disloyal buyers seek bargains wherever they can find them. So the network effect continues to grow.

5. The effective communication. Two priorities dominate eBay's operational strategy: keeping its buyer/seller community happy, and keeping its massive site up and running. From the start, eBay has been, first and foremost, a community. To this day, the company maintains a high degree of communication with its customers via posted bulletins, interactive message boards and the unusual accessibility of its top-level executives. At the same time, software tools automatically regulate trust in the community. The company's feedback system, which at one time was vulnerable to tampering, has been tightened and serves as a self-regulating mechanism that keeps eBay's marketplace integrity high.

6. Learning from Disaster. eBay's second main business priority—keeping the site up and running—was galvanized in the summer of 1999, when a catastrophic systems failure blacked out the entire auction site for 22 hours. The company lost millions in transaction fees and billions in market value as investors dumped shares. Two results of the Big Crash remain paramount to this day: first, eBay's realization that remaining "up" on a 24/7 basis is a mission-critical business imperative; second, the hiring of Maynard Webb as CIO who is widely considered to have been eBay's white knight in the time of its greatest need, the man who fortified the site's stability.

7. Diversified categories. When assessing eBay's dominance, the company's role in building out certain product categories also should not be underestimated. Naturally, the auction giant must follow its sellers to some extent in determining its product directory. eBay did not invent Beanie Babies, for example, though it enabled a brisk business in trafficking them. This means that when eBay notices a swell of activity in a previously overlooked category, it works to promote it. The best current example is eBay Motors, which brought in $3 billion in 2002. Home electronics (US $2.2 billion), home appliances and furniture (US $1.4 billion), and baby merchandise (50% growth in 2002 over 2001) also have grown robustly, thanks to the company's stewardship. eBay is transacting business at a rate that represents only about 3% of the capacity of its 18,000 categories. So there is plenty of room to grow—especially beyond the U.S. borders.

8. Universal garage sale. Indeed, globalization has played a big part in eBay's recent success and will remain a vital part of the company's strategy going forward. International business already accounts for about 15% of eBay's total revenue which is expected to either equal or outdistance the U. S. market. Though some products and services are dependent on behavior characteristics of market groups or nationalities, they are not so with eBay since it is highly extensible.

Conclusion

eBay is probably the best hands-on example of how the Internet has changed commerce. People have been talking about this for a good number of years now. eBay might be the first example where a commerce site has actually been built around a community where people are exchanging information and exchanging goods, services and merchandise. People with traditional businesses found that eBay was so enticing, so much fun and in many ways profitable that they created a brand new business for themselves on eBay. They've left behind their profession or careers and started a new business on eBay. Those are demonstrations where people have really changed their lives and changed the way that they are doing things and the way commerce is conducted.

eBay has transformed from a boutique specialty site into a rival-stomping juggernaut—the "Walmart of online auctions". If it can continue to pull the right strings, fulfill the need of its enormous and diverse community, and keep its website technology aim at the lowest common denominator, it is likely to retain its invincible status.

Case Analysis

也许你对 eBay 并不是非常熟悉,但如果说它相当于"美国的淘宝",是否让你觉得有几分亲切? 的确,就商业模式而言,eBay 与淘宝十分相似:都是基于双边市场的 C2C 平台模式①。但从交易模式上看,eBay 却与淘宝大相径庭:它采取网上竞拍的交易模式,即用户在线对目标商品或服务进行竞价,优胜者根据事先约定获得拍卖标的②。eBay 诞生于电子商务萌芽阶段,在后来几十年激烈的竞争中为什么它能脱颖而出,成为美国乃至全球最知名的拍卖网站? 对其原因的分析正是本案例分析的侧重点。

eBay 的成功首先应归功于它独特的商业模式。前面的案例分析已经证明了商业模式对于电商企业成功的重要性,然而商业模式的选择却没有一定的标准。实践经验告诉我们,成功的企业在选择商业模式时往往遵从一个准则:了解用户的需求,并从中寻找能满足这种需求的最佳模式。eBay 的成功再次印证了这一点:创始人 Pierre Omidyar 从自己寻找小众商品的过程中发现,不少人都有在网上交易闲置商品的需求,

---

① 也有部分 B2C,但占比很小。
② eBay 的商品除了竞拍还可以用直接明码标价的"一口价"方式获得,但绝大多数用户仍然倾向于前者。

于是创建了 eBay,为人们自由进行商品交易和信息交流提供了网上空间。eBay 的 C2C 模式的优点显而易见:首先,它不需要存货。与亚马逊的 B2C 网上书店不同,eBay 搭建平台吸引买卖双方自由进行供求匹配,完成交易,并从中获取交易中介费。它并不需要直接向买方提供商品,而只是扮演交易中介的角色,商品交易产生的采购、库存、物流配送等成本均由交易双方自行承担,降低了平台的运营成本;其次,eBay 为卖家尤其是中小卖家提供了一个有效的销售渠道。它类似传统的"跳蚤市场",但却借助因特网打破了时空限制,从而为卖家更快地传递产品信息,吸引更多的潜在客户,更重要的是,相比跳蚤市场,它的成本更低。因此,eBay 能吸引大量的卖家尤其是中小卖家也就不足为奇了。大量卖家的入驻,丰富了网站的商品种类,也增加了它对买家的吸引力,这就是前几章所说的网络效应。再次,为了延续这种网络效应,增强客户的"黏性",eBay 借助商品信息发布、互动信息留言板等手段加强与客户的交流,并依靠安全的支付系统 Paypal、用户评分系统等一系列措施建立了一个互动良好,相互信任的虚拟交易社区。

　　eBay 的成功还应归功于它的先发优势和双边平台所带来的网络效应。eBay 成立于 1995 年,是与亚马逊诞生于同一时期的电商企业。尽管也是从事网上零售,但它选择了与亚马逊不同的商业模式 C2C 电子商务,这一市场在当时几乎处于空白。也正是因为如此,eBay 抓住了市场先发优势,迅速壮大,终于发展为全球知名的拍卖网站。另一方面,eBay 充分激发了双边平台的网络效应。如果平台企业希望享受到网络效应的益处,则必须使双方用户规模达到"临界数量(critical mass)",即能让平台维持生存和增长的最低数量。eBay 通过免费等手段吸引了大量的买家和卖家到网站上进行自由交易,并使用户规模突破了临界数量,从而实现了业务的快速增长。不仅如此,先发优势和网络效应还使 eBay 在竞争中占据优势,轻松化解了来自雅虎拍卖、亚马逊拍卖等后来竞争对手的威胁,最终在网上拍卖领域一枝独秀。

　　除此之外,eBay 的商业模式及其业务范围决定了它的可拓展性,迄今为止,它的业务已经遍及全球 190 多个国家和地区,拥有超过 1.6 亿的买家,这无疑是它的一大优势,也是它持续吸引更多交易者的基础。当然,eBay 在发展过程中也遭遇了不少问题,如:交易安全、技术故障等。幸运的是,eBay 善于从问题中吸取教训,总结经验,这将为它的可持续发展奠定基础。

Section 5
Case Analysis Preparation
第五节　案例分析前的准备

　　Since case analysis is a process requiring materials, attitude and ability, you have to prepare in advance:

1. Skim the case quickly to get an overview. The quick overview should give you a general impression of the situation, issues and problems that you need to cope with like "What organization is the case about? What happens in the organization? What are the results? and so on".

2. Read the questions of the case carefully and try to remember them or write them down so that you don't have to turn the pages forward and backward while reading the case thoroughly for the second time.

3. Review all the information presented in the exhibits. Usually, the exhibits indicates some important information which is crucial to materially affect your diagnosis of the situation.

4. Collect the supplementary materials if it is necessary. Sometimes, if you are not familiar with the case, collecting extra materials is a good way since it provides you more information. All the related materials online and offline like websites, books can be helpful.

After preparing for the case analysis well, you can begin a complete case analysis.

Summary（本章小结）

O2O is a new business model combining the online shopping and the offline transactions. O2O model usually provides information, services, booking discount and pushes the messages to Internet users, who in return will be converted into the customers of the particular offline business partners. The business model is particularly suitable to consumer goods and services, such as food and beverage, fitness, movies and beauty salon.

Groupon is a deal-of-the-day website that features discounted gift certificates usable at local or national companies. It is a typical O2O firm. Groupon works as an assurance contract using ThePoint's platform: if a certain number of people sign up for the offer, then the deal becomes available to all; if the predetermined minimum is not met, no one gets the deal that day. This reduces risk for retailers who can treat the coupons as quantity discounts as well as sales promotion tools. Groupon makes money by keeping approximately half the money the customer pays for the coupon. Besides, Groupon's business model satisfies consumers' curiosity and willingness to get larger discount. Since its foundation, Groupon has achieved its goals in a short term. Its success should be attributed to entering the market in the right time, being adaptable to consumers' shopping habits, easy access to Internet and guaranteed service, focusing on O2O services and word-of-mouth effect.

Ctrip is a platform, founded in 1999, for hotel accommodations, airline tickets and pre-packaged-tours in China. Ctrip targets on its services primarily at business and leisure travelers who do not travel in groups. In all transactions it acts as the sole agent. Ctrip aggregates information of hotels and flights and enables its customers to make hotel and flight bookings. Ctrip adopts the business model which shortens the value chain, establishes a successful travel information platform and enables the suppliers to lower the marketing cost. All these strategies enables low-cost travel.

eBay is an American multinational corporation and e-commerce company, providing C2C and B2C services via Internet. eBay is an online auction service that allows users to sell merchandise and prospective buyers to place bids on a wide variety of items. The duration of an auction can last anywhere from a few days to a few weeks. Throughout the duration of the auction, bids are accumulated. At the end of the auction, the bidder with the highest bid is then awarded the item. Although eBay started its business in the United States, the online auction has expanded its service to over thirty countries around the world. The items up for bid range from trading cards to automobiles. eBay actually plays the role of a broker which connects sellers with buyers. eBay's success should be attributed to critical mass, vanquished competition, lack of inventory, business channel, the effective communication, learning from disaster, universal garage sale and diversified categories.

In order to make an effective case analysis, we should prepare for it in advance. Skim the case quickly, remember or write down the study questions for the case carefully, review all the information presented in the exhibits and collect the supplementary materials are the four things in preparation.

Exercises & Tasks（练习与任务）

Exercises

1. How to describe the relationship between O2O and B2C?
2. How does OTAs like Ctrip shorten the travel service value chain?
3. What are the pros and cons of online aunction?
4. What should you prepare for a case analysis?

Tasks

Pick a firm with new e-commerce model and prepare a 20-minute presentation. The presentation should at least include:

1. Background introduction of the enterprise;
2. Pros and cons of its business model;
3. Conclusion.

Part II E-Commerce Infrastructures

第二部分 电子商务的基础架构

Chapter 4 Supply Chain and Logistics
第四章 | 供应链与物流

 Learning Objectives（学习目标）

After finishing this chapter, you should be able to:
1. Understand the concept of supply chain and logistics;
2. Identify how e-commerce influences supply chain and logistics;
3. Explain the critical success factors of Apple's SCM;
4. Analyze the problems with Jingdong's logistics;
5. List the basic case analysis methods.

 Introduction（内容简介）

Like other enterprises, e-commerce merchants have to control the cost to maximize profit. In practice, an e-commerce merchant has to control the cost of materials or commodities as well as the cost of delivery. It involves managing the chain from material procurement to products delivery efficiently. The chain is called as supply chain and the delivery is involved in logistics.

Chapter 4 is composed of 5 sections. The brief introduction to supply chain and logistics is made in section 1. Three supply chain and logistics cases are offered respectively in section 2, 3, and 4. Section 5 focuses on the case analysis methods.

Section 1
Supply Chain and Logistics
第一节 供应链与物流

▶ Key Words

1. supply chain 供应链
2. logistics *n.* 物流
3. material *n.* 物资,原料

▶ Supply Chain

Supply chain is the flow of materials, information, money, and services from raw material suppliers through factories and warehouses to the end customers[①]. Supply chain activities transform natural resources, raw materials, and components into a finished product that is delivered to the end customer. In a mature supply chain system, used products may re-enter the supply chain at any point where residual value is recyclable.

E-commerce, as a new business model, benefits supply chain in three aspects:

1. E-commerce shortens the supply chain. In a traditional retailing supply chain, customers can only purchase goods at the retailer's location; while with e-commerce, they can contact the suppliers directly.

2. E-commerce smoothes the supply chain by reducing problems in the flows of material, money, and information. Usually, the problems with supply chain are caused by information management. For example, the delay of information transmission may cause the rising procurement cost. E-commerce benefits supply chain by virtue of information technology by which information of products, materials and money can be transferred from one node to another quickly. As a result, the problems in the traditional supply chain management can be avoided effectively.

3. E-commerce facilitates the restructuring of supply chains. Traditionally, a complete supply chain contains five nodes: suppliers, manufacturers, distributors, retailers and customers. The more nodes involved in the supply chain, the higher managerial cost may occur. E-commerce, with the direct sale model, obviously shortens the original supply (Figure 4-1).

---

① R. Kelly Rainer, Casey G. Cegielski, *Introduction to Information Systems: Enabling and Transforming Business*(3rd Edition), Wiley Publish, 2010: pp. 334.

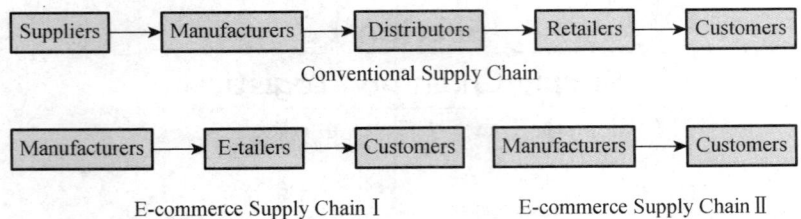

Figure 4-1　E-Commerce Restructures Supply Chain

▶ *Logistics*

Evolving since the 1960s, logistics refers to the operations involved in the efficient and effective flow and storage of goods, services, and related information from point of origin to point of consumption. The resources managed in logistics can include physical items such as food, materials, animals, equipment and liquids, as well as abstract items such as time, information, particles, and energy①. Logistics is usually a portion of supply chain.

What does e-commerce bring to logistics?

1. Logistics cost can be lowered with e-commerce. Under e-commerce business model, it is not necessary for the products to move from the upstream suppliers to wholesalers to retailers and finally to consumers. It can be offered to end customers directly from suppliers. Besides, digital goods do not need offline delivery. Therefore, the repeated transportations can be avoided.

2. The flow of information is more efficient. By virtue of information technology, especially computer network, all the information can be transmitted quickly and accurately. For example, a customer is allowed to track the package online anytime.

3. Higher quality and efficiency of logistics are required by e-commerce. One of the reasons that people prefer online shopping lies in the speed of transactions. E-commerce requires the commodities delivered in the right time, at the right place and at the most reasonable cost.

---

① https://en.wikipedia.org/wiki/Logistics

Section 2
Apple—Winner of "Best Supply Chain Management"
第二节 苹果——"最佳供应链管理"获得者

Key Words

1. capitalization *n.* 资本化
2. distribution *n.* 分销
3. inventory turnover *n.* 库存周转次数
4. inventory *n.* 存货
5. obsolete *adj.* 陈旧的
6. synchronize *vt.* 使同步
7. nitty-gritty *adj.* 根本的

Case

Background[①]

Founded by Steve Jobs, Steve Wozniak, and Ronald Wayne in April 1976, Apple Inc. (Hereinafter referred to as Apple) initially aimed to develop and sell personal computers. Nowadays, it has become an American multinational corporation that designs, develops, and sells consumer electronics, computer software, online services and personal computers.

Apple is the world's largest information technology company by revenue and the world's second-largest mobile phone manufacturer after Samsung. On November 25, 2014, in addition to being the largest publicly traded corporation in the world by market capitalization, Apple became the first U.S. company to be valued at over $700 billion. In March 2015, Apple was announced to be added to the Dow Jones Industrial Average. As of 2014, Apple employed 72,800 permanent full-time employees, maintained 437 retail stores in fifteen countries, and operated the online Apple Store and iTunes Store, the latter of which was the world's largest music retailer.

Apple's worldwide annual revenue in 2014 totaled $182 billion. According to the 2014 edition of the Interbrand Best Global Brands report, Apple was the world's most valuable brand with a valuation of $118.9 billion. For the fiscal quarter ending December 26, 2015, Apple reported revenue of $74.6 billion and net profits of $18.4 billion. Those totals were driven by record fourth quarter sales of iPhone, iPad and Mac. Services—which consists of things like the app store, iCloud, AppleCare, and Apple Pay—grew 26% year over year to $6.05 billion. "Other Products", which includes the

---

① https://en.wikipedia.org/wiki/Apple_Inc.

Apple Watch and Apple TV, grew its revenue 62% year-over-year, bringing in 4.3 billion this quarter[①]. From 2011 to 2014, Apple continuously ranked No.1 of "The Best Supply Chain" launched by Gartner.

Apple's Supply Chain[②]

1. Supply Chain Planning at Apple

Supply Chain Planning at Apple is the classic example of New Product Development Process (NPD). It's the integration of R&D, marketing and various function under supply chain management. Apple accelerates the new product introduction by acquiring licensing and third party businesses (Figure 4-2). The whole process looks very similar to that of other industries. Interesting point is that Apple has to make pre-payments to some suppliers to secure strategic raw materials.

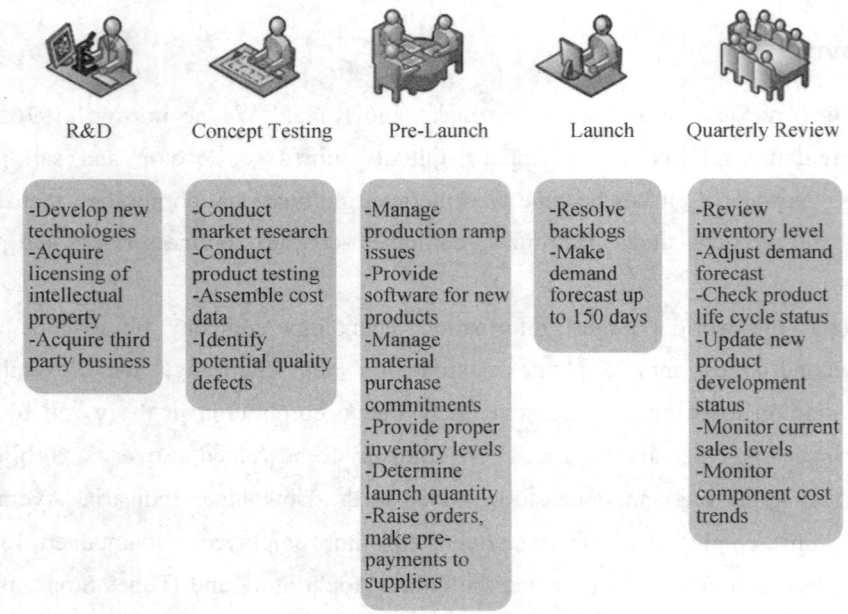

Figure 4-2 Supply Chain Planning at Apple

Supply Chain Map (Figure 4-3) is the way to express large system from points of origin to points of consumption in simple to understand manner. Information from annual report is also used to produce Apple Supply Chain Map.

Apple purchases raw materials from various sources then gets them shipped to

---

① Apple's Process Improvements Make it a Global Supply Chain Leader, http://www.spreadbird.com/apples-process-improvements-make-it-a-global-supply-chain-leader/, 2016-06-29.

② Is Apple's Supply Chain Really the No.1? A Case Study, http://www.supplychain247.com/article/is_apples_supply_chain_really_the_no._1_a_case_study, 2013-09-02.

assembling plant in China. From there, assembler will ship products directly to consumers (via UPS/Fedex) for those who buy from Apple's online store.

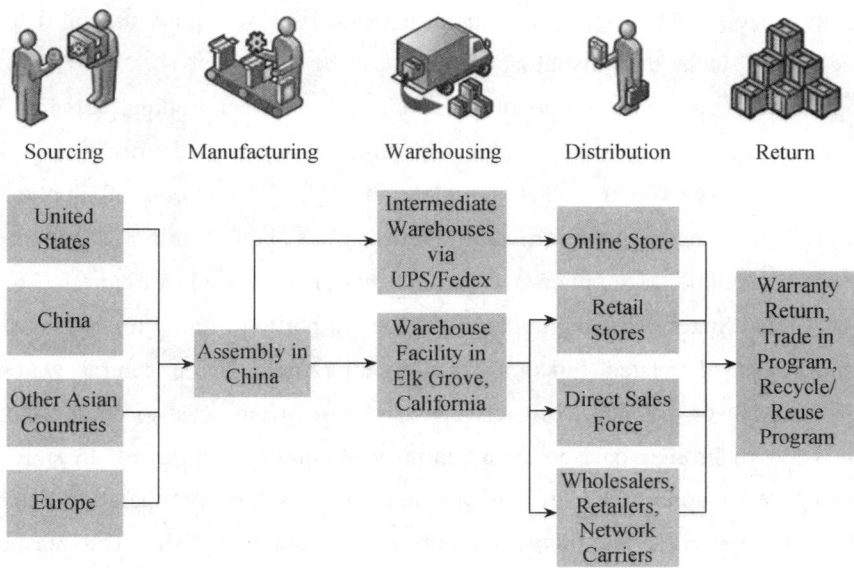

Figure 4-3 Apple's Supply Chain Map

For other distribution channels such as retail stores, direct sales and other distributors, Apple keeps products at Elk Grove, California (where central warehouse and call center are located) and supplies products from there. At the end of products' life, customer can send products back to nearest Apple Stores or dedicated recycling facilities.

2. How Complex is Apple's Supply Chain?

Inventory Turnover is a traditional financial measure to determine how efficient a company uses its financial resources to create sales, the higher number is the better. Supply chain professionals also use this metric in inventory management function. Generally accepted calculation is: Cost of Goods Sold / Average Inventory.

Figure 4-4 shows that inventory turnover of Amazon and Apple is 10 times and 59 times respectively (cost of goods sold of digital content and downloadable products are

Figure 4-4 Inventory Turnover Amazon vs. Apple

excluded). That means, their respective inventory period is 36.5 days and 6.19 days (365 days/inventory turnover, the lower number is the better). From the face value, Apple seems to be more efficient. Apple is now marketing company with no manufacturing facility but Amazon is a distributor of general merchandise. It's pretty natural that Amazon has to keep more stocks then inventory turnover can be much lower.

Supply chain management is about the relationship between trading partners. Working closely with strategic suppliers will bring competitive advantage to the firm. Apple said that they had about 156 key vendors across the globe in 2013. This amount of suppliers is quite manageable. According to this information, Amazon has about 3 million suppliers in total. Top 5% of this is 300,000 suppliers, way more than that of Apple (Figure 4-5).

In the United States, transportation cost is the big portion of total logistics cost. Then, good management of related function is essential. Apple has a central warehouse in California but Amazon has approximately 28 warehouses from coast to coast. What Apple has to do is to synchronize data between central warehouse and its own 246 stores as well as customers. With appropriate level of automation, this kind of operation can be done efficiently. For Amazon, the thing is more complicated than that. The reason is that Amazon distribution environment must be mathematically solved through optimization method. Typically, it has to determine how many facilities it should have, where serves which market, items/quantity stored in each location, how to manage transportation between warehouse-to-warehouse and warehouse to customers in order to minimize cost and increase service level (Figure 4-6).

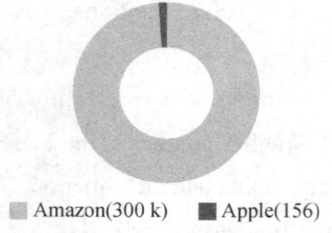

Figure 4-5　Suppliers Amazon vs. Apple

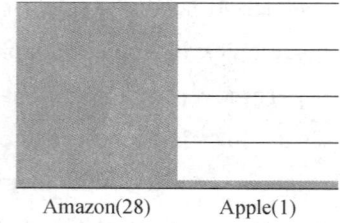

Figure 4-6　Number of Warehouse Facilities Amazon vs. Apple

Stock Keeping Unit (SKU) is another indication of supply chain complexity. One model of phone but different software inside is considered different item/SKU. According to this, Amazon has about 170 million items on its catalog. About 135 million items are physical products. For Apple, they have about 26,000 items (rough estimate, subject to change). The point is that, if a demand forecast has to be made, which one will be more difficult, 135 million items or 26,000 items?

Product life cycle is how long you can sell products. From rough estimate, Amazon has some seasonal products such as summer ware. They can only sell it for 3 months, at most. The life of Apple's key products are way more than 12 months. It is very difficult for short life cycle products to estimate demand (Figure 4-8).

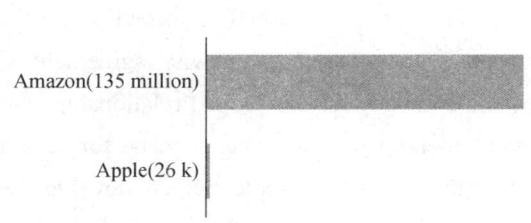

Figure 4-7　Number of SKUs Amazon vs. Apple

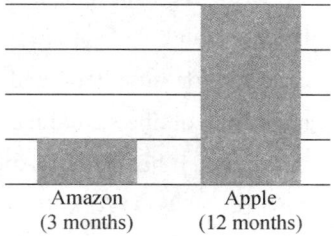

Figure 4-8　Product Life Cycle Amazon vs. Apple

The results from the analysis of Apple's supply chain indicates that it is not easy to manage its supply chain well. After all, there are many challenges to overcome: collaborations with suppliers may encounter problems; inventories can become obsolete or exceed anticipated demand; some components are currently obtained from single or limited sources; some custom components are not common to the rest of the industries; supply chain disruption such as natural and man-made disasters can be serious. Facing these challenges, how does Apple win "the best supply chain"?

What Enables Apple "The Best Supply Chain"?[1][2][3]

1. Complete "Mission Impossible". In 2006, Apple design guru Jony Ive decided to add a new feature for the next MacBook—a small dot of green light above the screen, shining through the computer's aluminum casing to indicate when its camera was on. However, it's physically impossible to shine light through metal. Ive called in a team of manufacturing and materials experts to figure out how to make the impossible possible. The team discovered it could use a customized laser to poke holes in the aluminum small enough to be nearly invisible to the human eye but big enough to let light through. The team of experts found a U. S. company that made laser equipment for microchip manufacturing which, after some tweaking, could do the job. Each machine typically goes for about $250,000. Apple convinced the seller to sign an exclusivity agreement and bought hundreds of them to make holes for the green lights that later shined on the

---

　　① Adam Satariano, Peter Burrows, Apple's Supply-Chain Secret?, *Bloomberg Businessweek Magazine*, 2011-11-03.
　　② Bisk, Apple's Process Improvements Make It a Global Supply Chain Leader, http://www.usanfranonline.com/resources/supply-chain-management/apples-process-improvements-make-it-a-global-supply-chain-leader/#
　　③ Clara Lu, Apple Supply Chain—The Best Supply Chain in the World, https://www.tradegecko.com/blog/apple-had-the-best-supply-chain-in-the-world-for-the-last-four-years-here-is-what-you-can-learn-from-it

company's MacBook Airs, Trackpads, and wireless keyboards. Most of Apple's customers have probably never given that green light a second thought, but its creation speaks to a massive competitive advantage for Apple's operations.

2. Effective suppliers management. Apple took steps early on to manage its global supply chain and the suppliers within it. The company established a formalized list of expectations for suppliers and quickly moved on to creating exclusivity agreements in exchange for volume guarantees. Over time, the company has developed relationships with suppliers, which has helped Apple quickly scale operations to customer demand for existing and new products. Working with its supply chain partners, Apple helped develop new manufacturing processes, some of which have been the subject of patents filed by the company. Although outsourcing provides Apple with advantages, it doesn't come without risk. Outsourcing can leave a company vulnerable to disruptions in key links of its supply chain, potentially caused by anything from natural disasters to changes in international trade agreements. Therefore, Apple also made a strategic decision to partner with manufacturing companies that understand Apple's products require different technologies and approaches, which often must be accommodated with very little lead time. Additionally, Apple diversified product assembly companies as part of process improvements. Apple has moved toward more manufacturing partners since the production of iPhone 6 and Apple Watch as it has been looking to reduce the risks of shortages and other vendor issues that could slow or stop production. By increasing the number of companies it works with, Apple reduced the risk of relying on one company and opening itself up to production stalls and business fails. For example, Apple kept its options open when it came to selecting manufacturing partners for the iPhone 6 and the Apple Watch by broadening the number of companies it contracted with. Lower costs could potentially be an advantage for Apple, as multiple companies compete for further business with Apple.

3. Massive procurement. This is the world of manufacturing, procurement, and logistics in which the new chief executive officer, Tim Cook, excells, earning him the trust of Steve Jobs. Apple has built a closed ecosystem where it exerts control over nearly every piece of the supply chain, from design to retail store. Because of its volume—and its occasional ruthlessness—Apple gets big discounts on parts, manufacturing capacity, and air freight. Apple was thought to have "taken operational excellence to a level never seen before". This operational edge is what enables Apple to handle massive product launches without having to maintain large, profit-sapping inventories. It also makes the company be criticized for high prices to sell its iPad at a price that very few rivals can beat, while still earning a 25% margin on the device.

4. Buy out all the resources. Apple began innovating on the nitty-gritty details of supply-chain management almost immediately upon Steve Jobs's return in 1997. At that

time, most computer manufacturers transported products by sea, a far cheaper option than air freight. To ensure that the company's new, translucent blue iMacs would be widely available at Christmas the following year, Jobs paid $50 million to buy up all the available holiday air freight space. The move handicapped rivals such as Compaq that later wanted to book air transport. Similarly, when iPod sales took off in 2001, Apple realized it could pack so many of the diminutive music players on planes that it became economical to ship them directly from Chinese factories to consumers' doors. When an HP staffer bought one and received it a few days later, tracking its progress around the world through Apple's website. That mentality—spending exorbitantly wherever necessary, and reaping the benefits from greater volume in the long run—is institutionalized throughout Apple's supply chain, and begins at the design stage. Engineers in Apple sometimes spend months living out of hotel rooms in order to be close to suppliers and manufacturers, helping to tweak the industrial processes that translate prototypes into mass-produced devices. For new designs such as the MacBook's unibody shell, cut from a single piece of aluminum, Apple's designers work with suppliers to create new tooling equipment. The decision to focus on a few product lines, and to do little in the way of customization, is a huge advantage.

    5. Efficient inventory management. Keeping as little inventory on hand as possible is very important since costs with warehouses and competitors possible hits. Technology manufacturers can't afford to keep too many products in stock because a sudden announcement from a competitor or a new innovation could change everything and suddenly bring down the value of products in inventory. Apple also demonstrates its value of "pursuit extreme" in inventory management. For instance, Tim Cook shut down 10 of the 19 Apple warehouses to limit overstocking, and by September of 1998 inventory duration was down from a month to only six days. By 2013, Apple kept only one central warehouse in perfect data sync with the approximately 250 owned stores. Foreseeing sales levels accurately and not having excess inventory are absolutely crucial in the computer industry, especially when new products quickly cannibalize the old. Not having too many SKUs helps correct forecasting (in 2013, Apple had 26.000 SKUs, way less than other technology manufacturers). And forecasting demand doesn't come only in the form of what products your customers will buy, but also on what kind of technologies will be in demand for the next coming years, allowing the company to reduce costs with suppliers by placing orders for longer term. This also leads to creating enough demand for suppliers, so that other competitors can not order the components and hence limiting imitations. Although Apple was always pushing to have fast inventory turnover, it made a change in 2011 of not rushing selling. The change was implemented with the launch of the iPad 2 and consisted of selling the much-awaited products the second day after they were delivered to shops, despite the customer ques in front. This measure was taken to make sure inventory tracking runs smooth and there are no errors to lead to inventory inaccuracies.

有效的库存管理。由于仓储成本的原因,保持尽量低的库存是很重要的。技术制造商无法承受高库存是因为竞争对手策略的变化和技术创新的出现都可能导致库存产品的价值下跌。苹果在库存上面也显示了它"追求极致"的价值理念。比如,提姆库克将苹果的仓库数量从19个减少至10个,并在1998年9月将仓储周期从1个月缩短至6天。截至2013年,苹果仅保留了1个中心仓库并使其与大约250家门店保持数据同步。精准预测销售并保证没有超额库存对计算机行业而言是至关重要的。较低的SKU使苹果能正确进行销售预测。需求预测不仅涉及顾客未来的购买还关系到接下来几年中市场的技术发展走向。这意味着制造商必须提前与供应商预约采购,以避免竞争对手购买同样的部件并进行仿制。尽管苹果一直推行快速库存周转,它在2011年仍然实施了一项"非急售"变革。这项改革与iPad 2同步推出,要求所有待售商品必须在到达门店后的第二天起售。这项措施也是为了确保库存跟踪能顺利进行,避免库存误差。

6. High investment. When it's time to go into production, Apple wields a big weapon—more than $80 billion in cash and investments. In 2011, the company said it planed to nearly double capital expenditures on its supply chain in the next year, to $7.1 billion, while committing another $2.4 billion in prepayments to key suppliers. The tactic ensures availability and low prices for Apple—and sometimes limits the options for everyone else. Before the release of the iPhone 4 in June 2010, rivals such as HTC couldn't buy as many screens as they needed because manufacturers were busy filling Apple orders. To manufacture iPad 2, Apple bought so many high-end drills to make the device's internal casing that other companies' wait time for the machines stretched from six weeks to six months. Life as an Apple supplier is lucrative because of the high volumes as well as painful because of the strings attached. When Apple asks for a price quote for parts such as touchscreens, it demands a detailed accounting of how the manufacturer arrives at the quote, including its estimates for material and labor costs, and its own projected profit. Apple requires many key suppliers to keep two weeks of inventory within a mile of Apple's assembly plants in Asia, and sometimes doesn't pay until as long as 90 days after it uses a part. Not every supplier gives in. A major parts manufacturer declined a $1 billion payment from Apple that required the supplier to commit much of its manufacturing capacity to Cupertino's products because Apple's bargaining tactics tended to exert downward pressure on prices, leading to lower profits and margins. While deals featuring $1 billion in cash up front were basically unheard of, the company didn't want to be too dependent on Apple—and didn't want to help it deflate prices.

7. Strict confidentiality. Apple's control reaches its crescendo in the leadup to one of its famed product unveiling, a tightly orchestrated process that has been refined over years of Mac, iPod, iPhone, and iPad debuts. For weeks in advance of the announcement, factories work overtime to build hundreds of thousands of devices. To track efficiency and ensure pre-launch secrecy, Apple places electronic monitors in some boxes of parts that allow observers in Cupertino to track them through Chinese factories, an effort meant to

discourage leaks. At least once, the company shipped products in tomato boxes to avoid detection. When iPad 2 debuted, the finished devices were packed in plain boxes and Apple employees monitored every handoff point—loading dock, airport, truck depot, and distribution center—to make sure each unit was accounted for. Apple's retail stores give it a final operational advantage. Once a product goes on sale, the company can track demand by the store and by the hour, and adjust production forecasts daily. If it becomes clear a given part will run out, teams are deployed and given approval to spend millions of dollars on extra equipment to get around the bottleneck. Apple's enormous profits—its gross margins were 40% in the third quarter of 2011, compared with 10 to 20% for most other hardware companies—are in large part due to this focus on supply chain management, which is sure to remain a priority.

Apple has been insisting in using supply chains as a strategic weapon in business. When implementing the strategy, it always emphasizes efficiency and pursuits extreme. Just as a catchphrase used by Cook, the new CEO, said, "Nobody wants to buy sour milk." That can, to some extent, explain "Best Supply Chain Management" of the company.

Case Analysis

长久以来,当我们谈及苹果公司(以下简称"苹果")的成功,更多地关注它极富创造性的产品及其带给用户的上佳体验。实际上,对于这家收入最高,市场遍布全球15个国家,员工超过7万人的信息技术公司而言,杰出的供应链管理是它成功的重要原因。从2011年到2014年,苹果连续4年在Gartner评选的"最佳供应链"企业中蝉联榜首。这也激发了我们的好奇,对这家知名企业的供应链管理成功的原因一探究竟。

第一,苹果建立了一套完整而成熟的供应链系统。这套系统涵盖了产品设计、制造、销售、退货等一系列完整的步骤。以苹果的明星产品iPhone和iPad为例,其整个供应链流程简单概括起来就是:苹果在美国总部完成产品设计,并向上游供应商购买原材料和零部件,然后将其运往分别位于中国大陆郑州和成都的两家工厂组织生产,并针对不同渠道的客户组织发货:对于网上订货的客户,该公司选择联邦快递等第三方物流企业直接将产品送到消费者手中;对于线下购买(如:旗舰店)的客户,苹果则将产品先运至各仓储中心,再发往零售商店。苹果在各大零售点设有专门的回收设施完成产品回收。

第二,杰出的供应商管理。苹果的产品质量有口皆碑,这在很大程度上得益于它杰出的供应商管理。苹果的产品除了设计之外的其他流程均采取外包方式,因此选择优质且合适的供应商是关键。苹果通常选择多家拥有丰富的产品生产装配经验的供应商,并借助自身的行业影响力促进供应商之间的竞争以降低采购成本。苹果还与供应商签订独家的大批量长期采购合同,以获取成本和质量优势。随着时间推移,苹果与供应商之间建立了良好的合作关系,实现了"双赢":苹果能随时根据客户需求调整生产规模,供应商则能从长期的大批量采购订单中获益。例如,有些供应商在苹果的帮助下开发了新的生产流程,其中一些甚至申请了专利。优化的供应链管理不仅降低了外包带来的风险,也保证了产品质量。

第三,大量而极端的采购。大批量采购可以获得价格优惠,因此成为制造商们降低成本的常用方法。苹果的不同之处在于,它不仅大量采购,而且往往采用独家买断的方法将某种资源据为己有。这不仅体现在原材料采购中,也体现在物流配送过程中。苹果曾经为了赶在圣诞节前将其最新型的 iMac 电脑配送到位,预订了所有的运输航班,使其竞争对手无法进行产品配送。这种大量而极端的采购方式虽然看起来不近人情,但的确使苹果降低了采购、制造和运输成本,阻碍了竞争对手进入市场,获取了市场先机。这其实也是其"做到极致"的企业文化的体现。

第四,有效的存货管理。存货是供应链管理的关键环节,为了降低存货成本,企业应该使其存货数量在保证供货的前提下维持在尽量低的水平。苹果一直致力于大幅度降低存货,减少仓储中心数量。例如,其现任 CEO 库克就曾将仓储中心从 19 家减少至 10 家。实践证明,这种做法是行之有效的:苹果的库存周转期仅为 5 天,仅为同行的1/4 或 1/2,意味着它可以在不到一周的时间内将仓库存货清空。苹果的存货管理不仅有效降低了库存成本,加速了资金周转,而且帮助它精确预测销量,从而制订合理的生产计划。

第五,强有力的资金和品牌支持。苹果能连续多年荣膺"最佳供应链管理"企业,除了上述几个直接原因之外,还有两个间接原因:一是资金支持,二是品牌优势。经过多年成功的经营,苹果拥有强大的资金实力,这有利于它投入大量资本,实现供应链管理及优化。例如,苹果有实力进行原材料和零配件的预约采购,从而保证后续的生产供应,并在一定程度上阻碍了竞争对手获取同样的资源。除此之外,在供应链管理中,苹果自身的品牌优势是一项重要的无形资产。苹果的品牌知名度有利于它寻找和吸引优质的供应商,并在议价谈判中获取优势。尽管苹果的强势与严苛在业界众所周知,但仍然无法阻止供应商与其合作的热情,因为对方是苹果,与它合作意味着收入和自身知名度的提升。

苹果的供应链管理之所以成功,是因为它将其作为一项重要的战略武器,并将"强调效率"和"追求极致"贯彻始终,最终所向披靡。

Section 3
Jingdong—Leading Logistics, Winning E-Market
第三节 京东商城——引领物流,赢得市场

Key Words

1. magneto-optical *n.* 光盘 2. skyrocket *vi.* 飞涨
3. third-party logistics *n.* 第三方物流 4. controversy *n.* 争议

5. abundant *adj.* 丰富的,充裕的   6. prospectus supplement *n.* 招股文件

 Case

Background

JD. com or Jingdong Mall, formerly 360Buy, is a Chinese electronic commerce company headquartered in Beijing. It is one of the largest B2C online retailers in China by transaction volume. The company was founded by Liu Qiangdong in July 1998, and its B2C platform went online in 2004. It started as an online magneto-optical store, but soon diversified, selling electronics, mobile phones, computers, etc. Jingdong Mall changed the domain name to 360buy. com in June 2007, and to JD. com in 2013. Jingdong supplies 40.2 million products covering 13 categories now①.

China's e-commerce market continues to skyrocket with estimates of 2020 online sales likely to peg at $1.7 trillion②. However this growth has placed pressure on the logistics infrastructure resulting in delivery issues since most e-commerce retailers tend to rely on the top ten largest Chinese domestic express providers. Not only are some express providers expanding service offerings into the warehousing segment but many of these providers are also launching their own e-commerce websites. Facing the challenge from logistics, Jingdong decided to spend 350 million yuan building its own logistics system in 2007.

Why Self-Built Logistics?③④

Unlike other e-tailer such as Taobao depending on third-party logistics, Jingdong focuses on self-built logistics. When Liu Qiangdong, CEO of Jingdong, decided to build the self-owned logistics system at the expense of 350 million yuan in 2007, the controversy seemed unavoidable. The reasons that Jingdong chose self-built logistics lie in:

1. Amazon's success in self-built logistics system sets a benchmark for numerous e-commerce enterprises. Actually, Jingdong is not the first e-commerce firm building its own logistics system. The model of self-built logistics system is American online retailer Amazon, which invests a lot in building logistics system relying on its high IT technology. In addition to meeting its own demand for logistics, it also provides supply chain

---

① https://en. wikipedia. org/wiki/JD. com
② Mike O'Brien, Chinese Ecommerce Market Pegged at $1.7 Trillion by 2020, http://multichannelmerchant. com/news/chinese-ecommerce-market-pegged-1-7-trillion-2020/, 2017-03-03.
③ Yolanda Zhang, Chinese E-commerce's Self-built Logistics, Capital Game or General Trend?, http://en. pedaily. cn/Item. aspx? id =217819, 2011-08-12.
④ T Racking, Self-built Logistics Warehouse Have Advantages, http://www. t-racking. com/news/self-built-logistics-warehouse-have-advantage/, 2015-02-27.

management services to other enterprises. Such a model has become a development direction of Chinese e-commerce enterprises.

2. Competition in service and cost control boost logistics building of e-commerce enterprises. The competition of all kinds of e-commerce enterprises is intensified, evolving from the competition of single products and price to the service competition. In order to attract users and to increase users' faithfulness, e-commerce enterprises try to enhance the user experience through the "last mile" construction. In addition, although the logistics system requires large funding in the short run, in the long run, enterprises can save costs by means of logistics system management.

3. Holiday mode is challenging the existing logistics system. Every year, when Spring Festival is approaching, the courier and delivery capacity shortages are inevitable. As lots of part-time couriers go back to hometown for vacation, the number of couriers on duty declines sharply. As a result, the delivery has to be delayed or even refused, which causes the customers' dissatisfaction. The phenomenon is prominent especially for the e-commerce companies outsourcing their logistics. For example, many small and medium-sized retailers on Taobao have been obsessed by the complaints and low rating from the customers due to the inefficient delivery in holiday. With self-built logistics, Jingdong can keep normal operation even during the special days like Spring Festival since it doesn't have to depend on third party logistics. Besides, the self-built logistics system enables the enterprise to not only track all the parcels on delivery but also collect customers' data so as to accurately capture their need.

4. Self-built logistics enables more control. Self-built logistics allows e-commerce enterprises to track the whole process of delivery so as to control quality and efficiency better. Besides, without the dependence on third-party logistics, the enterprises can focus on the innovation of logistics service, which satisfies customers' demand better. Actually, all the personalized logistics services launched by Jingdong are based on its own logistics system.

5. Self-built logistics system benefits reverse logistics. Product return or replacement has been a tough part of online retailing as it requires the resources integration and systems docking between the e-commerce platform and the logistics system. With self-built logistics system, the process becomes easier because the process only involves single firm.

By the first quarter 2016, Jingdong's self-built logistics had been able to handle about 98% orders delivery, 90% of which could be delivered same-day or next day[①]. With the support of the logistics system, Jingdong's customer satisfaction rate greatly surpasses that of the peers.

---

① 沙水,时势造京东:自建物流战略一剑封喉,http://www.sohu.com/a/76793599_116457, 2016-05-23。

SWOT Analysis of Jingdong's Self-built Logistics

Though the statistics has shown the effectiveness of self-built logistics system, it doesn't mean the model is perfect. A SWOT analysis helps us to understand Jingdong's choice clearly.

Strengths

1. Abundant financial resources. It spends lots of resources such as money, human resources building a self-owned logistics system. System building will become "mission impossible" without sufficient financial supports. Fortunately, early 2011, Jingdong successfully financed 1.5 billion U.S. dollars from six investors including Digital Sky Tech from Russia and Tiger Fund. The adequate capital becomes the solid base of self-built logistics system.

2. Complete control over logistics including R&D and implementation. To build such a complex system requires high-level technical forces. Jingdong has its own R&D workforce who successfully developed critical products. For example, Jingdong owns a mature ERP system by which a customer is able to check product, inventory and delivery information anytime, everywhere. The excellent workforce ensure the efficiency and effectiveness as well as the control of the critical technologies.

3. Outstanding sales ensuring the delivery demands. The self-built logistics system is time and money consuming. In addition to the external financing, it needs the outstanding enterprise performance to cover the high costs. Jingdong's annual revenue increased from 10 million yuan in 2004 to 10.2 billion yuan in 2010. The annual compound growth rate reaches 217.27%. In 2017, Jingdong had 292.5 million annual active customer accounts and gained net product revenues of 331,824 million yuan (approximately 51,000 million U.S. dollar)[1].

4. Personalized service assuring customers' satisfaction. To increase convenience and flexibility for customers, Jingdong launched some innovative delivery services such as 211 Program, Next-Day Delivery. Since May 31, 2013, Jingdong's customers have been able to receive orders placed before 3 p.m. the same evening between 7 p.m. and 10 p.m. through the company's self-operated delivery network. The new service expands on the same-day delivery option in Jingdong's 211 program, which previously required orders to be placed by 11 a.m.. Jingdong also launched "Three-Hour Delivery", an option for customers who want to receive their products within three hours of placing an order. Jingdong's last-mile delivery network offers customized delivery options to its customers,

---

[1] 2017 Annual Report, ir.jd.com/phoenix.zhtml?c=253315&p=irol-reportsannual

including same-day, next-day, and timed delivery, in more than 150 cities across China, with a wide variety of payment options, like cash on delivery. They are the improvements in Jingdong's long-standing commitment to providing customers first class service, from their ordering experience to their speedy and convenient delivery options[①].

Weaknesses

1. Possible risks of financial supports. Due to the long cycle and high expenses of self-built logistics, Jingdong's logistics strategy probably suffers risks such as lack of capital and over-budget. Jingdong had 110,000 employees by the end of 2015, almost 70% of whom belonging to the logistics system. According to Liu Qiangdong, CEO of Jingdong, the workforce is expected to break through 1 million in the future[②]. The rising workforce will not only lead to the higher operation cost, but also challenge the existing managerial system. Meanwhile, Jingdong's B2C businesses grew rapidly in the past few years, which means more investment on website maintenance, personnel recruitment. Can Jingdong bear the burden?

2. Single model causing low efficiency. Because Jingdong's self-built logistics only serves the products sold by itself or affiliated merchants, it causes the low rate of logistics utilization—only 50%-60%, which is far away from the average 80%.

Opportunities

1. The growing online consumption ensures the demand for logistics. In 2013, Jingdong pulled in over $16 billion in sales. Some other numbers for the site also prove the point: over 140 million registered users; over 100 million users using its mobile shopping apps; about 220 million page-views from PC-based shoppers[③]. The rising online sales indicates that more customers shop on Jingdong, which generates lots of demand for logistics. As a result, the logistics system in building can be utilized efficiently.

2. The improving infrastructures in China. As we know, the efficient delivery depends on not only the effective information, fund and personnel management, but also the quality of infrastructures. Even though there are excellent logistics teams and adequate investment, the quality of logistics may be dissatisfied due to the poor infrastructure. It can not be changed by a single private enterprise. Fortunately, Out of all the infrastructure

---

① Jingdong Launches "Night Delivery" and "Three-Hour Delivery" Options, https://www.prnewswire.com/news-releases/jingdong-launches-night-delivery-and-three-hour-delivery-options-209632901.html, 2013-05-31.

② 刘强东说京东员工总数将超百万,规模堪比富士康, http://www.redsh.com/a/20160721/101903.shtml, 2016-07-21。

③ Steven Millward, Chinese E-store Jingdong Set to Pull in over $16 Billion in Sales in 2013, TECHINASIA, 2013-12-23.

sectors, the effort to improve the country's roads has received the strongest impetus and investment from Chinese government, which will benefit Jingdong's logistics implementation.

3. The rapid development of technologies. The new technologies such as RFID and AI(artificial intelligence) have been applied to logistics, which will improve the quality and efficiency of delivery. Thanks to these technologies, Jingdong's self-built logistics system can serve its e-commerce more efficiently.

Threats

1. Logistics competition with opponents. Taking into account the various problems of third-party logistics, domestic shopping sites generally begin to construct self-built logistics system. Relying on third-party logistics for a long time, Alibaba also began to construct self-built logistics system. In June 2010, Taobao, controlled by Alibaba Group, officially introduced "Big Taobao Logistics Plan". In January 2011, Jack Ma, Chairman of Alibaba Group, announced that Alibaba would spend hundreds of billions of RMB in establishing a national logistics system with partners. Phase one of the project would be investing 20 billion yuan in building the national-wide warehouse system that covers seven major regions in China including northeast, north, east, south, middle, southwest and northwest. Amazon began to build its shipping capacity in China in 2007. By September 2011, Amazon had owned four logistics centers in Beijing, Guangzhou, Suzhou and Chengdu as well as a shipping team, a distribution center and a call center. Amazon's self-established shipping company is named "Millennium Amazon. cn Shipment" which is now responsible for majority of Amazon's order shipment. In July 2011, Amazon officially opened its third-party seller platform in China. It means sellers don't have to invest in any expensive infrastructure such as warehousing and logistics but just focus on the products, while Amazon takes care of the warehousing, logistics, return, exchange, refund and other customer services. As the largest local online bookstore in China, Dangdang used third-party logistics services at early stage. With rapid increase in services, Dangdang started to build warehouses in different places, but is still using third-parties for shipping services. In February 2011, Dangdang took the lead to establish a shipping service company which Dangdang held a certain stake, in order to build an open logistics platform and provide e-commerce companies with services ranging from warehousing, distribution and packaging, and COD (Collect-on-Delivery) services in over 1,200 cities[①].

2. Rising logistics cost. China's logistics costs climbed 11.4% year on year to reach 9.4 trillion ($1.51 trillion) in 2012, according to a report by China Federation of

---

① Chinese E-commerce Giants' Hype on Logistics, Businessinsider. com, 2011-09-20.

Logistics and Purchasing (CFLP). Although the growth rate shed seven percentage points from 2011, total logistics costs accounted for 18% of the nation's GDP in 2012, compared with 17.8% in the previous year. The report attributed high expenditure in 2012 to rising costs for labor, fuel and tolls of roads and bridges: labor costs surged 15% to 20% on average, fuel prices tripled from that in 2000, while road charges made up one third of the total logistics costs[①].

3. High pressure on delivery. Since Jingdong's self-built logistics system covers most of the delivery and complies with the requirement like "211 program", it leads to a high workload. With the rising online ordering, the pressure on Jingdong's logistics will increase greatly.

4. Skepticism on Jingdong's self-built logistics which causes the pressure on the implementation of logistics system. Actually, when Liu Qiandong, CEO of Jingdong proposed the self-built logistics plan in 2011, many people doubted it. The opponents argued that the system cost too much money and the ROI (Return of Investment) was uncertain. Besides, they also worried that the high expenses of the system probably affected the existing businesses. Though Liu insisted on the self-build logistics project, the external skepticism may become the pressure which influencing the progress of the system building.

How Is Jingdong's Logistics Going?

Self-built logistics enables a complete delivery process and high quality services. With the rapid development of electronic business, logistics has become a vital "link in the various courier companies to enter the 'semi-closed' state", self-built electric providers highlight the advantages of logistics warehouse. By June 2015, Jingdong had owned 7 logistics centers all over the country, 166 large warehouses in 44 Chinese cities, 4,142 delivery spots and self pickup stations, covering 2,043 districts and counties[②]. The effective logistics system enables the innovations such as 211 Program, Next-Day Delivery, which improve the quality of services and customers' satisfaction. By now, Jingdong has successfully built a complete logistics system dominated by self-built logistics and a good brand image of high efficiency and quality due to its excellent logistics services. Jingdong logistics is serving the customers by 4 delivery modes:

1. FBP

FBP is a full colocation delivery mode. Under this mode, an affiliated merchant posts the product information on Jingdong's website and begins stock. Jingdong is responsible for

---

① Logistics costs remain high in China: report, http://www.globaltimes.cn/content/760979.shtml, 2013-02-08.
② 京东物流实现"极速达"的四种模式, 搜狐财经, 2016-09-01.

products preparation; invoice and delivery right after an order is made online. After the deal is completed, Jingdong makes a settlement with the merchant to share the revenue. The merchant tracks the stock information so as to make an instant replenishment. Because the merchant begins stock in advance, the mode is most efficient so as to achieve the goals such as "211 program".

2. LBP

LBP is a half colocation delivery mode under which an affiliated merchant only needs to package and send products within 12 hours and deliver them to Jingdong's distribution center within 36 hours rather than make stock in advance. As a partner, Jingdong is in charge of delivery and customer service so as to alleviate its inventory. The merchant is responsible for products preparation right after an order is made online. This mode increases the merchant's transport cost and decreases the delivery efficiency since all the products are required to transfer to Jingdong's distribution center.

3. SOPL

Differing from LBP, SOPL mode requires an affiliated merchant to complete the whole logistics process but delivery. Jingdong only provides the delivery service, which reduces Jingdong's inventory and logistics costs. Like LBP, this mode lowers the delivery efficiency that probably causes customers' dissatisfaction.

4. SOP

Under SOP mode, an affiliated merchant is responsible for the whole process from products preparation to delivery and customer service. Jingdong only provides a mature platform which allows the merchant to manipulate the logistics process within 12 hours. Jingdong has little logistics load and cost since the merchant handles everything.

Though encountering skepticism, Jingdong's self-built logistics system has shown its effectiveness and Jingdong has been devoting to perfecting the system so as to supply high-quality services to its customers.

Case Analysis

从 2004 年成立至今,京东在不到 15 年的时间里成长为中国第二大的 B2C 电子商务企业,令人惊叹。它为什么能在竞争如此激烈的环境中脱颖而出? 其中一个主要的原因就在于它杰出的物流管理。物流被称为"电子商务的最后一公里",京东正是在这"最后一公里"中以高效优质的服务赢得了顾客的信赖,成功建立起自己的品牌。因此,本案例的重点就是基于 SWOT 分析,对京东物流进行全面的分析。

如本章第一节所述,物流体系的构建模式分两种:自建物流及物流外包,两种模式各有优缺点。这意味着企业在构建物流体系时,面临两种选择,选择哪种模式将在很大程度上影响其未来的运营。2007 年,面对日益增长的物流需求和顾客对已有物流服务的不满,成立仅仅3年的京东做出了一个大胆的决定:自建物流,这意味着当时年营业收入不足5亿元人民币的京东需要投资3.5亿元构建自己的物流体系。京东的这一举动引起了极大争议,绝大多数人并不看好这一疯狂之举。然而,这一决定做出9年之后,2015年京东全年营业收入达到1 813亿元人民币,物流配送业务线的员工超过60 000人①。从统计数据和京东近年来的发展情况看,当年看似疯狂的决定是行之有效的。那么,如果我们将时光倒流,回到京东做决策的时点,又应该如何在两种模式中进行选择呢?一个完整的SWOT分析可以帮助我们。

首先,京东自建物流的第一个优势就是它有强有力的资金支持。投资3.5亿元构建自己的物流系统,这意味着京东必须有丰富的资源储备,包括资金、人力和设施等,否则项目随时可能变成"不可能的任务"。幸运的是,京东自创立以来良好的销售业绩以及品牌知名度为其融资奠定了基础。2011年,经过艰苦的沟通,京东成功地从6个投资者手中融资1.5亿美元,为其自建物流提供了资金来源。除了资金投入,京东复杂的物流系统开发还需要专业人才来完成。京东之前开发ERP等信息管理系统的人才与经验得到了充分利用,实现了企业对系统开发到系统实施的全程控制,保证了系统的质量。京东自建物流的初衷是为了满足日益增长的网上订单所带来的物流需求,这样耗时费力建设的系统如果得不到充分利用,将造成极大的资源浪费。幸运的是,京东超过200%的网上销售增长率及其不断扩大的用户规模保证了物流系统的使用率,真正实现了物有所值。除此之外,京东一直致力于创新的个性化物流服务的开发,以"211限时达"为代表的一系列个性化配送服务的推出不仅充分发挥了自建物流体系灵活的优势,而且满足了不同客户的需要,用户满意度也得到了提升。

其次,京东自建物流的劣势也是显而易见的:资金及人力短缺的风险是其第一个劣势。作为一项高投入、长周期的项目,京东自建物流最大的风险就是资金的短缺,一旦风险发生,项目可能随时中止。事实上,京东在2011年成功融资之前,也的确经历了资金短缺的惊险时刻,差点让这个项目夭折。另外,物流从本质上看是一个劳动密集型的行业,它需要大量的人力投入,尤其是面对中国复杂的城市交通和地形分布,配送人员必不可少。近年来,随着劳动力工资的上涨,配送的人力成本也急剧上升,这对于拥有60 000多名配送员工的京东而言是一项巨大的开支,如果处理不当,它甚至可能阻碍企业的发展。另外,过于单一的物流模式是京东的第二个劣势。京东的自建物流主要承担其自营商品和部分入驻商家产品的配送服务,还有不少入驻商家出于成本的考虑会采用其他的第三方物流服务。这可能对京东物流的利用效率产生影响。

最后,京东自建物流遇到了好的机遇:网上购物的快速增长,中国对基础设施建设的大量投入以及以人工智能、物联网等为代表的新技术的问世都为其自建物流系统的良好运行提供了必要的条件。但是,阿里巴巴等竞争对手的积极跟进,不断上升的物流成本和快速增长的物流需求以及外界对京东自建物流的质疑都可能对其构成威胁。

事实胜于雄辩,京东自建物流已逐渐步入正轨,并成为其未来发展的坚实基础,京

---

① 沙水,时势造京东:自建物流战略一剑封喉,http://www.sohu.com/a/76793599_116457,2016.5.23.

东以其高质量且极富特色的物流配送服务赢得了电子商务的"最后一公里",而它不断推出的诸如 FBP, LBP, SOPL 和 SOP 等创新服务也在满足消费者多样化的需求。

Section 4
Yihaodian—Winning by Supply Chain
第四节 1号店——供应链致胜

Key Words

1. commodity *n.* 日用品
2. genuine *adj.* 真实的
3. autonomy *n.* 自治
4. fulfillment *n.* 执行
5. replenish *vt.* 补充
6. nascent state *n.* 原生态

Case

About Yihaodian

Yihaodian is a Chinese online grocery business founded by Gang Yu and Junling Liu in July 2008. As a B2C e-commerce website, Yihaodian provides people with a platform to shop groceries online. In 2008 when Yihaodian entered the e-commerce market, the market was being dominated by e-commerce companies like Alibaba, Taobao and Dangdang, which seized one domain in e-commerce respectively: Alibaba for B2B, Taobao for C2C and Dangdang for B2C. After analyzing the situation at that time, the two co-founders found that there lacked a well-known online super market. Therefore, they eventually decided to develop the B2C market by introducing a specialized category—commodity, to the marketplace[①].

In May 2011, the retail giant Walmart first invested in Yihaodian, aiming to integrate its logistics to Yihaodian's supply chain. In 2012, Walmart announced its further investment in Yihaodian under the approval of Chinese Ministry of Commerce, which let Walmart become the biggest shareholder of Yihaodian (51.3% of shares). In July 2015, Walmart announced full ownership of Yihaodian, solidifying the online retailer as a central part of its strategy in the region. Meanwhile, the co-founders of Yihaodian announced their departures. With full ownership of Yihaodian, Walmart planed to invest in both

---

① https://en.wikipedia.org/wiki/Yihaodian

accelerating e-commerce and creating a seamless experience for customers across online, mobile and stores①.

Yihaodian has been growing fast since its foundation: when it was founded in 2008, it owned only 3,000 SKUs (Stock Keeping Unit), one catalog, 5,000 square meter warehouse, and 60 employees. However, it has experienced a rapid growth since then (Figure 4-9).

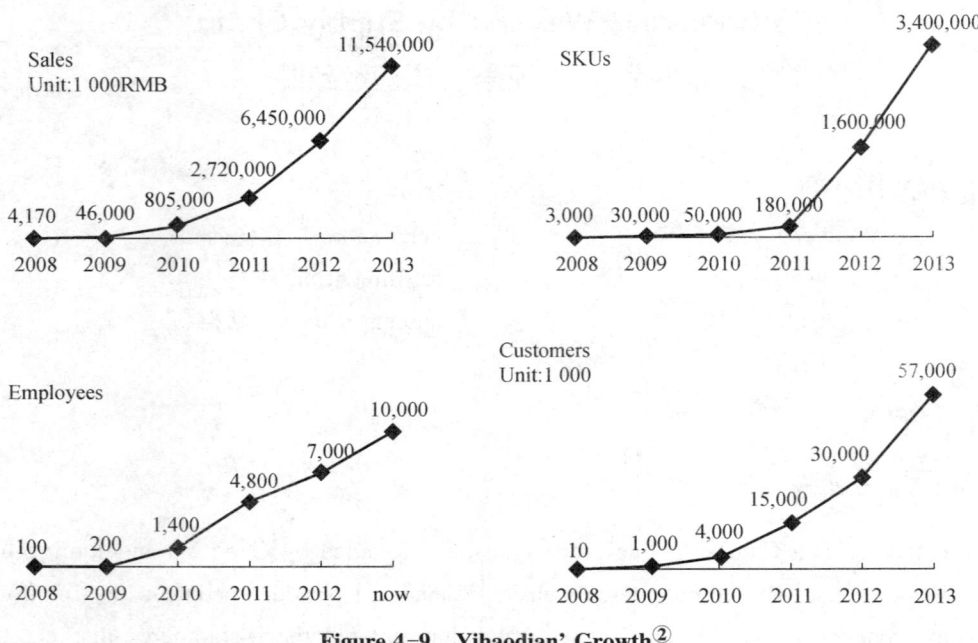

Figure 4-9 Yihaodian' Growth②

Since its foundataion, Yihaodian has quickly become a challenger to the extant e-tailers like T-Mall and Dangdang. Its performance in the past few years drew lots of attention: Yihaodian doubled its product offerings to 8 million in 2014; Yihaodian turned over its entire inventory in 10 days by early 2015, down from 50 days when they started.

Why Does Yihaodian Stand Out from Competition?③④

It is well known that the competition in retailing especially e-tailing is extremely fierce. Facing the powerful competitors, why does Yihaodian stand out? Several reasons can explain it:

---

① Sarah Nassauer, Laurie Burkitt, Wal-Mart Takes Full Ownership of Chinese E-commerce Venture Yihaodian, Forbes, 2015-06-23.
② http://slideplayer.com/slide/8920979/
③ Marios Michaelides, Walmart's Online Success in China with Yihaodian.com, LinkedIn.com, 2015-05-10.
④ How Yihaodian Has Become Very Successful in E-commerce in China?, http://ecommercechinaagency.com/yihaodian-become-successful-e-supermarket-china/, 2014-10-29.

1. Expanding product line

Yihaodian expanded rapidly the range of classes offered: it initially focused on food, beverage and household products, the range has been extended to cosmetics and electronics since 2009. The clothes are the last category that Yihaodian bet on. By January 2014, Yihaodian had provided 8 million products and brought in more goods from abroad.

Yihaodian now has its customer base in the tens of millions (more than 60 million in early 2014). The company employs 10,000 persons, most of whom are allocated to the deliveries. Since China allowed the sale of over-the-counter medications online in 2014, Yihaodian has become the first to obtain a license to sell such products. By now, Yihaodian has been allowed to sell 25,000 medications and health care products.

2. Partnering with Walmart

In 2011, Yihaodian and Walmart reached an agreement, which was thought a financial strategy. The agreement that Walmart takes a 51% stake provides cash for development investments required by the growth of the company. The cooperation with Walmart can further increase the Yihaodian's power of bargaining with its suppliers. The two enterprises cooperated through the exchange of information about their contracts with suppliers—all information that can be used in negotiations. Yihaodian thus indirectly benefits from the firepower of Walmart. By virtue of the cooperation with the largest retailer, Yihaodian receives valuable assistance from Walmart on two essential components of business: price and range of products offered.

3. High speed delivery and customer service

Like many Chinese companies, Yihaodian assures its initial development with the first-tier cities and the richest provinces—which are also the coastal provinces. The company has 70% of its business on the coast. Penetration rates are twice as high in the first-tier cities than in cities of the second level. With over 20 fulfillment centers and hundreds of delivery stations across China, Yihaodian can offer same-day or next-day delivery for the majority of its items. Yihaodian has even started setting up shipping centers in individual apartment complexes, such as Shanghai's Zhongyuan Liangwancheng which houses over 50,000 residents. And Yihaodian also provides delivery within an hour for the customers in Shanghai. In March 2013, Yihaodian launched fresh food (such as fruits and vegetables) delivery service in Shanghai and expanded the service to Beijing five months later in order to further tap the online grocery market.

According to the statistics, Yihaodian was expected to increase its revenue by 4 or 5 times if residents' living standard keeps increasing. The rapid growth should be partially attributed to Yihaodian' focus on customer satisfaction. Most of Yihaodian's customers are the people owning good educational background and high income, who have the higher requirements of customer service. Therefore, Yihaodian follows its clients closely, learns about their requests and solves the problems instantly. According to Yihaodian's data, the rate of dissatisfied consumers was drastically decreased constantly from 40% (first quarter 2011) to 3.7%.

4. Focusing on genuine, quality products

Yihaodian always emphasizes products quality such as brand, expiration date and packing. Due to Yihaodian's efforts to quality, consumers' trust in Yihaodian's products has been built. Despite baby milk powder scandals, Yihaodian dominated this sector with a 37% market share in 2013.

5. Constantly launching innovative products and services

In May 2014, Yihaodian launched "Yi Finance" which offers insurance and loans to its suppliers, affiliated merchants, partners and consumers online. For example, "Yi Guarantee Loan" offers the loans no more than six months to the suppliers within three minutes. In addition, Yihaodian launched the brick and mortar stores where customers can visit and browse the products Yihaodian offers online. The strategy has been proven effective since sales from surrounding residents of these stores doubled. It protects the innovation by filing patents and limiting the spread of sensitive knowledge within a group bound by secrecy.

6. Complete autonomy from suppliers

As an e-tailer, the reactivitivity between Yihaodian and its suppliers is increasing because in this emerging sector, speed is of the essence. Yihaodian establishes an order fulfillment system. In the control room, there are sixteen screens that allow the real-time tracking of orders, traffic, activity by region or by product categories, etc. For example, when a screen displays a word which is the result of client's requests analysis, the company captures the trend instantly. These tools enable Yihaodian to target on consumers more accurately than what can be done in stores, and most importantly, they help to set up business operations whose effect can be displayed immediately just as fast promotions. Yihaodian is also in a position to give a huge amount of information to its suppliers. Though the early steps were made towards PCs, the growing number of smart phones and tablets in China has become an engine of development for the company.

7. Building the supply chain system based on the characteristics of Chinese e-commerce

Unlike in the U.S., grocery shopping in China is frequent and repetitive. Therefore, one of the key factors to satisfy the need is building an efficient supply chain system[①]. Instead of imitating the peers, Yihaodian firstly analyzed the unique characteristics of Chinese e-commerce based on its nascent state and Chinese intrinsic

---

① Dixit, Shailja, E-retailing Challenges and Opportunities in the Global Marketplace, *IGI Global*, 2016.

cultural behaviors:

1) Cash on delivery (COD) is still a popular way of payment because some consumers do not trust either e-commerce providers or online payment system and others have been used to the exchanges by cash. However, once they find both payment system and the website are secure, they shift toward shopping online immediately and become a loyal group. For example, when Yihaodian was launched in 2008, more than 70% orders were paid by COD, but in 2014 the percentage dropped to less than 20%.

2) "The Last mile" delivery mainly depends on electric bicycles and motorcycles. The vast territory and the complex traffic in China prevent the regular delivery tools like trucks from transporting quickly. The small-sized vehicles like electric bicycles and motorcycles can work better on Chinese roads. Besides, the logistics industry is very fragmented in China, with the likes of UPS and Fedex in China, it is unable to provide nationwide coverage and qualified service.

3) Chinese shoppers' behavior is quite different from Western consumers. For example, online shoppers in the U.S. are used to opening one window at a time and flipping back and forth via navigation buttons, but Chinese online shoppers prefer that each click opens a new window allowing them to navigate a site by jumping between several windows. The user interface of e-commerce websites in the U.S. are usually very simple and clean with plenty of images, but Chinese shoppers favor crowded websites with information and links all packed into one page providing the impression of a high-energy shopping atmosphere. Yihaodian's first homepage was simple and clean, mimicking that of such model websites in Western countries, but after receiving the users' feedback, it quickly made changes[①].

4) In general, Chinese consumers are very price sensitive, which leads to Chinese e-commerce a promotion driven business. Shoppers do not yet value the concept of "time is money". Whereas, in Western countries, shoppers are willing to pay considerable fees for expedited delivery, which is rare in China.

Usually, the large e-commerce companies choose to build their own logistics capabilities to ensure a better customer experience and to facilitate faster growth, while the small and medium e-commerce companies take advantage of third party logistics to low the cost. Differing from either one, Yihaodian started its own logistics system alongside with 30 third party logistics partners in 2011, allowing it to cover the entire nation. Such a decision was based on the fact that more than 60% of the customers' complaints were focused on delivery services. Not long after that, Yihaodian's logistics services began to

---

① Yu Gang, Co-founder: How China's Yihaodian Sees E-commerce, https://www.cnn.com/2013/09/17/business/on-china-yihaodian/index.html, 2013-09-17.

bear fruit with a significantly improved customer experience and 10% improvement in its CSAT (customer satisfaction) score.

In 2012, Yihaodian launched the Service by Yihaodian (SBY) model to provide its merchants with logistics, marketing, platform, and data services. Through SBY, Yihaodian's last mile delivery fleet serves not only its own customers, but also the merchants who sell through their own website or through other marketplace platforms. The strategy helps it to reduce the last mile delivery cost further.

Supply Chain Management of Yihaodian[①]

E-commerce brings logistics both opportunities and challenges: the drastically rising e-commerce creates more demands for logistics; on the other hand, e-commerce requires more for the quality and efficiency of logistics. For example, the trading volume on "Single's Day" is 4 or 5 times of that on regular days, which puts the huge pressure on logistics. How to cope with the stress? How to deliver the fresh products to the end consumers as soon as possible? How to utilize the appropriate vehicles to realize the efficient delivery, avoiding the possible fines due to the transportation restrictions? When solving the problems encountered by all the e-tailers in supply chain management, Yihaodian makes a successful demonstration. It boasts an industry-leading supply chain management system in the Chinese B2C e-commerce sector. In October 2012, Walmart announced to increase investments in Yihaodian. One of the major reasons for the move is the leading supply chain management of the Chinese company. How does Yihaodian make it?

Both of the two founders previously worked in the international enterprises such as Dell and Amazon, which accumulates rich experiences and management skills for Yihaodian's businesses. Particularly, Gang Yu, one of the founders, was the vice-president of Worldwide Procurement of Dell and he also had acted as the vice-president of Global Supply chain at Amazon before joining Dell. Besides, in this company, 10% of workforces are engineers of information technology, which enables the in-house IT developments (with the exception of software finance and accounting). The company controls all the internal computer systems of suppliers, warehouses, delivery, customer, etc. The excellent personnel and the powerful IT systems build the solid base for Yihaodian's supply chain management. Besides, Yihaodian adopts some effective measures to construct its supply chain system:

---

① scmking 链客, 1号店供应链系统解析, http://mp.weixin.qq.com/s?__biz=MzA5NjU2MTEzMw==&mid=205547992&idx=3&sn=9c260dd96ab0f829283db69f5dc23a90&scene=5&srcid=0921W6xJB2VKzB0iGDYtIjrl#rd, 2015-05-21。

1. Building the open supply chain platform—FBY[①]

Yihaodian launched its open supply chain platform named "Service by Yihaodian" in June 2012. Only half a year after the platform's launch, this platform attracted over 400 suppliers.

The platform mainly targets traditional enterprises who want to tap the e-commerce sector but lack e-commerce operating ability. With this service, these enterprises are able to share Yihaodian's platform, covering system integration, cloud-based marketing, viral promotion tools, warehousing, and logistics, so as to realize a full online operation. Meanwhile, with the open supply chain platform, Yihaodian can improve its own supply chain operating efficiency and lower its costs. The company is also able to offer more product categories and expand into a wider market (Figure 4-10).

Figure 4-10　Yihaodian's Open Supply Chain Platform[②]

2. "The 7 NOs" warehouse policies in picking

Picking is an important step of fulfillment process. Yihaodian proposed "The 7 NOs" warehouse policies so as to improve the efficiency of picking:

1) No Waiting. It means there is no idle time for fulfillment;

2) No Moving. It refers to taking good advantage of conveyor belt and Automatic Guided Vehicles so as to reduce manual moving;

3) No Walking. It means Yihaodian prioritizes the picking routing to shorten the route;

4) No Thinking. It requires the fulfillment prioritization to realize zero decision from operators;

---

① Yihaodian's Open Supply Chain Platform Gains Over 400 Partners in China, ChinaRetailNews.com, 2012-12-11.

② www.yhd.com

5) No Seeking. Searching a commodity from the huge warehouse is difficult and time-consuming. To solve the problem, people usually divide the warehouse into different storage zones and code them based on an order. Yihaodian uniforms the coding rules of storage zones so as to make the zones information clear and reduce the seeking time;

6) No Writing. paperless operation is not only efficient but also beneficial to environment protection;

7) No Inspecting. By virtue of Warehouse Management System (WMS) and RF (Radio Frequency) systems, Yihaodian can easily check whether a product is in the right zone, whether the product in a specific zone owns the closer expiration date and whether the product in the zone has been damaged or frozen. Because the inspection has been completed by the automatic system, operators only need to pick the products rather than inspect them manually. The inspection based on the automatic systems ensures the accuracy and efficiency of picking.

3. The attempts at "The Last Kilometer"

Logistics has been regarded as "The Last Kilometer" of e-commerce, which means offline delivery is critical for e-commerce. When handling logistics, Yihaodian encounters the problems that are usually faced by its peers: the terrible transportation infrastructure, the sky-high rent downtown and the obscure transportation regulations which may cause the fines for utilizing the prohibited vehicles. To solve the problems, Yihaodian develops "The Mobile Delivery Station" mode that sets the specific communities and parking lot of complex as its temporary delivery stations that enable the van to park. Besides, by virtue of home-developed tools, the delivery, cash and receipts can be completed in the temporary delivery stations.

4. Prioritizing delivery routes

The higher requirements of delivery also challenge Yihaodian's supply chain management. For example, the routes prioritization in the same-day delivery or the door-to-door product returning can not completely depends on manual operations. Fortunately, Yihaodian's supply chain management system can prioritize the fulfillment process and realize the efficient delivery. For example, on November 12, 2014, one delivery staff created a record which had been incredible a year ago—delivering 4,275 products in one day. The mission impossible is achieved by Yihaodian's effective supply chain management.

5. Focusing on inventory management

Inventory is a problem obsessing most retailers, which, if is not conducted well, may lead to the catastrophic result. How to balance between inventory turnover and customer experiences is very important. Yihaodian makes some successful attempts which enable it to achieve the inventory turnover period of 10 days.

1) Sales forecast model. Due to the online promotion, price changes and competitors' activities, it is hard to forecast e-commerce sales precisely. Building the sales forecasting model is the first step of e-commerce supply chain management. Yihaodian has been focusing on modeling and the forecast model developed has achieved weekly forecast accuracy of 88%. The effective forecast model benefits Yihaodian's supply chain management greatly.

2) Automatic replenishment program which replenishes inventory based on the sales forecast system. Considering IT system can not handle everything especially in online promotion, Yihaodian does not fully depend on the automatic replenishment system. Instead, it also imports people's experiences during the replenishment decision as a supplement. As a result, both backlogging rate and out of stock rate are improved.

3) Bad stock management system. Low inventories are bad because this means your business does not have enough resources to pull in its potential profit. On the other hand, a stockpiled inventory is equally as bad because it represents money that is just sitting there not being moved, which makes it a waste of resources. The bad stock management system is able to trigger a delivery, allot and allocate cargo so as to avoid the stockpiled inventory.

> 译 不良库存管理系统。过低的库存并非上策,因为这可能意味着企业因为缺货而丧失盈利机会;过高的库存同样不利,因为它占用了企业资金,造成资源浪费。不良存货管理系统能促进货物的配置、运送以避免存货积压。

Based on the demand forecast system, inventory management system, logistics integration of front-end and order fulfillment system, Yihaodian builds an effective supply chain management system which ensures it an efficient "Last Kilometer".

Where Is Yihaodian's Future?

Though Yihaodian outstands in China's e-commerce by virtue of the effective SCM, there are still some problems which may become the obstacles for its development. For example, since Walmart announced full ownership of Yihaodian in July 2015, Yihaodian suffered the serious resign boom—some core staff including the two founders left Yihaodian due to the strategic adjustment. By October 2015, the number of resigned employees had surpassed one thousand. The resign boom not only hurted the existing SCM but also impacted the morale greatly. After the acquisition, Yihaodian's glory did not reappear as expected. As Walmart's online grocery business, Yihaodian has been struggling to gain traction in China in the red sea of deep pocketed local B2C e-commerce players. Unfortunately, Yihaodian threw in the towel and was sold to e-commerce Jingdong in June 2015. According to the agreement, Jingdong took over Yihaodian online and Walmart acquired a 5% stake in Jingdong. Walmart retained the Yihaodian direct sales business, but rather than operated its own online store entirely, it became a retailer inside Yihaodian.

Actually, it has been five times that Yihaodian's host was changed since its foundation. In 2008, 80% of Yihaodian's share was sold to Ping An, Chinese local insurance company, to gain cash and customer resources; due to the inconsistent strategy, Yihaodian sold 17.7% of its share to the retailing giant—Walmart to realize its business expansion in 2011; in 2012, Walmart increased its share to 51.3%, becoming the largest shareholder of Yihaodian which is the third time that Yihaodian's host was changed. After three years, Walmart took full ownership of Yihaodian, which caused the personnel vibration. The investment was expected to help Walmart target on China's fast-growing online market at a time when largely brick and mortar retailers were feeling the pinch of competition from online rivals and a slowing of the world's second-largest economy. Unfortunately, the expectation was not achieved, which led to the fifth equity transfer and Jingdong's full ownership of Yihaodian. After the five sells, Yihaodian's strategy, organization structure has changed a lot, which influence its operation greatly. Will Yihaodian be sold again in the future? How will it keep its strengths of SCM? Where is Yihaodian's future? All the questions need to be answered.

Case Analysis

1号店的案例令人印象深刻的有两点：一是它自行构建的高效的供应链系统；二是它自成立以来被屡次转手的收购历程。

尽管苹果和1号店都是因出色的供应链管理脱颖而出，但两者显然有所不同：前者是制造商，因此它的供应链管理贯穿了从原材料采购、生产制造到产品零售的全过程；后者是纯线上的零售商，它的供应链因为不涉及生产制造，相对较短，但它会面临困扰大部分零售商的库存问题，以及线上零售需要面对的物流配送问题。对于这两个问题，1号店通过出色的上下游供应链管理进行了有效解决。

首先，1号店的供应商管理非常出色。作为供应链的第一个环节，采购非常关键，而选择合格的供应商则是这一关键环节的核心。1号店的电商零售业务主要包括自营业务和平台商家的电商业务。相应地，它的供应商有两类：一类是上游的生产商，另一类是进驻1号店的平台商家。对于第一类供应商，1号店坚持选择品牌知名度高，商业信誉度好的厂商，例如宝洁；对于第二类，1号店则采取了两项措施来保证供应商的质量：第一，设定进驻门槛，过滤掉低质量的供应商。1号店的商家在入驻平台时需要交纳会员费，商家负责自己网店的运营。一般而言，一家平台入驻商需要构建1—4个人的团队进行网店设计、客户服务和营销管理等，而物流配送则可以选择与1号店或第三方物流合作。粗略估计，一家1号店商家每年需要交纳10 000—100 000元不等的会员费，约5 500元的市场费以及1%—10%不等的销售提成，再加上营销、物流等费用，每年的运营成本就是一笔不小的支出,而这恰恰形成了入驻1号店平台的门槛,保证了入驻商家的质量。其次,为供应商提供金融支持。由于买方市场以及企业本身的议价能力不强,不少供应商尤其是中小型生产商经常面临货款无法及时到账,现金流不足的窘况,企业无法及时进行研发和扩大再生产,甚至因为资金链断裂陷入危机。针对这一情况,1号店推出了"1号金融",专门为其供应商提供融资服务,这样不仅解决了供应商的资金问题,也令1号店的资本价值得到发挥。1号店监管和扶持双管齐下的方法有效地保证了供应商的质量,也相应地保证了产品质量。

其次,本土化的供应链实现了供应链管理理论的"落地"。尽管供应链管理在中国已经普及,但其概念及管理理念则源自美国。与很多企业的做法不同,1号店并没有直接复制国外供应链管理的做法,而是在仔细分析了中国电子商务及电商供应链的特点之后,构建了符合企业实际的高效的供应链系统。除此之外,1号店还推出了"1号服务",为供应商提供物流、营销、平台及数据服务。

最后,有效的供应链管理措施提高了管理效率。1号店推出了一些有效的措施,提高了供应链上游至下游的管理效率。例如,针对货物分拣的"七不"原则提高了分拣效率,优化物流路径节约了配送时间,销售预测模型将库存周转期缩短至10天。

尽管1号店自成立以来成长迅速,其有效的供应链管理不仅提升了运营效率,降低了成本,也令其成为网上零售行业中的佼佼者,但是频繁地被收购导致该企业战略不稳定,也使其在供应链管理上的优势被削弱。自成立以来,1号店已经经历了5次易主,平安保险、沃尔玛、京东相继获得了它的部分或全部所有权。频繁的所有权更替已经影响到企业的战略规划、组织架构以及人员变动,也相应地影响到运营的其他方面。1号店急需寻找一条更适合自己的、稳定的发展路径,以保持并进一步发挥它原有的优势。

Section 5
Case Analysis Methods
第五节　案例分析方法

  Generally speaking, case analysis is known as a qualitative study, which commonly asks questions of who, what, where, when, why and how. It is used to collect in-depth data in a natural setting where the researcher has little or no control over the events and with a real life context. There are different types of case analysis methods like SWOT analysis, PETS analysis and comparative analysis[①].

  SWOT analysis is a strategic planning technique used to help a person or organization

---

  ① https://en.wikipedia.org/wiki/

identify the Strengths, Weaknesses, Opportunities, and Threats related to business competition or project planning. It is intended to specify the objectives of the business venture or project and identify the internal and external factors that are favorable and unfavorable to achieving those objectives.

PEST analysis describes a framework of macro-environmental factors used in the environmental scanning component of strategic management. It is part of an external analysis when conducting a strategic analysis or doing market research, and gives an overview of the different macro-environmental factors to be taken into consideration.

Comparative analysis is a methodology in social science that aims to make comparisons across different cases. It is the act of comparing two or more things with a view to discovering something about one or all of the things being compared. This technique often utilizes multiple disciplines in one study.

The method selected depends upon the nature of the question being asked and the goals of the case analysis. In this book, we focus on SWOT analysis and comparative analysis and show the applications by the virtue of cases.

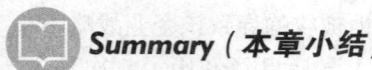

Summary (本章小结)

Supply chain is the flow of materials, information, money, and services from raw material suppliers through factories and warehouses to the end customers. Supply chain activities transform natural resources, raw materials, and components into a finished product that is delivered to the end customer. In sophisticated supply chain systems, used products may re-enter the supply chain at any point where residual value is recyclable. Logistics refers to the operations involved in the efficient and effective flow and storage of goods, services, and related information from point of origin to point of consumption. Logistics is usually a portion of supply chain.

Apple is an American multinational corporation that designs, develops, and sells consumer electronics, computer software, online services, and personal computers. As the world's second-largest information technology company by revenue after Samsung Electronics, as well as the world's third-largest mobile phone maker, Apple has a complicated supply chain. Its success should primarily be attributed to the outstanding supply chain management. Fortunately, Completing "mission impossible", massive procurement, buying out all the resources, deep pockets and strict confidentiality enable its "Best Supply Chain Management".

Jingdong, starting as an online magneto-optical store, has grown up to a diversified online shopping mall, selling electronics, mobile phones, computers. It is one of the largest B2C online retailers in China by transaction volume. Logistics is called as "The Last Mile of e-commerce". With the growth of Jingdong's online businesses, the pressure from logistics also increases. Liu Qiangdong, CEO of Jingdong decided to build the self-owned logistics system at the high expense in 2012, which caused the controversy. Jingdong has the obvious strengths for self-building logistics such as abundant financial resources and the weaknesses such as possible risks of financial supports. Regardless of its excellent performance in logistics services, Jingdong's self-built logistics still suffers the controversy.

Yihaodian is a Chinese online supermarket founded in 2008. As a business-to-consumer (B2C) e-commerce website, Yihaodian has successfully established its brand strength since its foundation. Particularly, Walmart's investment in Yihaodian since 2011 benefits its resource integration and business reputation. Yihaodian's achievements can be attributed to its focus on product line expansion, partnership with the well-known partners, high speed delivery and customer services, constantly innovating and complete autonomy from suppliers. A critical reason that Yihaodian outstands is its effective supply chain management based on the characteristics of Chinese e-commerce. One the one hand, the excellent personnel and the powerful IT systems build the solid base for Yihaodian's supply chain management. On the other hand, Yihaodian adopts some effective measures such as building the open supply chain platform and prioritizing delivery routing—FBY to construct its supply chain system. As a result, Yihaodian has established a supply chain system including the functionalities of logistics, suppliers, platform and data services. Nevertheless, there are still some problems which can not be ignored. Actually, it has experienced five host changing since its foundation, which impacted its strategy and morale. How to find a stable way of development is critical for this e-tailer.

There are different types of case analysis methods like SWOT analysis, PETS analysis and comparative analysis. The method selected depends upon the nature of the question being asked and the goals of the case analysis.

 Exercises & Tasks (练习与任务)

▶ *Exercises*

1. How do you explain the relationships between supply chain and logistics?
2. What are the necessary factors for the successful supply chain management?
3. How do you explain the advantages and disadvantages of Jingdong's self-built logistics?

▶ *Tasks*

Choose a case of e-commerce supply chain or logistics and prepare a 20-minute presentation which should include:

1. Background introduction to the enterprise;
2. Analyze its supply chain or logistics, e.g. pros and cons, the causes of success or failure;
3. Conclusion.

Chapter 5
第五章

New Technologies Changing E-Commerce
改变电子商务的新技术

 Learning Objectives（学习目标）

After finishing this chapter, you should be able to:
1. Define the three new technologies including cloud computing, big data and mobile technology;
2. Identify the impacts of cloud computing, big data and mobile technology on e-commerce by virtue of case analysis;
3. Describe how cloud computing is becoming a new profit source of Amazon;
4. Explain how Netflix leverages big data in its operation;
5. Identify the strengths, weaknesses, opportunities and threats of Autonavi when it expands from a map to a platform;
6. Explain SWOT analysis.

 Introduction（内容简介）

    Nowadays, the new technologies like cloud computing, big data and mobile technology are playing even more significant role during the development of e-commerce. Some enterprises leveraging them (like Amazon) in operation have found new profit source.

    Chapter 5 is composed of 5 sections. The brief introduction to the new technologies changing e-commerce is made in section 1. Three cases involving the application of the three technologies are offered respectively in section 2, 3, and 4. Section 5 focuses on a case analysis method—SWOT analysis.

Section 1
New Technologies Changing E-Commerce
第一节　改变电子商务的新技术

▶ Key Words

1. architecture *n.* 架构
2. velocity *n.* 速度

E-commerce is the exchange of products and services via Internet. From the perspective of system, it is composed of two layers: one layer is the technical architecture made up of hardware and software; the other layer is the business transactions based on the technical architecture. The technical architecture is the base of e-commerce. And only on the base of the technical architecture, can the e-commerce business modes and marketing strategies be realized. In addition, the security and stability of technical architecture are the prerequisite of online products and services exchange.

Since 2007, three new technologies have drawn people's attention and are regarded as the important technologies changing e-commerce. The three technologies include: cloud computing, big data and mobile technology.

1. Cloud Computing

There has not been a universal definition of cloud computing since the concept was proposed by Google in 2007. According to Google, cloud computing is the practice of using a network of remote servers hosted on the Internet to store, manage, and process data, rather than a local server or a personal computer[①]. Cloud computing, a new computing model, is making a significant impact on e-commerce:

Firstly, cloud computing enables e-commerce enterprises to rent rather than purchase hardware and software, which helps them to decrease the cost of system building. Particularly, the charging mode of "pay-as-service" is very flexible, which helps an e-commerce company to pay for the resources based on the demand.

Secondly, cloud computing solves the problem of resources utilization efficiency. For an e-commerce company, it is necessary to invest in the software and hardware to maintain the operation. With the company's growth, the investment will be increased. However, the utilization efficiency of the invested infrastructure is low. The statistics shows that the average utilization efficiency of IT is no more than 10%. Cloud computing enables the

---

① www.google.com

businesses to integrate the idle IT resources (e. g. server) on the far end platform and rent them to the customers. This mode on the one hand reduces the operation cost of an e-commerce company and prioritizes resources allocation on the other hand.

Thirdly, cloud computing enables the new backend service model for e-commerce enterprises. All the IT resources such as hardware, software, data and infrastructure are offered to e-commerce enterprises as service by virtue of the cloud platform. An e-commerce company is allowed to get access to the IT resources just like the utility services (e. g. electricity) on the cloud platform and pay for them. It does not require the high expenses on devices purchase and each firm is able to choose the appropriate IT resources through renting. In another word, the emergence of cloud computing brings the new service philosophy and model which enables the lower cost and changes the traditional IT licensing mode. Cloud computing sets the e-commerce enterprises free from the complicated technical architecture planning, designing and maintaining and enables them to focus on the core businesses.

Fourthly, cloud computing is influencing e-commerce business strategies. Since the emergence of cloud computing, some e-commerce firms like Amazon, Google have begun to expand their business to cloud computing and involve cloud computing in their long-term strategies.

Finally, cloud computing is influencing the structure of e-commerce industrial chain. Traditionally, the e-commerce industry chain is composed of the hardware supplier, software developer, Internet service provider, system integrating provider, service supplier, e-commerce enterprise and customer. Each member of the industry chain fulfills its own responsibilities. When cloud computing is migrated into e-commerce industry, one cloud service provider can supply almost all the necessary products and services to an e-commerce website. As a result, the structure of e-commerce industry chain will be changed. On the one hand, an e-commerce enterprise doesn't have to purchase IT resources. Instead, it just rents the cloud services needed. Thus, the margin of traditional IT firms (e. g. IT service provider) in the chain will be squeezed. They may cooperate with a cloud service provider and become its "backend" which offers the necessary infrastructure services for the provider. The e-commerce enterprise will be directly served by the cloud service provider rather than the IT firms group. Further, with the popularity of cloud computing, the end users who buy the hardware or software products from the traditional e-commerce websites will probably transfer to the cloud computing platform which offers all the IT resources as services. That means the IT resources market of the traditional e-commerce website will be partly shared by cloud computing. The e-commerce enterprises lacking the core competencies will have to exit from the market. Eventually, the e-commerce industry chain will be restructured.

2. Big Data

Big data is a broad term for data sets so large or complex that traditional data processing applications are inadequate. The Internet generates big data each second such as consumers behavior data or online transaction data.

There are 4 characteristics of big data:

1) Volume. That means the big volumes of data. Everyday big data generated by the Internet can occupy 168 million DVDs.

2) Variety. That means the numerous types of big data such as pictures videos and so on.

3) Velocity. That means the fast data processing which is called as "The One Second Law".

4) Value. That means the high values contained in data. Particularly, the valuable data account for less than 1% of big data. Extracting the 1% data is just like sift sand for gold. So big data requires the better data processing technologies.

E-commerce enterprises can improve their business with big data in the following areas[1]:

1) Optimized product portfolio. The analysis of large amounts of structured customer data allows detailed target group analysis. Based on the results, the portfolio of an online shop can be adapted user-specific. Particularly, large online vendors can scale their offerings with big data better and meet specific customer need. Big data also allows to predict customer need and enable a future optimization of the product portfolio. So with big data it is possible to optimize the stock costs.

2) Optimized prices. Thanks to big data, data mining and real-time analyzes are possible. An online retailer can dynamically adjust the price of a product. Due to the high transparency of the internet, it is necessary to have competitors always under observation and adjust its own price in order to remain competitive. Big data offers comprehensive market analysis for a dynamic pricing policy.

3) Optimized online store. Due to the use of big data and fast webserver technologies, it is possible to provide dynamic websites. So different start pages or landing pages can be displayed depending on the region or target group. Furthermore, different preferences regarding the product range for men and women can be displayed.

4) Optimized online advertising. Due to big data and programmatic buying online retailers' advertisements can be targeted on their customers precisely. With a look-a-like modeling it is possible to reach new customers. Real time advertising is cheaper and more effective than advertising in the past. Therefore with big data online retailers can reduce

---

[1] Björn Radde, Big Data: Future of E-commerce, Linkedin, November 12, 2014.

advertising costs and increase their media reach.

5) Optimized customer service. If a customer is dissatisfied with a product and complained by phone or e-mail. It will be a big advantage if a service employee can use the complete customer history enriched by some social media information about the customer during the telephone call. This scenario is possible with big data. The variety of valuable background information offers a customer support team possibilities to improve a customer relation significantly.

3. Mobile technology

Mobile technology is the technology used for cellular communication. Mobile code division multiple access (CDMA) technology has evolved rapidly over the past few years[①]. Since the start of this millennium, a standard mobile device has gone from being no more than a simple two-way pager to being a mobile phone, GPS navigation device, an embedded web browser and instant messaging client, and a handheld game console. Many experts argue that the future of computer technology rests in mobile computing with wireless networking[②].

When mobile technology is applied to e-commerce, a new e-commerce type—mobile commerce (m-commerce) is generated. In general, any e-commerce done in a wireless environment, especially via the Internet, can be called as m-commerce which has two characteristics differentiating it from other forms of e-commerce:

1) Mobility: users carry cell phones or other mobile devices to realize the instant connections.

2) Broad reach: people can be reached at any time, everywhere.

Section 2
Cloud Computing—New Profit Engine of Amazon
第二节　云计算——亚马逊的利润新引擎

Key Words

1. scalable *adj.* 可测量的　　　　2. deployment *n.* 部署
3. terminate *vt.* 终结　　　　　　4. peter out 逐渐减少

---

① www.google.com
② https://en.wikipedia.org/wiki/Mobile_technology

Case

Background

Since it was proposed by Google in 2007, cloud computing has attracted a lot of attention. Cloud Computing is a term that is called as the extension of grid computing, a computing mode, and it enables the dynamic computing capacity, storage capacity, network exchanging capability and information service capability. After realizing the huge potential of this new computing and serving mode, some IT service suppliers have been striving to make profit by virtue of cloud computing and Amazon is one of them.

Before launching AWS, Amazon developed unique software and services based on more than a decade of infrastructure work for the evolution of the Amazon e-commerce Platform. This was dedicated software and operation procedures that drove excellent performance, reliability, operational quality and security all at very large scale. At the same time, Amazon realized that offering programmatic access to the Amazon Catalog and other ecommerce services was driving tremendous unexpected innovation by a very large developer ecosystem. The thinking then developed that offering Amazon's expertise in ultra-scalable system software as primitive infrastructure building blocks delivered through a services interface could trigger whole new world of innovation as developers no longer needed to focus on buying, building and maintaining infrastructure. The previous experience showed that the cost of maintaining a reliable, scalable infrastructure in a traditional multi-datacenter model could be as high as 70%, both in time and effort, and require significant investment of intellectual capital to sustain over a longer period of time. The initial thinking was to deliver services that could reduce that cost to 30% or less. Amazon also found that compute utilization in most cases, enterprise as well as startups, was extremely low (less than 20% and often even lower than 10%) and was often subject to significant periodicity. Providing these services in an on-demand fashion using a utility pricing model had the potential to radically change this[①].

In 2006, Amazon officially launched Amazon Web Services (AWS) which provides online services for other web sites or client-side applications. Most of these services are not exposed directly to end users, but instead offer functionality that other developers can use in their applications. All services are billed based on usage, but how usage is measured for billing varies from service to service. They include Amazon Elastic Compute Cloud (EC2) and Amazon Simple Storage Service (S3).

---

① Werner Vogels, How and Why Did Amazon Get into the Cloud Computing Business?, https://www.quora.com/How-and-why-did-Amazon-get-into-the-cloud-computing-business

AWS Pricing Model[①]

AWS offers a range of cloud computing services. There are three fundamental features a customer pays for with AWS: compute, storage, and data transfer out. These characteristics vary slightly depending on the AWS product it is using. These are fundamentally the core characteristics that have the greatest impact on cost. Although the customer is charged for data transfer out, there is no charge for inbound data transfer or for data transfer between other Amazon Web Services within the same region. The outbound data transfer is aggregated across AWS services and then charged at the outbound data transfer rate. This charge appears on the monthly statement as AWS Data Transfer Out. A customer (usually an organization) pays for exactly the amount of resources it actually needs and utility-style pricing model helps to save money as the below:

1. Pay as you go. A customer replaces its upfront capital expense with low variable cost and pay only for what it uses. There is no need to pay upfront for excess capacity or get penalized for under-planning. For compute resources, a customer pay on an hourly basis from the time it launches a resource until the time the customer terminates it. For data storage and transfer, the customer pays on a per gigabyte basis. The customer can turn off its cloud resources and stop paying for them when it doesn't need them. With a pay as you go model, a customer can adjust its business depending on need and not on forecasts, reducing the risk of over provisioning or missing capacity. Besides, by paying for services on an as needed basis, the customer can redirect its focus to innovation and invention, reducing procurement complexity and enabling your business to be fully elastic.

2. Pay less when you reserve. For certain products like Amazon EC2, a customer can invest in reserved capacity which is available in 3 options—All up-front (AURI), Partial up-front (PURI) or No up-front payments (NURI). In that case, it pays a low upfront fee and get a significantly discounted hourly rate, which results in overall savings up to 75% (depending on the type of instance you reserve) over equivalent on-demand capacity. When the customer buys reserved instances, the larger the upfront payment, the greater the discount. To maximize the savings, the customer can pay all up-front and receive the largest discount. The customer can also choose to spend nothing up front and receive a smaller discount, but allowing it to free up capital to spend on other projects. By using reserved capacity, an organization can minimize risks, more predictably manage budgets, and comply with policies that require longer-term commitments.

---

① How AWS Pricing Works, https://d1.awsstatic.com/whitepapers/aws_pricing_overview.pdf, 2016-03.

> **译** 对于 AWS 中的某些产品如 Amazon EC2,用户可以通过3种方式来预订资源用量:全部预付、部分预付以及非预付支付。如果选择预付,用户可以享受小时费率的优惠,这样可以节约高达75%的成本。用户预付金额越高,得到的优惠就越多。用户也可以选择非预付的支付方式,这样虽然获得的优惠较少,但却可以将资金用于支付其他项目。使用预订用量有利于组织降低风险,更有计划地管理预算以及遵守组织的长期承诺。

3. Pay even less per unit by using more. A customer saves more as its usage increases. For storage and data transfer out, pricing is tiered, meaning the more the customer uses, the less it pays per gigabyte. For compute, the customer gets volume discounts up to 10% when it reserves more. Besides, as an organization evolves, AWS also gives options to acquire services that help to address its business need. For example, AWS' storage services portfolio offers options to help to lower pricing based on how frequently an organization accesses data and the performance needed to retrieve it.

4. Pay even less as AWS grows. Most importantly, Amazon is constantly focused on reducing its data center hardware costs, improving its operational efficiencies, lowering its power consumption, and generally lowering the cost of doing business. These optimizations and AWS's substantial and growing economies of scale result in passing savings back to a customer in the form of lower pricing. Since 2006, AWS has consistently lowered prices (45 price drops as of August 1, 2014).

Benefits of AWS[①]

Amazon AWS's simple web service interface allows a client to obtain and configure capacity with minimal friction. It provides a client with complete control of its computing resources and lets a client run on Amazon's proven computing environment. Amazon AWS reduces the time required to obtain and boot new server instances to minutes, allowing a client to quickly scale capacity, both up and down, as its computing requirements change. Amazon AWS changes the economics of computing by allowing a client to pay only for capacity that a client actually uses. Amazon AWS provides developers the tools to build failure resilient applications and isolate themselves from common failure scenarios:

1. Elastic Web-Scale Computing. Amazon AWS enables a client to increase or decrease capacity within minutes, not hours or days. A client can commission one, hundreds or even thousands of server instances simultaneously. Of course, because this is all controlled with web service APIs, its application can automatically scale itself up and down depending on its need.

---

① Amazon EC2, https://www.amazonaws.cn/en/ec2/

弹性的网络规模化计算。使用 AWS，用户每分钟都可以自由增加或减少资源用量。用户可以委托一台、上百台或者上千台服务器处理计算任务。当然，由于这种计算是由网络服务应用程序界面控制的，其规模可以根据需求进行调节。

2. Completely Controlled. A client have complete control of its instances. A client has root access to each one, and a client can interact with them as it would any machine. A client can stop its instance while retaining the data on its boot partition and then subsequently restart the same instance using web service APIs. Instances can be rebooted remotely using web service APIs. A client also has access to console output of its instances.

 全面控制。用户对虚拟机有完全控制权。它可以进入虚拟机的根目录，可以和其中任何一台机器交互，也可以随时暂停这些虚拟机而同时将数据保留在启动区中，并在随后使用网络服务应用程序界面重启系统。虚拟机也可以通过网络服务应用程序界面远程重启，用户可以获取控制台输出。

3. Flexible Cloud Hosting Services. A client have the choice of multiple instance types, operating systems, and software packages. Amazon AWS allows a client to select a configuration of memory, CPU, instance storage, and the boot partition size that is optimal for its choice of operating system and application. For example, its choice of operating systems includes numerous Linux distributions, and Microsoft Windows Server.

4. Designed for use with other Amazon Web Services. Amazon AWS works in conjunction with Amazon Simple Storage Service (Amazon S3), Amazon Relational Database Service (Amazon RDS), Amazon SimpleDB and Amazon Simple Queue Service (Amazon SQS) to provide a complete solution for computing, query processing and storage across a wide range of applications.

5. Reliable. Amazon AWS offers a highly reliable environment where replacement instances can be rapidly and predictably commissioned. The service runs within Amazon's proven network infrastructure and data centers. The Amazon AWS Service Level Agreement commitment is 99.95% availability for each Amazon AWS Region.

6. Secure. Amazon AWS works in conjunction with Amazon VPC to provide security and robust networking functionality for its compute resources. Its compute instances are located in a Virtual Private Cloud (VPC) with an IP range that a client specify. A client decides which instances are exposed to the Internet and which remain private. Security Groups and networks Access Control List (ACLs) allow a client to control inbound and outbound network access to and from its instances. A client can connect its existing IT infrastructure to resources in its VPC using industry-standard encrypted IPsec VPN connections. A client can provision its AWS resources as Dedicated Instances. Dedicated Instances are Amazon AWS Instances that run on hardware dedicated to a single customer

for additional isolation.

7. Inexpensive. Amazon AWS passes on to a client the financial benefits of Amazon's scale. A client pays a very low rate for the compute capacity a client actually consumes due to the four charging models:

1) On-Demand Instances—On-Demand Instances let a client pay for compute capacity by the hour with no long-term commitments. This frees a client from the costs and complexities of planning, purchasing, and maintaining hardware and transforms what are commonly large fixed costs into much smaller variable costs. On-Demand Instances also remove the need to buy "safety net" capacity to handle periodic traffic spikes.

2) Reserved Instances—Reserved Instances provide a client with a significant discount (up to 75%) compared to On-Demand Instance pricing. There are three reserved instance payment options (No Upfront, Partial Upfront, All Upfront) that enable a client to balance the amount a client pay upfront with its effective hourly price. The Reserved Instance Marketplace is also available, which provides a client with the opportunity to sell Reserved Instances if its need changes (i.e. want to move instances to a new AWS Region, change to a new instance type, or sell capacity for projects that end before its Reserved Instance term expires).

3) Spot Instances—Spot Instances allow customers to bid on unused Amazon AWS capacity and run those instances for as long as their bid exceeds the current Spot Price. The Spot Price changes periodically based on supply and demand, and customers whose bids meet or exceed it gain access to the available Spot Instances. If a client has flexibility in when its applications can run, Spot Instances can significantly lower its Amazon AWS costs.

4) Dedicated Hosts—An Amazon EC2 Dedicated Host is a physical server with EC2 instance capacity fully dedicated to customers' use. Dedicated Hosts can help the customers address compliance requirements and reduce costs by allowing them to use the existing server-bound software licenses like Microsoft Windows Server, Microsoft SQL Server or other software licenses that are bound to VMs, sockets, or physical cores, subject to the license terms.

8. Easy to Start. A Client can quickly get started with Amazon AWS by visiting AWS Marketplace to choose preconfigured software on Amazon Machine Images (AMIs). It can quickly deploy this software to AWS via 1-Click launch or with the AWS console.

Many organizations has benefited from AWS since it was launched. For example, The New York Times, a very popular newspaper chose AWS when it planned to transform all the TIF data into PDF data. As a result, it only cost 3,000 U.S. dollar to achieve the goals. The powerful computing ability of cloud computing enables the drastically reduced data transformation cost. Another similar example is from Eli Lilly & Co., a big medical company. Using AWS, Eli Lilly & Co., decreased the cost of data analysis to $89, which usually spent more than one million dollars before.

AWS Is Becoming A New Profiting Source of Amazon

Ten years after its launch, AWS continues to grow rapidly and has become the company's most profitable segment.

After generating $8.9 billion in revenue for Amazon in 2015, AWS generated $2.6 billion in revenue during the first quarter of 2016, representing 64% year-over-year growth (Figure 5-1). AWS has become a profit bright spot for Amazon. The segment's operating income, after stock-based compensation, reached $604 million during the first quarter of 2016, generating about 67% of the company's operating income. That was better than the company's North America commerce segment (US $588 million operating income) or international (US $121 million operating loss). By September 30, AWS has generated $861 million in net revenue for the first three quarters of 2016. And its year-to-year sales increased by 55%, with the margin rate of 26%①.

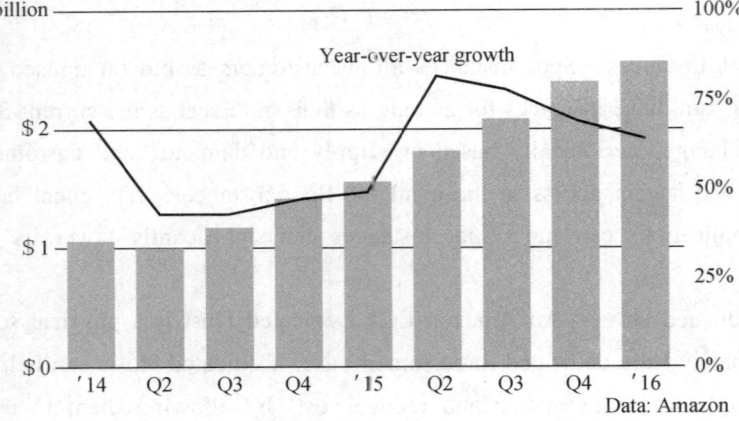

Figure 5-1　AWS Quarterly Revenue and Growth②

AWS pioneers the business of hosting computer servers for companies like Netflix and the Central Intelligence Agency. It has become the go-to provider for a generation of startups, government agencies and other corporations seeking to offload computing power to Amazon's thousands of servers. In other words, AWS is supporting Amazon's sprawling, 20-year-old business that spends billions of dollars in an effort to upend traditional brick-and-mortar retail by providing customers nearly everything imaginable in

---

① 亚萌, 亚马逊最赚钱 AWS 业务添三大 AI 工具, 这里是亮点和售价一览表, 雷锋网, 2016-12-01。
② Jay Chapel If Your CFO Hasn't Already Told You to Control AWS Costs, (S)he's About To, https://www.parkmycloud.com/blog/cfo-control-aws-costs/, 2016-06-09.

as quickly as one hour[①].

Problems Encountered by AWS

Today, Amazon Web Services (AWS) has become the undisputed leader of the public infrastructure-as-a-service (IaaS) market. And as more and more organizations realize the massive business agility benefits of public IaaS, it is difficult to envision any near future that doesn't have Amazon as a critical infrastructure provider to an increasing number of companies. But it does not mean that AWS poses no problem.

1. Price-cutting strategy will peter out. In fact, Amazon has been using price cuts as a club to beat up its competitors, leveraging its massive economies of scale as it plays the "Walmart" of the cloud. Indeed, such price reductions squeeze the margins of competitors, struggling to keep up—but they also squeeze Amazon's margins as well. And regular pricing can never go to zero or the company will lose money regardless of its massive scale. As a result, price drops will asymptotically level out over time at best—or even give way to price increases, as inflation inevitably trumps downward pricing pressure[②].

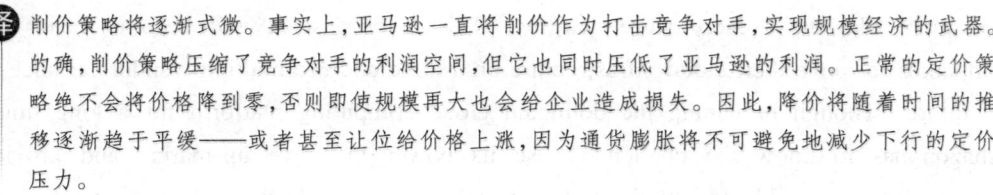
削价策略将逐渐式微。事实上,亚马逊一直将削价作为打击竞争对手,实现规模经济的武器。的确,削价策略压缩了竞争对手的利润空间,但它也同时压低了亚马逊的利润。正常的定价策略绝不会将价格降到零,否则即使规模再大也会给企业造成损失。因此,降价将随着时间的推移逐渐趋于平缓——或者甚至让位给价格上涨,因为通货膨胀将不可避免地减少下行的定价压力。

2. Single service model is challenged by competitors. While Amazon continues to focus on IaaS, one of its competitors—Microsoft, the number two position behind Amazon, doubles down on Platform-as-a-Service (PaaS) as well as Software-as-a-Service (SaaS) offerings like the popular Office 365. Actually, it is not enough for AWS to iteratively improve the public IaaS market that it created. Because while public IaaS delivers great business agility to companies, there are even greater agility gains to be had beyond today's best-practices public IaaS deployments. Specifically, the next innovation seems to be in moving from servers-as-cattle to no servers at all, which will affect IaaS offered AWS greatly. Though AWS seems to understand what the future holds (e.g. it launched Lambda—serverless compute), its ability to compete effectively is held in check by the way it is built. And it will continue to be held back unless Amazon changes some fundamental aspects of AWS. An analysis even shows that instead of being the leader,

---

① Greg Bensinger, Cloud Unit Pushes Amazon to Record Profit, *The Wall Street Journal*, 2016-04-28.
② Jason Bloomberg, Five Reasons Why The Amazon Cloud Has Lost Its Silver Lining, https://www.forbes.com/sites/jasonbloomberg/2016/11/27/five-reasons-why-the-amazon-cloud-has-lost-its-silver-lining/# 5fd3cf364b94, 2016-11-27.

Amazon is a distant follower. For example, Facebook—a company that did not exactly pitch as a cloud powerhouse, currently owns a company that does serverless better than AWS.

3. Possible technical risks. On September 20, 2015, AWS suffered database problems which affected Netflix and other web sites relying on Amazon's public cloud infrastructure. Starting early morning, the AWS status page noted DynamoDB database issues at the company's huge US-East data center complex in Ashburn, Virgina. As of noon, the database service was still reporting increased error rates responding to Application Programming Interface (API) calls. That means outside services that rely on AWS to send instructions to their own applications were out of luck. As of 11:16 a.m., Amazon said it was seeing that service recover but typically once a service like this was disrupted, the restart and recovery took time.

Justs as Jeff Bezos said "your margin is my opportunity." AWS, the service operating at a rapid run rate and owning millions of active customers, is expected to seize more opportunities in the future. Meanwhile, the challenge can not be ignored since the current margins on cloud computing will continue to erode every year and it will eventually look more like the grocery store margins. This is because it will become easier for companies to move their cloud infrastructure on a dime and use multiple vendors at once in the future. Though remaining the dominant cloud computing platform for a long time, Amazon has to know the challenge, use its power to move up-market and provide additional services with potentially higher margin because it is the only large technology company that is used to competing in very low margin space.

Case Analysis

亚马逊一直以来是作为知名的网上书店为大家所熟知,我们曾经在第一章讨论过这家企业,并提及它已经成为全球顶尖的三大云服务商之一。这一章的案例分析就聚焦于该企业的云计算服务——AWS。案例分析的重点在于三个部分:亚马逊为何要发展云服务? AWS 的收费模式是什么? 为什么说 AWS 正成为亚马逊的利润新引擎?

首先,AWS 的推出最初源于亚马逊希望为其内部的专业团队提供一个可扩展的软件系统作为企业基础架构的一部分,以便激发更多的创新。然而,这个系统的高维护成本和低利用率迫使亚马逊不得不想出更有创意的解决方案。与此同时,它发现传统 IT 系统的高成本和低利用率困扰着很多企业。为什么不寻找一种好的解决方案为大家服务呢? AWS 因此应运而生。由此可见,AWS 诞生的初衷并非如我们想象得那么复杂,就是为了解决亚马逊内部的技术问题。至于后来成为专属于企业客户的商业化云服务也算是"无心插柳柳成荫"的结果。这也告诉我们,企业通常是问题导向的思维,创新的推出是为了解决问题,而不是为了创新而创新。

其次，AWS 的定价模式打破了企业通过购买获取 IT 资源的传统，转而采用租赁的方式提供 IT 服务，实现了从所有权到使用权的转变。AWS 采用"即用即付"的收费模式，客户仅需为其所使用的 IT 资源付费，而不需要花高价购买这些资源。在这种模式下，客户不仅避免了由前期预测所导致的 IT 高投入的风险，而且可以根据自身需求选择个性化的服务。AWS 还为客户提供"预订低价"、"量大低价"以及"服务更新低价"等优惠措施，为企业尤其是中小企业降低了 IT 成本，提高了资源使用率。

最后，AWS 灵活低廉的定价模式、安全可靠以及简单易操作的特性使其自问世以来成为不少企业云服务的首选。随着它的品牌知名度的提高，AWS 为亚马逊带来了越来越多的收益，也成为该企业新的利润源泉。即使面对着激烈的市场竞争、业务规模增长与服务降价，AWS 自推出以来表现亮眼，一直保持强劲增长。除了案例中的统计数据以外，最新数据表明，AWS 的利润贡献已经占据公司总体利润的近 90%，大大超出了其零售业务带来的收益。也是得益于 AWS 的亮眼成绩，亚马逊这家以零售起家的电商企业非但没有遭遇大部分零售商的利润瓶颈，反而在 2017 年总体市值首次突破 800 亿美元，而其总裁贝佐斯也凭借着 500 亿美元的个人资产成为世界上最富有的人之一①。正因为如此，有人将 AWS 比喻成亚马逊孕育的一枚"金蛋"。

面对云服务利润空间压缩，微软等竞争对手的强势崛起以及技术风险等问题，AWS 这枚"金蛋"能否继续发光并维持亚马逊在云服务领域的主导地位，不仅取决于它本身的服务质量，还取决于亚马逊的产品策略。可以肯定的是，亚马逊将利用这一利润引擎发掘更多的盈利点。正如贝佐斯所说"企业的利润就是我们的机会"。

Section 3
Big Data—Power Source of Netflix
第三节 大数据——Netflix 的力量来源

1 Key Words

1. streaming media *n.* 流媒体
2. hit *n.* 成功
3. trailer *n.* 预告片
4. series *n.* 连续剧，系列剧
5. scenery *n.* 舞台布景
6. episode *n.* 集
7. genre *n.* 流派
8. synergistic *adj.* 协同的，协调的
9. piracy *n.* 剽窃
10. prefabricate *vt.* 预先构思

---

① 捷克互联网，亚马逊 90% 的利润来自 AWS 云计算究竟有多大的利润空间？，http://baijiahao.baidu.com/s？id＝1566310562352625＆wfr＝spider＆for＝pc,2017-05-03。

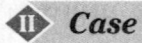 Case

Background

Netflix, founded in 1997, is an American provider of on-demand Internet streaming media available to viewers. As an Internet subscription service company, it provides subscription service streaming movies and TV episodes over the Internet, and sends DVDs by mail. Netflix obtains content from various studios and other content providers through fixed-fee licenses, revenue sharing agreements and direct purchases. It markets its service through various channels, including online advertising, broad-based media such as television and radio, as well as various partnership. It started its subscription-based digital distribution service in 1999, and by 2009 it had offered a collection of 100,000 titles on DVD and had surpassed 10 million subscribers. As of April 2018, Netflix had 125 million total subscribers worldwide, including 56.71 million in the United States①.

Netflix is neither the first nor the unique streaming media, it should be strictly defined as a data-driven company. It distinguishes itself from the peers by launching the original programming. "House of Cards" is one of the originally programmed plays, which makes Netflix well-known. The play is so successful that the former President Obama is its huge fan. Why is the play so popular? The answer is big data, which is also the power source of the e-commerce company. Let's take a look at the secrets behind Netflix's hit.

How Did Big Data Help Netflix to Make a Decision of Investment? ②

In 2011 Netflix made one of the biggest decisions they would ever make. They outbid top television channels like HBO and AMC to earn the rights for a U.S. version of "House of Cards", giving them 2 seasons with 13 episodes in each season. At a cost of $4 million to $6 million an episode, this 2-season price tag was over $100 million. Netflix had undoubtedly made other big investments before (shipping centers, postage costs, etc.), but nothing like this was on the content side. why did they make such a big bet, and how did it add analytic factor to the decision? As what chief communications officer, Jonathan Friedland said: "Because we have a direct relationship with consumers, we know what people like to watch and that helps us understand how big the interest is going to be for a given show. It gives us some confidence that we can find an audience for a show like House of Cards."

Before green-lighting House of Cards, by virtue of data analysis, Netflix knew that a

---

① https://en.wikipedia.org/wiki/Netflix
② Johnathan Cabin, How Netflix Uses Analytics To Select Movies, Create Content, and Make Multimillion Dollar Decisions, https://blog.kissmetrics.com/how-netflix-uses-analytics/, 2013-05-17.

lot of users watched the British version of "House of Cards" well. Those who watched the British version "House of Cards" also watched Kevin Spacey films and/or films directed by David Fincher. Each of these 3 synergistic factors had to contain a certain volume of users since Netflix had a lot of users in all 3 factors. This combination of factors had a lot of weight in Netflix's decision to make the $100 million investment in creating a U. S. version of "House of Cards".

Particularly, with the data it owned, Netflix made a "personalized trailer" for each type of Netflix member, not a "one size fits all" trailer. Generally, before a movie is released or TV show premiers, there's typically one or a few trailers made and a few previews selected. Netflix made 10 different cuts of the trailer for "House of Cards", each geared toward different audiences. The trailer you saw was based on your previous viewing behavior. If you watched a lot of Kevin Spacey films, you would saw a trailer featuring him. Those who watched a lot of movies starring females would saw a trailer featuring the women in the show. And David Fincher fans would saw a trailer featuring his touch.

What is the result of Netflix's decision? —"House of Cards" brought in 2 million new U. S. subscribers in the first quarter of 2013, which was a 7% increase over the previous quarter. It also brought in 1 million new subscribers from elsewhere in the world. According to The Atlantic Wire, these 3 million subscribers almost paid Netflix back for the cost of "House of Cards".

How Does Netflix Take Advantage of Big Data in Programming?①②

Let's take a look at how TV shows are traditionally approved. Networks③ receive hundreds of pitches from writers and producers. The networks then request scripts for a few of these and then order 20 to 30 pilots. Once the pilots are produced, they are presented to executives and sometimes focus groups to predict how successful the show might be. What is the success rate for the shows that see the light of day? Despite such an exhaustive process, only about one show out of three is renewed for a second season, according to publicly available data from 2009–2012.

 让我们看看传统电视节目的审批流程。广播电视网收到来自编剧和制作人的上百个节目构思后,会要求其中部分提供剧本,并选出其中20—30部拍成试播集。试播集拍好以后放给节目主管或试映群体看,以预测该剧未来的播出效果。那么节目成功播出的比例有多高呢? 2009—2012年的公开数据显示,3部当中只有1部能成功播出。

---

① How AWS Pricing Works, https://d1.awsstatic.com/whitepapers/aws_pricing_overview.pdf, 2016-03.
② Harsha Hegde, Netflix And Its Revolutionary Use Of Big Data, http://dataconomy.com/2014/09/netflix-and-its-revolutionary-use-of-big-data/, 2014-09-22.
③ 即 television networks 广播电视网,是电视系统运营商,在广播电视网时代包括了主发射站和各地的中继站以及本地的接收系统。

Netflix, which was a new entrant into original programming, licensed five original series to date. Four of them, including "House of Cards", had been renewed for subsequent seasons which gave Netflix an 80% success rate with original programming, compared to the 30% to 40% success rate for networks. These shows were primarily picked by running data mining and other algorithms against the vast user behavior data available to determine the size of the possible audience and thereby the likelihood of success. Data analytics plays a significant role in Netflix's original programming and movies recommendation.

1. Analytics at Netflix

The core job of analytics is to help companies gain insight into their customers. Then, the companies can optimize their marketing and deliver a better product (without analytics, companies are in the dark about their customers). Analytics gives businesses the quantitative data they need to make better, more informed decisions and improve their services. So how does Netflix use analytics? Netflix has millions of worldwide streaming customers, which allows Netflix to gather a tremendous amount of data. With this data, Netflix can make better decisions and ultimately make users happier with its service.

Suppose you're watching a series like "Arrested Development", Netflix is able to see (on a large scale) the "completion rate" of users. For example, the people at Netflix could ask themselves "How many users who started "Arrested Development" (from season 1) finished it to the end of season 3?" Then they get an answer. Let's say it's 70%. Then they ask "Where was the common cut off point for users? What did the other 30% of users do? How big of a "time gap" was there between when consumers watched one episode and when they watched the next? We need to get a good idea of the overall engagement of this show." Netflix then gathers this data and see user trends to understand engagement at a deep level. If Netflix finds that 70% of users watched all seasons available of a cancelled show, that may provoke some interest in restarting "Arrested Development". It knows there's a good chance users will watch the new season.

Besides, Netflix tracks your activities on its site like: when you pause, rewind, or fast forward; What day you watch content (Netflix has found people watch TV shows during the week and movies during the weekend.); Where you watch (zip code) content; What device you use to watch content (Do you like to use your tablet for TV shows and your Roku for movies? Do people access the Just for Kids feature more on their iPads, etc.?); Your searches, browsing and scrolling behavior. Netflix also looks at data within movies. It takes various "screen shots" to look at "in the moment" characteristics which may be the volume, colors, and scenery that help Netflix find out what users like. Netflix checks when users' credits roll so as to see what users do afterward. Do they leave the app or go back to browsing? Because if users leave the app after watching a show, that may mean they are more likely to cancel. Through the analytics, Netflix may know how much content users need to watch in order to be less likely to cancel. For instance, Netflix knows "If we can get each user to watch at least 15 hours of content each month, they are 75% less likely to cancel. If they drop below 5 hours, there is a 95% chance they will cancel."

Owning these data, Netflix can ask itself: "How do we help users watch at least 15 hours of content per month?" One idea is enabling post-play, which automatically plays the next episode of a TV show unless the user opts out. For movies, show movie suggestions (based on the rating of the movie just watched) right after the credits start rolling and allow users to press "play" right from that screen. Netflix can add this feature to the web and mobile apps through analytics.

2. The recommendation algorithm

As part of the on-boarding process, Netflix asks new users to rate their interest in movie genres and rate any movies they've already seen. Based on the rating, Netflix offers movie recommendations soon after credits start (or, for television shows, it automatically plays the next episode). Netflix's recommendation depends on the self-developed personalization algorithms that aim to accurately predict what users will watch next. For Netflix, helping users to discover new movies and TV shows they'll enjoy is integral to its success.

If people run out of movies they want to watch and have no way to find new movies, they'll cancel. It's important that Netflix puts a lot of focus on making sure it has an accurate algorithm for this rather than having users rely on outside sources to find new movies. Does the recommendation algorithm work well? Since 75% of viewer activity is based on these suggestions, it seems that the algorithm works pretty well for them.

Possible Problems with Netflix's Big Data Application

Though Netflix's big data adoption has become a classic paradigm, some problems and concerns with its application should be noted:

1. Conflicts between big data and creativeness

For years Netflix has been analyzing what customers watched last night to suggest movies or TV shows that we might like to watch tomorrow. Now it is using the same formula to prefabricate its own programming to fit what it thinks we will like. These innovative productions might be troubling because they pave the way for more calibrated and uniform content, denying the disruptive novelty of digital TV. But if our future TV programming coincides perfectly with our tastes and habits, how TV can surprise us anymore?

The same funnel will narrow the curiosity of viewers as well as their desperate need for learning and exploring new horizons. The success of this new kind of production remains in the capacity of entertainment players to take risks and use big data as a launching pad to cutting-edge creations. It is the role of content producers to push consumers out of their comfort zone and use big data as an incentive to expand their field of vision.

2. Piracy

"House of Cards" is one of the first forays into original programming by Netflix and its success, which should be greatly attributed to its big data applications. The hit show has changed the company's perception in the mind of the consumer. Netflix is no longer considered just an aggregator of popular content from other networks and has come of age as a provider of engaging and interesting content on its own. However, House of Cards' growing popularity has also led to unwanted attention in the form of piracy. Piracy-tracking firm Excipio reported that the show's season three was downloaded illegally around 682,000 times within the first 24 hours of being available on torrent services. The show was also pirated in other countries like China, Canada and the United Kingdom. Piracy is impacting Netflix's revenue since subscribers may not be interested in viewing these shows at Netflix's paid platform when they can get the same shows for free.

Besides, concerns about users' privacy also exist. Given that Netflix is in the business of recommending shows or movies, might its algorithms tilt in favor of the work it commissions as it goes deeper into original programming? It brings to mind how Google got crossed up when it began developing more products, and those began showing up in searches. And there are concerns that the same thing that makes Netflix so valuable—it knows everything about us—could create problems if it is not careful with our data and our privacy though many people think the trade is worth it.

Where Is Netflix Going in the Future?

1. Online streaming

There is very clear shift of video consumption to the Internet, and Netflix is one of the companies leading this change. The company's DVD subscribers are declining and future growth will come from streaming subscribers. Eventually the company would like to replace all of its physical DVDs with online library.

2. International expansion

Netflix entered Canada towards the end of 2010 with its streaming-only service. In 2011, it witnessed good adoption in Canada and consequently expanded to Latin America. In early 2012, Netflix launched its streaming service in the U. K. and Ireland. Following that success, the company also expanded to Nordic countries of Norway, Sweden, Denmark and Finland. Netflix expanded its service to The Netherlands by late 2013 and launched in Germany, Austria, Switzerland, France, Belgium and Luxembourg by late

2014. Currently, Netflix has subscribers in around 50 countries. While the international market presents a huge potential, it also presents obstacles such as low broadband penetration and speeds, local competition and content licensing complications.

3. Increasing competition in online streaming

Netflix has been facing increasing competition in online streaming. Along with Amazon and Hulu, Blockbuster and Comcast have also entered this space. Dish and Sony launched their own internet MVPD (multichannel video programming distributor) services. The growing competition can not only put pressure on Netflix's subscriber growth, but also increase content costs due to bidding by competitors.

4. Growing focus on improving content and increasing original content

Netflix's original content has improved perception of the overall brand. The company's original programming has garnered critical acclaim by scoring multiple Emmy, Golden Globe and Academy Award nominations and several wins in the past few years. Shows such as "House of Cards" and "Orange Is the New Black" are drawing lots of audience and attracting customers to sign up. Netflix has effectively marketed these exclusive shows to maintain its subscriber momentum.

Case Analysis

美剧《纸牌屋》自2012年推出以后大获好评,甚至赢得了2013年美国电视剧界的最高奖——艾美奖的两项大奖。这部剧集引人注目不仅是因为它创下的高收视,更是因为它的幕后推手——Netflix,一家在线提供影视资源的电子商务企业。这家打造出2012年大热剧集的企业居然不是人们印象中的影视制作公司,而是看起来和电视剧制作没什么关系的电商企业的确让人大跌眼镜。Netflix为什么可以打造出《纸牌屋》这样成功的剧集?它成功背后的秘密是什么?它在经营中又面临哪些问题?这些问题都值得我们进一步探究。

众所周知,《纸牌屋》是20世纪90年代英国BBC广播公司推出的热门剧集,Netflix为什么偏偏选中了这部剧集进行翻拍?它又如何保证这项1亿美元的投资能获得回报?答案就是大数据。简单来说,Netflix通过大数据分析,发现《纸牌屋》很受欢迎,而喜欢这部剧集的观众同时又是著名导演大卫·芬奇和奥斯卡影帝凯文·西派斯的拥趸。根据大数据分析的结果选择最适合的剧集,挑选最适合的导演和演员,Netflix推出的美版《纸牌屋》一炮而红也就在情理之中了。

当然,要进行深度案例分析,我们不能把注意力仅仅放在《纸牌屋》上,而应该进一步挖掘Netflix是如何在节目制作中巧用大数据的。在竞争激烈的美国电视剧制作行业,从开始的构思、剧本挑选到后面的拍摄,一般仅有30%—40%才能与观众见面(这还不算后续几季的进一步筛选),而Netflix保持了约80%的上映率。它是如何做到的?事实上,Netflix主要在两个环节巧用大数据来保证高成功率:用户行为分析和剧集推荐。

首先，需求分析的重要性不言而喻，企业能否赚钱很大程度上取决于它能否真正了解用户需求。传统的需求分析通常是针对客户群体而不是个体，这种粗放式的需求分析往往无法精准捕捉每个用户的个性化需求，而这恰恰是大数据所能弥补的。Netflix 遍布全球的大量用户每天能为它提供上亿条数据。用户在网站或是 App 上的每一次搜索、浏览、暂停、回放都被这些数据精确而完整地记录下来，再结合用户的性别年龄等个人信息进行分析，Netflix 就能得到用户需求的完整"画像"：你喜欢何时观看影视作品？你喜欢什么样的节目？你通常观看节目的时间有多长？……基于这个"画像"，Netflix 能够为每位用户量身打造最适合的产品和服务。其次，Netflix 利用大数据进行节目推荐。产品推荐是电商网站的常用营销策略，它对 Netflix 这样的流媒体而言显得尤为重要，因为如果无法持续地吸引用户的注意力，用户很快就会下线甚至放弃网站或 App。正如 Netflix 的专家所说："如果用户能在我们的网站或 App 上持续观看节目长达 15 小时以上，那么他们继续留下来的可能性将增加 75%。"但是，推荐什么样的节目最合适呢？Netflix 通常会询问用户喜欢的节目类型，并收集用户对节目的评分记录，然后利用它自主开发的数据算法进行分析，以预测用户接下来的观影需求，并基于分析的结果实施节目推荐，例如，为用户自动播放下一集节目。对 Netflix 在制作节目的两个环节巧用大数据的流程进行梳理可以发现，收集数据、分析数据和做出决策是应用大数据的一般流程。需要强调的是，大数据应用的核心并非数据本身，而是收集和分析数据并由此做决策的人。

Netflix 的案例也告诉我们，尽管已经有大数据应用的成功案例，但它并非万能。自它诞生以来，有关这项技术的争论从未停止。例如，有人担心完全基于大数据来制作节目可能会削弱企业的创新能力，减少有创意的节目给观众带来的惊喜。另外，类似 Netflix 的流媒体因为数据涉及用户隐私问题而备受争议，而它本身也因为用户的非法下载行为而饱受困扰。如何在发掘大数据的价值和降低这项技术带来的风险之间平衡是 Netflix 未来需要正视的问题。

Section 4
Autonavi—Building a New Portal of Mobile Life
第四节　高德——打造移动生活新门户

Key Words

1. navigation *n.* 航行
2. portal *n.* 门户网站
3. aerial *adj.* 空中的
4. photogrammetry *n.* 摄影制图法
5. fusion *n.* 融合

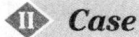 **Case**

Foundation

AutoNavi Software is a corporation of digital map content and navigation and Location-based Solutions (LBS) in China, which was founded in 2001. In February 2014, Alibaba Group Holding Ltd, China's largest e-commerce firm, offered to buy AutoNavi Holdings Ltd in a deal valuing the Chinese digital mapping and navigation firm at $1.58 billion. Alibaba, which already owned 28% of AutoNavi, has been trying to expand its product line-up to better compete with Chinese rivals Tencent and Baidu①.

Products and Services

AutoNavi is a provider of navigation digital map and location-based services in China, with Class A qualification certificate for digital navigation map production and Class A aerial photogrammetry qualification certificate. It has passed ISO9002, CMMI Level 3 and TS16949 qualification. Many international enterprises such as BMW, Audi and Apple are its clients. Due to its excellent performance in map services, AutoNavi became the unique official navigation digital map and application sponsor authorized and appointed by Shanghai World Expo Bureau and 2010 World Expo②.

Its main products and services include:

1. Automotive Navigation. AutoNavi provides wide-coveraged, rich and accurate digital map for more than 10 major automobile brands like Audi, BMW, Benz and VW, covering approximately 100 models with more than 50% market share in China in-dash navigation map market. It also provides an integration solution of navigation digital map and navigation engine to more than 10 PND customers including Shinco, Malata, Mio, Siemens, etc.

2. Government & Enterprise Applications. AutoNavi provides various solutions for government and enterprise customers, including aerial photogrammetry, 2D and 3D geographical information data, 3D digital city management and exhibition platform and Wei Zhi Tong software, Data Earth, etc.

3. Wireless & Internet Location-Based Services. AutoNavi provides various location-based services and solutions for wireless and Internet customers, including basic map data, API services, mobile phone navigation software, MiniMap software, location-based value

---

① Alibaba Offer for AutoNavi Values Digital Map Firm at $1.58 billion, https://www.reuters.com/article/us-autonavi-offer/alibaba-offer-for-autonavi-values-digital-map-firm-at-1-58-billion-idUSBREA190XB20140211, 2014-02-11.
② http://chzt.sbsm.gov.cn/accessory/201009/1284962360144.pdf

added service, etc. It also provides various solutions for telecom carriers, including digital map data, POI platform, GIS platform, etc.

How Does Autonavi Generate a Map?

In general, AutoNavi's map generating process is composed of 4 steps:

1. Demand planning and product defining. During the process of product research and development, demand analysis is necessary. Particularly, a map involves many possible applications for customers such as navigating, group buying and so on. Therefore, AutoNavi has to accurately capture customers' need so that the map and the applications can satisfy their demands well. Besides, a clear product definition is required since it helps to position the product accurately.

2. Production planning. This step focuses on data collecting such as data acquisition by vehicle, data acquisition by walking, business customer information acquisition, Internet information acquisition, aerial photogrammetry measurement and satellite image acquisition. AutoNavi typically collects data by walks. For the places that aren't accessible by walks, AutoNavi uses a car. Data acquisition by walks means AutoNavi hires people who utilize PDA or camera with map data to collect data as much as possible. This way is especially suitable for suburban data acquisition. For suburbia or western cities, AutoNavi usually uses a car for data acquisition. This way is high efficient but it can not collect the deep information.

3. Data production which includes the production of navigation data and value-added data. The navigation data production involves road mapping, POI, background, pictures, real-time traffic, 3D cities and so on. The value-added data integrate the dynamic information. POI, a Point of Interest, is a specific point location that someone may find useful or interesting. An example is a point on the Earth representing the location of the Space Needle, or a point on Mars representing the location of the mountain, Olympus Mons. Most consumers use the term when referring to hotels, campsites, fuel stations or any other categories used in modern (automotive) navigation systems. Due to the fast change of POI, AutoNavi updates it periodically. For example, POI collection for first-tier cities such as Beijing is usually implemented four times a year, while it is done once a year for the hot cities such as Hangzhou, and once in several years for western cities. In addition to POI collection, AutoNavi also updates data through the feedback from users' mobile devices. For instance, once AutoNavi receives the information of location changes, it will check and correct the existing POI.

4. Data fusion. After data conversion and compiling, AutoNavi releases the data on vehicle navigation, mobile navigation, LBS and government or business applications.

> **译** 数据融合。在进行数据转换和编译测试后,高德地图就将其实时发布在汽车导航、移动导航、互联网位置服务以及政府企业应用上。

Autonavi'S Expansion—From Map to Platform

AutoNavi began its businesses from a digital map. It has become a well-known map and navigation service provider. However, AutoNavi is not satisfied with being a bottom data service provider, it has been aiming to establish a portal or platform combining navigating, searching, group buying, logistics, LBS and O2O services. What are the strengths and weaknesses of AutoNavi to build such a comprehensive platform? A SWOT analysis can tell the answer.

1. Strengths

1) Excellent capabilities of mapping. As a leading provider of navigation digital map, AutoNavi owns Class A qualification certificate for digital navigation map production and Class A aerial photogrammetry qualification certificate. The qualification is AutoNavi's core competence as well as the support for its expansion. After all, there are only two qualified fundamental data providers in China.

2) Solid customer base. As a professional in digital map and navigation, AutoNavi has built a solid customer base. Many famous enterprises such as Apple, BMW, Audi are its loyal customers. The cooperation with the high brand recognition firms provides a guarantee for AutoNavi—the services quality of AutoNavi is trustworthy. The faithful customers are the potential customers for AutoNavi's new applications since it is easy for them to accept the new services offered by AutoNavi.

3) Internet and mobile Internet services are playing more significant roles in AutoNavi's businesses. For a long time, vehicle navigation service has dominated AutoNavi's businesses. In 2012, the revenue from vehicle navigation service was about 570 million yuan, accounting for 57.6% of total turnover. However, the situation has changed since 2013. The percentage of vehicle navigation service dropped from 74% in 2010 to 45% in Q1 2013[①]. Meanwhile, LBS accounted for 40% of AutoNavi's turnover (Figure 5-2). AutoNavi has realized that the Internet especially the mobile Internet will be a huge market. The enterprises that seize the opportunity will lead the future mobile Internet market. Besides, with the popularity of mobile devices such as smart phone, people are inclined to substitute navigation applications on smart phones for traditional vehicle navigation devices. It indicates that the future competition will focus on the value-added applications behind navigation rather than the unitary navigation services.

---

① 刘登:"高德:从地图进,从地图出",《商界(评论)》,2013(6):pp.42-45.

Fortunately, the rising Internet-based businesses such as LBS make it possible that AutoNavi converts from a unitary digital map into a comprehensive platform.

高德互联网及移动互联网营收增长情况

	2011 Q1	2011 Q2	2011 Q3	2011 Q4	2012 Q1	2012 Q2	2012 Q3	2012 Q4	2013 Q1
高德互联网及移动互联网营业收入(万美元)	370	540	880	950	990	1 100	1 110	1 550	1 390
同比增速(%)	109.1	112.6	239.3	158	166.6	104.5	26.2	63.4	40.4
上述两项营业收入在高德总营业收入中所占比例(%)	14.68	16.62	26.19	27.37	27.73	27.36	27.61	35.55	40.52

Figure 5-2　AutoNavi's Internet and Mobile Internet Businesses Growth[①]

2. Weaknesses

1) Unitary brand image. It takes AutoNavi more than 10 years to successfully build its brand image—a professional digital map and navigation service provider. Because AutoNavi has been focusing on the fundamental map data services so much that users have a fixed and unitary impression on AutoNavi. Consequently, it is hard to change the image in a short time even though AutoNavi has worked hard on the comprehensive platform.

2) Insufficient active users. Monthly Active Users (MAU) is one of the ways to measure the success rate of online social games and social networking services. Typically, MAU is measured by counting the number of unique users during a specific measurement period, such as within the previous 30 days. Compared to its competitors like Baidu, AutoNavi owns less MAU. According to the statistics, by 2012, Baidu's MAU had surpassed 100 million, 3 times as many as AutoNavi. Lack of active users may limit AutoNavi's growth.

3. Opportunities

1) The rapid growth of mobile Internet. According to the statistics, Chinese netizens volume reached 649 million, 85.8% of which is mobile phone users by the end of 2014[②]. The fast development of Internet especially mobile Internet means the huge market for AutoNavi which will benefit its development.

2) The exit of Google Map. In 2012, Google exited from China due to the license problem. For some time, Google map was a big threat for AutoNavi. Google's exit means a powerful competitor retreated from Chinese market. This creates a wonderful chance for AutoNavi's development.

---

① 刘登:"高德:从地图进,从地图出",《商界(评论)》,2013(6):pp.42-45.
② The 34th Report of Chinese Internet Development, CNNIC, June, 2014.

4. Threats

1) Threats from competitors such as SiWeiTuxin and Baidu. Though Google map exited from Chinese market, the threats are still existed. Actually, as the other fundamental map data service provider, SiWeiTuXin has been a huge threat for AutoNavi. Their market share for a long time has been almost even. For example, the vehicle navigation revenue of SiWeiTuXin was 419 million yuan, not far away from AutoNavi's 570 million yuan[①]. In addition, in terms of brand recognition, the number of active users, Baidu is superior to AutoNavi.

2) Customers have not been used to paying for Navigation services. AutoNavi's platform is based on its original navigation service. However, with the popularity of the navigation applications attached to mobile phones, customers has been used to them since they are convenient, efficient, particularly, they are free! This will cause a big pressure on AutoNavi's navigation service.

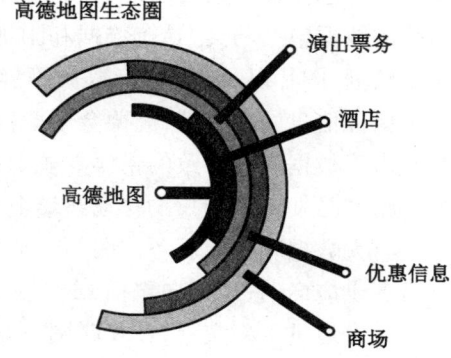

Figure 5-3　AutoNavi's Ecosystem[②]

AutoNavi plans to establish a map-centered ecosystem (Figure 5-3). This ecosystem will provide the comprehensive services including hotel reservation, shopping guide, entertainment and discount information. As long as the ecosystem is built, people will be allowed to enjoy the all-around services.

Case Analysis

相比本章的前两个案例,高德的案例对很多人而言会更有亲切感,因为它被大量地运用在我们的生活中,甚至成为人们必不可少的智能助理。对于这个案例,我们关注的重点应该在高德基于大数据的地图产生流程以及对高德由位置服务提供商向综合性平台拓展的SWOT分析。

通过阅读案例,我们可以发现,高德的地图产生流程包括4个步骤:需求分析、数据规划、数据生产和地图发布。与一般人的想象不同,高德并没有直接进入地图制作环节,而是首先进行用户需求分析,为什么?因为人们使用高德地图并非只为了导航,而且还包括它所提供的购物、美食、娱乐等其他与生活相关的功能。因此,了解用户的偏好、口味以及购物习惯是高德,这家中国领先的数字地图内容、导航和位置服务解决方案提供商的首要任务。除此之外,高德将它的产品不仅仅定位为简单的地图而是人们

---

① 刘登.高德:从地图进,从地图出[J].商界(评论),2013(6):42-45.
② 朱丽.高德的地图攻略[J].中外管理,2013(6).

生活的智能助理。也是因为如此，必须准确地了解用户需求，才能及时为其提供所需要的服务。随着移动互联网技术的普及，位置服务(LBS)市场的竞争变得异常激烈。一旦产品给用户带来的体验不佳，用户只需要在手机或平板电脑上轻松删除就可以永远舍弃它。反之，一旦用户习惯了某款 LBS 产品，它将很难被取代。正因为如此，高德才在需求分析上花费如此多的功夫。在数据生产环节，高德尝试了与众不同的数据收集方法：考虑到中国的地形和交通状况复杂，高德并没有像谷歌一样全程依靠车载方式采集数据，而是采用了人工步行和车载相结合的方式采集数据。这种灵活的数据采集方式能更好地保证所收集的地图数据的准确性和即时性，为后续的地图发布奠定了基础。高德的数据包括两类：导航数据和附加价值数据。前者包括道路地图、POI(兴趣点)、背景数据、图片以及 3D 城市数据等静态数据；后者则是指实时交通状况等动态数据。为了保证信息的即时性，高德会定期根据 POI 和用户移动设备的反馈进行数据更新，以避免由于数据陈旧导致的错误导航引起消费者不满。完成了关键的前两个环节，高德最终将产品发布到用户的移动终端上为其服务。

有大数据和移动服务这两项武器在手，高德显然并不满足于仅仅做一家领先的位置服务供应商，它计划向包括 LBS 服务、租车、智能设备、环保以及 O2O 服务在内的综合性平台迈进。事实上，在互联网行业构建多边平台已经成为趋势，但这种拓展并非适合每家企业。SWOT 分析可以帮助我们更好地理解高德的拓展策略。首先，高德出色的地图服务是它的明显优势，也是它的核心竞争力。只要高德保持自己在这一领域的优势，它就可以继续在中国数字地图市场占据主导地位。这也说明对于企业而言，产品质量才是其赢得竞争的根本。另外，在位置服务领域经营了二十多年的高德拥有坚实的客户基础，并成功塑造了自己的品牌形象，这不仅是它的另一个显著优势，也成为它吸引阿里巴巴的重要原因。其次，活跃用户不足是高德的劣势之一，因为活跃用户是衡量互联网服务成功与否的重要指标。在这方面，高德显然落后于它的竞争对手百度，这甚至引发了 2016 年两者之间的争论。而这场争论所揭示的不仅是高德所面临的威胁，更是整个位置服务行业缺乏统一的技术标准的尴尬。值得庆幸的是，中国移动互联技术的快速发展，谷歌地图的退出，以及被阿里巴巴成功收购也给高德带来了良好的发展机遇。

Section 5
Case Analysis Methodology—SWOT Analysis
第五节 案例分析方法解析——SWOT 分析法

SWOT analysis is a tool for auditing an organization and its environment. It is the first stage of analysis to help marketers to focus on key issues. SWOT stands for strengths, weakness, opportunities and threats. Strengths and weakness are internal factors while opportunities and threats are external factors[①].

A Strength could be:

1. Your specialist marketing expertise;
2. A new, innovative product or service;
3. Location of your business;
4. Quality processes and procedures;
5. Any other aspect of your business that adds value to your product or service.

A Weakness could be:

1. Lack of marketing expertise;
2. Undifferentiated products and service (e.g in relation to your competitors);
3. Location of your business;
4. Poor quality goods or services;
5. Damaged reputation.

An Opportunity could be:

1. A developing market such as Internet;
2. Mergers, joint ventures or strategic alliance;
3. Moving into new market segments that offer improved profits;
4. A new international market;
5. A market vacated by an inefficient competitor.

A Threat could be:

1. A new competitor in your home market;
2. Price wars with competitors;
3. A competitor has a new, innovative product or service;
4. Competitors have superior access to channels of distribution;
5. Taxation is introduced on your product or service.

There are some Simple rules for a successful SWOT analysis:

1. Be realistic about the strengths and weaknesses of your organization;
2. Analysis should distinguish between where your organization is today, and where it could be in the future;
3. Be specific, avoid gray areas;
4. Always analyze in context to your competitors. E. g. better or worse than your competitors;
5. Keep your SWOT short and simple and supply necessary explanation for your idea.

---

① http://www.marketingteacher.com/swot-analysis/

Summary（本章小结）

The three technologies including cloud computing, big data and mobile technology are thought as the new technologies changing e-commerce. Cloud computing is not a brand new computing mode. It is the evolution and extension of the traditional distributed computing and grid computing. As a new compute model, cloud computing influences not only the e-commerce enterprises but also the e-commerce industrial chain. Big Data refers to the collection of data sets so large and complex that it becomes difficult to process using on-hand database management tools or traditional data processing applications. The Internet generates big data each second such as consumers behavior data or online transaction data. There are 4 characteristics of big data which are called as "The 4Vs". Big data can be used in e-commerce like anticipatory purchases, data-driven decisions and personalized offers. Mobile technology is the technology used for cellular communication. When mobile technology is applied to e-commerce, a new e-commerce type—mobile commerce (m-commerce) is generated. M-commerce has some attributes like mobility and ubiquity.

Amazon Web Services (AWS), allows users to rent virtual computers on which to run their own computer applications. Its pricing model allows a customer (usually an organization) to pay for exactly the amount of resources it actually needs. Many organizations prefer EC2 due to its benefits like elastic web-scale computing and flexible cloud hosting services. AWS appears to be growing and becoming a new profit engine of Amazon. All the element services from AWS can be combined to build robust data platforms for storing, processing and analyzing e-commerce marketing data.

Netflix is an American provider of on-demand Internet streaming media available to viewers. As an Internet subscription service company, it provides subscription service streaming movies and TV episodes over the Internet and sending DVDs by mail. Netflix distinguishes itself from the peers by launching the original programming which is typically data-driven as well as audience-oriented and it can even ask producers of original programming to find new actors if the suggested ones don't have a history of impressing the online audience. "House of Cards" is the play which makes Netflix well-known. Netflix's hit on "House of Cards" should be primarily attributed to its programming process based on big data. The process is composed of collecting data, analyzing data and recommending the most suitable movies based on data analysis. Big data is a precious treasure for Netflix which helps it to build a better service for users and become a more cost-efficient business by reducing waste and avoiding "shots in the dark". Due to the technical or managerial limitation, there are still some problems with big data such as piracy and the conflicts between big data and creativeness.

AutoNavi Software, as a corporation of digital map content and navigation and location-based solutions (LBS) in China, provides automotive navigation, government & enterprise applications and Wireless & Internet location-based services. In general, AutoNavi's map generating process is composed of 4 steps: demand analysis, production planning, data production which includes the production of navigation data and value-added data, and data fusion. AutoNavi has been aiming to establish a portal or platform combining navigating, searching, group buying, logistics, LBS and O2O services. On the one hand, AutoNavi has the strengths including excellent capabilities of mapping, solid customer base and mobile Internet services. Meanwhile, the rapid growth of mobile Internet and the exit of Google Map provide the opportunities for AutoNavi; on the other hand, the weaknesses such as unitary brand image and insufficient active users can not be ignored. Besides, AutoNavi should pay attention to the threats from competitors and customers' habits.

SWOT analysis is a tool for auditing an organization and its environment. It is the first stage of analysis to help marketers to focus on key issues. SWOT stands for strengths, weakness, opportunities, and threats. Strengths and weakness are internal factors while opportunities and threats are external factors. When making a SWOT analysis, you should ensure your attitude is objective. And keep your SWOT short and simple, and supply necessary explanation for your idea.

 Exercises & Tasks（练习与任务）

▶ *Exercises*

1. What is cloud computing? What are the influences of the technology?
2. Why do we call cloud computing "The new profit engine of Amazon"?
3. How do you define big data and describe its characteristics?
4. How does big data benefit Netflix's operation?
5. What are the characteristics of mobile technology?

▶ *Tasks*

Choose a case of the application of new technology in e-commerce and prepare a 20-minute presentation which should include:

1. Background introduction to the enterprise and its new technology application;
2. Analyze its new technology application. E.g. pros and cons, the causes of success or failure;
3. Conclusion.

Part III Online Marketing

第三部分 网络营销

Chapter 6 Personalization & Customization
第六章 个性化与定制化

 Learning Objectives（学习目标）

After finishing this chapter, you should be able to:
1. Define and differentiate personalization and customization;
2. Grasp the methods by which a firm can realize products/services personalization;
3. Analyze the strengths and weaknesses for LightInTheBox to implement personalization;
4. Explain how Mogujie implements personalization by virtue of online social community;
5. Learn about how NIKEiD realizes customization;
6. Describe the basic case analysis process.

 Introduction（内容简介）

Personalization and customization are two important marketing strategies. Though they look similar, the two terms have different focuses. What are the differences between the two concepts? How to realize personalization or customization so as to improve customers' loyalty in practice? These questions are answered in this chapter.

Chapter 6 is composed of 5 sections. The brief introduction to personalization and customization is made in section 1. Three related cases are explained respectively in section 2, 3, and 4. Section 5 focuses on case analysis process.

Section 1
Personalization and Customization
第一节 个性化与定制化

Key Words

1. personalization *n.* 个性化
2. customization *n.* 定制化
3. overt *adj.* 公开的
4. covert *adj.* 隐蔽的
5. solicit *vt.* 征求

Personalization

1. What is personalization?

Personalization, just like tailoring the clothes according to each customer's individual demand, refers to the matching of services, products, and advertising content to individual consumers. Personalization has been proven an effective marketing strategy of satisfying customers' need better, strengthening customer relationship, increasing a company's profit and realizing differentiation.

2. How to realize personalization[①]?

There are two steps for personalization implementation:

1) Constructing user profile. For personalization, the matching process is based on what a company knows about the individual user. This knowledge is usually referred to as a customer profile, which defines the customer's requirements, preferences, behaviors, and demographic traits. Therefore, the ways to build an effective customer profile can be used as the strategies to realize personalization:

• Solicit information directly from the user. This usually means asking customers to fill in a questionnaire;

• Cookie. It is not a snack but a data file that is placed on a user's hard drive by a web server to collect information about users' activities at a site, frequently without disclosure or the user's consent;

• Perform marketing research. Research the market using tools such as web mining;

• Build from previous purchase patterns. This is a method usually utilized by the merchants since it is easy to operate.

2) Collaborative filtering. Once constructing user profile, a firm can apply

---

① Efraim, Turban. David King. 王建译.《电子商务导论》,人民大学出版社,2006 年。

personalization through different methods. One of them is collaborative filtering that uses customer data to predict, based on formulas derived from behavioral studies, what other products or services a customer may enjoy; predictions can be extended to other customers with similar profiles. There are different three variations of collaborative filtering:

- Rule-based filtering. A company asks the consumers a series of yes/no or multiple-choice questions. The questions may range from personal information to the specific information the customer is looking for on a specific web site. Certain behavioral patterns are predicted using the collected information.

- Content-based filtering. Vendors ask users to specify certain favorite products. Based on these user preferences, the vendor's system will recommend additional products to the user.

- Activity-based filtering. Filtering rules can be built from watching the user's activities on the web.

Customization

1. What is customization?

Customization, a term related to personalization, refers to changing the delivered products or services based on a user's preferences or prior behavior.

2. Why customization? [1]

1) Every customer is their own market. Since the late 1980s many consumers have desired products that meet their exact need. No longer does "one size fits all". Customers expect it and are willing to pay for it. The heterogeneity of consumers' need has expanded and offered brands a tremendous opportunity. As a result, enterprises can profit from exploiting heterogeneity across customers' need.

2) Consumers are more expressive. Individuals have long expressed themselves through various forms of media such as the clothing they wear, the car they drive, and the food they eat. Particularly, social media services such as Twitter and Facebook have made it easier for people to effortlessly express themselves to their friends. Today, self-expression through user generated content (UGC) is quickly moving to self expression through user generated products (UGP). For UGP, this consumer-driven movement has already started in product categories such as apparel, footwear, and accessories.

3) Customization is the new loyalty. Every brand wants loyalty programs. These programs increase consumer spending, retention and lifetime customer value. The problem with most loyalty programs is that they force the customer to make decisions that are non-

---

[1] Erik Eliason, 3 Reasons Why Mass Customization is the Future of Consumer Products, https://www.huffingtonpost.com/erik-eliason/mass-customization_b_1313875.html, March 21, 2012.

utility maximizing. What customers are seeking now is customization—products made to order. Customers that customize a product are more likely to be brand advocates and repeat purchasers, completing the loyalty loop.

Personalization vs. Customization

Personalization and customization are so similar that the two terms are often confused with each other. Therefore, it is necessary to distinguish them (Table 6-1).

Table 6-1　Personalization *vs.* Customization①

Attributes	Personalization	Customization
Initiator	system-initiated	user-initiated
How to?	Automatic personalization systems gather user browsing behavior data by two ways—overt & covert; Directly asking users for their personal information covertly "observing" user behavior by placing cookies in browsers	Features a number of affordances that allow users to make changes to the form and content of the interfaces.
Examples	Automatic changes of web pages to accommodate advertisements based on individual user's need	Different skins of input method

Section 2
LightInTheBox—Personalized Wedding Gown Services from China
第二节　兰亭集势——来自中国的定制婚纱服务

Key Words

1. apparel *n.* 服装
2. gadget *n.* 小配件
3. outwardly *adv.* 向外地
4. crank *n.* 曲柄
5. pop *vi.* 突然出现
6. lid *n.* 盖子
7. stock-up *n.* 备货
8. homogeny *n.* 同质

---

① Sundar S S, Marathe S S. Personalization versus customization: The importance of agency, privacy, and power usage, *Human Communication Research*, 2010, 36(3): pp. 298-322.

Case

Background

LightInTheBox is a global e-tailer that delivers products directly to consumers around the world by virtue of B2C model. The business model of LightInTheBox was inspired by *The World Is Flat*, a book by Thomas Friedman. With the realization that e-commerce lent itself well to the theories in the book, the founders of LightInTheBox decided to build a company that would take advantage of China's manufacturing and supply chain. In 2007, LightInTheBox was founded by Guo Quji, the former CSO of Google in China, and his partners. Initially, LightInTheBox focused on B2B small trade. Since its online wedding gown retailing began in 2009, LightInTheBox has offered customers a convenient way to shop for a wide selection of lifestyle products at attractive prices. LightInTheBox offers products in the three core categories of apparel, small accessories and gadgets, and home and garden.

The name of LightInTheBox originated from a popular toy in Western countries—jack-in-the-box which is a children's toy that outwardly consists of a box with a crank. When the crank is turned, it plays a melody, often "Pop Goes the Weasel". At the end of the tune there is a "surprise", the lid pops open and a figure, usually a clown or jester, pops out of the box. Since LightInTheBox concentrates on the consumers in Western countries, naming the website after a well-known toy is a good choice. It enables the consumers to remember the name easily.

As of March 31, 2013, LightInTheBox had more than 220,000 product listings, and added an average of 14,000 products each month in the preceding three months. Net revenues in the second quarter of 2013 were \$72.2 million, an increase of 52.6% from \$47.3 million in the same quarter of 2012. On June 6, 2013, LightInTheBox opened for trading on New York Stock Exchange[①].

LightInTheBox integrates the resources from the excellent enterprises to support its personalized products and services: it uses global online marketing platforms such as Google and Facebook to reach consumers, accepts payments through major credit cards and electronic payment platforms such as PayPal, and delivers goods via major international couriers, including UPS, DHL and FedEx. During almost ten years since its foundation, LightInTheBox has established its brand strength successfully and attracted numerous customers overseas. In 2015, it ranked No. 1 in "Top 20 Chinese Online Shopping Websites in English"[②].

---

① https://en.wikipedia.org/wiki/LightInTheBox
② Top 20 Chinese Online Shopping Websites in English, http://www.shops-in-china.com

Personalized Services of LightInTheBox

1. The tailored products. LightInTheBox enables the customers to order the tailored products. The personalized products can be delivered to them after some time, which satisfies each individual consumer's personal demands. Wedding gown consumption, for example, is huge in the U. S.. Each bride desires a unique as well as fantastic wedding gown. However, most of them can not afford the expensive personalized wedding gowns designed by those famous designers such as Vera Wang. The wedding gowns sold by the boutique are usually designed with universal sizes and styles which can not distinguish a girl from the peers. Moreover, they are not cheap. LightInTheBox seizes the wonderful opportunity. It accepts the online orders for wedding gowns and finds the medium and small suppliers in China to produce. After 2-4 weeks, the tailored wedding gowns based on the customers' individual demands are delivered to them.

2. The pick-up service for order returns in the U. S.. If there are some quality problems with the products, what should I do? Do not worry about it, you can get the free pick-up service for returns specified to the orders over a specific price. LightInTheBox customer service has a new UPS pick-up parcel service for customers in the United States who have orders valued over $50 which need to be returned for quality related reasons.

3. Shopping in multi-language. LightInTheBox now supports 23 languages, giving customers in different countries a better shopping experience. The multi-language supporting website is able to aid the customers from different countries to complete the online shopping easily. Furthermore, in 2016, LightInTheBox launched its App which allows a consumer to tap into the amazing line of products to purchase items on the website in 19 languages.

4. LightInTheBox Wedding Planner App. LightInTheBox released a personalized new app called "InTime". This is a multi-user collaborative wedding planning aid that allows customers to easily pool wedding ideas and plans with their friends and family (Figure 6-1).

Figure 6-1　The InTime Wedding Planning App[①]

---

① https://en.wikipedia.org/wiki/LightInTheBox

The personalized strategies make an effect: LightInTheBox rates 5/5 stars by almost 8,000 consumers according to resellerratings.com. Its personalized products and services enable it to win the customers. "I love to shop at LightInTheBox to be a serious company and that honors its commitments. Always put the products I buy in a sturdy container and conserves very well my products. Prices are very attractive and the selection is quite large.... On a whole, I like the company and like to do business with her. I want to do more shopping there,"① a customer said in the review. In 2016, LightInTheBox reported 10% year-to-year sales growth on Black Friday②.

SWOT Analysis of LightInTheBox's Personalization Services

Implementing personalization is not easy for most retailers. Satisfying each individual customer's need means the rising costs, the innovative managerial model and the solid technical base. A complete SWOT analysis can assist us to understand the strengths, weaknesses, opportunities and threats encountered by LightInTheBox, the successful wedding gown e-tailer, during the process of personalization.

Strengths

1. B2C model benefits personalization. Compared to C2C or B2B model, B2C model enables LightInTheBox to face the end consumers directly and capture their need more accurately and efficiently. In addition, B2C model helps LightInTheBox to supervise the quality of products and services effectively. For example, LightInTheBox usually receives customers' suggestions or requirements on wedding gowns through the network and instantly adjusts the designing based on his or her need.

2. Data analysis aids LightInTheBox to understand consumers' demands accurately, building the solid base of personalization. The online transactions generate lots of data related to consumers' habits and preferences. For example, consumers in South America prefer watching TV over mobile phone. These data are collected and analyzed. As a result, LightInTheBox applies the useful information extracted from big data to personalization.

3. Internet-based media assists the sales growth of LightInTheBox personalized products and services. As the former co-founder of Google China, Guo Quji effectively takes advantage of Google's excellent search engine advertising services—Adwords. By virtue of keyword search, the brand of LightInTheBox reaches numerous consumers

---

① http://tbdress-reviews.blogspot.com/2016/04/?m=0, April 2016.
② LightInTheBox Holding Co., Ltd., LightInTheBox Reports 10% YoY Sales Growth on Black Friday, https://www.prnewswire.com/news-releases/lightinthebox-reports-10-yoy-sales-growth-on-black-friday-300370426.html, Nov 30, 2016.

rapidly. As of middle 2013, LightInTheBox delivered several million keywords in 17 different languages at Google. In March 2013, the clicks from Google accounted for 45% of the total visits of LightInTheBox. Besides, LightInTheBox utilizes social networks such as Facebook to make the effective propagation. According to Hitwise, Facebook contributes 3% clicks to LightInTheBox. The third way by which LightInTheBox implements its marketing strategy is alliance distribution. LightInTheBox supplies ads content and tools which attracts consumers to its partners such as eBay. As long as a user makes website visits and purchases on LightInTheBox through a partner's website, LightInTheBox will pay commission. This method contributes 5.51% clicks (Figure 6-2).

www.lightinthebox.com北美地区流量来源			
Upstream	Websites	Domain	Clicks March 2013
1	Google	www.google.com	45.58%
2	Facebook	www.facebook.com	3.06%
3	eBay	www.ebay.com	2.97%
4	Yahoo! Search	search.yahoo.com	2.61%
5	Bing	www.bing.com	2.24%
6	Ask	www.ask.com	2.16%
7	Yahoo! Mail	mail.yahoo.com	2.01%
8	Amazon.com	www.amazon.com	1.75%
9	YouTube	www.youtube.com	1.02%
10	Shopzilla	www.shopzilla.com	0.79%
			数据来源：Hitwise

Figure 6-2 The Flow Source of LightInTheBox in North America①

4. Structuring the innovative supply chain model. For a retailer, managing its upstream supply chain is critical. How to balance cost and efficiency of supply chain? LightInTheBox adopts the innovative solutions:

1) Purchasing from the manufacturers directly, cutting off the intermediaries. Personalized services may lead to the rising operation cost. To control the cost, LightInTheBox purchases 70% of its commodities directly from the manufacturers instead of wholesalers, decreasing the procurement cost (Figure 6-3).

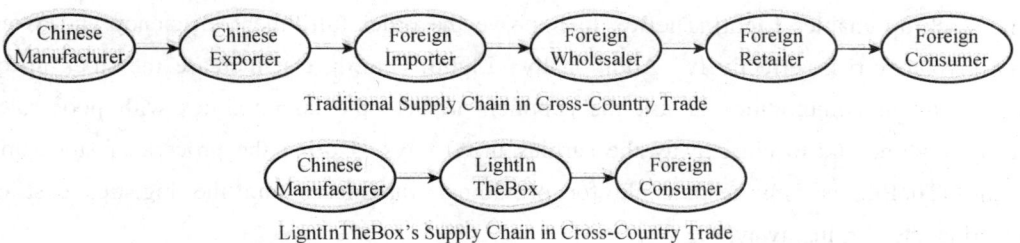

Figure 6-3 Traditional Supply Chain vs. LightInTheBox's Supply Chain

2) Selecting the excellent suppliers and signing at least one-year contract. Usually, large enterprises are unwilling to undertake personalized orders since they will decrease economy of scale. The small and medium enterprises are interested in the orders but their products are probably unqualified due to the limited resources or managerial problems. After the careful investigation, LightInTheBox chose the candidates who have small scale and the excellent ability of learning and signed at least one-year contracts with them. As a result, the

① 李妍,兰亭集势商业模式篇(二):营销费用为何这么高? http://xueqiu.com/8689584849/23673111, 2013.

stable supply and product quality can be ensured. Actually, the chosen suppliers perform well in both quality and efficiency: the cycle from product design to consumption drops from 18 months in a traditional firm to 3 months in LightInTheBox; and the procurement minimum declines from 100,000 for the general firms to 3,000 for LightInTheBox.

3) Participating in the production process which ensures the high quality of products. Retailers barely take part in the production process. LightInTheBox does this because its personalization focuses primarily on wedding gowns which provided by the small and medium sized suppliers in Suzhou, China. Limited to the suppliers' management and manufacturing capabilities, there exist risks of product quality. To assist the suppliers to improve quality and efficiency, LightInTheBox establishes an internal experts team who is involved in the production process and in charge of quality and efficiency improvement.

4) Made-to-order model enables the production based on an individual consumer's need. After receiving the online orders, LightInTheBox instantly informs the suppliers to produce based on the customer's need. Due to the good collaboration between LightInTheBox and its suppliers, most orders can be fulfilled within 10 or 14 days and delivered to the warehouse. For the products with the standard specifications, the order fulfillment can be completed within 48 hours.

5) Stock-up increases the efficiency of order-fulfillment and decreases the risks. Since the forth quarter 2011, LightInTheBox has required part of its suppliers to stock up on particular commodity in case of unexpected orders. The stock-up is placed in the warehouses of LightInTheBox while not being counted in stock. Only after they are orderd by customers, can it be counted in the revenues and cost of LightInTheBox. Obviously, the stock-up enables LightInTheBox to improve the order fulfillment efficiency and avoid the inventory risks effectively. Additionally, LightInTheBox can increase the stock-up of the well-sold commodities or ask the suppliers to take the commodities with poor sales away anytime and to clear away the surplus in 90 days. During the process of stock-up, LightInTheBox is only responsible for providing warehouses and the logistics cost of clearing the surplus away.

> **译** 备货机制提高了订单执行效率，降低了风险。兰亭集势和供应商的合作关系在2011年第四季度发生了独特的变化，从那时起，兰亭开始要求部分供应商提前备货，备货需存放至兰亭自己的仓库，而且这部分备货不计入兰亭集势的库存，只有当用户下单后，这部分资产的所有权才转至兰亭集势，计入兰亭集势的营收和成本。很明显，通过供应商"提前备货"，兰亭集势提高了订单处理的效率，同时有效避免了库存风险。不仅如此，兰亭集势还可以根据商品受欢迎程度，要求供应商加大特定商品的备货，或是随时要求供应商将销量不佳的商品库存拿走，以及在90天内将商品剩余库存拿走。整个备货过程中，兰亭集势只负责提供仓库空间以及支付供应商将剩余库存运走时的物流开支①。

---

① 李妍，兰亭集势商业模式篇（一）：独特的供应链管理，http://xueqiu.com/8689584849/23673111, 2013.

6) Experts who know well the markets both in China and America. For example, Guo Quji, CEO of LightInTheBox, has the wonderful experience in the Internet field. His work experience in Google, Amazon and Microsoft enables him to know the market, managerial models and customers of B2C e-commerce. Wen Xin, the co-founder, has the work experience in Bokee.com and Blogdrive.com. As the leaders who grew up in China and have the work experience in USA, the founders of LightInTheBox have the capability of understanding the markets, customers and suppliers in China and America well. As a result, they can seize the opportunities and make the correct decisions.

7) Financial supports. Just when LightInTheBox was founded, it gained the venture financing from the famous investors such as Xu Xiaoping, the co-founder of New-Oriental in China. The financial supports not only enables the entrepreneur capital but also shows the investors' confidence for the future of LightInTheBox.

5. New revenue stream can support LightInTheBox's personalization. Personalization strategy is effective as well costly. Fortunately, LightInTheBox turns selling technology into additional revenue streams, which can support its personalization expenses. In November 2016, LightInTheBox announced to provide an e-commerce technology it developed in house to other merchants. LightInTheBox had used the system over the past eight years before that. The ERP system is designed for online and offline distribution companies, including retail and wholesale businesses, and it handles order, procurement, product category, supplier and inventory management. It is designed for small and large distribution companies that handle millions of orders per year and manage thousands of suppliers. By virtue of open-source software, the ERP system can be deployed on several major cloud platforms like Amazon Web Services (AWS)[①].

Weaknesses

1. Possible problems with product quality and partnership may affect the online sales negatively. LightInTheBox is a retailer rather than a manufacturer. Even though it adopts a managerial system to supervise the products quality, it is unavoidable that the products with quality problems influence customers' trust on the website.

2. Intellectual property problems. Due to the limited investment, personnel and technologies, part of wedding gown suppliers in Suzhou copied the existing design, which led to the intellectual property claims. This problem probably affects LightInTheBox's reputation unless it is solved well.

3. Product homogeny. This problem usually occurs to the retailing industry since it is

---

① Katie Evans, LightInTheBox will sell its enterprise resource planning system to other merchants, Internetretailer.com, 2016-11-14.

hard to differentiate the consumption commodities. How to differentiate its products from those of competitors is a big challenge encountered by LightInTheBox.

4. High expenses of marketing vs. low customer stickiness. According to the financial report of LightInTheBox, the ratio of marketing cost to net revenue from 2010 to 2012 was respectively 38.5%, 33.1% and 26.7% (Table 6-2). Though the ratio had been dropping, it was still very high compared to the B2C peers such as Amazon (3.9%) and vip.com (4.7%)①. On the other hand, compared to its peers, LightInTheBox's customer stickiness is still low. The causes lie in two aspects: 1) its customers are price sensitive, which may cause the "customer transferring" due to the lower prices; 2) wedding gown is a special commodity whose repeated consumption frequency is low.

Table 6-2 LightInTheBox's Marketing Expenses—Net Revenues Ratio②

	2010	% of Net Turnover	2011	% of Net Turnover	2012	% of Net Turnover
Marketing Plan	18,747	31.90	28,611	24.60	43,955	22
Marketing Personnel	3,860	6.60	9,854	8.50	9,463	4.70
Totals	22,607	38.50	38,465	33.10	53,418	26.70

Opportunities

1. Growth of netizens enables the rising sales online. According to Internet World Stats, Internet users in the world had reached 4.2 billion, with the penetration rate of 54.4%, by December 2017③. The rising number of netizens provides lots of potential clients for e-tailing.

2. Popularity of mobile network makes the personalization easier. By December 2017, two-thirds of the world's 7.6 billion inhabitants had owned a mobile phone④. Mobile phone especially smart phone allows people to gain access to the Internet easier and take advantage of the Apps to enjoy personalized products or services.

3. Economy slow-down in western countries forces consumers to find low-price products. Only one year after LightInTheBox's foundation, financial crisis broke out which led to the economy depression in Western countries. As a result, consumers prefer the lower price commodities. Wedding gowns, for example, are usually priced higher than ordinary commodities. High price plus lowered incomes forces Western consumers to look

---

① 李妍,兰亭集势商业模式篇(二):营销费用为何这么高? http://xueqiu.com/8689584849/23673111, 2013.
② 埃弗瑞姆·特伯恩(Efraim Turban),戴维·金(David King)著,王健改编,《电子商务导论》,中国人民大学出版社,2006年。
③④ https://www.internetworldstats.com/stats.htm.

for the wedding gowns with the superior cost performance, which is a good opportunity for LightInTheBox.

4. Rapid development of the Internet technology makes personalization possible. There are two prerequisites for personalization implementation: one is the fast information transmission which enables the efficient communication between sellers and buyers; the other is the sufficient products storage and circulation channel which make the massive personalization possible. LightInTheBox, by virtue of the Internet technology and B2C business model, allows consumers to gain the personalized products and services.

Threats

1. The profit margin of LightInTheBox is decreasing due to the rising salary and inflation in China. In the past few years, Chinese workforce cost has been increasing. This plus inflation, will lead to the rising operation cost of LightInTheBox.

2. LightInTheBox's revenue will be influenced significantly once the policy and economy of Western countries change since its businesses depend too much on these countries.

3. The strong competitors. Witnessing LightInTheBox's success, more competitors have enter the market. These new comers such as milanoo.com and osell.com perform well in capital, personnel and logistics. They will become the significant threats for LightInTheBox.

Suggestions for LightInTheBox

1. Strengthen intellectual property management. As mentioned above, intellectual property probably becomes an obstacle for LightInTheBox's development. Wedding gown is a kind of commodity involving copyright. Chinese suppliers lack the legal awareness due to educational background and the immature legal system in China, which can explain why they copy the existing design at little expense. LightInTheBox has to pay much attention to the problem because it is a wedding gown e-tailer focusing the oversea market.

2. Optimize supply chain management so as to keep its strengths with low price. LightInTheBox has benefited from its efficient supply chain management. To keep its strength, LightInTheBox should optimize the supply chain management further. For example, decreasing the marketing expenses percentage.

3. Expand its markets to the regions except for Western countries. Since its foundation, LightInTheBox has been concentrating on Western markets. However, with the new competitors' entry and the market's changes, it will be harder for LightInTheBox to keep the high profit margin. Therefore, it is necessary for LightInTheBox to explore new markets and deliver its beautiful personalized wedding gowns to more consumers in different countries.

Case Analysis

对于本案例,我们的分析重点应该放在兰亭集势如何实现婚纱的定制服务及其实现这种服务所具备的条件。前者侧重该企业的个性化产品和服务策略,后者则侧重于 SWOT 分析。

个性化策略的有效性已经被无数案例所证明,如何实施这些策略才是管理者关注的焦点。兰亭集势的做法可以给我们提供启示:个性化策略应该贯穿产品的整个生命周期——从产品设计到销售。兰亭集势从成立之日起就注定与一般的品牌商不同,它根据个体消费者的需求为其量身打造所需的婚纱及周边产品。兰亭集势在其官网上提供款型式样繁多的婚纱供消费选择,消费者根据自己的喜好选择心仪的产品并下单,这看起来似乎与一般的网上购物没有区别。然而,就是在下单这一步,消费者可以留下身高、体重、肤色等个人信息,并提出对布料选择、版型、配饰等的个性化要求。订单被传送至后台,远在中国苏州的婚纱生产工厂按照顾客的要求为其量身打造个性化的婚纱,并在 2—4 周内将其交到消费者手中。消费者提出设计要求,工厂据此组织生产,就这样,兰亭集势分别在产品设计和生产阶段实现了个性化。在产品配送阶段,兰亭集势仍然不忘个性化,它根据各地顾客不同的消费习惯推出个性化的配送服务。例如,在成立之初就针对西方国家的消费者推出了免费退货服务:如果消费者对产品质量有任何不满,可以享受免费上门收件的退货服务。除此之外,兰亭集势还设计了多语种的官方网站和 App 来满足不同消费者的需求。正因为它的个性化策略覆盖了所有的产品和服务,兰亭集势才能吸引来自全球各地的众多客户。

个性化策略要想有效,需要高投入。企业是否具备实施该策略的资源?实施过程中可能面临的风险是什么?通过对兰亭集势实施个性化策略的 SWOT 分析,我们可以归纳出企业实现产品和服务个性化的必要条件:首先,企业需要选择一种有利于实施个性化策略的商业模式。兰亭集势的 B2C 模式不仅使它能直接与消费者互动,从而捕捉其需求,而且能有效监管产品和服务的质量。其次,企业需要获得客户数据来精准捕捉消费者需求,这是实施个性化策略的另一个先决条件。每天在兰亭集势的官网和 App 上注册、浏览和购物的客户留下了大量的数据,这些数据成为企业精确分析每个消费者的偏好、购物习惯的宝贵资源。正是借助有效的数据分析,兰亭集势得以精准捕捉消费者的需求,并为其量身打造产品和服务。再次,企业需要选择合适的渠道进行个性化产品和服务的宣传推广。例如,借助谷歌的关键词搜索和与 eBay 建立的分销联盟,兰亭集势将其产品和服务的信息迅速推送给客户。最后,也是非常关键的一项条件——创新。让客户参与产品设计和产品服务定制化等创新不仅帮助兰亭集势成功地在供应链管理的成本和效率之间实现平衡,而且令个性化得以实现。那么,一家企业如果拥有上述 4 项条件,是否就一定能实施个性化策略呢?答案是不一定。因为企业本身的劣势及其面临的威胁必须纳入考量。例如,兰亭集势一直为人所诟病的知识产权问题以及低客户黏性的问题都有可能削弱其个性化策略的实施效果。除此之外,对于高度依赖西方发达国家市场的兰亭集势来说,当地宏观政策的变化、政治环境的改变以及法律法规的出台都可能影响其策略实施的效果。

Section 3
Mogujie—Personalization Based on Online Community
第三节 蘑菇街——基于网上社区的个性化

Key Words

1. collocation *n.* 搭配
2. eponymous *adj.* 齐名的
3. fragment *n.* 碎片
4. re-organize *vt.* 再组织

Case

Background

Founded in 2011, Mogujie, which means "Mushroom Street" in English, is a shopping guide website that combines online shopping and online socialization. Mogujie focuses on women's fashion and aim to provide all the female consumers better purchase decision. Chen Qi, its founder, used to be the founder of Taobao UED (User Experience Design) and in charge of Taobao's new business exploration such as logistics. In 2010, Chen Qi founded Juandou.com, a community e-commerce services platform, after quitting the job in Taobao. Juandou.com profits through recommending the Taobao's hyperlinks on the online community websites. As long as a consumer clicks the hyperlinks on a community website and makes the transaction, Juandou.com can get commission from the sales. However, Chen Qi found that transation conversion rate on the online community websites was low and decided to found a new online community combining shopping and socialization, that is, Mogujie.

Only one year after its foundation, Mogujie owned 6 million registered users, 1.6 million daily active users and more than 70 million Page View (PV). At the end of 2013, it reported monthly sales of over 300 million yuan ($48 million), with more than 60% from App①. By 2014, Mogujie had owned 130 million users, with 8 million daily active users. In 2014 the annual turnover was $560 million, and the company had more than 1,000 employees and the post money valuation of Mogujie was more than $1 billion②.

Rather than other online vendors, Mogujie does not neither sell products itself nor has inventory, it builds a socialization platform where registered users can create a photo

---

① Sramana Mitra, Billion Dollar Unicorns: Mogujie's E-Commerce Pivot Pays Off, https://www.linkedin.com/pulse/billion-dollar-unicorns-mogujies-e-commerce-pivot-pays-sramana-mitra, November 11, 2015
② https://en.wikipedia.org/wiki/Mogujie

collage, post and comment on favorite shoes, apparel, and accessories. The platform allows users to communicate and make profit by directing to some e-commerce vendors such as Taobao and JD. com. Mogujie's business model seems similar to Pinterest, an eponymous photo sharing website. However, Pinterest focuses on the photo display rather than the conversion from photos to online transactions like Mogujie.

Mogujie targets the female consumers from 20 to 30 years old. The online shopping process on Mogujie includes 4 stages: finding, comparing, buying and sharing. A customer can search the products with key words. When there is more than one result matching the key words, the customer can gain the advices and comments from the peers in the community and makes the purchase decision. Each customer is encouraged to provide the recommendation for shopping and the feedback for a specific product. Besides, she can also share the experiences of make-up, clothing and appearance designing.

Why Does Mogujie Adopt Personalization?

E-commerce enables consumers to search useful information of shopping quickly, but also it makes the decision-making harder due to too much information. Generally speaking, peers' experience or suggestions play an important role during the process of purchase decision-making for female consumers. Mogujie provides such a platform which supplies guidance for consumers' purchase behavior and a free space where helpful information on shopping can be shared.

Compared to the standardized products or services, personalization usually costs more since it aims at each individual customer's demands. External and internal forces enable Mogujie's personalization:

1. Business model. Mogujie does not provide products for end customers directly. Instead, it plays the role of "shopping guide" and "social sharing platform" that offers information such as products, prices and services so as to assist consumers to make the optimal decision. It effectively solves the problems that consumers fail to know their real need when there are too many choices online.

2. Technical base. Personalization means a firm captures customers' need based on historical data and tailors products and services for consumers. It requires understanding an individual consumer's need and reacting fast. By virtue of the Internet and data processing technologies, Mogujie is able to capture each customer's needs through the online behavior data and give the most suitable recommendation based on data analysis.

How Does Mogujie Realize Personalization?

Personalization refers to tailoring products or services based on an individual customer's need. As a shopping as well as socialization website, Mogujie recommends the most appropriate commodities for each individual customer by virtue of online community. Mogujie realizes personalization by three methods:

The first one is helping customers to make a choice. When there are many options online, it is time consuming and difficult for a consumer to make the final decision. By virtue of online community, Mogujie aids her to decide:

1. What to buy? —A customer can use the experience of shopping or dress collocation from other community members for reference. For example, you can search Mogujie to find your favorite coat collocation (Figure 6-4).

Figure 6-4 Coat Collocation on Mogujie[①]

2. Where to buy it? —The customer is directed to a specific website (e.g. Taobao) to make the purchase. For example, by clicking the picture, you will be directed to the website (here is Taobao) which provides the light-blue sweater of the collocation above and you can get detailed information of the product (Figure 6-5).

3. How to Share your experience? —A customer is encouraged to share experience by providing the recommendation for shopping and the feedback for a specific product. The experience sharing enables you to gain extra credits.

The second one is the "FOR Model". The "FOR" is the abbreviation of three words: Fragmenting, Organizing and Re-organizing[②]. It refers to Mogujie's model helping to judge consumers' behavior:

1. Fragmenting. The product content provided by Mogujie is fragmented, That is, the

---

① act.mogujie.com
② 王晓东:"蘑菇街:帮助选择",《商学院》,2012(5):pp.36-37.

Figure 5-5 Detailed Information of Clothes[①]

website pushes the short and accurate information to each customer to aid her shopping behavior. Particularly, in the mobile internet era, people are inclined to read the information over mobile phone. Due to the screen size and limited time, fragmented information usually attracts attention more effectively. For example, a posted Sina micro blog is composed of one picture and a paragraph with no more than 140 characters.

> 译 碎片化。蘑菇街提供的产品内容是碎片化的,即网站通过简短而精确的内容推送帮助用户做出购买决策。在移动互联时代,人们更倾向于在手机上阅读信息,由于手机屏幕和阅读时间的限制,碎片化的信息通常更能有效吸引人们的注意力。例如,新浪微博的内容就是被碎片化为一张图片加上140字的简单描述。

2. Organizing. Fragmenting is not enough. Only when the fragmented information is organized, can it be valuable. For example, the information on Twitter is organized based on chronologically; the information on Pinterest is organized based on board. Mogujie organizes the fragmented information based on the pattern and content.

3. Re-organizing. The organized fragment on the website can be re-organized by users based on different purposes. That is, users are allowed to process the fragment such as restructuring. Forwarding the message to Sina micro blog is a typical example of re-organizing.

Based on the FOR model, Mogujie decides its advertisement referral. All the beautiful

---

[①] Figure 6-4 and Figure 6-5 are both from Mogujie.com

female products are "FORed" into: A picture +A text +A link.

The third way is leveraging opinion leaders. There are a group of special users who, called as "DaRen" in Chinese, are the opinion leaders of Mogujie community. They are the active users leading the fashion of the community and inspiring other users to shop online. They are very poplar in the community and play an important role during the process of users' online purchasing. Therefore, Mogujie always does its best to recommend these opinion leaders. Mogujie not only recommends DaRen to the new users but also displays their information on top of its official micro blog. Besides, Mogujie segments DaRen into sub-groups targeting different customers. For example, a make up DaRen is attractive for a user planning to buy some makeup. By August 2013, there had been 1,500 DaRens on Mogujie who recommended 2.1 million products, displayed 2.4 million pictures and owned 3 million fans. Opinion leader system enables All-Win: DaRens gain the sense of success by showing, sharing and participating; users gain helpful referrals for shopping; Mogujie boosts revenues by personalized recommendation.

The Effects of Mogujie's Personalization Strategy

Everything has two sides. How does Mogujie's personalization strategy affect its operation?

1. Positive impacts

1) Mogujie has become a popular online shopping website which owns 2.2 million unique visitors (UV), 100 million page view (PV) and more than 80 employees[1];

2) Mogujie has successfully built the brand of "community e-commerce" in China;

3) Mogujie's personalized services promote the sales growth of its partners such as Taobao.

2. Negative impacts

1) The rate of valid information is not high enough. 78% of product information is filtered due to the embedded advertisements;

2) The sales conversion rate of 8% is not high enough;

3) Depends too much on Taobao. Currently, Taobao is still the primary profit source of Mogujie. According to the statistics, 40% of Mogujie's customers flow to Taobao. Depending too much on a single website is probably risky for Mogujie.

Where Is Mogujie Going?

As venture capitalists and other investors become more cautious about putting high price tags on companies that are burning through cash to compete with rivals, startups in

---

[1] 张楠、可心、刘长乐:"美丽说和蘑菇街准能笑到最后",《中国市场》,2012(21):pp.46-47.

China are under pressure to consider teaming up with rivals.

In January 2016, Mogujie agreed to take over its competitor Meilishuo.com, which is backed by social network giant Tencent, to form a new company valued at roughly $3 billion. Mogujie's co-founder and Chief Executive—Chen Qi would manage the new company, which combined sales of 20 billion yuan ($3.05 billion) in 2015, according to the announcement. The acquisition was expected to be a "win-win" strategy since it helped to avoid competition and save lots of costs. And the new company aims to provide differentiated services and focus on its long-term goal instead of short-term rivalry[①].

Case Analysis

与前面的案例企业相比,蘑菇街的知名度显然没有这么大,但我们仍然选择它进行分析是因为它独特的商业模式和由此带来的个性化服务。

蘑菇街采取的是"社交+购物"的商业模式,这种商业模式的独特之处在于:第一,它的盈利模式与众不同。它扮演的是"导购网站"的角色,即并不向消费者出售商品,而是基于消费者需求,向其推荐适合的商品,并在交易成功以后从中获取佣金。除此之外,它也通过为商家提供网络广告服务来获取收入。第二,它的市场定位清晰明确。蘑菇街自诞生之日起就将自身定位为:针对年轻女性消费者的社交购物网站。在这家网站上,用户不仅能自由选择和购买自己心仪的商品,还能通过上传图片和文字分享自己日常化妆、穿搭等方面的心得,并由此积累极高的网上人气。众所周知,购物、美妆是女性感兴趣的话题,在网上讨论这些热门话题,分享自己的独到经验,不仅满足了用户希望分享和被关注的需求,而且也为有购物需求的消费者提供了决策支持。正是因为蘑菇街敏锐地捕捉到了女性消费者的需求,并据此明确了自身的市场定位,才能自成立以来实现快速增长。

如果说兰亭集势主要是在产品设计和生产环节实现个性化,那么蘑菇街则是在内容服务上实现个性化,并采取了三种措施:首先,创造了内容推荐的FOR模式,即碎片化、组织和再组织。蘑菇街认为,社交平台高效简短的内容分享特征决定了它上面的产品内容一定是碎片化的。比如微博上的"一切事物"被碎片化为140字的简单描述。碎片的丰富性也决定了这个产品最终平台化之后的基础规模。这些碎片看似不同,在形式上却是同构的,而同构的碎片很容易被以各种维度组织起来,形成完整的内容。如:有些社交平台上按标签(Tag)来组织碎片。这种组织一定是非常自由的,任何两块碎片,都有可能被组织到一起,这也为内容分享提供了更加多样化的形式和更加丰富的内容。当产品的信息碎片按某种形式组织好之后,社交平台的"转发"和"评论"功能还能允许用户用非常自由的手段重新组织信息碎片,将别人的信息碎片重组到自己的时

---

① Yue Wang, Chinese Fashion Site Mogujie Acquires Meilishuo In $3 Billion Deal, https://www.forbes.com/sites/ywang/2016/01/10/chinese-fashion-site-mogujie-acquires-meilishuo-in-3-billion-deal/#79e61733457d, Jan 10, 2016.

间线中①,尽可能充分地重复利用有限的内容,以此提升信息传播的效率和效果。也是基于该模式,蘑菇街把"所有美好的女性商品"碎片为一张图和一小段描述,不仅将信息高效地推送给用户,还因为简洁的内容适合手机浏览而广受青睐。其次,蘑菇街通过网站和App终端为用户提供商品浏览和搜索功能,帮助消费者快速进行购买决策:买什么?在哪里买?是否有人提供相应的经验分享?最后,蘑菇街借鉴了大多数社交平台的做法——利用"意见领袖"的影响力进行营销。这些被称为"达人"的意见领袖,在分享自己的美妆、服饰搭配心得的同时也"润物细无声"地推销了相关产品,而用户之间的每一次分享、转发和评论都在彰显蘑菇街这家社交购物平台的影响力。

Section 4
NIKEiD—Customized Services
第四节　NIKEiD——定制化服务

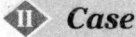 **Key Words**

1. athletic *adj.* 运动的
2. fluctuation *n.* 波动
3. satirical *adj.* 讽刺的
4. fruition *n.* 完成
5. cleat *n.* 鞋楔子
6. dilution *n.* 冲淡,稀释

Case

Background

Founded in 1964, Nike, Inc. is an American multinational corporation that is engaged in the design, development, manufacturing and worldwide marketing and sales of footwear, apparel, equipment, accessories and services. It is one of the world's largest suppliers of athletic shoes and apparel and a major manufacturer of sports equipment. Nike sponsors many high-profile athletes and sports teams around the world, with the highly recognized trademarks of "Just Do It" and the Swoosh logo.

In 2014, Nike's global revenue amounted to about $27.8 billion. From 2005 to 2015, Nike's revenue worldwide kept a stable growth though there was a little fluctuation

---

① 王晓东:"蘑菇街:帮助选择",《商学院》,2012(5):pp.36-37.

around 2008 due to the financial crisis (Figure 6-6)①.

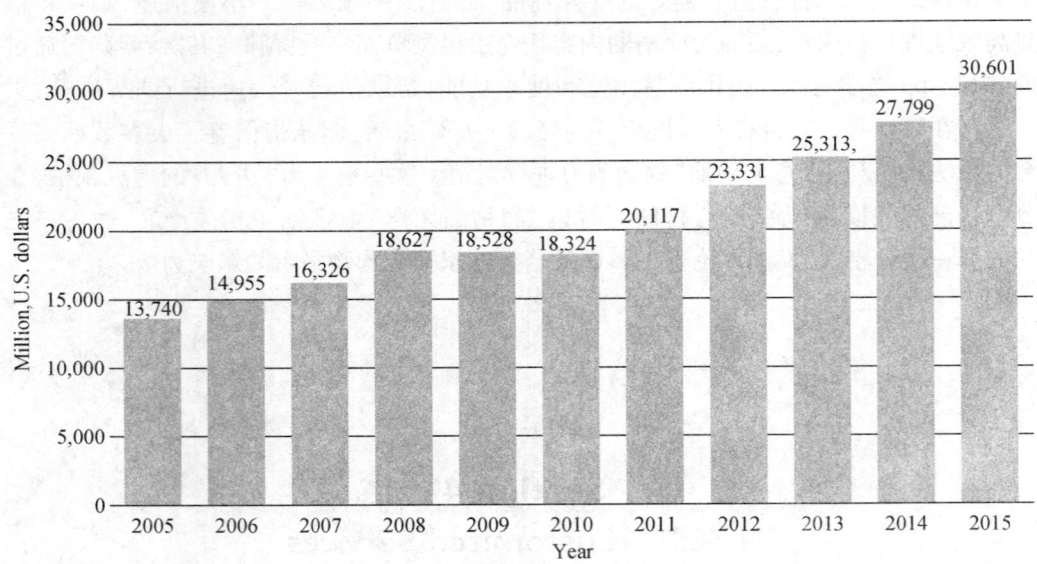

Figure 6-6   Nike's Revenue Worldwide from 2005 to 2015②

Nike's Marketing Strategies③

Nike promotes its products mainly by three methods: advertising, sponsorship and customization.

1. Advertising

In 1982, Nike aired its first national television ads during the broadcast of the New York Marathon. Since then, Nike has launched a series of wonderful commercials such as FuelBand Presents which wins Advertiser of The Year of The Cannes Advertising Festival 2012. Before that, it had received that honor twice respectively in 1994 and 2003.

Nike also has earned the Emmy Award for Best Commercial twice since the award was first created in the 1990s. The first was for "The Morning After", a satirical look at what a runner might face on the morning of January 1, 2000 if every dire prediction about the Y2K problem came to fruition. The second was for a 2002 spot called "Move", which featured a series of famous and everyday athletes in a variety of athletic pursuits.

The wonderful commercials contribute much to Nike's sales growth.

2. Sponsorship

Signing sponsorship agreements with celebrity athletes, professional teams and college athletic teams has been an important marketing strategy of Nike.

---

①② www. statista. com/statistics
③ https://en. wikipedia. org/wiki/Nike,_Inc. #Causes

Nike pays top athletes in many sports to use their products and promote and advertise their technology and design. Nike's first professional athlete endorser was Romanian tennis player Ilie Năstase. In June 2015, Nike signed an eight-year deal with the NBA to become the official apparel supplier for the league, beginning with the 2017 – 2018 season. The brand takes over for Adidas, which has provided the uniforms and apparel for the league since 2006.

Besides, Nike also participates in the charity activities which help it to build a good public image. In 2012, Nike was listed as a partner of the RED campaign, together with other brands such as Girl, American Express and Converse. The campaign's mission is to prevent the transmission of the HIV virus from mother to child by 2015.

The sponsorship not only improves Nike's brand awareness but also helps Nike to build its positive brand image.

3. Customization[1]

As an early adopter of Internet marketing, email management technologies, and using broadcast and narrowcast communication technologies to create multimedia marketing campaigns, Nike has been finding the ways to impress customers and shareholders by introducing new marketing strategies to increase its sales. It adopts customization to achieve the goals.

How Does Nike Implement Customization?

In 1999, Nike launched NIKEiD—a strategy that allows customers to create their own gear by a digital customization platform.

NIKEiD is a service that allows a consumer to customize the shoes exactly how he or she wants them. The customer is allowed to add the personal touch, design from scratch, or maximize the performance. As what Nike said, "Unleash your creativity, and discover Nike's most personal service." Joining in NIKEiD, the customer can put his or her own touch on the classic by dressing it up in the choice of nylon, original suede, mesh, leather, fleece and more new materials; the customer can also customize the tongue, which is something that's not too common on NIKEiD; the customer can either go with the traditional sewn or vintage open construction, which means it's not sewn shut around the edges so he or she sees the soft foam interior; last but not least the customer can select his or her own midsole[2]. All the customized shoes are delivered to the customer in 4–5 weeks and the delivery is free. Customers have to pay $170 for the option. The new service fits

---

[1] Erik Eliason, 3 Reasons Why Mass Customization is the Future of Consumer Products, 2012-03-21.
[2] Andres Carrillo, The Nike Internationalist Is Headed To NIKEiD, http://www.kicksonfire.com/the-nike-internationalist-is-headed-to-nikeid/, 2015-09-04.

in perfectly with Nike's focus on its direct-to-consumer, or DTC, strategy to bring more profits to the brand.

The shoes customization is classified into three types:

1. Add A Personal Touch. The customers is allowed to change a color or add his or her name, number or a motivational message to create a shoe that's all him or her. For example, for the light, strong LeBron XIII iD Basketball Shoe which features sock-like comfort plus thicker-than-ever Nike Zoom Air cushioning for maximum explosiveness in the paint, a customer can make it his or her own with exclusive graphics, materials, glow-in-the-dark options and a personalized name and number (Figure 6-7). The features include:

1) Get exclusive graphics. The NikeiD-exclusive Lake Erie graphic mimics the fluid properties of the great lake;

2) Add unique colors. A customer can choose metallic colors, or give the shoe an exclusive, two-tone color-shifting look on the court;

3) Glow in the dark. Turn heads at night with a glowing outsole, lace and swoosh.

Figure 6-7　Add A Personal Touch

2. Create A One-of-A-Kind. The shoe is a blank canvas. When every color is key and the customer sweats each detail, there's a world of options to explore (Figure 6-8).

Figure 6-8　Create A One-of-A-Kind

3. Gain A Competitive Edge. Take the training or game to the next level. The customer is allowed to change performance details like plates and midsoles which can help him or her jump higher, run faster, go farther. The features include:

1) Customize the colors. The customer can design his/her cleat with one or more colors to match the kit or stand out on the field. Opt for the Electro Flare treatment for a color-shifting effect;

2) Design the details. Make the swoosh stand out by choosing from a range of colors with or without a spray of black speckles. For even more personality, add speckled laces;

3) Choose your traction. Get the cleats built best for the game. Choose AG (artificial-grass) cleats for synthetic fields, FG (firm-ground) cleats for traction on short-grass fields, or SG-PRO (soft-ground) cleats for extra grip on soft ground in wet and sloppy conditions.

Figure 6-9　Gain A Competitive Edge[1]

The customized shoes launched by NIKE are so attractive that Chris Paul, a famous NBA star, admits that he has been addicted to Designing Custom Sneakers on NIKEiD: "No one is on NIKEiD more than I am... I try to design a shoe that is wearable straight from the store—take them out of the box and go play." Meanwhile, he says his favorite part of the design process is adding hidden details and nuances throughout the shoes[2].

SWOT Analysis of NIKEiD

Is NIKEiD a correct decision for Nike? What are the pros and cons of NIKEiD strategy? SWOT analysis can tell the answer:

Strengths

1. Well-known brand. As the largest sport shoes manufacturer with more than fifty-year history, Nike owns the remarkable brand strength. The well-known brand enables

---

[1] The pictures of Figure 6-7,6-8,6-9 are from Nike.com
[2] Riley Jones, Chris Paul Says He's Addicted to Designing Custom Sneakers on NIKEiD, http://news.yahoo.com/chris-paul-says-hes-addicted-170209372.html, 2015-10-01.

NIKEiD to acquire customers easily due to the high customer loyalty.

2. High quality. Customers focus on the comfort and wear-resistance of a pair of shoes, which are just the remarkable features of Nike's products. Nike's footwear has been well-known for its high quality. With this solid base, customers are inclined to trust NIKEiD and willing to join in the digital customization platform.

3. Customizability. Customization strategy may not work well for all the products. Tinker Tailor, a mass customization platform for designer fashion, allows customers to tweak runway pieces by designers. Orders are placed directly after the shows, but garments took three to four months to reach consumers. The company folded after less than a year in business[①]. Actually, online customization requires the outstanding production capabilities, high efficient delivery and the relative simple customization process. Fortunately, NIKEiD owns the abilities: more than fifty years production experience and the advanced production lines build the solid base of production; 4-5 weeks customization duration and the fast delivery enable the efficiency of the process; the customization involves the minor details such as colors, signs rather than the fundamental steps such as material selection, which makes the whole process relatively easy to implement.

4. Innovations in athletic footwear, apparel, equipment and accessories. The continuous innovations of products enable the numerous options for customization, which can satisfy customers' diverse demands.

Weaknesses

1. Cost burden. Usually, customization is at the expense of economies of scale. Unlike the mass production whose process is standardized and universal, customization means the production process is changeable so as to meet different need. Accordingly, the cost will rise. As what Magnusdottir—founder of Tinker Tailor said, "Building that manufacturing capability is certainly not a small task." Fortunately, for the largest sport-shoes manufacturer over the world, the extra cost of customization will not become a heavy burden.

2. Rising demand for customized shoes. The rising demand for customization is an opportunity one the one hand. However, it may bring the new challenge for Nike on the other hand—how to improve the productivity so as to satisfy the increasing demand. Nike has to balance between economy of scale and economy of scope.

3. Higher price limits the consumption. Compared to the common shoes provided by Nike, the products from NIKEiD charge the customers extra $170, which discourages the purchase.

---

① Kate Abnett, Will Mass Customisation Work For Fashion?, https://www.businessoffashion.com/articles/intelligence/mass-customisation-fashion-nike-converse-burberry, 2015-09-03.

Opportunities

1. The pursuit for self-expression and individual style. A new generation of consumers—used to the personalized nature of digital products like Facebook—may start to expect the same degree of customization from their physical products. This creates a market for NIKEiD.

2. The increasing netizens. More and more people have been used to ordering their favorite products online. Therefore, the digital customization platform of NIKEiD can get popular quickly.

Threats

1. Pressure from rivals. Nike's rival — Adidas also launched its customization service by which customers can to create their own shoes. This is a big threat for NIKEiD. Besides, some sports shoes manufacturers are mimicking the strategy after witnessing its effects.

2. The mindset of consumers. "We're so used to buying off the rack, we (women in particular) are so used to living with sacrificing our exact size requirements, we're so used to buying things on sale". For many consumers, changing the existing mindset is difficult. Besides, when customizing products, consumers my feel overwhelmed due to too much information of choice.

> 译 消费者的观念。"我们已经习惯于购买成品,我们(尤其是女性)已经习惯于牺牲自己的身材特征来迎合标准化的商品。我们已经习惯于购买打折商品。"改变这些消费观念是很困难的,而太多的选择维度又可能造成顾客的决策压力。当消费者在购买时尚商品尤其是奢侈品时,他们购买的其实是设计师或者品牌的时尚理念(并非他们自己的),他们觉得没有必要也没有信心去改变这种理念。对于时尚业而言,给消费者说太多设计流程也可能会冲淡品牌印象(因此也没必要)。

3. Design culture. With mass production, the emphasis during product development is on minimizing the variable cost of newly developed components. Manufactures usually focus on designing the sharable parts and compatible processes. However, customization requires the unique components satisfying each customer' need, which will change the existing design and production process and challenging the old design culture.

4. Value chain constraints. Reconfiguring a value chain that was originally conceived for massive production in order to accommodate a variable product mix can lead to a number of problems. An existing corporate purchase policy, for example, can make it difficult for a division to select new suppliers who are qualified to provide materials or components for customized products. Moreover, external structural constraints within suppliers and distribution channels can also become obstacles.

SWOT analysis implies that though there are some weaknesses and threats with Nike's customization, the intrinsic strengths of Nike and the opportunities enable its customization strategy.

How Does Customization Benefit Nike[①]?

1. The higher profits

Even though Nike didn't break down sales from NIKEiD outside of its total Direct-to-Consumer (DTC) sales, the company identified the initiative as a key part of its overall DTC channel strategy. The sports retailer targeted a goal of $5 billion in sales from the DTC channel by the end of fiscal 2015. The idea is that when Nike sells its products through a retailer, it is forced to sell products at wholesale prices, which allows the reseller to offer those products for a profit. By selling directly to the consumer, Nike can obtain the entire retail price itself, generating more revenue and profits in the process. This strategy has enabled the company to increase the contribution of sales from the DTC channel as part of its sales mix. In its the second quarter of 2015, sales from the DTC channel were up to 22% of its total revenue.

As the company's product mix tilts more in favor of DTC sales, the company's gross margins also rose. This is because it has greater ability to set prices and a higher per-item revenue leads to an increase in margins. In it's the first two quarters of 2015, the company's gross margins increased by 1.4 percentage points on a year-over-year basis. Growing sales of Nike's products from the online channel supported this trend.

2. The huge potential of the DTC Channel

In the early quarters of 2015, Nike's DTC revenue growth rate stayed close to 30%, driven by strong comparable store growth and the strong increase in online sales. The DTC channel is a higher margin segment as Nike does not have to share any of its revenues with intermediary. Delving further into Nike's DTC business, it can be found that its e-commerce business has been delivering strong quarterly growth in excess of 50%. Moreover, accounting for just over 20% of Nike's DTC revenues, the e-commerce business clearly has opportunity to grow.

3. Nike for the long-term win

By virtue of NIKEiD, Nike keeps proving how it can continue to increase its sales and profit, and how its dominant position doesn't mean the company has plateaued either in sales or innovation.

As offerings such as NIKEiD help to push Nike's overall online sales higher, both total sales and margins will improve, helping the company to become even more profitable. For investors, as well as for amateur shoe-designers, it's easy to see why NIKEiD is ultra-cool.

[①] Great Speculations, How NIKEiD Is Helping Nike's Push For Greater Profits, https://www.forbes.com/sites/greatspeculations/2015/07/09/how-nikeid-is-helping-nikes-push-for-greater-profits/#41d713094e65, 2015-07-09.

Case Analysis

　　定制化已经被证明是一种有效的营销策略,但是实施该策略对于像耐克这样的批量生产制造商而言并非易事。耐克实施定制化是否可行？如果可行,耐克应该如何实施该策略？这两个问题是本案例分析的重点。

　　SWOT 分析可以帮助我们解答第一个问题。首先,耐克作为有 50 多年历史的全球最大的运动鞋生产企业拥有最显著的优势——品牌知名度。相比传统的规模化生产,定制化会增加生产成本,削弱生产中的规模经济效应。为了保证这项投资有所回报,必须事先非常清楚客户需求。换句话说,必须保证一定数量的客户愿意为此项服务额外付费。幸运的是,耐克多年以来建立起的品牌知名度和客户忠诚度使客户尤其是年轻客户愿意尝试这项新服务。除了客户需求这个外因,耐克本身的生产能力是评估定制化是否可行的内因,即它能否实现客制化生产。耐克多年的运动鞋制造经验、先进的技术、高效的生产线以及具有专业技术的人员不仅保证了定制化生产的可操作性,也将其生产周期控制在合理范围内,再加上高效的物流配送、一如既往的产品高质量以及持续不断的创新,使 NIKEiD 这项定制化策略得以成功实施。当然,作为 SWOT 分析的组成要素,耐克实施定制化策略的劣势也不能忽略。定制化本身的明显劣势就是成本问题。基于个体消费者需求的定制化策略不仅意味着生产工艺流程的改变,还意味着资源投入的增加,这就是为什么不少大型制造商不愿意实施定制化生产的原因。但为什么耐克坚持定制化生产呢？这主要是因为耐克拥有雄厚的资金实力和成熟的生产技术,构成了策略实施的基础。同时,耐克公司勇于创新和冒险的企业文化也使 NIKEiD 项目得以开展。成本的上升导致的产品价格的提高是 NIKEiD 实施时必须考虑的另一个风险,因为它可能会压缩销量,对企业原有的定价体系也是一大挑战。值得庆幸的是,市场环境和消费观念的改变使大部分消费者仍然愿意为此支付额外的成本。诸如"每个顾客都是一个独立的市场"和"客户更有表达自我的需求"这样的趋势为 NIKEiD 提供了很好的机遇。尽管要面对竞争对手的威胁以及价值链资源约束,耐克的定制化服务总体上仍是有利可图的,这也是为什么它坚持实施 NIKEiD 项目。当然,结果是令人满意的:NIKEiD 项目的实施令耐克在销量和知名度方面都有所提升。

　　在实施 NIKEiD 的过程中,耐克并没有笃信"一招鲜走遍天",而是根据客户细分采取了三种不同的定制化策略:添加个人印记、设计自己的鞋型以及设计性能更优的鞋子。第一种策略允许客户选择鞋子的颜色或者在鞋子上添加名字及口号等细节,也是适用人群最广的一种策略;第二种策略由耐克提供白色帆布的鞋子,客户可在上面根据自己的喜好和想象力自由涂鸦。显然,这种策略比起第一种的定制化程度更高,给顾客自由发挥的空间更大,当然收费也更高;第三种策略则允许顾客对鞋底和夹层的设计提出自己的要求,并由耐克的设计师们评估后付诸实施。这也是定制化程度最高的一种策略。耐克的三种定制化策略不仅意味着针对人群的不同,也意味着消费者参与产品设计生产程度的差别,因此被称为"定制化的定制化"。由 NIKEiD 的成功我们可以发现,产品定制化是一个复杂的过程,它需要周密的设计和详尽的规划,不能盲目实施。

Section 5
Case Analysis Process
第五节 案例分析流程

The case analysis process is composed of four stages: individual preparation, case discussion, presenting case analysis and writing case analysis report.

1. Individual preparation. For individual preparation, you have to become acquainted with the information contained in the case, normally by reading, to follow an analytical and case solving process. It forces a reader to move into the position and role of the decision maker in the case and make good individual preparation which demands a high level of self-discipline and hard work.

2. Case discussion. Case discussion can be implemented in a small group (team) or in a class. No matter where the discussion is implemented, you should prepare for it in advance, actively participate in the discussion, listen to others carefully and express your points accurately. Case discussion can stimulate the opinion sharing, brain-storm and practise your communication skills.

3. Presenting case analysis. Usually, you need to propose your opinions on a case by presentation. An oral presentation principally relies on verbalizing your diagnosis, analysis, recommendations, visually enhancing and supporting your oral discussion with colorful, snappy slides.

4. Writing a case analysis report. After finishing a case analysis, you need show your analysis in report form. It requires the identification of the strategic issues and problems confronting the company, analysis of industry status and the company's situation, and a thorough action plan.

Summary（本章小结）

Personalization, as a marketing strategy, refers to the matching of services, products, and advertising content to individual consumers. It can satisfy customers' need better, strengthen the customer relationship, increase a company's profit and realize differentiation. The differences between personalization and customization lie in that the former is system-initiated while the latter is user-initiated. User profile and collaborative filtering are the two steps to realize personalization.

LightInTheBox, as a global online retail company, is a typical example of successful personalization. Since it began the online wedding gown retailing in 2009, LightInTheBox has offered customers a convenient way to shop for a wide selection of lifestyle products at attractive prices. LightInTheBox implements personalization through the tailored products, pick-up service for order returns, personalized web-designing in different language and wedding planner App. Realizing personalization is not easy for most retailers. Fortunately, B2C model enables LightInTheBox to capture the end consumers' need directly; data analysis aids LightInTheBox to understand consumers' demands accurately; Internet-based media assists drastic growth of LightInTheBox personalized products and services; and the innovative supply chain model ensures the quality of personalized products and services. Meanwhile, the growth of netizens, popularity of mobile network and rapid development of the internet technology provide a good opportunity for LightInTheBox's personalization. However, the problems like product quality, intellectual property, product homogeny and high expenses on marketing obsess LightInTheBox. The fierce competition, the policy restrictions from Western countries and the decreasing profit margin are the possible threats for LightInTheBox. Therefore, LightInTheBox should focus on intellectual property management, supply chain management and market expansion so as to keep its advantages in personalization.

Though it also focuses on personalization, Mogujie realizes personalization by virtue of online community, differing from B2C model of LightInTheBox. Founded in 2011, Mogujie is a shopping guide website which combines online shopping and online socialization. Mogujie does not sell product itself nor has inventory, it builds a socialization platform where all the users are free to communicate and get the recommendation of products from other e-commerce websites such as Taobao and Jingdong. The business model and technical base enable Mogujie to realize personalization. By virtue of online community, Mogujie aids each individual customer to decide what to buy, where to buy it and how to share experiences with friends. In addition, Mogujie adopts the FOR (Fragmentation, Organize and Re-organize) model which helps to judge consumers' behavior. Personalization has helped Mogujie to build the brand of "community e-commerce" and promote the sales growth. On the other hand, the problems like the low sales conversion rate are still obsessing Mogujie.

The case analysis process is composed of four stages: individual preparation, case discussion, presenting case analysis and writing case analysis report, each of which is respectively explained in the subsequent chapters.

 Exercises & Tasks (练习与任务)

▶ *Exercises*

1. What are the differences between personalization and customization?
2. How do you differentiate the personalization strategies between LightInTheBox and Mogujie?

3. Why does NIKEiD's customization succeed?

▶ Tasks

Choose a case of personalization/customization and prepare a 20-minute presentation which should include:

1. Background introduction to the firm and its personalization/customization;
2. How does it realize the product/service personalization/customization;
3. What are the effects of the personalization/customization (good & bad)?
4. You suggestions for the firm's personalization/customization.

Chapter 7 Online Advertising
第七章　网络广告

Learning Objectives（学习目标）

After finishing this chapter, you should be able to:
1. Define online advertising and identify different online advertising methods;
2. Characterize online advertising;
3. Understand how Adwords becomes the profit source of Google;
4. Explain why The Vancl Style can succeed;
5. Find the success factors of Xiaomi's microblog advertising;
6. Grasp the basic 5 parts of case discussion.

Introduction（内容简介）

Along with the development of the Internet technology, online advertising has prevailed. Some firms profit from providing online advertising services while others increase sales by leveraging its advantages like quick dissemination. Their practices indicate that online advertising is indeed an effective way of marketing and it is not easy to improve its effectiveness.

Chapter 7 is composed of 5 sections. The brief introduction to online advertising is made in section 1. Three online advertising cases are provided respectively in section 2, 3, and 4. Section 5 focuses on case discussion.

Section 1
Online Advertising
第一节　网络广告

> **Key Words**

1. advertising *n.* 广告
2. affiliate *vt.* 使加入
3. transmission *n.* 传播

> **Online Advertising**

Online advertising is a form of marketing and advertising which uses the Internet to deliver promotional marketing messages to consumers. It includes email marketing, search engine marketing (SEM), social media marketing, many types of display advertising and mobile advertising. Like other advertising method, online advertising usually involves the following participants:

1. Publisher, who integrates advertisements into its online content;
2. Advertiser, who provides the advertisements to be displayed on the publisher's content;
3. Advertising agency who helps to generate and place the advertisement copy.

Differing from traditional advertising, online advertising emphasizes interactive marketing that allows a consumer to interact with an online seller. It is characterized by:

1. Two-way communication. Under traditional advertising model, the information on products or services is sent to consumers and it is hard to get the feedback from the consumers accurately. Internet enables two-way communication in which information is sent to consumers and the feedback from the consumers can be acquired quickly by clicks or actual views.

2. Accurate targets. Vendors can target on specific groups and individuals. Data analysis helps vendors to target on the specific groups and individuals precisely so as to improve the effectiveness of advertising.

3. One-to-one advertising. Unlike traditional advertising targeting customer groups, online advertising can accurately send information to an individual customer by virtue of the tools like online survey or cookie, which makes one-to-one advertising possible.

In 2016, Internet advertising revenues in the United States surpassed those of cable television and broadcast television. In 2017, Internet advertising revenues in the United States totaled $83.0 billion, a 14% increase over $72.50 billion in 2016①.

---

① https://en.wikipedia.org/wiki/Online_advertising

▶ Why Online Advertising?

1. Rising number of netizens provides opportunities for online advertising. According to CNNIC, Chinese netizens had rose up to 668 million by July 2015[①]. The increasing netizens will bring more potential audiences for online advertisements, which probably leads to a bigger market. In 2017, China's online advertising revenue was approximate 400 billion yuan with a share larger than 50% in China's advertising market[②].

2. Internet is by far the fastest growing communication medium. No doubt, the Internet has the obviously higher transmission efficiency than traditional media such as TV. Additionally, with the emergences of smart ends and social media, people prefer the communication on the Internet anytime everywhere. Due to its efficiency and convenience, people would rather stick to the Internet, bringing opportunities for online advertising.

3. Advertisers are interested in a medium with such potential reach, both locally and globally. Breaking the geographic limits is one of the remarkable traits of the Internet. That means, by virtue of the Internet, advertisers' information can be transmitted in a much broader space and reach more potential customers.

4. Online advertisements are cheaper than those on other medias. Low price is another remarkable strength of online advertising. If your product information can be delivered to more customers at the lower price, why not? Besides, the advertisements on the Internet can be updated at any time with minimal cost.

5. Diverse advertising patterns. An online advertisement can be displayed as a text, picture, video, audio or flash. It can be delivered on multi-media platforms such as portals, e-commerce websites or social medias. Besides, online advertisements are easily embedded in games and entertainments.

6. Personalization. By virtue of the tools such as cookie, an advertisement can be tailored based on an individual customer's preference and delivered to him or her. As a result, the effectiveness of the advertisement can be improved.

▶ Categories of Online Advertisements[③]

The traditional online advertising methods include banner, e-mail and so on. And they are usually delivered on the portals or e-commerce websites. With the popularity of social media, advertisers found new delivery channels:

---

① CNNIC,第36次中国互联网络发展状况统计报告,2015年7月。
② China's Online Advertising Sector Data in 2017, http://www.iresearchchina.com/content/details7_40729.html, January 30, 2018.
③ 埃弗瑞姆·特伯恩(Efraim Turban),戴维·金(David King)著,王健改编,《电子商务导论》,中国人民大学出版社,2006年。

1. Banner. On a web page, a graphic advertising display linked to the advertiser's web page. It is classified into: keyword banners and random banners. The benefits such as one-to-one advertisement, multi-media capabilities enable banners to be frequently utilized in practice. However, the declining click ratio since viewers have become immune to banners is an obvious limitation.

2. Pop-under advertisements. An advertisement that appears underneath the current browser window, and users can see the advertisement when they close the active window. It is hardly used now because users have lost the interest in it.

3. Interstitials. An initial web page or a portion of it that is used to capture the user's attention for a short time while other content is loading. It can draw users' attention quickly but may annoy users due to the long loading time.

4. E-mail. The advertisements are sent to the potential customers directly by email. It used to be the most popular online advertising method due to the fast dissemination and low cost. However, with users' being tired of junk mail, the effectiveness of email advertising has been decreased greatly.

5. Paid search-engine inclusion. Several search engines charge fees for including URLs near the top of the search results. It can reach potential customers directly. An advertiser has to bid for the same search term, often causing the top of a search engine results page to look orderly.

6. Advertising on social media platforms. An advertiser delivers its advertisement directly on a social media platform. Information can be embed in a text, picture or video. The method originated from advertising in chat rooms to draw users' attention. With the pervasion of social media, advertising on social media platforms has been adopted frequently.

Section 2
Google Adwords—a Profit Source of Google
第二节 竞价排名广告——谷歌的利润源泉

Key Words

1. paid listing 竞价排名广告
2. eligible *adj.* 合格的
3. advert *n.* 广告
4. spiral *vi/vt.* 螺旋式上升
5. ad *n.* 广告(非正式)

▶ Case

Creation of Google Adwords[①]

Google, known as an American multinational technology company that specializes in Internet-related services and products is famous for its search engine. Since searching on google.com is free for users, how does the company make money? Actually, Google creates a business model which embeds online advertising service into the online search and allows advertisers to compete to display brief advertising copy to web users, based in part on keywords, predefined by the advertisers, which might link the copy to the content of web pages shown to users. The model is called as paid listing and the advertising service based on the model is Google Adwords launched in 2000.

AdWords offers pay-per-click (PPC), that is, cost-per-click (CPC) advertising, cost-per-thousand-impressions or cost-per-mille (or cost per thousand impression, CPM) advertising, site-targeted advertising for text, banner and rich-media ads, and remarketing (also known as retargeting). The AdWords program includes local, national and international distribution. Google's text advertisements are short, consisting of one headline of 25 characters, two additional text lines of 35 characters each, and a display URL of 35 characters. Image ads can be one of several different Interactive Advertising Bureau (IAB) standard sizes.

Service Expansion of Google Adwords[②]

Since it launched Adwords, Google has been making efforts to expand the services of its profit source so as to satisfy customers' need.

In 2003, Google introduced site-targeted advertising. Using the AdWords control panel, advertisers can enter keywords, domain names, topics, and demographic targeting preferences, and Google places the ads on what they see as relevant sites within their content network. If domain names are targeted, Google also provides a list of related sites for placement. Advertisers bid on a cost-per-impression (CPI) or cost-per-click (CPC) basis for site targeting. With placement targeting, it is possible for an ad to take up the entire ad block rather than have the ad block split into 2 to 4 ads, resulting in higher visibility for the advertiser. The minimum cost-per-thousand impressions bid for placement-targeted campaigns is 25 cents. There is no minimum CPC bid, however.

---

① http://en.wikipedia.org/wiki/AdWords
② Larry Kim, AdWords Enhanced Campaigns: Google Announces Big Changes to Mobile Ad Campaign Management, https://www.wordstream.com/blog/ws/2013/02/06/google-adwords-enhanced-campaigns, May 24, 2016.

In 2005, Google launched the Google Advertising Professional (GAP) Program to certify individuals and companies who completed AdWords training and passed an exam. Due to the complexity of AdWords and the amount of money at stake, some advertisers even hired a consultant to manage their campaigns.

In 2010, Google launched AdWords Express aiming at small businesses that attempts to reduce the difficulty of managing ad campaigns by automatically managing keywords and ad placement. AdWords Express also supports small businesses that do not have a website by allowing them to direct customers to their Google Place page.

In 2013, Google added enhanced campaigns for AdWords to "help advertisers better manage their campaigns in a multi-device world". The enhanced campaigns "show ads across devices with the right ad text, sitelink, app or extension, without advertisers having to edit each campaign for every combination of devices, location and time of day," and include "advanced reports to measure new conversion types".

In 2016, Google announced a bold and sweeping set of changes to their AdWords PPC(pay-per-click) management platform in a bid to greatly simplify mobile ad campaign management. All of the new AdWords Enhanced Campaign features was thought to greatly increase both mobile advertising adoption and Google's revenues from mobile search.

These changes affect all advertisers and fundamentally change the online advertising landscape.

How Does Adwords Work?[①]

Google designs some features and mechanisms which enable the effective works of Adwords:

1. Paid search

Paid search is the term for advertising within the listings of a search engine. These normally appear to the side or at the top of a SERP (Search Engine Results Page), the listing of results returned by a search engine in response to a keyword query. Google places a small yellow 'Ad' label on them (Figure 7-1).

Figure 7-1　Google Adwords Yellow Labels for Ads

---

① Christopher Ratcliff, What is Google AdWords and how does it work?, October 30, 2014
https://econsultancy.com/blog/65682-what-is-google-adwords-and-how-does-it-work/

2. Adverts based on keywords

Basically a firm is allowed to pick some keywords that a searcher might use on Google, then create an advert that will appear on the SERP based on those keywords (Figure 7-2).

Figure 7-2 Advert Based on a Keyword[①]

Of course the firm is probably not going to be the only company wanting to serve adverts to people who use those particular terms. Its rivals are also allowed to display adverts to the potential customers searching the same term. Whose adverts should be listed on the top of a search engine results page? Google Adwords employs an efficient as well as key mechanism—bidding.

3. Bidding

If a firm wants its ad to appear at all, it has to bid against other marketers on how much it is willing to pay Google AdWords every time a searcher clicks on its ads. Obviously the more its pay-per-click (PPC) the more likely its ad will appear in the search results.

The firm pays Google AdWords each time its ad is clicked. The price the firm is willing to pay for each click is called cost-per-click (CPC). The firm can pick a maximum bid amount, and if it chooses the automatic option, Google chooses the bid amount for it within its budget, and theoretically brings it the most clicks possible within that budget. There is also another less common option called cost-per-thousand-impression (CPM). This is where the firm pays the search engine for every 1,000 times its ad appears on the SERP. The user doesn't have to click-through. The firm can choose either method.

一旦用户点击了企业的广告,该企业就要为此向谷歌支付费用,这被称为按点击计费。企业可以选择 Google AdWords 的自动竞拍功能,这样系统可以按照其事先设置的竞价预算为其匹配最优点击次数。还有一种用得比较少的收费模式——按千次曝光计费,即企业按照其广告在搜索结果页面上每展示 1 000 次为单位付费,而不用考虑用户是否点击。

4. Quality score

Unlike other real-time bidding models, Google Adwords doesn't just take the highest bid into account, instead, it also uses a criteria called "quality score".

Google looks at how relevant and useful a firm's ad is to searchers and the search terms they've used. It also looks at how many clicks its ad has received previously, also known as its click-through-rate (CTR) and how relevant its landing page is. For instance, if a searcher types "Nike Air Max" and the firm's advert appears saying "buy Nike Air

---

① Both Figure 7-1 and Figure 7-2 are from www.google.com

Max here", once the ad is clicked this needs to lead the searcher directly to a page featuring Nike Air Max. If it just goes to its generic homepage, it's not good enough. The higher a firm's quality score, the better. In fact even if the firm's maximum bid is less than that of rivals, it still may appear above their ads if the quality score of the firm is better.

The time it takes for Google AdWords to look at all the relevant advertisers bidding for a search term, decide whether there will be an auction or not, hold that auction, work out which ad offers a mixture of highest maximum bid and quality score and finally serves that ad on the results page, is the time it takes for someone to type a search term into Google and receive the results, which is about 0.26 seconds.

5. Advertisement content restrictions

As of April 2008, Google AdWords no longer allowed for the display URL to deviate from that of the destination URL. Prior to that, Google paid advertisements could feature different landing page URLs to that of what was being displayed on the search network. Google expounded that the policy changed stems from both user and advertiser feedback. The concern prompting the restriction change is believed to be the premise on which users click advertisements. Users were in some cases, being misled and further targeted by AdWords advertisers.

As of December 2010, Google AdWords decreased its restrictions over sales of Hard Alcohol. It allowed ads that promote the sale of hard alcohol and liquor. This is an extension of a policy change that was made in December 2008, which permitted ads that promote the branding of hard alcohol and liquor.

1) Allowed keywords

Google has also come under fire for allowing AdWords advertisers to bid on trademarked keywords. In 2004, Google started allowing advertisers to bid on a wide variety of search terms in the U.S. and Canada, including the trademarks of their competitors and expanded this policy to the U.K and Ireland in May 2008. Advertisers are restricted from using other companies' trademarks in their advertisement text if the trademark has been registered with Advertising Legal Support team. Further, it is prohibited from advertising a book which uses a trademarked name in its title. For example, the advertising of a book related to Facebook is restricted from advertising on AdWords because it contains the word "Facebook" in its title. Besides, Google does require certification to run regulated keywords, such as those related to pharmaceuticals keywords.

2) Prohibited keywords

Google has a variety of specific keywords (or categories) that it prohibits, varying by type and by country. For example, the use of keywords for alcohol related products is prohibited in Thailand and Turkey; for gambling and casinos in Poland; for abortion services in Russia and the Ukraine; and for adult related services or products worldwide as of June 2014; From June 2007, Google banned AdWords from adverting for student essay-writing services, a move which was welcomed by universities.

6. AdWords distribution

All AdWords ads are eligible to be shown on www.google.com. Advertisers also have the option of enabling their ads to show on Google's partner networks. The "search network" includes AOL search, Ask.com, and Netscape. Like www.google.com, these search engines show AdWords ads in response to user searches, but do not affect quality score.

The "Google Display Network (GDN)" (formerly referred to as the "content network") shows AdWords ads on sites that are not search engines. Click-through rates on the display network are typically much lower than those on the search network and quality score for Display Network is calculated separately from search network.

Advantages and Disadvantages of Google Adwords[1][2]

Just like other services, Google Adwords has its own advantages and disadvantages. Combing these pros. and cons. helps us to understand and evaluate the online advertising service further.

1. Advantages

1) Results from AdWords can be instant. AdWords ads can be really helpful if a firm looks to drive traffic to the site quickly. AdWords is instant compared to SEO (Search Engine Optimization) which can take weeks, sometimes months to take effect. Additionally, a firm is allowed to use AdWords to test its ideas without committing to the whole SEO thing. It can test which keywords the firm wants to drive traffic for, which landing pages work, and the firm can learn a whole lot about its customers quickly.

2) Creating an AdWords campaign can be quick. A firm can be up and running on AdWords in a very short space of time. While there is a lot more to AdWords than just campaigns. Fox example, ad groups, keywords and ads are the building blocks. And the firm can set them up very quickly. Do a bit of keyword research, decide on the budget, set up a campaign and a few ad groups, write some killer ad copy, and the campaign begins. The ads will appear as soon as they've been approved, which could be instantaneous.

3) Fantastic exposure in the search results. Each firm has the chance to appear on the first page of the Internet's largest search engine as long as it wins the bidding. It means the

---

[1] Lauren Ahluwalia, Google AdWords: Pros and Cons, https://www.hallaminternet.com/google-adwords-pros-and-cons/, July 18, 2017.
[2] Google Adwords Pros And Cons For Small Businesses, https://contentgarden.org/google-adwords-pros-and-cons-for-small-businesses/, April 5, 2017

exposure which means almost everything for an online advertisement. If the products or services of the firm appear to someone who's actively searching, which may enable a successful transaction.

4) The budget is flexible and controllable. AdWords doesn't have to be expensive. Google AdWords averages a cost of about $1-2 per click, making it a relatively affordable advertising platform for just about any size business. This cost is an average across industries, however, meaning that there is a fair amount of variability. Some industries, like insurance, have a very high cost-per-click for most keywords, but most keywords within AdWords are relatively inexpensive. AdWords also allows a firm to choose which keywords it bids on, meaning that it can select keywords that are more budget friendly over more competitive, costly ones. This allows it to tailor the campaigns to the exact budget the firm has while creating optimal ads to maximize the return on investment.

5) The useful online advertising tools make campaigns easy to create. AdWords comes with a suite of tools that help a firm create ads, the best of which is the Keyword Planner. The planner helps the firm find keywords that will trigger the ads based on the attributes like the existing content on a webpage the firm wants to link the ads to, the industry, the average cost-per-click of the keyword, the average monthly searches involving that keyword and the competitiveness of that keyword. KeyWord Planner guides the firm through the process of selecting keywords for the campaign so that it ends up with the ones that will be the best fit for its particular campaign.

6) AdWords ads have increased in size. In 2016 the size of the text ads increased, meaning that a firm can get more bang for its buck, as the adverts are larger and take up more space in the search results. The ads have become increasingly engaging, with options to add site-links and structured snippet extensions, which means the ads can look better and more engaging than the organic listings.

2. Disadvantages

1) High learning curve. If a firm has never run a pay-per-click advertising campaign before, it may find that this kind of advertising boasts a high learning curve. It's relatively easy to create a campaign, but the campaign probably does not perform very well. It can be quite difficult to pick keywords that are appropriate to the type of campaign, to pick keywords that have the right level of competitiveness for the budget, and to create an optimal campaign in which the ads successfully convince people to click on them. Though Google rolled out Adwords Express, an easier-to-use version of AdWords in 2017, the firm either needs to hire someone who knows what they're doing or dedicates some time to learning the platform and how to create effective campaigns.

2) Spiraling costs. Since Google does online ads for a living, it will prompt a firm to increase the budget when the firm logs in and will show that how many more clicks the

firm will get if it does what Google recommends. The problem with this is that it can be easy to dump more and more money into AdWords only to find that the ads aren't converting search engine users into actual customers. Therefore, when using AdWords, it's important for an advertiser to keep a close eye on the two metrics: click-through-rate (CTR) and cost-per-acquisition (CPA). CTR is how many people actually click on the ads when compared to how many times they're displayed. CPA is how much it costs the advertiser to land a customer through its campaign. Though CTR can vary, the advertiser wants to achieve a rate of at least 2%-3%. 4% is considered a very good CTR for a campaign. As far as CPA, it depends highly on the type of product or service the firm advertises. If the firm is selling something that costs thousands of dollars for each unit, it will need a lot more clicks before it experiences a sale. If each unit is a few dollars, the firm needs to make sure it's not getting too many clicks for each customer it lands or it will lose all the profits to AdWords.

3) Competitive industries have higher Cost-per-click. If the competitors have already used Google AdWords, this might the reason why a firm wants to starts its own campaign. But the competition can be fierce, and as a result the cost-per-click is going up. If the keyword bid is too low then the ads could be relegated to page 2 or 3 of the search results, which means the ads could be ignored by the searchers.

4) The short shelf life. AdWords has a very short shelf life, which means if the firm has no budget, its ads will stop. Compared to it, SEO obviously is a longer term investment, with a longer shelf life.

5) Adverts have limitations. An advertiser is restricted by the amount of characters it is allowed. There are two 30 character headlines and one large 80 character description and a customizable display URL. And the advertiser ideally needs to include an attention-grabbing headline, keywords, benefits and a call to action in that too.

6) The landing pages need to be top-notch. Google looks at the quality of the landing pages, so a firm's website needs to be up to scratch in terms of relevancy to the search query. Ultimately, it can't just rely on AdWords to get the traffic, its landing pages need to be of a good quality and relevant to its ads, so the firm can't neglect its SEO. By improving its website's landing pages, the firm's Quality Score will increase, which means the less pay for the clicks.

7) Customer life cycle. If the products sold require the user to think, save and research the product, the firm may not see the ROI it was initially expecting. If the firm has been used to playing the long game, then AdWords can only help it to reach more potential customers.

> **Case Analysis**

　　Google Adwords 不仅是竞价排名广告的代表也是谷歌重要的利润源泉。自它 2000 年推出以来已经获得了业界和学界的大量关注,人们开始探讨 Google Adwords 是如何为谷歌赚取利润的?如何评价在线广告服务的优劣?因此,本案例分析的重点是 Google Adwords 的竞价排名广告机制及其优缺点。

　　Google Adwords 的运作机制简单而言就是将广告植入线上搜索之中,允许广告商通过竞价的方式将自己的广告在内容相关的搜索结果页面上显示。首先,谷歌将广告植入搜索结果中,并用黄色标签标识,这被称为竞价搜索。为了使自己的广告得以显示,广告商应事先挑选一些与广告相关的关键词,并基于关键词制作广告。这样当用户用这些关键词进行搜索时,广告就可以在搜索结果页面显示出来。对于大多数用户而言,他们只浏览前面几页的搜索结果,这就意味着广告出现在越前面的页面越能被注意到。但是,这些有利的页面位置是有限的,如何让自己的广告出现在好的广告位呢?这就涉及 Google Adwords 运作机制的第二步也是最关键的一步:竞价。广告商通过竞拍获得有利的位置,出价越高,越有可能获得有利的位置。但是,如果广告商出价虽高,但因其广告质量不佳而影响用户的搜索体验怎么办呢?为了解决这一问题,Google Adwords 巧妙地制定了质量评分体系来评价广告的价值。一则广告与用户搜索主题的相关性、对用户而言的有用性、广告的历史点击数(CTR)及其与载入页面的关联性都被纳入评分体系中。Google Adwords 将上述两项标准相结合,使出价和质量评分综合排名靠前的广告得以展示。除此之外,Google Adwords 还通过 Adwords 分销和广告内容限制来保证广告商和用户的利益:前者是将广告投放在 Ask.com 等知名的谷歌合作伙伴的网站上,以增加广告投放的渠道;后者则是过滤掉虚假或无价值的广告以保证搜索的质量。正是这种有效的运作机制保证了 Google Adwords 自推出以来一直广受青睐。

　　作为一项成功的广告服务,Google Adwords 有其自身的优缺点。它的第一个显著的优点就是高效率。它可以在用户输入搜索关键词之后几秒钟内就将广告展示在搜索结果页面中,并将用户引导至相应的网站,大大提升了广告信息传播的效率。同时,它还允许广告商快速创建广告活动,提升了营销效率。灵活性以及广告预算的可控性是 Google Adwords 的第二项优点。相比其他广告投放模式,Google Adwords 平均每次点击 1—2 美元的成本相对便宜,同时它还能根据企业的预算为其量身打造广告活动,以保证其投资回报最大化。这种模式对于预算有限的中小企业而言尤其具有吸引力。另外,谷歌的品牌知名度能保证广告的曝光率,而"关键词规划"等工具则能帮助企业简单高效地创建广告投放活动。这些都是 Google Adwords 的优势。

　　事物往往有其两面性,Google Adwords 自问世以来因上述优势广受好评,但也因为其自身的局限性而承受争议,甚至它自身的优势也可能变成劣势。比如,令 Google Adwords 自豪的快速创建广告活动的功能看起来效率很高,但广告的效果却往往差强人意。为提升广告效果,有些企业不得不聘请专业人士来利用这项功能创建广告活动,导致运营成本上升,也使Google Adwords本身低价的优势大打折扣。此外,尽管初期的广告投入较低,但为了提高广告用户的转化率,企业不得不加大后期投入,并密切关注广告的点击率(CTR)和用户行为付费率(CPA)。与此同时,激烈的行业竞争不仅使广告投放的成本上升,也令广告商陷入两难境地:是增加广告投入以保证有利的广告位呢还是减少投入而忍受广告的效果打折扣呢?另外,广告上架时间短以及客户生命周期长也削弱了Google Adwords本身效率高的优势:一旦广告商的资金不到位,谷歌就会立即停止其广告展示,加上广告客户转化率所需要的时间使Google Adwords并不适合那些客户生命周期较短的产品。当然,关键字广告对字数的限制也对广告文案的策划提出了更高的要求。

尽管Google Adwords有其自身的局限性,但必须承认,这项创建于2000年的广告服务不仅成为谷歌的利润源泉,更实现了网络广告模式的创新,也使它成为不少后来者(如:百度)的模仿对象。

Section 3
The Vancl Style—Vancl's Online Advertising
第三节 凡客体——凡客的在线广告

Ⅰ Key Words

1. apparel *n.* 服装
2. likes *n.* 好恶,爱好的事物
3. gimmick *n.* 花招
4. sensation *n.* 轰动
5. motto *n.* 座右铭

Ⅱ Case

About Vancl[①]

Vancl, founded in October 2007, is an Internet apparel brand in China providing men's and women's fashion products such as shoes, jeans, shirts, skirts, accessories, and other lifestyle goods at reasonable prices. Vancl is led by its founder & CEO, Chen Nian who also founded Joyo funded by top international VC companies, Vancl is mainly operated by the core team of Joyo. Its product designers come from around the globe, including Spain, Japan, and Korea. The company realizes cost effective operations by

---

① Unicorns 57/229—VANCL, http://www.franktop10.com/silicon-valley/610036/, June, 2017.

selling clothes on the Internet.

As an online retailer, Vancl competes with the likes of Taobao, Tmall and Jingdong. With no physical stores or distributors, Vancl sells directly to consumers online. The retailer distributes goods for cash-on-delivery across 1,100 Chinese cities. Setting it apart from other Chinese clothing retailers, online-only Vancl exclusively sells its own branded clothing—like Uniqlo or Gap—which is how it pulls off its most notable gimmick: letting customers model its clothes.

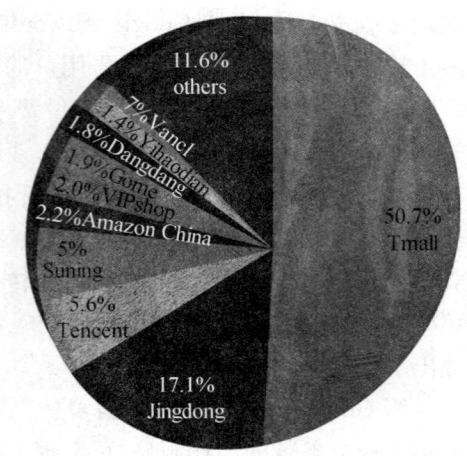

Figure 7-3 B2C Market Share of China B2C E-commerce Site by GMV②

In 2015, Vancl ranked No. 10 of The B2C top 10 in China though it suffered a big drop, losing over half of its market share by sales (Figure 7-3) ①.

Vancl's Growth

In October 2007, Vancl earned its first venture capital investment. In December 2007, the company received its second venture capital investment, followed by a third in June 2008. Company sales in December 2008 reached about 300 million yuan, becoming China's first B2C brand for men's clothes. In June 2009, the company entered the women's clothing industry and in August this year it also started to market footwear products, continually expanding its product lines. In 2014, Vancl closed a seventh round of funding. The company raked in $100 million, which was the same amount it raised in its last round in November 2013. The investment came from Temasek, Ceyuan, IDG Capital Partners and SAIF Partners. Vancl logo brought total financing to $522 million, with nearly half of that coming from a single round in 2011. Vancl had a rough 2012 when it diversified its catalog, but in 2013 the company hit the reset button and returned to its roots: clothing. Some of that money went into acquiring a handful of fledgling clothing brands and expansion into Vietnam③.

---

① Steven Millward, China's E-commerce Market to Hit $71 Billion in Sales in Q2: These Are the Top 10 E-stores, https://www.techinasia.com/china-E-commerce-market-share-stats-q2-2013/, 2013-08-28.

② www.iresearch.com.cn

③ Paul Bischoff, Chinese Fashion E-tailer Vancl Breaks Half-billion Funding Mark with Latest $100 Million Round, https://www.techinasia.com/chinese-fashion-etailer-vancl-breaks-halfbillion-funding-mark-latest-100-million/, 2014-02-10.

By 2009, of all self-operating B2C clothing websites, Vancl had ranked first with 28.4% market share, becoming the leader in China's B2C clothing industry, and only two years after its founding. Offering women's dresses, canvas shoes, jeans as well as other high quality goods at reasonable prices, the company provided many bargain products to Chinese netizens, causing a great sensation in China's clothing industry in 2009. As a result, it quickly became a symbol for online fashion with Chinese netizens. Thus far, the product lines of Vancl included men's wear, women's wear, shoes, accessories, and home furnishings. In the List of "Future Stars—Top 21 Emerging Enterprises with the Most Potential for Growth", selected by the magazine "China Entrepreneur" in 2009, Vancl ranked first in terms of its average annual growth of 1,475.48%[1].

Vancl's rapid rise has drawn extensive attention from both the media and the public. And people want to find the causes behind its rapid growth:

Firstly, most of the managerial personnel of VANCL are from Joyo, boasting rich practical experience in online marketing. Also, VANCL has quickly made itself a familiar name to netizens in China under a special marketing model utilizing plentiful online advertisements.

Secondly, Vancl's rapid growth should also be attributed to the explosive increase of China's e-commerce clothing industry. From 2007 to 2008, China's e-commerce clothing industry witnessed an explosive growth whereby clothing and accessories became a key focus of online shopping, with trading volumes ranking first of all kinds of commodities. According to iResearch in 2009, there were about 80 million online clothing shoppers in China. Because there were 338 million netizens in China and clothing was one of the most basic consumer goods, the potential consumer base was enormous. Besides, online clothes shopping accounted for 12.8% of the total online shopping volume, of which, the B2C clothing trading volume was about 2.4 billion yuan in 2009, up 99.8% year-on-year[2]. A Forrester report released in early 2015 estimated Chinese e-commerce market to grow 20% annually from $307 billion in 2013 to more than $1 trillion by 2019. The growth in the market is being driven by the penetration of Internet in the country as well as adoption of mobile devices[3].

Thirdly, Vancl has been insisting on high quality and fast production. Unlike some cheap products with low quality, Vancl always emphasizes products quality and attempts to provide the excellent products with high performance-price ratio. For example, in 2014 Vancl launched the 129-yuan shirt with the combination of non-ironing, announcing "Wear

---

[1] VANCL.com Evolves into Industry Leader Following Two Years of Success, PR Newswire, 2009-09-28.
[2] http://en.wikipedia.org/wiki/AdWords
[3] Billion Dollar Unicorns: Vancl On A Roller Coaster Ride, http://www.sramanamitra.com/2015/04/16/billion-dollar-unicorns-vancl-on-a-roller-coaster-ride/, 2015-09-16.

them right away. Just shake it out!"①. This shirt keeps the consistent style of Vancl—elegant, simple and comfortable and gained the favor of business group. Additionally, Vancl has been devoting to the fast production. Usually, it takes six to nine months to complete the process from designing, producing to putting the finished goods on the shelf in China. Vancl shortens the duration to seven days which is similar with Zara, a famous clothing brand. The shorter cycle enables Vancl to seize the timing of market entry, especially for the best sellers.

Fourthly, the excellent service throughout the process from sales to delivery. Vancl offers more than one sales channels which customers can choose freely. For example, part of customers prefer ordering by telephone which allows customers to supply product number and address and pay by cash on delivery. The process is simple and efficient. Besides, Vancl builds its own delivery team and provides the necessary training so as to ensure the high quality of services. Compared to the competitors, Vancl has stand out due to the logistics advantages.

Finally, the effective online advertising plays an important role in Vancl's growth. After realizing the fierce competition in the online apparel market, Vancl decided to emphasize online advertising so as to distinguish itself from the competition. Chen Nian, CEO of Vancl, pointed out that Vancl made so much effort to online advertising that the expenses accounted for more than 60% of its total advertising costs. The appropriate strategies and the effective propagation enable Vancl to build its brand strength quickly in China. Vancl has become a symbol of own branded clothing which represents energy, fashion, innovation and low-price for local youth.

Vancl's Online Advertising

To improve the effectiveness of online advertising, Vancl adopts the strategies which are imitated by the peers:

1. Taking advantage of the Internet media to build its brand and interacting with the customers

Differing from its peers like PPG who covers both online and offline media, Vancl has been focusing on the Internet media due to their low cost and high efficiency. From the initial official website and forum to the later blog and micro-blog, Vancl always instantly captures the new media and takes good advantage of them to deliver its advertisements. Vancl establishes a team in charge of media maintenance and information release. The information on new products, new technology, advertising spokesman, promotion and company development situation is released on the media instantly. The strategy not only

---

① Liao Wei, VANCL: From a myth to a white shirt, *China Daily*, 2014-10-14.

strengthens the communications between Vancl and its customers but also stimulates consumption and builds the positive enterprise image. In December 2011, Vancl made its advertising debut with microblog at Sina Mall. Vancl is the first settle-in firm at Sina Mall which implements promotion with microblog. Fortunately, the attempt succeeded, which encourages the peers to utilize the new medium for advertising.

2. Innovative copywriting[1]

Vancl's advertising process including choosing the spokesman, designing the copywriting and disseminating the advertisement has become a classic model of online advertising. Vancl selected the youth's favorite stars such as Han Han (Figure 7-4), Wang Luodan, Li Yuchun and Huang Xiaoming as its spokesman. Meanwhile, it designed an impressive slogan focusing on personality. For example, the slogan for Han Han—young persons' favorite author as well as a famous blogger is "Love Internet, Love freedom, Love getting up lately, Love night stall, Love racing car, Also love the sneaker of 59 yuan. I am not a flagman nor a spokesman of anybody. I am Han Han. I only represent myself. I am same as you—I am a Vancl." The copywriting is not only concise, humorous and easy to memorize but also emphasizes personality which is consistent with most young persons' need. As a result, the slogan was disseminated widely on the Internet and the name of Vancl was in turn well known and memorized by many people. No long after, Vancl renewed its endorsement contract with Han Han and launched a series of outdoor advertisement campaigns to promote its new collection in ten major cities. Viewing the wonderful effects of the ad campaigns, Vancl successively launched a series of copywriting, which also caused a sensation. In May 2011, the Huang Xiaoming version was launched online and forwarded more than 120,000 times by microblog. A series of

Figure 7-4　Han Han was Chosen as Vancl's Spokesman[2]

---

[1][2]　Oliver, Vancl launched its new advertising campaign, *Marketing China*, 2013-09-30.

slogans featuring the personality and positive spirit of VANCL made a splash on the Internet, and VANCL's brand influence reached its peak then. Vancl's online advertising is so successful that it is called as "The Vancl Style".

After a long time since Vancl launched its big advertising campaign, starring super famous blogger Han Han, Vancl launched another campaign only available in visual pictures, without videos in early 2013. This move enabled Vancl to reduce communication costs while still reaching people in the metro with effective posters visuals. The new campaign changed its previous design, from white background to black one but still keeping the red font with Vancl's motto. Not only had this design changed, but also the photo style totally moved to a different concept. Quite out of the traditional ads, using black and white photos with high detailed skin texture, the ad was not smoothed or refined. It is quite a bold strategy to choose such an idea.

In order to succeed with such concepts, Vancl partnered with the super trendy TV Show, the Voice of China, starring 5 famous participants of the program: Li Qi, Wang Tuo, Simon Chung, Zhu Ke and Yao Bei Na (Figure 7-5). Though the budget on this campaign obviously decreased in comparison to the previous one, it was broadcasted on screens in public areas. The campaign caught back people's eyes.

Figure 7-5　Vancl's Spokesman Zhuke and Yao Beina[①]

3. Combined delivery of advertisements[②]

As one of the earliest e-commerce enterprises, Vancl has been insisting on the high

---

① Oliver, Vancl launched its new advertising campaign, Marketing China, 2013-09-30.
② 张媛媛：“浅析电子商务企业的网络广告营销策略——以凡客诚品为例”，《广东经济》，2012(9)：pp.53-55。

investment in online advertisement. In 2011, Vancl's investment in online advertisement reached 500 million yuan. In 2012, Vancl ranked among "The Top 20 Advertisers", based on the investment in online advertising. Particularly, Vancl was the unique e-commerce firm among the 20 advertisers. Vancl adopts the combined strategy in advertisement delivery, that is, the advertisements are delivered to different types of channels so as to cover different groups. The channels include:

1) Comprehensive portal websites. The famous portals such as Sina, Sohu and Tencent have been an important delivery channel. The websites usually own the huge user groups, which enables the high exposure and awareness. Vancl covers all the famous portals in China in advertisement delivery. As a result, as long as a user logs on the website, he or she can see Vancl' advertisement, which helps the user to be familiar with Vancl' brand quickly.

2) Vertical websites. Vertical websites refer to the websites focusing on a specific field such as entertainments, finance and economy, vehicles, fashions and sports. These websites usually target on a specific customer group like vehicle owners, which enables the better effects of advertising. Vancl chooses the vertical websites whose themes are consistent with Vancl's motto such as young, fast and fashionable, which ensures the accuracy and efficiency of the advertisement delivery. In terms of advertisement type, Vancl combines graphics, flash and video advertisements to transmit the information on promotion and brand so as to import stream flow, improve clicks and purchases.

3) CPS affiliate. CPS (Cost-per-sale, sometimes referred to as Pay-per-sale), as an online advertisement pricing system, refers to the amount an advertiser pays for each sale generated by an advertisement. Under the CPS affiliate system, an advertiser delivers its ad code to a CPS affiliate platform which is responsible for sending the ad code to the numerous affiliate websites. The owners of the affiliate websites will decide whether to deliver the ad code to the websites based on their preferences. As long as the ad code on a specific affiliate website achieves a real purchase, the advertiser will pay the commission based on the agreement. Vancl establishs the good co-operations with the well-known CPS affiliate and websites, which benefits its online advertising including advertisement delivery, links tracking and sales recording. Once a deal is done through affiliate, Vancl pays the highest 18% commission. Due to the generous commission, about 4,000 websites have become Vancl's CPS affiliate, which improves Vancl's coverage online.

4) Social media. Considering the target customer—the youth, Vancl has been utilizing social media such as microblog for propagation. There are three groups opening their microblog related to Vancl on Sina Weibo: Vancl individual members, Vancl dealers and Vancl products communities. The microblog belonging to the three groups connects with each other and becomes the effective advertising forces for Vancl. Compared to the

traditional online medias such as official website, microblog has the obvious advantages[①]:

- Reaching the end customers initiatively. Unlike the official website which has to wait for customers' visiting, microblog can transmit the advertisements to the customers who follow Vancl's microblog initiatively.

- Interacting with customers effectively. A remarkable advantage of microblog is its interaction. On the microblog platform, consumers are allowed to inquire about the products, make the reviews, learn about the promotion campaign. On the other hand, by virtue of the interactions with consumers on microblog, Vancl is able to precisely capture consumers' need and make the correct decisions.

- Improving Vancl's brand awareness. As a popular social media, the powerful functionalities of forwarding and transmitting enable microblog to improve Vancl's awareness effectively. For example, the video of starring Han Han and Wang Luodan was disseminated widely, which not only improves Vancl's brand awareness but also attracts more potential customers.

Problems That Vancl's Online Advertising May Suffer

Though online advertising benefits Vancl a lot, there are still some problems which can not be ignored:

1. Ad blindness. According to the statistics, if someone has already seen an advertisement once, he or she wouldn't want to sit through it again with a high possibility. Unless the advertisement is so amazingly creative and interesting that viewer will loop that 3-15 minutes. Besides, all the consumers love that "Skip ad" option and get sort of annoyed when they have to wait 5 seconds to do so[②]. Currently, many website visitors are so inundated with online advertising that they experience ad blindness: Their eyes simply skip over the locations that banner advertising and other types of advertising are located, and may have a negative view of sponsored content. Though Vancl's advertisements cover many websites, the ad blindness probably impairs the effectiveness of online advertisements.

2. Ad blocking. All current versions of popular Internet browsers such as Google Chrome have access to ad blocking extensions. Instead of experiencing banner blindness and not seeing your ads, they completely block the ads from getting to their browser. By default, these extensions block a majority of ad servers and are updated to adjust to new ones on the market as well. With the explosive rising of online advertisements, more and

---

① 刘方:"凡客诚品的微博营销战略浅析",《新闻世界》,2011 年第 7 期。
② Parminderjit Kaur, Pros & Cons: Online video advertising, available at: http://www.marketing-interactive.com/pros-cons-online-video-advertising/, 2014-12-12.

more consumers have been bored with them. Therefore, Vancl's advertisements may be blocked by the tools.

3. Competition. Vancl has a great deal of opportunity on the Internet, but it also has a great deal of competition. It can't just set up an e-commerce site and expect the money to flow in. If Vancl doesn't have any way to set itself apart from its market, it is going to be drowning in a saturated market. Its online advertisements are likely to be displayed alongside competitors, so it's important that Vancl finds a way to stand out.

4. Distraction. The problem is particularly remarkable when an advertisement is delivered on a search engine. When a firm is advertising through a search engine or on a site that has a lot of content curation, its potential customers are getting distracted by dozens of things on the screen at once. The amount of traffic leaks can easily lead Vancl's online advertisements not to be as effective as they are.

5. Analytics learning curve. To completely take advantage of online advertising methods, Vancl needs to spend a lot of time tracking the data and adjusting its advertising by watching data tracking and other analytics programs. If it hasn't used this, there would a learning curve before Vancl understands how all of the data interact[1].

6. Weak economics. According to eMarketer, CPM of broadcast TV is $10.25, which is almost five times of online display (US $2.46). It's generally understood that while people are spending about 30% of their media consumption time online, only about 10% of media budgets are dedicated to online. Advertisers are spending money advertising in order to sell enough products or services at a profit to survive and thrive. If their products or services are high quality and valuable, they'll succeed—but only if enough potential customers know that their products or services exist, and if they can become educated enough to understand what the value is. Publishers are creating their own set of products in the form of some type of content that they hope consumers will ingest. They are also advertisers, selling the value of their content to the consumer. And in order to make enough money to create more valuable content to attract consumers, they need to profit from advertising that they sell. Right now the world is living on somewhat inverted principles. Much of the advertising being sold is not profitable enough to cover the production costs of the content that "hosts" it at any significant profit margin. For example, one of Vancl's senior manager pointed out that "The input-output ratio of our advertising is absolutely more than 1." This means that the vehicles that carry the ads—the content—are at risk of disappearing. And this means that the means for a company to put

---

[1] TopTenSM Staff, TEN PROS AND CONS OF ONLINE ADVERTISING, http://www.toptensocialmedia.com/social-media-social-buzz/ten-pros-and-cons-of-online-advertising/, 2014.

its message of value in front of a potential customer is eroding①.

> **译** 投入产出比不理想。统计表明,按照曝光度计费的标准,电视广告的成本几乎是网络广告的 5 倍。当人们在线上媒体花费 30% 的消费时间时,在网络广告上的投入却仅约占预算的 10%。广告商为广告投入是为了增加销售以盈利。如果他们的产品和服务质量足够好,那么投放广告就会成功,但这必须是在消费者知道该产品(服务)的存在或者了解其价值的情况下。媒体向消费者提供内容服务,同时他们也是广告商。为了能向消费者提供更多有价值的内容,他们必须从投放广告中赚取利润。目前很多广告的投入与产出是不成比例的。例如,凡客的资深管理者就曾指出,他们的广告投入产出比大于 1。这不仅意味着投放网络广告和内容的渠道正面临被淘汰的风险,而且说明企业向潜在客户投放信息的价值正在降低。

Just as what Chen Nian, CEO of Vancl, said, "When I make a style of shirts or down jackets that chain brands like Uniqlo would never dare to tailor, it means we have taken a big step toward our successful transformation. What we want is to become China's Uniqlo. But the difference is we are going to work as a dot-com company rather than run physical stores."②

Case Analysis

成立于 2007 年的凡客诚品(以下简称凡客)曾经以惊人的速度成为国内互联网时尚第一品牌,甚至改变了中国人的消费习惯。凡客早期的成功除了得益于它高效而高质量的生产以及出色的物流配送,也因为它抓住了 2007—2008 年中国线上服装零售市场快速增长的良好时机,针对消费者尤其是年轻人线上服饰消费的旺盛需求,适时地推出价廉物美的产品,成功占领市场并成为同类产品中的翘楚。尽管凡客后来因为种种原因迅速衰落,从顶峰时期的 1.3 万员工仅剩下 2016 年的 180 人③,但它早期的 29 元 T-shirt、49 元的帆布鞋、Polo 衫和 bra-T 等优质低价的产品仍然令人记忆犹新,而令这些产品以及凡客诚品这个品牌在中国迅速走红的正是它独具特色的互联网广告营销——也是本案例的分析重点。

一般而言,选择合适的代言人、设计广告文案以及选择合适的广告投放渠道是线上广告的基本要素。凡客广告最令人印象深刻的就是它极具创意的广告文案策划。广告文案是一则广告成败的关键,做得好的广告文案能令人眼前一亮,迅速扩大品牌知名度,并最终刺激消费。凡客广告文案的成功之处在于它准确地把握了目标客户群的心理特征,并传达了凡客的文化理念——做你自己,保持个性。这极大程度地满足了当时年轻人的心理需求,因此广告一经推出就迅速走红,这不仅带来了产品销量的增加,也令凡客诚品这个品牌的知名度迅速提高。除了响亮的广告语,凡客还选择了合适的代

---

① Eric Picard, Online advertising's 4 biggest problems, http://www.imediaconnection.com/content/23585.asp#singleview, 2009-06-24.
② Liao Wei, VANCL: From a myth to a white shirt, China Daily, 2014-10-14.
③ 红商网,凡客诚品的败局:十年走出一条发人深思的曲线,http://www.redsh.com, 2018-03-09

言人——韩寒。韩寒是当代知名的青年作家,也是知名博主,他出色的写作才华,极具个性的言论都令他一度成为青年人的偶像。而他一直以来崇尚自由、张扬个性的形象也与凡客的品牌文化不谋而合。韩寒的代言无疑对凡客广告起到了锦上添花的作用,同时也在潜移默化地利用"意见领袖"的影响力刺激消费需求。另外,凡客对广告投放渠道的布局也颇值得借鉴:除了在官网投放广告,凡客还选择了微博这种年轻人青睐的社交平台进行宣传推广,有效地利用了社交媒体的口碑效应,并在门户网站上高密度地播放广告,增加品牌的曝光度。凡客以重金打造的混合渠道投放策略不仅保证了信息的有效传播,也迅速提高了品牌知名度,但同时也给凡客造成了资金压力。

除了借鉴凡客的网络广告策略的成功之处,我们也应该规避网络广告中的常见误区,例如广告盲区、分散注意力以及投资回报率不理想等问题就给凡客实施网络广告策略造成困扰。

Section 4
Microblog Advertising—Xiaomi's Miracle
第四节 微博广告——小米的奇迹

I Key Words

1. defy *vt.* 挑衅
2. microblog *n.* 微博
3. handset *n.* 手机
4. razor-thin margins 微薄的利润
5. flash sale 限时抢购
6. debut *n.* 初次登台
7. drum up 招徕顾客
8. rapport *n.* 密切关系
9. resonate *vt.* 引起共鸣
10. like-minded *adj.* 志趣相投的

II Case

About Xiaomi

Xiaomi, a privately owned Chinese electronics company headquartered in Beijing, was founded in 2010 by Lei Jun. It designs, develops, and sells smartphones, mobile apps, and consumer electronics. According to Xiaomi's official explanation, the "MI" in the logo stands for "Mobile Internet". It also has other meanings, including "Mission Impossible" because Xiaomi faced many challenges that had seemed impossible to defy in its early days. Since the release of its first smartphone in August 2011, Xiaomi has experienced a rapid growth: As of the fourth quarter of 2017, Xiaomi became the fourth-largest smartphone maker by market share and even increased shipments of its devices as the overall market declined for the first time ever. At the end of 2017, Xiaomi beat its 100 billion yuan ($15.8 billion) revenue target①. It currently has 15,000 employees in China, India, Malaysia, Singapore and is expanding to other countries such as Indonesia, the Philippines and South Africa②.

During the past eight years, Xiaomi has been developing a wider range of consumer electronics, including a smart home (IoT) device ecosystem. However, its goals are obviously much more than the current businesses. Though being known for its affordable handsets, Xiaomi is not really banking on them and connected devices in general to make money. Its business model is described by Lei Jun as a "triathlon", where it invests in companies producing hardware and devices, sells the products through its online stores and offers services for product users on the internet. Though gadgets currently remain Xiaomi's major source of income, this is expected to change soon and the internet services will drive the bulk of its revenues down the road(Figure 7-6)③.

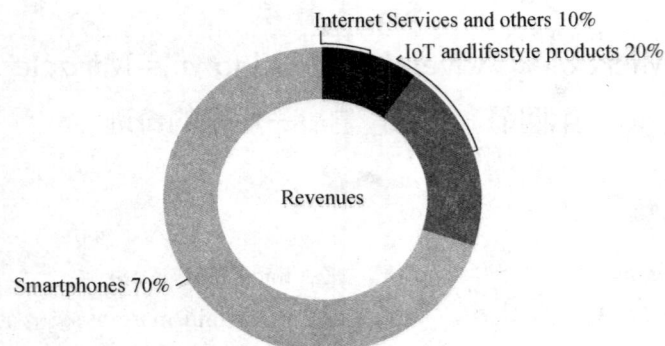

Figure 7-6　Xiaomi Revenue Breakdown 2017④

Xiaomi's Marketing Strategies

Xiaomi differentiates itself from the peers by adopting four special marketing strategies: online-only selling, razor-thin margins, online interaction community and active use of social media.

1. Online-only selling

Xiaomi does not own a single physical store and instead sells exclusively from its own

---

　　① Arjun Kharpal, Xiaomi says it hit its $15.8 billion revenue target in 2017 ahead of time, https://www.cnbc.com/2018/02/26/xiaomi-says-it-hit-its-15-point-8-billion-revenue-target-in-2017-ahead-of-time.html, Feburary 26, 2018.
　　② https://en.wikipedia.org/wiki/Xiaomi
　　③④ Rita Liao, For Xiaomi, the real money is not in gadgets, https://www.techinasia.com/xiaomi-ipo-business-model, May 2018.

online store. The online channel allows the company to reach the end customers efficiently and sell its smart phones in different markets like India, Brazil and Russia, keeping the cost base down and appealing to a tech-savvy audience. It also does away with traditional advertising and relies on social networking services as well as its own customers to help advertise its products.

2. Razor-thin margins[①]

The company is known for its high-spec smart phones, which can take on its premium rivals such as Apple and Samsung, but sells at less than half the cost. This comes at a price for Xiaomi which has an approximately 3% margins on its phones. Just as what Lei Jun said that the company priced the phone almost at bill-of-material prices, without compromising the component quality and performance compared to other premium smartphones. To profit from the narrow margin, Xiaomi sells a model for up to 18 months instead of the short 6 months used by Samsung to profit from the fall in the costs of components that occurs over time. It also profits by selling phone-related peripheral devices, smart home gadgetry, in addition to apps, online videos and themes. In the long term, the company sees the hardware sales just as a means of delivering software and services, as explained by a manager of Xiaomi, "We are an Internet and a software company much more than... a hardware company."

> 译 这家公司以其高品质智能手机而闻名,其手机具有几乎可与苹果、三星等媲美的功能,但售价却不到前两者的一半。这使小米手机的利润仅为3%左右。正如其负责人雷军所说,小米手机几乎是按成本价出售,但其质量和性能却并未打折。为了能从如此薄利中获益,小米延长产品生命周期,将一般手机的生命周期从6个月延长至18个月,以此获得更多收益。另外,它还通过提供手机周边产品、智能家居产品以及应用软件等来获取收入。小米将硬件销售作为其交付软件和服务的途径。正如小米对自己的定位一样,是一家"互联网和软件服务公司"。

Furthermore, by keeping a tight control over its stock, Xiaomi is able to place cheaper batch orders as demand dictates. Limited availability and flash sales ensure that supply never outstrips demand and help create a free marketing buzz around its products. Traditional OEMs usually have to incur large upfront productions costs in order to ship smartphones out to retailers all around the world, some of which may not sell. This is far more expensive than Xiaomi's model and it's the consumers that end up paying the difference. Xiaomi changes the game because it has such a strong image of affordability but with equally strong functionality for the phone.

3. Online interaction community

Xiaomi built an extensive online community so as to listen closely to customer

---

① Arjun Kharpal, What's Behind Rapid Rise of 'China's Apple' Xiaomi?, https://www.cnbc.com/2014/12/22/whats-behind-rapid-rise-of-chinas-apple-xiaomi.html, 2014-12-22.

feedback and have customers to test out upcoming features themselves. The approach allows Xiaomi to quickly act on feedback, release updates for their software every couple of weeks to keep their offering up-to-date and build a strong and loyal consumer base. This approach originated from Lei Jun's previous experience: when he pointed out some inadequacies of the products to Nokia and Motorola, 2 mobile phone giants of their time, they merely acknowledged the input, but never acted upon what he had said. "So I thought to myself, if I make a phone, you can tell me anything you wish for it or what's wrong. If it is justifiable, we will work on it immediately. I'll give you an update every week and you may even see your wishes come true within a week." In practice, Xiaomi's product managers dedicate a lot of time to browsing through the company's user forums. Once a suggestion is picked, it is quickly transferred to the engineers. Therefore features can turn from mere concept to shipping products in the span of a week. The company then ships a new batch of phones out every week on Tuesday at noon Beijing time, containing the new software builds and possible minor hardware tweaks. Xiaomi calls this process "design as you build".

4. Active use of social media

XiaoMi has been managing to harness the power of social media. It not only delivers advertising on microblog to broadcast messages and announcements but also actively engages with their customers on it. For example, Engineers are routinely encouraged to speak directly to consumers and use gathered feedback to refine software. Through its active role in social media, XiaoMi has also succeeded in building a dedicated fan base. Those Mi-fans are very active in social media and are, in some ways, similar to those hardcore Apple advocates that we are all familiar with. Mi-fans are always present at XiaoMi's product launches where they are known for loud cheering and applauding.

Xiaomi's Debut of Microblog Advertising[①]

Xiaomi's mascot is a bunny wearing an Ushanka (known locally as a "Lei Feng hat" in China) with a red star and a red scarf around its neck. In 2011, this bunny registered on Sina Weibo (microblog) and started its journey on microblog.

On December 19, 2012, Xiaomi undertook an e-commerce experiment to sell its handsets directly on the Sina Weibo microblogging site, while the link-up offered Sina a chance to test out its new WeiboPay e-payment service. On Sina Weibo, Xiaomi posted an advertisement of 100 Chinese characters which announced that Mi2 smart phones would be

---

① Josh Ong, Microblog commerce sees success in China, as Xiaomi sells 50,000 smartphones in 5 minutes on Sina Weibo, http://thenextweb.com/asia/2012/12/21/xiaomi-and-sina-weibo-E-commerce-experiment-succeeds-as-50000-smartphones-snatched-up-in-5-minutes/, 2012-12-21.

sold on December 19, 2012 and introduced the basic functionalities and price of the product (Figure 7-7).

【#小米手机2微博开卖# 转发狂送20台】新浪微博社会化网购首单，12月21日中午12点，5万台#小米手机2#微博专场销售。全球首款28nm四核手机，2G大内存，新一代背照式相机，1999元性价比之王。现在起至20日，关注@小米手机，转发@好友，每天10点-20点每2小时送出2台米2。微博预约 http://t.cn/zj9m34X

2012-12-19 09:54 来自新浪微博 转发(2658392) | 收藏 | 评论(819841)

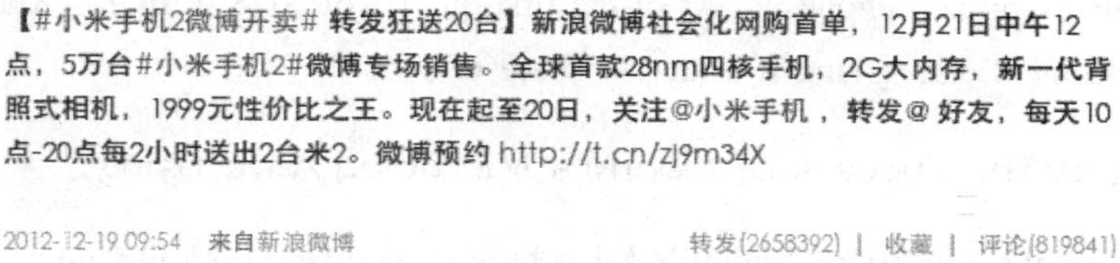

Figure 7-7 Xiaomi's Advertisement on Sina Microblog

The trial was successful, as the batch of 50,000 Mi2 smartphones sold out in 5 minutes and 14 seconds, according to Xiaomi. The sale received 810,000 comments, 1.3 million reservations and 2.33 million forwards on Weibo. The lucky 50,000 finalized their payment in 24 hours and the phones were shipped within two days. The success should be primarily attributed to the three groups behind the experiment: Xiaomi users, VIP bloggers and Sina microblog users (Figure 7-8). It is the three groups that commented, reserved and forwarded the advertisement, which resulted in a successful "Word-of-Mouth Marketing".

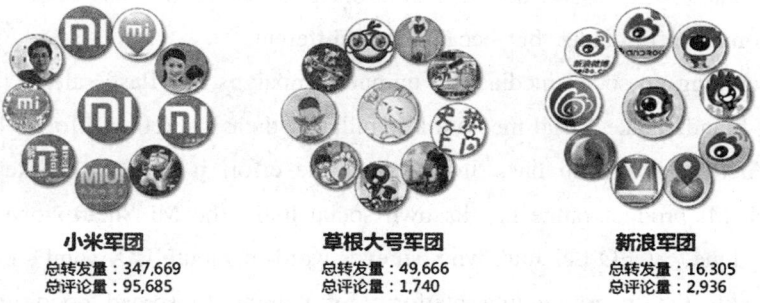

Figure 7-8 The Three Groups Contributing to Xiaomi's Advertising[①]

After tasting the sweetness of microblog marketing, Xiaomi employed the same strategy for its expansion to India. The company unveiled its first handset designed for exclusively for the Indian market on April 23, 2014. Indians bought 21.6 million smartphones in the fourth quarter of 2014, making it the world's third-largest smartphone market in terms of the number devices sold. Compared to ZTE and Huawei, the two well-known handset manufacturers in China, Xiaomi was a relative new entrant to the Chinese handheld market. To drum up interest for its India launch, Xiaomi accessed to India's social media to post teasers on its phone features and highlight its selling point—a longer battery life, the usual mid-range handset's high-resolution display in a form factor that's

① Both Figure 7-7 and Figure 7-8 come from http://36kr.com/p/200796.html.

comfortable to use one-handed. Xiaomi debuted in India in 2013. It also took a cue from Apple and set up "experience stores" across India, which would have their own in-house geek squad to fix broken phones①. As of the first quarter of 2018 in India, Xiaomi shipped over 9 million handsets, giving it a market share of 31%②.

What Causes The Success of Xiaomi's Microblog Advertising?③

Witnessing the success of Xiaomi's Microblog Advertising both in China and in India, it is important to find the reasons behind the success. Essentially, Xiaomi's microblog advertising leverages the power of word-of-mouth:

1. Creating a prerequisite that resonates with the target audience

Xiaomi began with a very simple idea: to offer high specs at low prices. It targets markets where technologically-savvy customers may not be able to afford top-of-the-line Apple or Samsung smartphones but seek higher quality devices than cheap knock-offs or clones.

It has distinguished itself by building a strong following around its custom operating system, MIUI. Fans eagerly await every update to their Mi phone's software for new, cutting-edge features not found on other Android phones. Now, fans seek it out not just because Xiaomi is affordable, but because it is different.

2. Leveraging on social media with unique campaigns like flash sales

Lots of brands make social media a key pillar of their marketing efforts, but few fully utilise it as deftly as Xiaomi has. Just look at the effort it put into marketing on Sina Weibo. Each Mi product range has its own social hub (the Mi Smartphone Hub has 11 million fans alone). CEO Lei Jun, who believes word-of-mouth is Xiaomi's key marketing strategy, credits the microblogging platform for helping to spread good reviews of its product.

More importantly, Xiaomi popularises flash sales as a means of generating hype online. The anticipation and urgency of the sales naturally drove many fans to share news about these sales on social media. By using word-of-mouth rather than just plain advertising, Xiaomi is able to sell its products efficiently and build its brand around its main mission of creating high specs at low prices.

3. Customizing the product and community outreach to the local market

---

① Kenneth Rapoza, Xiaomi To Make Things Even Harder For Apple In India, http://www.forbes.com/sites/kenrapoza/2015/04/21/xiaomi-to-make-things-even-harder-for-apple-in-india/3/, 2015-04-21.

② Prakhar Tripathi, Xiaomi Is No More An Underdog, Seized 31% of India Smartphone Market In Q1 2018, https://dazeinfo.com/2018/04/24/xiaomi-india-smartphone-market-q1-2018/, 2018-04-24.

③ Jared Tong, How Xiaomi Used Word-of-Mouth To Become China's Top Smartphone Vendor, https://www.referralcandy.com/blog/xiaomi-marketing-strategy/, 2016-01-14.

None of these efforts would have been effective had Xiaomi not demonstrated a great deal of sincerity and transparency, allowing them to adapt to local cultures. For example, It engaged Hugo Barra, a famous computer scientist, technology executive and entrepreneur, as Xiaomi's brand ambassador, having him to deliver product keynotes in markets like India to tremendous effect. Xiaomi has even built product features and marketing material around local issues, such as their unique MIUI feature to navigate India's Interactive Voice Response systems.

4. Fan festivals and meetups

It organises fan festivals and local meetups, building rapport within the local community and growing the fan base by encouraging fans to invite their friends along. And Xiaomi rewards such passion: Hugo Barra regularly visits fans, and staff personally autograph thank you cards. As a result, Xiaomi has built a tribe as fiercely supportive as Apple supporters.

5. Combining forces with like-minded brands to build hype

The Redmi Note was launched exclusively on QQ Zone, one of China's largest social networks and comprised of a predominantly geeky audience. The resulting public relationships coverage is a win-win for both parties. Xiaomi employed this strategy to great effect again when launching the Mi Note. It partnered with Uber to deliver the phones to customers. Even non-tech media covered this story, creating the kind of buzz only the combined forces of Xiaomi x Uber could. Other examples of partnership include: Microsoft Windows 10 on Mi4, Li Ning smart sneakers.

Microblog advertising, as an emerging marketing method, is still at its infant stage in China. With the dramatic growth of the Internet especially the mobile Internet users in China, microblog is going to popularize further. Xiaomi's success not only makes a good example of microblog advertising, but also indicates a huge opportunity for Chinese microblog advertising.

Case Analysis

小米从初创时的备受质疑到今天成为中国乃至全球都有一定影响力的智能手机和电子产品品牌花费了8年的时间。在这8年中,给人们留下深刻印象的不仅是它一直以来贯彻的"优质低价"的产品理念,贴近用户需求的产品设计和不断扩大业务版图的雄心,更是它巧妙的营销策略,尤其是别出心裁的广告。因此,本案例分析的重点就放在小米的营销策略以及它的微博广告成功的原因。

小米的营销策略可以借助4Ps理论进行剖析:首先来看小米的产品策略。众所周知,小米的产品价格亲民。但小米并未因为低价而降低对产品质量的要求,相反,它一直奉行"优质低价"的理念:出色的电池续航能力、高质量的手机屏以及坚固耐用的手机外壳……这些产品质量上的优势令小米在一众国产智能手机中脱颖而出,并有赶超三星等国际知名品牌的趋势。再来看小米的价格策略。小米一直采取低价策略,它的手机利润仅为3%左右,用雷军的话来说,就是几乎是以成本价在销售。低成本策略并非长久之计,为了弥补低价带来的利润损失,小米采取了三个办法:一是通过有效的促销手段提升销量,实现规模经济效益;二是延长产品生命周期,将一般手机的生命周期从6个月延长至18个月,以此获得更多收益;三是提供手机周边产品以及内容服务,例如通过应用软件来获取收入。小米已经将硬件销售作为其交付软件和服务的途径。正如小米对自己的定位一样,是一家"互联网和软件服务公司"。第三是小米的渠道策略。小米自诞生之日起就采取了纯线上销售的策略。这一策略不仅使企业能将优势资源集中在一个渠道,利用互联网低成本和没有时空限制的优势实现高效的市场拓展,而且能借助互联网快速获得顾客反馈,及时捕捉消费者需求。最后是小米最为人津津乐道的促销策略,也是本案例分析的另一个重点。小米的促销策略主要包括两个方面:构建网上互动社区和充分发挥社交媒体的力量。一方面,小米构建了用户论坛等网上互动社区以便于随时倾听消费者的意见和建议,产品经理随时浏览用户在论坛上的发言,并将其中有价值的意见转发给工程师使其及时在产品中得以体现。这种让用户参与产品设计生产的做法与互联网年代"生产消费者"的理念不谋而合。另一方面,小米则充分利用社交媒体信息传播快速广泛的优势,投放广告和与用户互动。这种做法不仅帮助小米迅速建立起庞大的用户群体——米粉,而且借助"米粉"的点赞和转发创造了小米在微博广告中的奇迹。

小米2012年12月在新浪微博上投放广告所创造的"米2"的销售奇迹令人记忆犹新。微博广告是网络广告的新手法,通过手机我们每天可以看到上千条微博广告,但这其中令人印象深刻的却是凤毛麟角。小米的这条广告不过100来字,没有华丽的辞藻,没有响亮的口号,通篇只是对"米2"的性能、价格和发售时间进行了简单说明。为什么这样一则看似平淡的广告却帮助小米创造了销售奇迹呢?我们能从中学到什么经验呢?首先,理解你的目标客户的真正需求。广告的主要目的是宣传产品和劝说购买,如果连客户的需求都不清楚,那么广告投放的效果将大打折扣。很长一段时间,中国的消费者在购买智能手机时经常遭遇这样的尴尬:高端手机(如iPhone)质量功能不错但价格昂贵,令人无法承担;价格亲民的手机,质量却往往令人不敢恭维。小米优质高价手机的问世不仅解决了这种尴尬,而且填补了需求空白。因此,小米在微博广告中重点突出米2的优越性能和亲民的价格,有效地激发了消费者的兴趣。其次,利用社交媒体平台的传播效应提升促销策略的效果。在此之前,不少品牌都尝试过使用社交媒体营销,但能与小米媲美的却并不多。小米巧妙地在微博广告中传达"闪购"的信息,不仅限定了销售数量——5万台,还告知消费者将定时送出2台"米2"手机,再加上用户的积极转发和评论,极大地提高了消费者的期望值,刺激了他们的购买欲。再次,构建高忠诚度的粉丝群,以奠定良好的用户基础。社交媒体的传播效应是以用户流量为基础的,要提升微博广告的效果需要数量庞大的用户基础。小米一方面利用过硬的产品和广泛的宣传吸引了一批用户,另一方面则通过米粉节、粉丝见面会等方式和用户保持频繁交流,并通过赠送小米员工亲笔绘制的感谢卡,与手机发烧友的偶像"Hugo Barra"的零距离互动等方式拉近和用户之间的距离。这些措施不仅有助于提升其忠诚度,还可以通过口碑效应吸引更多的用户入群。最后,小米还通过和知名企业合作的方式进行品牌的宣传和推广。例如,和QQ以及优步的合作不仅进一步扩大了小米的品牌知名度,也实现了双方的合作共赢。

Section 5
Case Discussion
第五节 案例讨论

In general, a case discussion includes 5 parts[1]:

1. Start. There are different ways to start a case discussion such as asking the solution to the case or defining an issue.

2. Issue identification. This step requires you to identify the important issues in a case.

3. Case data analysis. The tools, techniques, concepts and theories are used to help the quantitative and qualitative analysis.

4. Alternatives and decision. For this step, you are asked to generate the alternatives, discuss the respective merits in depth, identify the discussion criteria, present the arguments and justify the decisions.

5. Action and implementation plan. Not all the discussions require the implementation plan. It depends on whether the instructor emphasizes an implementation plan and whether there is enough time left.

A case discussion not only provides you an opportunity to show your points, but also enables you to practice the communication skills. It is very important to actively join in the case discussion. The following list includes the tips you should pay attention to in case discussion[2]:

1. Make a conscious effort to contribute rather than just talk. There is a big difference between saying something that builds the discussion and offering a long-winded, off-the-cuff remark that leaves your peers wondering what the point is.

---

[1] Louise A. Mauffette-leenders, James A. Erskine, Michiel R. Leenders, *Learning with Cases*, Ivey Publishing (Fourth Edition), 2008:pp.78-82.

[2] Rudyard Kipling, A Guide to Case Analysis, https://highered.mheducation.com/sites/dl/free/.../guide_to_case_analysis.pdf

2. Give supporting reasons and evidence for your views. The expressions like "My analysis shows" and "The company should do... because..." are encouraged.

3. Use the data and information to explain your assessment of the situation and to support your position. In making your points, assume that everyone has read the case and knows what it says, avoid reciting and rehashing information in the case.

Summary (本章小结)

Based on the philosophy of interactive marketing, online advertising attempts to disseminate information through the Internet in order to affect a buyer-seller transaction. Three parities including publisher, advertiser and advertising agency are usually involved in online advertising. Online advertising is characterized by two-way communication, targeting on specific groups and individuals, and the capability of one-to-one advertising. People prefer online advertising due to its strengths like lower cost, diverse advertising patterns and personalization. There are different types of online advertisements. With time's going by some types like email advertisement have been barely used while new types like social media advertisement are popularizing.

As a paradigm of paid listing, Google AdWords enables advertisers to compete to display brief advertising copy to web users, based in part on keywords. Advertisers pay when users divert their browsing to seek more information about the copy displayed, and partner websites receive a portion of the income they generate. Since its launch, AdWords has evolved into Google's main source of revenue. Google extends AdWords services such as launching site-targeted advertising so as to serve the customers better. AdWords is so successful that some merchants such as Baidu mimic the model. The location of an ad on the search list depends on not only the bidding price an advertiser offers but also the quality score, that is, how relevant and useful a firm's ad is to the searchers and what search terms it uses. Regardless of its success, Google Adwords is suffering the threats from its competitors. Google Adwords owns the advantages (e.g. No limits for keywords) and disadvantages of paid listing (e.g. the possible fake information).

Vancl, as an Internet apparel brand in China founded in 2007, impresses people due to its online advertising—The Vancl Style. Vancl's success in advertising should be attributed to taking advantage of the Internet media to build its brand and interact with customers, innovative copywriting and combined delivery of advertisements. Though online advertising benefits Vancl a lot, there are still some problems which can not be ignored including ad blindness, ad blocking, competition, distraction, analytics learning curve and weak economics.

Xiaomi is a Chinese electronics company which designs, develops, and sells smart phones, mobile apps, and consumer electronics. Xiaomi has become a well-known smart phone brand and developed a wide range of consumer electronics ten years after its foundation. The brand strength of Xiaomi should be greatly attributed to its successful online advertising strategy—delivering advertisements by virtue of microblog. On December 19, 2012, Xiaomi undertook an e-commerce experiment to sell its handsets directly on the Sina Weibo microblogging site. The trial succeeded. Xiaomi employed the same strategy for its expansion to India and the success replayed. As an advertising method, microblog advertising also has two sides: It is easy to implement, enables effective interaction between sellers and buyers. However, the disadvantages such as requiring large number of fans and the limited dissemination effect can not be ignored.

As the second stage of the case analysis process, case discussion is very important since it benefits your analysis, expression and communication skills. A case discussion is composed of 5 parts including start, issue identification, case data analysis, alternatives and decision, and action and implementation plan. Besides, this chapter supplies the tips you should pay attention to like making a conscious effort to contribute rather than just talking.

Exercises & Tasks (练习与任务)

Exercises

1. How do you explain the popularity of online advertising?
2. How does Google Adwords become a profit source of Google?
3. Why does "The Vancl Style" succeed?
4. What can you learn from Xiaomi's microblog advertising?

Tasks

Choose a case of online advertising and prepare a 20-minute presentation which should include:

1. Background introduction (e.g. what is the ad about? Who makes the ad? What are the effects of the ad?...)
2. Analyze its advantages and disadvantages.
3. Conclude the elements that a good online advertisement should own or the lessons that a good online ad should avoid.

Chapter 8 第八章

Interactions Between E-Commerce and Social Media
电子商务与社交媒体的相互作用

 Learning Objectives（学习目标）

After finishing this chapter, you should be able to:
1. Define and categorize social media;
2. Describe the characteristics as well as pros and cons of social media;
3. Understand why social media like Tudou and Wechat popularizes rapidly;
4. Explain and compare the business model of Facebook and Tudou;
5. Identify how WeChat monetizes social media services;
6. Understand the ways to make a good presentation.

 Introduction（内容简介）

Social media has penetrated into businesses and people's lives in the past few years. How to integrate it with e-commerce and dig new values not only becomes an important task for many enterprises but also facilitates a new model—social commerce.

Chapter 8 is composed of 5 sections. The brief introduction to social media and social commerce is made in section 1. Three related cases are explained respectively in section 2, 3, and 4. Section 5 focuses on case presentation.

Section 1
Interactions Between E-Commerce and Social Media
第一节 电子商务与社交媒体的相互作用

▶ Key Words

1. equivalent *n.* 等价物
2. immediacy *n.* 即时性
3. invaluable *adj.* 无价的
4. perpetuate *vt.* 使不朽

▶ Definition

Social media are computer-mediated tools that allow people to create, share or exchange information, ideas, and pictures/videos in virtual communities and networks. They are "a group of Internet-based applications that build on the ideological and technological foundations of Web 2.0, and that allow the creation and exchange of user-generated content"①.

Social commerce is a subset of electronic commerce that involves social media, online media that supports social interaction and user contributions to assist online buying and selling of products and services. More succinctly, social commerce is the use of social network(s) in the context of e-commerce transactions②.

▶ Classification of social media

With the popularzity of mobile devices like smart phones, people typically gain access to social media services via downloading services that offer social media functionality to their mobile devices. Mobile social media applications can be differentiated among four types③:

1. Space-timers (location and time sensitive): Exchange of messages with relevance for one specific location at one specific point in time (e.g. Facebook Places);

2. Space-locators (only location sensitive): Exchange of messages, with relevance for one specific location, which are tagged to a certain place and read later by others (e.g. Yelp);

3. Quick-timers (only time sensitive): Transfer of traditional social media

---

① https://www.sor.org/learning/document-library/somerad-guidance-radiography-workforce-professional-use-social-media/introduction-what-social-media

② https://en.wikipedia.org/wiki/Social_commerce

③ Ramesh Kumar Miryala, Trends, Challenges & Innovations in Management, *Zenon Academic Publishing*, 2015 (3): pp. 264.

applications to mobile devices to increase immediacy (e. g. posting Twitter messages or Facebook status updates);

4. Slow-timers (neither location, nor time sensitive): Transfer of traditional social media applications to mobile devices (e. g. watching a YouTube video).

Besides, Thomas Crampton and his team put together an info-graphic to explain some of China's Social Media equivalents. This graphic classifies social media in China into sixteen types based on the functionalities (Figure 8-1)①.

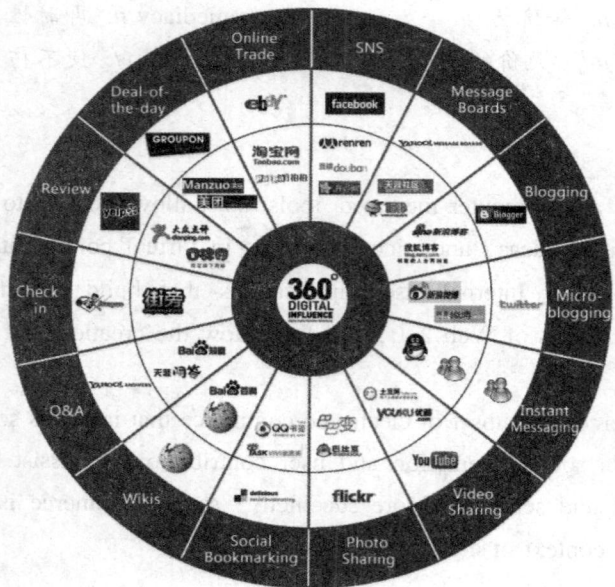

Figure 8-1　China's Social Media②

▶ *Characteristics*③

Some of the properties that help differentiate social media and industrial media are:

1. Quality. In industrial (traditional) publishing—mediated by a publisher—the typical range of quality is substantially narrower than in niche, unmediated markets. The main challenge posed by content in social media sites is the fact that the distribution of quality has high variance—from very high-quality items to low-quality, sometimes abusive content.

2. Reach. Both industrial and social media technologies provide scale and are capable of reaching a global audience. Industrial media, however, typically use a centralized

---

①② Thomas Crampton, Infographic of China's Social Media Equivalents, http://www. huffingtonpost. com/thomas-crampton/infographic-of-chinas-soc_b_721239. html, May 25, 2011.
③ https://en. wikipedia. org/wiki/Social_media

framework for organization, production, and dissemination, whereas social media are by their very nature more decentralized, less hierarchical, and distinguished by multiple points of production and utility.

3. Accessibility. The means of production for industrial media are typically government and/or corporate; social media tools are generally available to the public at little or no cost.

4. Usability. Industrial media production typically requires specialized skills and training. Conversely, most social media production requires only modest reinterpretation of existing skills. Technically, anyone with access can operate the means of social media production.

5. Immediacy. The time lag between communications produced by industrial media can be long (days, weeks, or even months) compared to social media (which can be capable of virtually instantaneous responses).

6. Permanence. Industrial media, once created, can not be altered (once a magazine article is printed and distributed, changes can not be made to that same article) whereas social media can be altered almost instantaneously by comments or editing.

▶ Pros and Cons of Social Media[①]

Pros:

1. Social media creates new social connections. The main purpose of social media is to be able to stay connected to friends and families in today's fast paced and ever changing worlds. Everyone is able to rekindle old friendships, share family photos, and special events in his or her life with just about everyone he or she knows, at the same time.

2. Finding people with common interests. Social media is also a great way to meet entirely new people. Everyone can seek out groups that are focused towards the special interests and hobbies and connect with local people that share the same interests. Members of social media like Facebook discuss their health conditions, share important information, and resources relevant to their conditions while creating strong support networks.

3. Invaluable promotional tool. Companies, artists, and musicians can reach an impossibly large and diverse amount of people using social media sites. This allows them to promote and market themselves and their products in a way that has never been seen before.

---

① 10 Advantages and Disadvantages of Social Networking, http://futureofworking.com/10-advantages-and-disadvantages-of-social-networking/, June 2, 2015.

4. Information spreads incredibly fast. Breaking news and other important information can spread like wildfire on social media sites. Important things like recalls or storm information are all communicated and taken seriously very quickly.

Cons:

1. Perpetuates false and unreliable information. Just like stated above, anything can spread to millions of people within hours or days on social media. This also, unfortunately, includes things that are false or made up. This information can cause panic and severe misinformation in society.

2. Causing major relationship problems. Online social interactions with social media have not only been starting new relationships, but ending many others. It is very simple to communicate and share pictures or plans with a person on social media and keep it completely under wraps. This new temptation has been driving wedges into people's real life, offline relationships, often time ending them for good. Social media puts trust to the limit.

3. Cyber bullying is a growing problem. Having access to people's lives at all times is not always a good thing. A new trend of cyber bullying is wreaking havoc all across the world. This is especially true with young kids. They are publicly harassing one another, and posting mean or slanderous things which are broadcasted to the entire cyber world.

4. The addiction is real. One of the biggest problems with the social media craze is that people are becoming more and more addicted to using it. It is the number one time waster at work, in school, and at home. It has caused people to have literal withdraws from their social networks.

Section 2
Facebook—From Social Media to Social Commerce
第二节　脸谱网——从社交媒体到社交商务

Key Words

1. colloquialism *n.* 口语
2. scrutiny *n.* 详细审查
3. adeptness *n.* 熟练
4. crappy *adj.* 蹩脚的

Case

About Facebook[①]

Facebook is an online social networking service headquartered California. Its website was launched on February 4, 2004, by Mark Zuckerberg, a Harvard University student with his college roommates and fellows. The founders initially limited the website's membership to Harvard students, but later expanded it to colleges in the Boston area, the Ivy League, and Stanford University. It gradually added support for students at various other universities and later to high-school students. Since 2006, anyone at least 13 years old has been allowed to become a registered user of the website, though the age requirement may be higher depending on applicable local laws. Its name comes from a colloquialism for the directory given to it by American universities students.

After registering to use the site, users can create a user profile, add other users as "friends", exchange messages, post status updates and photos, share videos and receive notifications when others update their profiles. Additionally, users may join common-interest user groups, organized by workplace, school or college, or other characteristics, and categorize their friends into lists such as "People From Work" or "Close Friends". Facebook's offerings for the online users include:

1. Facebook web and mobile app. These apps enable people to share their opinions, ideas, photos, videos, and other activities with friends and followers.

2. Instagram. It is a mobile application that enables people to take photos or videos, customize them with filter effects, and share them friends and followers. Facebook acquired Instagram in April 2012.

3. Facebook Messenger. It is a mobile-to-mobile messaging application available on iOS, Android, and windows phone devices.

4. Whatsapp. It is a cross-platform mobile messaging application that Facebook acquired in October 2014.

Facebook had over 1.44 billion monthly active users as of March 2015. Due to the large volume of data users submit to the service, Facebook has come under scrutiny for their privacy policies. Facebook held its initial public offering in February 2012 and began selling stock to the public three months later, reaching an original peak market capitalization of $104 billion. As of February 2015, Facebook reached a market capitalization of $212 Billion.

---

① https://en.wikipedia.org/wiki/Facebook

Business Model[①]

Facebook's revenue grew from 7.87 billion in 2013 to 40.7 billion U.S. dollars in 2017. That year, Facebook accumulated a net income of 15.9 billion U.S. dollars, ranking first among social media companies in annual revenues (Figure 8-2)[②]. How does Facebook make money?

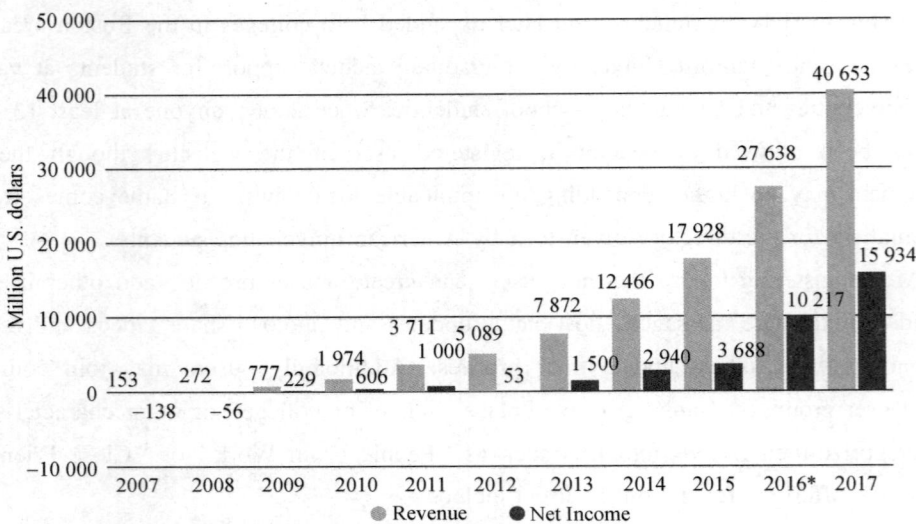

Figure 8-2　Facebook's Annual Revenue and Net Income from 2007 to 2017[③]

Currently, the majority of Facebook revenues are generated via advertising—the shift towards e-commerce and online marketing has not been more evident than in 2016 yet. Other revenue-generating factors are payment service for developers, online marketing and online promotion during events such as the U.S. election in 2016, during which online advertising played a major role.

1. From advertising

Most of Facebook's revenue comes from advertising. A big part of Facebook's pitch is that it has such a huge user group and owns so much information of its users that it can more effectively target on those who will be responsive to the content. Facebook offers advertising placements over its website and mobile app to the marketers to help them reach people on Facebook based on a variety of factors such as age, gender, location, and interests. In addition to Facebook, marketers can buy ads on Instagram and on other

---

① Jitender Miglani, How Facebook Makes Money?, https://revenuesandprofits.com/how-facebook-makes-money/, June 9, 2015.
②③ Facebook's Annual Revenue and Net Income from 2007 to 2017 (in million U.S. dollars), https://www.statista.com/statistics/277229/facebooks-annual-revenue-and-net-income/, 2018.

websites and applications such as Audience Network, Atlas, and Liverail (Figure 8-3).

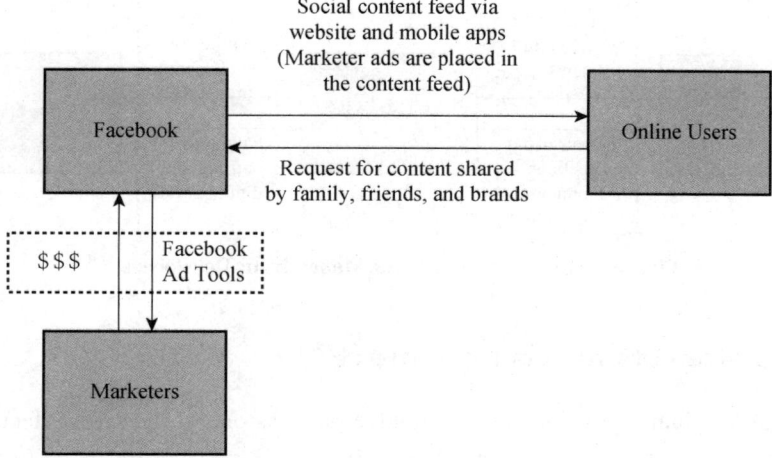

Figure 8-3 Facebook Makes Money from Advertising[①]

However, Facebook generally has a lower Click-through-rate (CTR) for advertisements than most major Web sites. According to BusinessWeek.com, banner advertisements on Facebook have generally received one-fifth the number of clicks compared to those on the Web as a whole, although specific comparisons can reveal a much larger disparity. For example, while Google users click on the first advertisement for search results an average of 8% of the time (80,000 clicks for every one million searches), Facebook's users click on advertisements an average of 0.04% of the time (400 clicks for every one million pages). The cause of Facebook's low CTR has been attributed to younger users enabling ad blocking software and their adeptness at ignoring advertising messages, as well as the site's primary purpose being social communication rather than content viewing. Though owning low CTR, Facebook's advertisement is good compared to its peers. A study found that, for video advertisements on Facebook, over 40% of users who viewed the videos viewed the entire video, while the industry average was 25% for in-banner video ads. In February of 2015, Facebook announced that it reached 2 million active advertisers with most of the gain coming from businesses.

2. From developers

Facebook offers a set of development tools and application programming interfaces (APIs) to the developers to help them create web and mobile apps for the Facebook platform. When users purchase virtual and digital goods from the developer apps, Facebook

---

① Jitender Miglani, How Facebook Makes Money?, https://revenuesandprofits.com/how-facebook-makes-money/, June 9, 2015.

receives a fee from the developers for the use of its payment infrastructure (Figure 8-4).

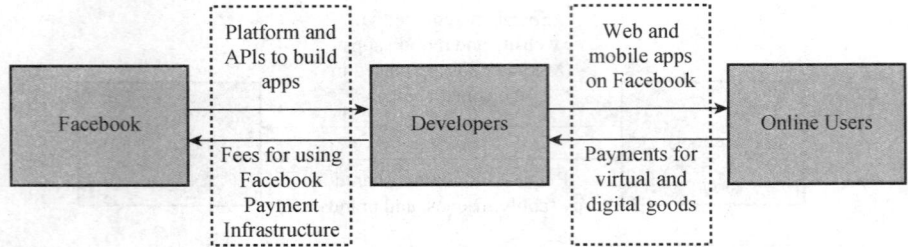

Figure 8-4   Facebook Makes Money from Developers①

Facebook's Attempts to Social-commerce②③

Facebook originally positioned itself to advertisers as one of the most effective ways of driving traffic and retaining viewership. Yet Facebook finds itself in a position where instead of simply promoting products and services, it can also act as the payment portal to them, hence the rise of social commerce. Besides, there are positive signs for Facebook that social commerce could become a vital contributor to the company's income going forward, with statistics suggesting payments through social networks in 2016 accounted for 30% of digital sales in South East Asia following Facebook partnership with the payments company Qwik. Facebook's social commerce attempts include two phases: being an e-commerce operator and being a social outlet for users.

1. E-commerce operator

Facebook first entered the online commerce space in February of 2007 with the launch of their virtual gift shop. Users loaded up on Facebook credits and purchased virtual gifts such as images of balloons and teddy bears to be posted on other user's walls, typically for $1.00 each, with the opportunity to add a personalized message to each gift. Facebook gifts gained traction and generated $40 million dollars in sales in 2008. To expand its virtual gifts shop, Facebook launched Credits program which was initially used as a way for Facebook users to purchase virtual goods through the Facebook gift shop with virtual currency. Further, Facebook slowly opened up Credits to third-party developers. The purpose is for developers of applications, like FarmVille and other large social games, to integrate Facebook's Credits product directly into their applications. While this may appear to be a successful product, Facebook decided to shut down their virtual gift site in 2010 to

---

① Jitender Miglani, How Facebook Makes Money?, https://revenuesandprofits.com/how-facebook-makes-money/, 2015-06-09.
② Samantha Harrison, Facebook. Will f-commerce be the future of E-commerce?, http://www.onlineeconomy.org/facebook-will-f-commerce-be-the-future-of-E-commerce, 2011-10-20.
③ Tomio Geron, What Is Facebook's Future As An E-commerce Platform?, Forbes, 2011-04-12.

focus on other priorities. Since then, Facebook pursued other commerce avenues—such as payment or the ability to purchase items from store's Facebook pages. None of these, however, has taken off.

Why is e-commerce of the platform with over 800 million active users not as successful as it is in social media? The first reason is the traits of products. Since Facebook is a communication tool and place for people to share their thoughts with one another, the products which are more "inherently social" are obviously sold well on Facebook. For example, books, DVDs, movie and event tickets are successful because these products are fundamentally about interaction with friends, which makes them a natural for Facebook. Similarly, selling for peer-to-peer marketplaces is also useful because people would more readily trust buying or selling from a friend or friend-of-a-friend than a stranger online. But other products such as sweater are not so inherently social.

The second reason is that Facebook doesn't make shopping any easier, instead, it simply provides another click-through step in the process of online shopping. Because of this, there has been virtually no traction of users shopping on Facebook for things other than virtual goods. Facebook's core asset is its open graph—the map of connections that Facebook users create with friends and online content. Facebook has started sharing the data with outside applications—letting other vendors track Facebook users' activity or leverage an individual's social network since 2007. This further delayed Facebook's entry into social commerce as it provides even less incentive for users to shop through Facebook rather than directly with stores.

On October 19, 2011, Facebook entered into a digital payment partnership with eBay which allows third party developers to incorporate Facebook's open graph when building applications on eBay's X. commerce platform. This formalized channel which allows all application developers to leverage Facebook's key asset is further evidence that Facebook did not prioritize driving users to purchase items through Facebook's interface.

Facebook began to steer away from online commerce after it recognized that its primary purpose is to be a social outlet for users. It is a great source of brand building for merchants—a way to share information, provide exclusive offers and access, and increase awareness but has not served as a strong driver of traffic for online commerce.

2. Social outlet for users[①]

In July 2014, Facebook announced that it was testing a Buy button that appears on ads and Page posts from a select group of businesses in the U. S. The company was not necessarily hoping to become the next Amazon. Instead, it had been trying to make mobile ads more effective so that it can charge more money for them. Generally, shoppers who

---

① Seth Fiegerman, Why Facebook and Twitter Are Embracing E-commerce, mashable. com, 2014-07-21.

click ads on their phones are less likely to actually buy something. When they click through to the advertiser's mobile site, it's usually harder to use than the regular website. So they end up leaving without buying, which means a lower "conversion rate" in advertising terminology. So brands pay less money for those ads (and potentially buy less of them).

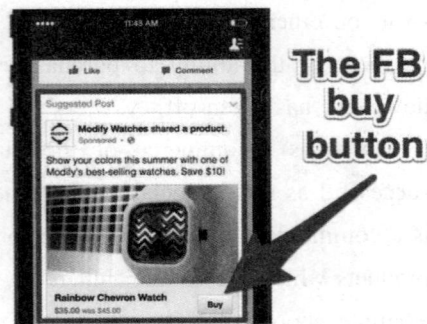

Figure 8-5　The BUY Button on Facebook①

Buy button which keeps the shopper contained on the original site with a more frictionless checkout experience should lead to more people actually completing their purchases. Higher conversion rate means advertisers will be willing to pay more for mobile ads. The new feature highlights the overlapping commerce ambitions of Facebook. Facebook is a powerhouse for advertising and virtual goods with 500 million people using the service to communicate and share information with their friends (Figure 8-5).

 购买按钮，它令购物者不用打开新网页即可享受无缝衔接的结账体验，这样将提升消费者的购物转化率。高转化率也意味着广告商更愿意在脸谱网上投放广告。这项新功能显示了脸谱网涉足电子商务的野心。5亿用户每天在脸谱网上交流分享信息，这令它成为广告和虚拟商品的"能量室"。

Besides, Facebook wants companies to update their Facebook pages with a collection of their products. The idea is that users will be able to browse and shop from these pages. Users can click on an item they are interested in and it will expand with pricing and sizing options and a Buy button (Figure 8-6).

Figure 8-6　The New Shops Section on A Brand Page②

---

①②　Jillian D'Onfro, Facebook's last push into ecommerce was a disaster, but it's gearing up to try again, http://www.businessinsider.com/facebook-ecommerce-2015-8, 2015-08-16.

By introducing commerce options on site, Facebook helps to bring in additional revenue streams, assuming they eventually take a cut of sales or charge to implement the Buy buttons. But the bigger goal for the social network is to use commerce as a way to boost engagement among users by giving them more reason to stay on site as well as provide an additional selling point to advertisers. But are people as eager to click "Buy" as they are to click "Share" on Facebook? Actually, users spend time on a social network checking for news and personal updates doesn't mean it is in the mindset to make an impulse buy. What should Facebook do if it desires to embrace social commerce better?

How Should Facebook Integrate Social Media with E-commerce[①]?

There are some suggestions for Facebook to move forward to social commerce:

1. Leveraging the mobile dominance. Despite the previous failure, there is an opportunity for Facebook to try again because people spend a majority of their logged-in Facebook hours on their phones, instead of on desktop computers. Forrester study shows that consumers spend over 85% of their smart phone time on apps, with each person only dedicating heavy usage to about five of them (Figure 8-7). Consumers may have liked brands' desktop sites better than the F-commerce experience, but most of the mobile web is pretty crappy, which gives Facebook a new chance to shine.

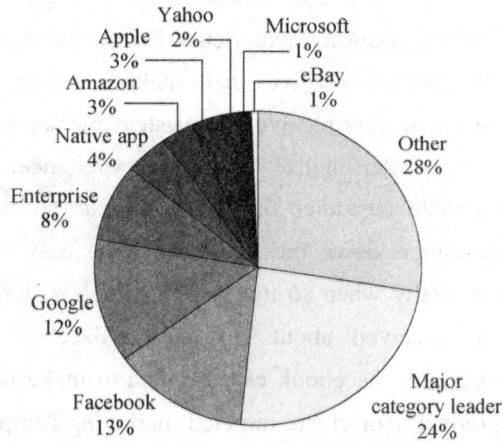

Base: 1,721 US online smartphone owners(18+)

Figure 8-7 Conusmers' Time in Apps[②]

2. Targeting small and medium sized businesses. Facebook owns a larger share of smart phone time than any other tech company: If 84% of the consumer time spent on apps is spent on just five downloaded apps, Facebook is probably one of them. So for a small-to-medium sized business that wants to put its catalog in front of more people, having a Facebook store would make sense because that's where people are spending their time. This makes Facebook even more attractive for those small and medium sized merchants. Therefore, although Facebook's first commerce efforts included major companies and it expects the new iteration of shops to draw some big clients, too—it clearly seems to be targeting smaller retailers this time around.

---

①② Steven Macdonald, 8 Ways to Optimize For Customer Experience, http://customerthink.com/8-ways-to-optimize-for-customer-experience/, 2015-09-18.

3. Optimizing customers' experience on mobile. According to Google, 42% of people use smart phones to aid shopping research while they are actually in the shopping store. As mobile become an increasingly popular platform for customers to browse websites and businesses online, it's impossible to ignore this channel when enhancing customer experience. After all, it is the key channel where the customers are spending most of their time today. Facebook should optimize customers' experience on mobile so as to attract and keep them.

1) Pay attention to platform performance. Maintaining platform performance to ensure the best experience possible for online shopping is crucial. To do this successfully, regular optimization tests are required. Facebook should make the necessary changes to improve things like loading times and responsiveness which will reap greater results for the overall customer experience.

2) Optimizing customer experience is about more than just focusing online. It's about creating a unified experience for people at every stage of their journey with the business. Whether this involves them making contact via the platform, e-mail or over the phone, it's vital that they receive a consistent message.

3) Personalize customer experience. Modern technology allows a firm to store valuable customer data, which can be used to create more personal experiences for customers down the line. It can be easy to lose a personal connection with the clients, especially when so much of business is done online. But with the information discovered and received about customers, Facebook can create individualized experiences. For example, Facebook can use data to make future recommendations about other services and products, or create targeted marketing campaigns to build loyalty and trust. However, it is important to ensure that the data is used appropriately and securely.

4) Ensure the secure payment. Some consumers don't trust Facebook to handle payments. Once potential customers get there, they'll need to feel comfortable sharing their personal information with Facebook. A survey shows both Pinterest and Facebook as new payments platforms that consumers feel hesitant about (Figure 8-8).

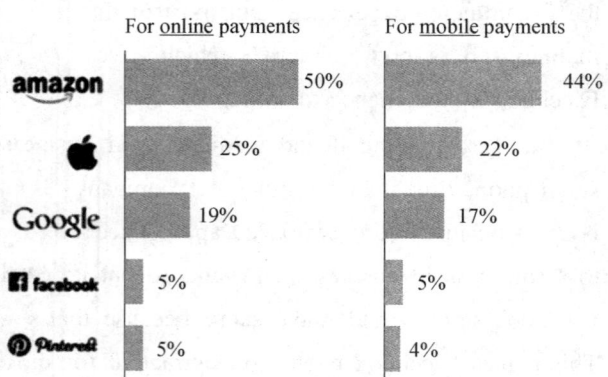

Figure 8-8　Payment Platforms Where Customers Are Willing to Share Personal Information[①]

---

① www.PYMNTS.com

Facebook said that it would not try to make money from Messenger until it becomes an organic, common way for people and businesses to communicate. That could be the real goal here: Once people start buying things directly from brands' Facebook pages, they'll have a lot more reason to start communicating with those brands on Facebook. And that could help turn Messenger into Facebook's next billion-dollar product.

Case Analysis

自从社交媒体崛起以后，Facebook可以说是其中当之无愧的明星。这家成立于2004年，并于2012年成功上市的社交网站因其独特的平台模式、惊人的成长速度吸引了无数人的目光。尽管2018年初的用户数据泄露事件将其推到了舆论的风口浪尖，但不可否认它为虚拟社交所做的努力以及在此过程中所体现的"连接、共享、平等"的互联网精神。本案例分析的重点在于Facebook的商业模式以及它从社交媒体到社交商务所做的尝试。

从本质上来讲，Facebook与谷歌一样，也采取了基于双边市场的平台模式连接两边的客户群：一边是免费注册和使用平台的广大用户，另一边则是在平台上投放广告的广告商。这就决定了它的收费模式与大多数双边平台一样：向一边的客户群收费，而对另一边客户群则保持免费。因此，广告收入是Facebook的主要收入来源：广告商通过付费在Facebook的PC端或移动端平台上投放广告，引导目标客户进行购买。除此之外，收取应用程序支付服务费也是Facebook的一项重要收入来源：与苹果应用商店一样，Facebook上面有大量的App软件，用户下载这些App需要向程序开发商付费，而付费是通过Facebook的系统，因此需要向其支付一定的服务费。既然广告收入是Facebook的主要收入来源，那么它凭什么吸引众多的广告商愿意为之付费呢？这是因为它有一项宝贵的资源：庞大的用户群体以及他们产生的数据资源。广告商可以在该平台上投放广告并借助社交网站口碑营销的优势将信息高效地传递给用户，刺激其购买欲；同时，借助大数据分析，广告商可以了解用户的年龄、性别、偏好及购物习惯等特征，在此基础上进行广告的精准投放，以此提高广告的投放效果。当然，具有双边市场特征的Facebook还能发挥网络效应的优势，通过向一方收费同时向另一方免费的方式，将广告商和用户吸引到平台上进行资源的自由匹配：越多的用户将吸引越多的广告商来此平台投放广告，反之亦然。当双边的客户规模达到"临界数量"时，网络效应的威力就会真正显现，从而实现平台的爆发式增长。

作为知名的社交平台，Facebook显然并不满足于靠广告收费维持生存的模式，自创立以来一直试图从社交媒体向社交商务转型，并经历了两个阶段：一开始，Facebook试图自建电子商务，并开设了虚拟的礼品商店，用户可以在其中购买和互赠虚拟礼物，由此为平台带来收入。为了丰富商品和服务种类，Facebook又推出了虚拟货币，并将礼品商店向第三方的商家开放。然而，这些尝试并未如人们预期的那样成功。原因是什么呢？一方面是因为商品的特点。并非所有的商品都适合在社交平台上出售，只有那些具有"内在社会化"特征的商品(如:图书)才适合,因为它们能在人们社交中发挥作用。另一方面,Facebook 缺少社交商务的运营经验。它推出的功能并没有令网上购物变得容易,却适得其反让用户在复杂的购物流程前面望而却步。吸取了第一个阶段的教训,Facebook 在第二阶段将自身重新定位为用户的社交商务渠道,不再自营电商,而是推出新的功能以促进供求双方的交易。例如,推出"BUY"按钮将用户引导至购物站点,并通过无缝衔接结账功能提升其购物体验,也相应地提高了用户转化的成功率。

很明显,Facebook 从未满足于仅仅做一个社交网络平台,相反,它一直试图挖掘社交网络更多的价值。作为社交商务领域的新手,Facebook 可以从利用移动互联、瞄准中小企业以及优化用户的移动端购物体验等方面入手实现顺利转型。

Section 3
Tudou—Everyone Can Be a Director of Life
第三节 土豆网——每个人都是生活的导演

Ⅰ Key Words

1. podcast *n.* 播客
2. couch potato *n.* 成天在沙发上看电视的人
3. clip *n.* 视频片段
4. the lion's share 最大份额
5. bandwidth *n.* 带宽
6. amateur *adj.* /*n.* 业余的/外行
7. immense *adj.* 巨大的
8. premiere *n.* 首映
9. derivative *adj.* 衍生的,派生的

Ⅱ Case

Foundation of Tudou[①②]

In 2005, inspired by YouTube, a website revolutionizing the world of online video, Gary Wang and Marc van der Chijs started a similar service for Chinese audiences. They founded Tudou, a website for video blogging. Tudou went live on April 15, 2005, just a few months after YouTube's launch. The website was named after a kind of ordinary vegetable not only because the name is interesting but also it positions as a podcast website originating from "couch potato". Tudou aims to provide an open media sharing platform where

---

① https://en.wikipedia.org/wiki/Tudou
② http://www.alexa.com/siteinfo/tudou.com

ordinary people are allowed to upload their original audios, videos and other media works.

The team self funded with $100,000 and then raised seed funding of $500,000. Soon afterwards, it changed the site's focus to the uploading and sharing of TV clips and other videos. It generated many views and its performance gave investors the confidence to provide $8.5 million in financing in 2006.

As a local media-sharing website in China, Tudou is influencing the users overseas so much that some of them call it "Chinese YouTube" though Chinese visitors are still dominating Tudou's audience. In terms of audience demography, female visitors obviously dominate Tudou's audience groups, which indicates that female users are more inclined to browse on Tudou to find the interesting video resources such as series. Besides, college students make up the largest audience group of Tudou.

Rapid Growth[①]

Tudou has experienced a rapid growth since its foundation, which is even out of the expectations of the founders. Initially, only five audios were uploaded. The daily video clips uploaded rose up to 20,000 quickly and Tudou became the podcast website with the highest daily visits and the most users in China only three years after its foundation.

As of the summer 2007, Tudou became one of the fastest growing websites on the Web, growing from 131 million to 360 million video clips per week in just three months. 55 million video clips were viewed daily on Tudou, with an additional 20,000 new videos uploaded every 24 hours. The website owned nearly 40 million visitors per month.

By middle 2007, Tudou had owned over 50% of the Chinese online video market. Tudou reached 95 million monthly unique visitors as of June 2009, and 170 million as of June 2010. Tudou soon controlled 50% of the online video market in China. Its popularity is aided by the fact that users can share videos and watch them across multiple devices. Its success enabled more funding, including $57 million in 2008 and $50 million in 2010. In 2011, Tudou went public successfully.

In 2012, Tudou and Youku announced a billion dollar merger and founded Youku Tudou. This alliance was thought an important milestone for Tudou's growth. Since then, Youku Tudou has become China's largest online video site with serves 500 million users per month in 2014, half of YouTube's reach[②]. Youku Tudou describes itself as a "leading multi-screen entertainment and media company in China" and as "China's leading Internet television platform."

---

① https://en.wikipedia.org/wiki/Social_commerce
② Kaylene Hong, China's Youku Tudou Now Serves 500 Million Users Per Month, Half Of Youtube's Reach, TNW News, 2014-08-20.

In 2015, e-commerce giant Alibaba announced that it completed its takeover of Youku Tudou. Valuing Youku Tudou at $5.40 billion, Alibaba paid $27.6 per New York Stock Exchange-listed ADS (American Depositary Share). As Alibaba and Jack Ma's Yunfeng fund already owned close to a fifth of the company, Alibaba paid $4 billion for the outstanding shares through its YK subsidiary①.

By December 2016, Youku Tudou② had owned 30 million subscribers and published more than 50,000 new videos each day, including amateur content such as videoblogging and original videos, movie and TV clips, and music videos. Unregistered users can watch videos on the site, while registered users are permitted to upload an unlimited number of videos, using online and Windows-based upload tools.

Business Model③

1. Video content sources

Tudou collects videos mainly from two sources: user-generated content (UGC) and self-produced videos. The former has been dominating the content on the website because Tudou bets that the UGC model can achieve higher user loyalty at a lower cost.

When it was initially founded, Tudou was very similar to the American video sharing website YouTube, where users upload almost all of the content. Like YouTube to start, Tudou included both pirated content as well as user-generated content (UGC). As copyright law started to be seriously enforced on China's Internet, Tudou removed pirated content and started spending significant money acquiring the rights to various shows. To further optimize its UGC platform and enhance users' enthusiasm for creating original content, Tudou organized some campaigns like "Tudou Film Festival", "Orange Box" and "The Sixth Warehouse" to attract talented users to produce content for its platform. This is also a core focus of Tudou's R&D activities. It also launched an "Original Picture Platform", which can restore the resolution of uploaded videos and attract advertising.

In contrast to the YouTube and Hulu models, Tudou also produces its own professional content. Examples include self-produced dramas and "Tudou Filming", an attempt to enrich its content offerings. This practice is actually becoming increasingly common for Chinese video sites.

2. Revenue sources④

---

① Patrick Frater, Alibaba Completes $4 Billion Takeover of Youku Tudou, http://variety.com/2016/biz/asia/alibaba-completes-youku-tudou-takeover-1201746908/
② For simpleness, we call the website "Tudou" at the rest of the case.
③ 袁苏明:"土豆网的商业模式分析",《企业技术开发月刊》,2009年7月。
④ iChinaStock, Analysis: Tudou's Business Model & Revenue Breakdown, http://www.businessinsider.com/analysis-tudous-business-model-and-revenue-breakdown-2011-8, 2011-08-16.

As a typical two-sided platform, Tudou charges the two parties of transactions: advertisers and users. Initially, Tudou charged advertisers while providing free services for users because the latter are more price sensitive. That is why Tudou relied entirely on online advertising for revenue before 2010. After Tudou gradually built its brand image, it attempted to find additional revenue streams which involved users charging. Since 2010, it has developed three more charging services: copyright distribution, mobile video services and VIP membership. Currently, Tudou acquires its revenues from four businesses:

1) Advertising.

For Tudou, advertising accounts for the lion's share of revenues. Tudou offers online advertising services mainly through third-party advertising agencies. Advertisers are allowed to insert their brand advertisements into both the start and the end of a video generated by a podcast. The advertisers pay for the advertising, which is distributed between Tudou and the podcast. To increase the effectiveness of advertising, Tudou adopts the personalized model. Tudou's advertising system analyzes an individual user's taste and preference based on his or her registration information and browsing history and pushes the most suitable advertisement for the user. For instance, Tudou usually pushes the advertisements of makeups, clothes or shopping malls for a young female user.

In addition to in-show commercials, mini-page commercials, banner ads, text links and product placement, Tudou also offers event sponsorship commercials and interactive commercials. Tudou made an investment plan of 500,000 yuan for each episode of self-produced dramas. Product placement in those dramas has become Tudou's new form of advertising.

Facing the fierce competition in the online advertising, Tudou differentiates its advertising service from the following aspects[①]:

- More about brand advertising, less about direct marketing. Although some targeted advertising is available with Tudou, the options are quite limited. As opposed to YouTube, the platform seems to be unable to target on specific users based on their preferences or browsing history. Instead, Tudou is still focused on blanket advertising by pursuing the largest possible audience, similar to traditional media such as TV or newspapers. However, an inherent disadvantage of such approach is obvious—it can not capture the target customers accurately. For example, displaying Porsche ad to a student or a soccer mom would be a complete waste of Porsche's advertising dollars.

- Limited value of the analytics. Just as with YouTube, Tudou makes basic analytics available to its customers. The data includes viewers' demographics, geo-location,

---

① How Does Advertising on Youku Work, Sampi.co, http://sampi.co/how-does-advertising-on-youku-work/, 2018-03-07.

browsing technology, language, operating systems, etc. If the targeting options are not yet well developed, the practical value of such statistics has its limitations. It seems that Tudou does know how to display ads relevant to what a viewer is presently watching but can't show them based on recent browsing history—something that Youtube or Google's Adsense does quite well.

● Great multitude of ad options. The ads can be displayed in various shapes and forms: from videos to banners which can be both static or animated, as well as text links and buttons. Those are often referred to as "hard advertising". Other forms include product placements in in-house produced content, or branded viral videos all of which are collectively known as "soft advertising". The price depends on the type of an ad, where and how it is displayed, and what scheme is chosen by a client. The most expensive ads are the ones that are displayed near the top of the page and those that are larger in size as opposed to smaller ones or those that are visible only after scrolling.

● For big spenders only. Advertising prices have not significantly changed since 2012 and they varied wildly depending on the type of ads. There are three basic schemes: CPM (Cost-per-thousand-impressions), banners in various locations on the site, ads displayed with the video being watched which could be pre-roll, mid-roll and post-roll as well as pause ads. Table 8-1 shows the list prices for banner ads on Youku Tudou and there is no low budget option clearly.

Table 8-1 The List Prices for Banner Ads on Youku Tudou[①]

Banners ads on homepage	RMB/day
Large ad in margin near page top	250,000
Video ad in "Recent Originals"	250,000
Banner ad near section break	120,000
Small text ad near mid-page	30,000

2. Copyright distribution

Copyright distribution refers to the business model that a company resells the exclusive copyright purchased from the creator of an original work so as to acquires margins. Copyright distribution has become one of Tudou's new revenue sources since the third quarter of 2010. In the second half of 2010, copyright distribution brought 2 million yuan ($300,000), about 0.7% of total revenue.

---

① How Does Advertising on Youku Work, Sampi.co, http://sampi.co/how-does-advertising-on-youku-work/, 2018-03-07.

3. Mobile video services

In January 2010, Tudou partnered with China Mobile to offer mobile video on-demand service. Mobile phone users can watch original video programs on Tudou through a monthly plan or pay-per-play viewing. Tudou and China Mobile share the revenue.

In 2010, the service contributed 19.1 million yuan ($2.9 million), accounting for 6.7% total revenue in 2010. In 2010, the number of users of Tudou on China Mobile reached 15.8 million and the total number of views reached 27.7 million. After completing its fifth round financing for $50 million in 2010, Tudou expressed that the money financed in this round would be spent on upgrading mobile terminals and developing its mobile businesses.

Since September 2010, Tudou has become an online video website that supports Apple iOS 4, Android, Symbian, Windows Mobile and Java. Meanwhile, Tudou signed cooperative agreements with mobile phone hardware manufacturers like Blackberry, Motorola, Nokia and Samsung to preinstall Tudou's mobile phone application.

4. VIP membership

Charging the members is another revenue source. Considering that Chinese users have not got use to paying for the videos online, Tudou only charge the members for the access of part videos. Paying 20 yuan per month, a user can enjoy the services like free movies, discount of online ordering and advertisements blocking.

Tudou's Way to Future

China's massive online video market is diverse, with the top five including LeTV, Tencent Video, Sohu.com, Youku Tudou and iQiyi and numerous small players. Facing the immense competition, Tudou should adopt the following strategies to solidify its achievements:

1. Technical support. Technical support including bandwidth and servers is the prerequisite of Tudou's operation. With the rising videos uploaded and the users' higher requirements of viewing experiences, more sufficient bandwidth and servers are required. Accordingly, the cost will rise greatly. For Tudou, its operation costs are composed of three parts—bandwidth, servers and propagation. Bandwidth is the highest expense because Tudou has to spend much on bandwidth to accommodate the media works uploaded by the users. According to the statistics, Tudou's bandwidth cost is even the sum of bandwidth cost of Sina, 163 and Sohu. Besides, as a content service website, Tudou spends lots of money purchasing exclusive content every year to attract viewer. Particularly, as a video-sharing website, Tudou sometimes has to pay for an awkward expense due to copyright infringement. Therefore, how to balance between cost and technology will be a problem encountered by Tudou.

2. Quality of contents and services. As a video-sharing website, quality of the works uploaded is the base of Tudou's operation. Only the works with high quality can attract the users for a long time. Due to the technical or monetary limits, the original works with high quality posted on Tudou have not dominated the website. Fortunately, Tudou is trying to improve the quality of contents such as excellent works exhibition, which will benefit Tudou's brand strength. Besides, due to the fierce competition, Tudou should differentiate its contents and services so that users can stick to the website. The model of buying programs from third-parties should be changed since it is too costly and lacks the exclusivity. An effective way is developing its own internal ecosystem that will encourage individuals and small companies to make their own video, which then will become exclusive property of Tudou.

3. Cooperation with traditional media. Though online video-sharing is popularizing, part of people still stick to the traditional media such as TV and movies. To attract more users, Tudou should cooperate with traditional media. For example, launch the online movie preview or premiere.

4. Aiming at mobile end. Mobile end is gaining more importance for the company along with the dramatic growth of Chinese mobile Internet. In 2014, Tudou revealed that its mobile daily video views passed 400 million. For the second quarter 2014, over 30% of the company's revenue was generated from mobile, and there has been "solid progress" in its subscription services with 379% growth year on year[①].

5. Brand rebranding. Rebranding is a marketing strategy in which a new name, term, symbol, design, or combination thereof is created for an established brand with the intention of developing a new, differentiated identity in the minds of consumers, investors, competitors, and other stakeholders[②]. Actually, Tudou has made the rebranding attempts since 2015. In August 2015, Tudou announced that the video streaming site began rebranding, marking a significant strategic shift from its previous focus on traffic and traditional video content to self-produced content. The company decided to invest tens of billions (RMB) in the next three years to construct a culture and entertainment ecosystem. For a long time, Tudou's revenue mainly comes from ads during videos. The transformation allows the company to increase earnings from content marketing and consumers, which is mainly derived from subscription-based service and interactive live entertainment. As the first step towards this goal, Tudou announced investments in a raft of five startups that may contribute to the construction of a professional community:

---

① Kaylene Hong, China's Youku Tudou Now Serves 500 Million Users per Month, Half of YouTube's Reach, https://thenextweb.com/asia/2014/08/20/chinas-youku-tudou-now-serves-500-million-users-per-month-half-of-youtubes-reach/, 2014-08-20.

② https://en.wikipedia.org/wiki/Rebranding

> 品牌重塑。品牌重塑是一种营销策略，即以新名称、术语、符号、设计或各项元素的整合在消费者、投资人、竞争对手以及其他利益相关者心目中为现有品牌创造一个新的形象。土豆自2015年开始进行品牌重塑，宣布进行从流量和传统视频内容向用户产生内容的重大战略转变，并计划在接下来的3年中投入上百亿资金建立一个文化娱乐生态系统。很长一段时间，土豆网的收入主要来自视频广告，这一转型为公司找到了从内容营销和消费者身上获利的新路径。除此之外，土豆宣布投资了5家围绕其构建专业社区目标的初创企业，包括：

1) Jiae. com specializes in marketing trend-setting, innovative design products. It helps designers and global brands launch new products, build brand awareness, and expand market reach in China. Jiae is responsible for assisting Tudou's efforts in developing derivative products based on video content produced the investor to support its e-commerce business;

2) AcFun is an ACG (animation, comic, game) video portal that is characterized by the popular Danmu or "Bullet Curtain" service, which engages audiences by providing live comment displays for online video comment sharing. Copyright issues have long been a headache for "Bullet Curtain websites" as they commonly host or link to pirated videos to display user commentaries on the same screen. Before this tie-up, Youku Tudou and AcFun just settled a piracy suit in March 2015. The investment was used to purchase copyrighted content and cooperate with content providers. Tudou announced that it would completely support AcFun in financing, content and production of animated films;

3) Joyme is a mobile game station focused on strategies, information, gift bag stores, game platforms, mobile apps and more. In 2015, The company raised its series C funding led by Tudou with participation from Chinese mobile gaming company Ourpalm;

4) Rongyi Education is an educational services provider that offers training courses for actors, film producers, artist agents and marketing talents. Tudou's investment brought the parties together to foster more professional talents for the music, gaming and animation industries;

5) Logical Thinking is a knowledge-based networking community for China's younger generations. It interacts with followers through various means including WeChat subscription accounts and talk shows.

Along with efforts to advance its original content by partnering with premium content providers, Tudou has made a lot of efforts to develop user-generated content and self-produced content. According to data from the company, in-house content now accounts for more than 50% of its traffic from both of its video streaming sites. Over ten self-produced programs, such as Rage Comics and Logic Thinking have hit a market valuation of over 100 million yuan. In addition to its ambitious push into self-produced content, the Alibaba-backed online video giant is hopping onto the virtual reality bandwagon, investing in the development of original VR content.①

Case Analysis

相比 Facebook，土豆网这个品牌对我们而言更加熟悉，因为不少人在生活中就是它的忠实用户。这家创立于 2005 年的视频网站一直是国内同行中的佼佼者，尤其是 2012 年与当时知名度相当的优酷网合并之后更是如虎添翼，成为中国视频网站中的知名品牌。"每个人都是生活的导演"曾经是土豆网的一句经典广告词，也反映了它的基本理念——用视频记录生活，并在土豆网表达和分享。对于这个案例，我们的分析重点只需集中在两点：土豆网的商业模式以及它未来的发展方向。

土豆网的商业模式主要从两个层面进行分析：产品层面和收入层面。土豆网作为内容提供商，它的产品就是视频。与 YouTube 等大多数视频网站类似，土豆网的视频主要来自于用户自发上传的资源，也就是所谓的用户产生内容（UGC），在该网站视频中占主导地位。UGC 的优势在于可以降低网站的运营成本，后者只需要提供视频资源自由分享和匹配的平台即可，但劣势也十分明显，那就是版权问题。由于所有的视频资源都是用户自发上传，网站很难对其内容一一审查，侵权问题时有发生，土豆网也曾遭遇这样的尴尬。鉴于此，土豆网投入重金组织各种活动鼓励用户制作和分享原创视频。这些活动的开展不仅优化了土豆网的视频质量，而且提升了网站知名度。除此之外，土豆网还自己投资制作网剧，为自身提供了新的视频来源。收入模式是土豆网商业模式分析的另一个重点。该网站有 4 个收入来源：网络广告、版权分销、移动视频服务以及 VIP 会员服务，其中网络广告是其主要的收入来源。土豆网的网络广告服务主要借助第三方广告代理商进行，广告商可以在视频的首尾两端投放广告，所支付的广告费由土豆网和代理商分成。土豆网深知自己的一大优势是用户数据，因此充分发挥这一优势基于数据分析精准了解每个用户的需求，并基于此向其推送个性化的广告。自 2010 年起，土豆网将版权分销作为一项新的收入来源，通过向第三方转售其已经购得版权的视频来获取收入，这种模式操作简单，但网站对市场需求要有精准的预测以保证转售的成功率。早在 2010 年，土豆网就和中国联通达成合作，提供移动端的视频服务，也使移动视频服务成为该网站又一项新的收入来源。事实证明这项决策是正确的，因为它与接下来几年中国移动互联网应用的爆发式增长完美契合。当然，作为拥有全球 3 000 多万会员的平台，会员费也是其不可忽略的一项收入来源。针对中国用户习惯使用免费视频的现状，土豆网的会员费涵盖了观看最新视频以及视频去广告等服务，每月 20 元人民币的价格也很亲民。

尽管土豆网已经成为中国视频网站的知名品牌，但是面对瞬息万变的市场和激烈的竞争，未来应该何去何从是本案例分析的第二个重点。土豆网首先应该加固技术基础。一方面随着用户规模的扩大和上传视频的增加，尤其是移动互联技术令制作和上传视频更加便利，土豆网需要增加带宽和服务器以满足快速增长的数据载荷。因为一

---

① Emma Lee，Youku-Tudou Rebrands During Agressive Original Content Push，Technode.com，2015-08-06.

且因为技术问题影响了用户的观看体验,很可能因此造成客户流失;另一方面,提升技术必然导致运营成本上升,这会使本来就在带宽和服务器上投入巨大的土豆网面临更大的成本压力。如何在成本和技术之间寻求平衡是土豆网未来将面临的一大挑战。其次,提高内容服务的质量。作为视频网站,视频的质量是土豆网生存的基础,而要在众多的同类网站中脱颖而出土豆网必须实现产品的差异化。这意味着土豆网应该坚持"原创视频"的策略,采取更多的措施鼓励个人和中小企业拍摄高质量的原创视频,以形成网站的核心竞争力。再次,土豆网应该积极和电视等传统媒体合作,实现优势互补,吸引更多用户,扩大品牌影响力。第四,抓住移动互联网快速增长的时机,推出更多适合移动端用户的产品和服务,增加用户粘性。最后,2012年与优酷的合并为土豆网带来了重塑品牌的机遇,这不仅意味着品牌名称的改变,更意味着通过创新实现品牌内容和形象的更新,为大众呈现一个更具活力的视频网站。

Section 4
WeChat—Digging the Value of SNS
第四节 微信——挖掘社交网络服务的价值

Key Words

1. standalone *adj.* 独立的
2. moments *n.* 微信朋友圈
3. monetization 货币化
4. pave *vt.* 铺设
5. pricey *adj.* 高价的
6. steal a march 先发制人

Case

About Wechat[①]

WeChat is a mobile text and voice messaging communication service developed by Tencent in China, first released in January 2011. It is the largest standalone messaging app by monthly active users. WeChat began as a project at Tencent Guangzhou Research and Project center in October 2010. The original version of the app, "Weixin", was invented by Xiaolong Zhang, and named by Ma Huateng, Tencent CEO. In April 2012, Weixin re-branded as WeChat for the international market. By November 2016, WeChat had owned 846 million monthly users.

---

① https://en.wikipedia.org/wiki/WeChat

The app is available on almost all the mobile phone systems such as Android and iOS, and there are also Web-based, OS X and Windows clients but these require the user to have the app installed on a supported mobile phone for authentication.

The initial features provided by WeChat focused on instant messaging and public accounts. With the rapid growth of WeChat, extra features were developed. As a result, there are seven popular features with WeChat[①]:

1. Instant Messaging. Wechat supports different ways of instant message, including text message, voice message, walkie talkie and stickers. Users can send pictures, videos, namecards, coupons, lucky money packages or positions to one of his contacts, or share them with friends in a groupchat.

2. Public Accounts. Wechat supports users to register as a public account, which enables them to push feeds to subscribers, interact with subscribers and provide them with service. By December 2016, the number of Wechat public accounts had reached 12 million[②]. Public accounts of organizations can apply for a verified official public accounts. In China, Wechat public accounts have become a common service or promotion platform for government, news media and companies. Specific public account subscribers use the platform for service like hospital pre-registration, visa renewal or credit card service.

3. Moments. Moments is WeChat's main social media feature. Basically, it's like a mix of Facebook and Twitter that lies on top of the base WeChat experience. Moments enables a user to maintain his/her own profile where the user posts things likes photos and status updates. The user can also comment and like posts made on his or her friend's Moments page. The main selling point is the enhanced privacy which, for example, allows a user to do things like control which of his/her friends can see what he or she like and comment on. Since Facebook is banned in China, a service like WeChat moments helps to fill in the gap.

4. WeChat Pay. WeChat Pay is a payment feature integrated into the WeChat app, users can complete payment quickly with smart phones. WeChat has Quick Pay, QR Code Payments, In-App Web-Based Payments and Native In-App Payments. All these payment tools fulfill the full range of scenarios customers' expectation under different payment situation. Combined with WeChat official accounts, WeChat Pay supports O2O consumption experience and provides professional Internet solutions for physical business. WeChat Pay supports major currencies like GBP, HKD, USD and JPY settlement. For

---

① Rahil Bhagat, 5 WeChat Features That WhatsApp Should Really Use, Forbes, September 29, 2016.
② Craig Smith, 94 Amazing WeChat Statistics and Facts, http://expandedramblings.com/index.php/wechat-statistics/April, 2017.

unsupported currencies, trade can be made through settlement on U.S. dollar. Facebook did not allow people to send money over Facebook Messenger until 2016. Compared to it, WeChat has been ahead of the curve for years, allowing payments via the app's WeChat Pay feature.

5. WeChat Shake. Shake is a very simple concept with far-reaching consequences. It allows users to connect with the world around them by simply shaking their phone. Shake Nearby uses Bluetooth beacons to connect users to relevant Official Accounts near the place they are visiting. Aside from the "people" and "TV shows" shake modes, there is also a "nearby" mode. In the west, this might seem like a strange concept but in China, it is a great way for young people, who have just left their rural homes to travel to the big megacities like Shanghai and Shenzhen, to meet new friends. In fact, some stories have proved that the feature may even help a user find true love.

6. WeChat Game. One of WeChat's most popular features is its integrated gaming platform which was introduced to WeChat in 2013. WeChat's parent company, Tencent, is the world's largest gaming company so it makes sense that WeChat is looking to leverage Tencent's expertise to bring gaming to the platform. WeChat users can visit the in-app app store to download games, launch games from within the app and then take advantage of WeChat's social features to add a more social dimension to the gaming experience. Particularly, WeChat's games are way more than simple 2D-pixel art style titles. Some titles, like Thunder Raid and Dragon Warrior are fully fleshed out 3D experiences that feel almost console-like in terms of technical quality.

7. Go Dutch. People usually feel frustrated after a joyful dinner when they get a long complicated bill with multiples items, tax charges, service charges and the like, then dividing it up, making sure the right amount and denomination of money. WeChat's Go Dutch feature circumvents this frustration by doing all the math for the people and allowing them to pay exactly what they owe, via the app, to any of the contacts using the WeChat Pay feature. With the feature of Go Dutch in WeChat Wallet, people can set the title, the amount (limit to 10,000 yuan) and the number of people to pay. Money can be paid by scanning QR code or a chat thread. At the same time WeChat sends a message showing who has paid and who hasn't from the payment page.

Why Is WeChat So Popular?

WeChat has experienced a rapid growth since its launch. Four factors cause WeChat's popularity:

1. The right entry timing. The 3G technology enables the connection between mobile phone and the Internet, which means users are allowed to get access to the Internet anytime everywhere with their mobile phones except for personal computers. The emergence of 3G

technology converts the traditional mobile phone with the feature of talking into a "mini-PC" by which people are able to talk, write, play games and browse on the Internet. However, for a long time, there has not been a suitable instant message software working on the mobile phones yet. Though China Mobile in 2006 made an attempt on Fetion (Chinese: Feixin)—an instant message software, it did not gain the first-mover advantages due to the limited users and the inappropriate marketing strategies. Besides, the instant message applications such as QQ and MSN have popularized. However, they are designed for on PC-end. The telecommunication market called for an instant message application specified to the mobile-end then. WeChat released in 2011 which combines talking and writing in communication and is compatible to different mobile phone systems as well as different telecommunication platforms (e.g. China Unicom) attracted lots of users rapidly. WeChat is not the first instant message software in China. However, it is because Tencent seizes the right timing to enter the market and satisfy customers' need can WeChat succeed rapidly.

2. Low price. WeChat's ubiquity and success in China should be primarily attributed to its low price which lows the telecommunication cost for Chinese people. For a long time, Chinese consumers have been complaining the high telecommunication cost. People have to pay 0.1 yuan per text message and even more for a calling. The emergence of WeChat allows people to communicate for free by downloading an application. With WeChat, users are charged for mobile data usage which is much cheaper than texting fee. The mobile data usage can be used for browsing, downloading and uploading activities within the App only. Particularly, users can use WeChat for free when there is Wi-Fi accessible. WeChat—the instant message application with more features and lower price attracts users rapidly.

3. Multi-functionalities. The multi-functionalities of WeChat satisfy users' diverse need. WeChat supports not only the communications by text, picture, audio and video but also the circle of friends built by the users. Additionally, in version 5.03 WeChat imports new features including "Shake & Shake" and "Scan & Scan" which support the communications among strangers. The new features are especially attractive for the young people because they can make new friends with the features. Actually, WeChat aims to establish a compositive platform combining SNS, games and e-commerce. The platform with multi-functionalities will attract more users.

4. The strong users stickiness. Actually, WeChat is not the unique instant message software for mobile-end. Its success should be partially attributed to the solid customer base built by Tencent QQ (QQ). As the most popular instant message software released in 1999, QQ had owned 843million monthly active users by August 2015. Therefore, it is easy for Tencent to leverage its large user base of hundreds of millions of QQ users to

migrate them across to WeChat, as all that is needed to sign up is a QQ account. According to the statistics, 77.46% WeChat users come from QQ. The local users' existing relationship with Tencent makes it easier for WeChat to steal a march on its competitors in China as it is easy to get started. Once the readymade users get access to WeChat, the network effect is realized. Imagine that the people in your social network communicate with WeChat, how can you keep yourself away from the new platform?

Monetization of WeChat's Services[①]

As the most popular mobile instant message platform, how does WeChat monetize its service? Or in another word, how does WeChat make money? As a popular social service platform, WeChat monetizes its services in 5 ways:

1. In-app purchase

In-app purchase is the first feature introduced by WeChat in order to generate revenue. In 2012, Tencent introduced stickers users have to pay for. The serial stickers of Chibi Maruko-Chan, originating from a classic anime character with constant and solid IP value, are one of the most popular and widely-used stickers on WeChat. WeChat stickers, as a typical example of In-app purchase, serve a special part in the ecosystem of WeChat. The creators of these creative stickers get paid by WeChat, and therefore their works are available to millions of users for free.

Figure 8-9　Chibi Maruko-Chan Stickers on WeChat[②]

---

① Thibaud, 5 ways WeChat will monetize its tremendous user base, http://marketingtochina.com/5-ways-wechat-will-monetize/, 2014-09-06.
② Huge Business Behind WeChat Stickers, http://www.tmtpost.com/1003831.html

Later on, games were introduced on the Chinese version of the platform. The Chinese mobile gaming market is huge and growing. Chinese mobile game market size in 2016 was $8.4 billion, rising to $14.4 billion in 2021①. Obviously, embedding mobile games in WeChat enables Tencent a deep well of new revenue and market occupancy. WeChat supports payment systems that allow users to purchase games and make in-app payments, and take a cut of revenue in the process. In this way, the games with high profitability like Candy Crush prove a lucrative addition to Tencent's app revenue. For example, in 2015, the gaming company generated more than $2 billion from just four mobile games②.

2. E-commerce

In May 2014, Tencent launched "WeChat stores" which enables service public accounts to sell products directly to customers through WeChat. Merchants are allowed to set up online shop within the WeChat stores. The system supports e-commerce features including product upload, products management, order management, product display management and customer complaint management. After the success in China, WeChat planned to offer its e-commerce platform for British companies to use to sell goods in China in early 2017. It would then start operating in other markets such as France and Germany③.

With the development of mobile technology, Chinese consumers are willing to pay for services and content on their mobile. As a result, WeChat incorporates payment options allowing users to buy items directly from WeChat official accounts with just one-click. The integration of online payment and e-commerce delivers brands opportunities for merchants to interact and engage their consumer base and optimizes the consumer experience. Since Chinese new year of 2014, WeChat has started creating buzz with "red packet" that people could share in friends groups and which would randomly split gift-money between group members. WeChat later started promoting very aggressively its cab-booking function, "Didi dache", by offering huge discounts both to the cab drivers and to the passengers.

3. Financial services

WeChat has two advantages in financial services: Firstly, Tencent launched third-party payment system—TenPay (Chinese: Cai Fu Tong) in 2005. Tenpay has become the second largest third-party payment platform, ranking only second to Alipay. Its readymade

---

① 2017 China Mobile Games Market Report—Research and Markets, https://www.businesswire.com/news/home/20170920006058/en/2017-China-Mobile-Games-Market-Report, 2017-09-20.

② BI Intelligence, Tencent adds Supercell games to Wechat and QQ, http://www.businessinsider.com/tencent-adds-supercell-games-to-wechat-and-qq-2016-7, 2016-07-08.

③ Madhumita Murgia, Tencent Expands WeChat's E-commerce Platform in Europe, https://www.ft.com/content/983693ac-1543-11e7-b0c1-37e417ee6c76, 2017-03-30.

customers build a solid base for WeChat financial services. With the launch of payment system—WeChat Payment (Chinese: We Xin Zhi Fu), the customer base of mobile payment was also founded. Particularly, it can compete against AliPay from e-commerce company Alibaba. Secondly, Tencent launched Li Cai Tong, a platform which provides a variety of financial services such as opening account, purchasing financial products and checking balance in January 2014. Actually, Yu'e Bao, an investment product offered by Alababa paved the way for Li Cai Tong: as customers start storing more and more money into their electronic wallets, the next step is to provide them with financial services. Users can put their money into the product, which invests in funds. There is no minimum amount, and customers can withdraw their cash anytime. When an ordinary demand deposit in savings accounts at major banks offers an interest rate of just 0.35% a year, Li Cai Tong offers an annual interest of about 6% and still allows depositors to withdraw their money at any time.

4. Advertising

WeChat advertising, the program enabling companies to display promotional messages on users timeline or at the bottom of WeChat Official Account articles, is another important revenue source for WeChat. WeChat advertising enables brands to grow WeChat Official Account followers, drive traffic to website and generate App downloads. There are 3 major types of WeChat advertising: WeChat Moments Advertising, WeChat Banner adverting and WeChat Key Opinion Leader advertising. Of the 3 types of WeChat advertising, WeChat moments is the most popular method. Marketers are allowed to deliver text, picture and videos Ads on WeChat Moments and charged based on impression (Figure 8-10).

Figure 8-10 WeChat Moments Advertising[1]

For example, an advertiser creates a scheme for advertising on personal WeChat Moments. In Shanghai and Beijing, it leverages 600 individual accounts, each with at least 500 friends. The price of posting on individual's moments ranged from 10 yuan to 400 yuan per post. Advertising through such a network reaches over 300,000 WeChat users. However this is a very manual process. What Tencent Moment advertising brings is a much more sophisticated way to reach the user timeline by directly buying access from WeChat. Minimal entry price (both foreign companies and Chinese companies) of WeChat Moment

---

[1] Huge Business Behind WeChat Stickers, http://www.tmtpost.com/1003831.html

Advertising is 50,000 yuan and CPM (Cost-per-thousand impression) changes based on city size and ads types (Table 8-2)①.

Table 8-2 CPM of WeChat Moment Advertising②

City size	Text & Pictures Ads CPM(RMB)	Video Ads CPM(RMB)
Core city	150,000	180,000
Large city	100,000	120,000
Others	50,000	60,000

5. Enterprise accounts

In September 2014, Tencent announced the launch of company accounts which are specifically designed to support internal operations of a company. With an enterprise account, a company is able to create many "sub-accounts" for different tasks which enables better structure information, send unlimited number of messages, send all kind of documents and store sensitive data on secure proprietary servers to avoid any data theft issues.

These accounts are extremely pricey for the companies using them. These accounts might become another successful move for WeChat on the way of monetization.

Future of Wechat

WeChat, undoubtly, has become the most popular mobile social media platform in China. How much longer can the popularity remain? What are the possible opportunities and challenges faced by WeChat?

1. Opportunities

The first opportunity is its continually growing user base, which should be primarily attributed to the increasing number of mobile Internet users in China. Besides, the number of users outside China is also rising. WeChat is getting traction in the countries and regions like Malaysia, Singapore, Hongkong and Taiwan. Though WeChat outside China is currently mostly confined to regions having a significant Chinese-speaking population, its expanding market is unarguable. Therefore, these enticements have prompted many brands to rush onto the platform. They set up an account, they write an article, they publish it and they wait for those client-delighting engagement stats to roll in.

The second opportunity is service expansion which enables WeChat to expand to new services. Since its foundation, WeChat has been devoting to its service expansion based on users' need. For example, it only supported text and picture based chat initially. And then

---

①② Tingyi Chen, Advertising on WeChat: a Step by Step Guide, https://walkthechat.com/advertising-on-wechat-moment, April 10, 2017.

it developed new services such as voice and video-based chat based on users' need. Particularly, WeChat launched mobile payment in 2014, which popularizes rapidly and becomes a growing threat to Alipay. With the fast development of mobile internet technology, users' demands are changing even more quickly and frequently. The changing demands will provide a chance for WeChat's service expansion.

2. Challenges①

The first challenge is managing the expanding platform. Originating from a two-sided platform connecting users in messaging, WeChat expands its sides by adding extra features gradually: the moments, e-wallet, WeChat payment and mini-apps. Today, WeChat has been called a "super app" combining a variety of functions. Meanwhile, it also has grown up to a multi-sided platform bridging users, third party apps developers, hardware manufacturers and advertisers. A Platform is known to be home to network effects: once the platform reaches a critical mass of users on its various sides, it is ensured to "take it all", leading to exponential growth. It is through the diversification of the services that WeChat inspires network effects and grows up to a multi-sided platform. A multi-sided platform means more opportunities as well as more problems. How to ensure everything is under control? How to balance among different sides? What strategy should be adopted to keep the customers from different sides? These problems are unavoidable.

The second challenge is the threats even the violent reactions from the formidable opponents. If the access to third party content was to be increasingly performed by Tencent's WeChat instead of Google's Android and Apple's AppStore, then the latter two's platforms would gradually lose control over their multi-sided market, weakening a leadership position built on inter-mediating these multiple sides. Consequently, WeChat is in a unique position to overthrow the existing platform thanks to its mini-apps. The potential is huge, but can it be fully realized? Netscape, the once cross-OS Internet browser market leader started to develop an over-the-internet OS. The move led its rival— Microsoft to react violently, bundling Internet Explorer with Windows, killing Netscape in a couple of years. Even though WeChat is able to overthrow Google and Apple, the two companies can still counter-attack. For example, they could bundle their OS with a certain number of value-adding apps or leverage their current leadership position.

The third challenge is the concerns from WeChat's business users. Currently, the biggest concern from the organizations doing businesses on WeChat is whether Tencent, WeChat's parent company, would for real open the platform, other than copy their features and then beat them. Besides, other concerns include: an official account can not collect

---

① Jullien Legrand, overthrowing digital platforms: lessons from WeChat, http://parisinnovationreview.com/2017/01/15/overthrowing-digital-platforms-wechat/, 2017-01-25.

audience data sets directly and analyze them as it likes; WeChat's mechanism isn't favorable for application distribution; third parties have to follow rules set or adjusted from time to time by WeChat. For example, official accounts previously were allowed to send three messages a day to followers. But WeChat reduced the quota into one per day after claiming three would flood users. Currently only a small number of verified accounts are allowed to send two a day. WeChat's infrastructure hasn't been stable enough. If the concerns can not be solved, it may cause the loss of business users.

The last possible challenge is the censorship from governments. In recent years, Chinese social media platforms are required to censor their users by authorities. For WeChat, censoring users' content would be a costly affair, and it would require more complicated filtering technology. Unlike Sina Weibo, which is text-based, WeChat would have to find a way to filter multimedia content such as voice messages too. Additionally, WeChat has to cope with the censorship problems from its foreign markets. For example, WeChat was blocked by Moscow's communications and media regulator on May 5, 2017. Because Russia required internet service providers to register with related government bodies while Tencent "had a different understanding" on this issue. Russia revised its data privacy law in 2015, and stipulated that all companies processing personal data of Russian citizens must store it on servers within Russia and provide it to law enforcement if necessary. Companies that fail to comply will be banned. Though WeChat was allowed to go back online in Russia after the app was taken offline, it should pay more attention to the censorship rules.

> 译 最后一个可能的挑战来自政府。近年来,国内相关主管部门要求社交媒体平台进行内容审查。对微信来说,审查用户发布的内容不仅成本高,而且对过滤技术也有较高要求。与微博基于文本的内容不同,微信必须找到过滤多媒体内容的方法。除此之外,微信也面临国外政府的审查。例如,2017年5月5日,微信被莫斯科通信和媒体主管部门屏蔽,这是由于俄国要求因特网服务提供商必须通过相关政府机构注册,而微信对此有"不同理解"。俄国于2015年修改了数据隐私法,规定所有公司必须将俄国公民的数据存储在俄境内的服务器中,如有必要需要将其向司法机构开放。企业如有违规,将被禁止服务。尽管微信将APP下线后被恢复了在俄境内的服务,但它应该更多关注相关的审查制度。

Originating from a mere instant messaging app, WeChat has found the effective ways to monetize the socialization services and grown up to a comprehensive platform combing the features of social media, e-commerce, games and payment. We can envision that it will bring us more surprises while facing more challenges.

Case Analysis

对不少的中国人而言,微信已成为必不可少的通信和社交工具,除此之外,它也是生活中常用的支付、理财、游戏平台。这个起源于即时信息的移动端应用为何能在短时间内迅速风靡？作为对消费者免费的多边平台又是如何挖掘社交服务的价值的？仔细分析这个案例能帮助我们回答这两个问题。

微信的快速成长首先应该归因于它对传统短信的颠覆。很长一段时间，中国的消费者不得不使用形式单一的短信进行移动端的即时信息沟通，并且为每一条短信支付0.1元的成本。尽管后来陆续出现了其他的文本即时信息工具，但都存在明显的局限性：飞信的问世尽管可以实现 PC 端和移动端的即时沟通，但形式仍然单一，且由于中国移动的宣传不力，它并没有真正流行起来；QQ 和 MSN 尽管普及率较高，但它们在很长一段时间都仅能支持 PC 端的交流。有没有兼顾廉价、形式多样、适用于移动端的即时信息工具呢？2011 年，微信的推出填补了这一需求空白，也实现了自身的快速普及。它不仅能提供包括文本、图片、视频、音频在内的多种沟通方式，更重要的是基于流量计费的它相比传统的短信沟通成本低到几乎可以忽略不计。这款廉价而灵活的社交应用适时地出现，润物细无声地满足了消费者对社交工具的几乎所有设想，它的风靡也就不足为奇了。在市场上的首秀大获成功以后，微信接下来并非高枕无忧，相反，它必须面对更大的挑战：如何留住用户，保持高市场渗透率？以多功能服务满足用户的不同需求是微信采取的主要策略：除了已有的多形式的即时信息沟通，朋友圈的功能满足了用户分享的需求；"摇一摇"和"扫一扫"实现了陌生人的沟通，拉近了人与人的距离。微信通过频繁的功能迭代不断满足用户的需求，并持续获得成功。此时的微信已经俨然成为中国知名度最高的社交网络平台。然而，微信的幕后推手——腾讯显然并未满足于此，它陆续将金融、电商、游戏等更多的功能嵌入微信中，不仅提高了服务的附加价值，增强了用户粘性，而且巧妙地实现了平台从双边向多边的拓展。

对于消费者而言，微信的下载和使用均是免费的，这个看似对消费者十分慷慨的平台是如何实现服务的货币化呢？换句话说，它是如何赚钱的呢？与 Facebook 类似，基于双边市场的微信仍然采用了对一边收费，而对另一边免费的平台策略。对消费者免费是为了获得平台流量，而由此造成的利润"损失"必须要通过其他途径弥补。与其他社交平台一样，微信的主要收入仍然来自广告。微信在短期内积累了规模庞大的客户群，这足以吸引广告商投放广告。更重要的是，随着客户群规模的进一步扩大，更多的广告商会被吸引进来，而一旦客户数量达到临界值，网络效应就会形成，带来的收入也会增加。除了广告，程序内购买是微信挖掘社交网络服务价值的另一项措施。微信将动漫表情和游戏嵌入平台功能中供消费者购买，并从销售收入中获得利润分成。例如，微信曾经和著名日本动漫《樱桃小丸子》的创作者合作，提供该动漫形象的微信表情供用户在沟通时使用，这种方式一方面令即时信息沟通更加生动和丰富，另一方面也有助于提高用户的忠诚度。开设微店服务以挖掘社交网络服务的电商价值是微信做出的又一项重要决策。微店是类似淘宝的 C2C 电商平台，它面向所有的消费者和付费商家开放，以便双方在其中进行自由的商品交换。显然，微店是又一个双边平台的例子，它将零售商和消费者联系在一起，促成双方的交易，并向商家收取一定的中介服务费。微店并非零售商涉足电商的唯一渠道，他们也可以通过付费注册企业公众号的方式吸引消费者关注,借此将其引导至购物站点完成交易,并借助公众号完成消息推送,内部管理等任务。这种方式虽然便利,但收费较高。除此之外,微信还推出了"类余额宝"的草根理财产品——理财通。用户可以将闲散资金存入理财通账户进行投资理财,不仅没有投资门槛,而且还可以随存随取,极大地方便了用户。很明显,微信起源于社交平台,却在不断地向金融、电商、游戏等重要领域拓展,未来将形成一个更加庞大的综合性商业生态圈。

Section 5
Case Presentation
第五节 案例分析演示

▶ Purposes of Case Presentation

There are many reasons why students are asked to give presentations and these will be influenced by the academic course and situational and organizational factors. The purpose and circumstances of a case presentation will influence its style, content and structure. Generally, a case presentation is used for the following purposes:

1. Developing a deeper understanding of a topic or text;
2. Covering specific areas of the curriculum in more detail;
3. Explaining an experiment or managerial process;
4. Showing your opinion on a specific problem or topic.

The content of a case presentation is usually focused on a topic area relevant to a course or module being studied. This may involve new research and knowledge that extends how the topic has previously been taught by teachers. It may also involve "repackaging" knowledge already covered or further exploration of the topic by looking at different perspectives. Sometimes, these types of case presentations are used to explore areas of a curriculum in greater detail than has been covered in lectures. This helps the presenters to develop deeper knowledge and the audience to broaden their understanding of the topic[①].

---

① Barbara Chivers, Michael Shoolbred, *A Student's Guide to Presentations: Making your Presentation Count*, SAGE Publications, 2007: p.4.

Suggestions for Effective Presentations[①]

Whatever the type of presentation, there are some common elements and requirements to take into account so as to make an effective presentation:

1. Organize your presentation. Since presentation is usually completed by a group, an effective organization is necessary. It includes who says what, in which order and how to make smooth connecting link. Special attention should be devoted to your opening to arouse class interest and attention as well as your conclusion as it may provide a lasting impression.

2. Prepare well. Preparation is crucial for an presentation especially you're your debut. A good preparation helps you to review the case, comb your opinions, find the bugs and make the necessary supplement and in turn build self-confidence. When preparing your presentation, you should remember: leave a slide showing an outline of the presentation, one or more slides showing the key problems and strategic issues that management needs to address and try to use exhibits if they are available.

3. Use memory props. Unavoidably, you usually feel nervous when making an presentation in public. A memory props is helpful at this time. An outline of your key points, cue cards, succinct overhead transparencies or computer generated graphics will serve as a guide to your presentation while preserving your ability to react to the audience and allowing for some spontaneity.

4. Keep it simple. Only the key points will be remembered anyway. So keep your structure or outline simple.

5. Use quality visual aids. During the course of a presentation, it is hard to attract and keep audience' attention. Therefore, you have to find a way to make your presentation interesting. Illustrating your presentation with quality and pertinent visual aids is an effective way. Effective use of slides, transparencies or computer graphics as well as videos may not only impress your audience but also save time.

6. Rehearse. To prepare for the possible accidents in an presentation, a rehearsal is necessary. Make sure that your rehearsal is not just for content but also for style of delivery, eye contact, poise, timing, linking between various presenters and use of visual aids. Besides, you should try to anticipate your audience reaction during a rehearsal. If you spend some time in trying to anticipate the questions from the audience, you will be in a better position to defend your positions.

[①] Louise A. Mauffette, James A. Erskine, Michiel R. Leenders, *Learning with Cases* (*Fourth Edition*), Ivey Publishing, 2008:pp.105-106.

Summary（本章小结）

Social media refers to the websites and applications that enable users to create and share content or to participate in social networking. Social media is usually categorized according to different criteria. For example, Andreas Kaplan classifies the existing social media into four types based on location or time sensitive. Thomas Crampton classifies social media in China into sixteen types based on the functionalities. Social media popularizes so fast because it owns some advantages over the industrial media such as quality, reach, frequency and immediacy. As a new media, social media is unavoidably criticized by public due to the problems of fake information, privacy, cyber bullying and addiction.

Launched in 2004, Facebook is an online social networking service platform which enables users to create a user profile, add other users as "friends", exchange messages, post status updates and photos, share videos, receive notifications when others update their profiles, and join in the common-interest user groups. The social media platform initially limited to Harvard students soon expanded to other college students and high-school students. Facebook held its initial public offering eight years after its foundation, reaching an original peak market capitalization of $104 billion. Unsatisfied with the profits from advertising, Facebook expanded its businesses to e-commerce with the launch of their virtual gift shop. Facebook's core asset is the map of connections that Facebook users create with friends and online content which has been shared with outside applications—vendors track Facebook users' activity or leverage an individual's social network. Facebook has recognized that its primary purpose is to be a social outlet for users. It is a great source of brand building for merchants—a way to share information, provide exclusive offers and access, and increase awareness but has not served as a strong driver of traffic for online commerce.

Tudou is a video-sharing website in China, where users can upload, view and share video clips. Tudou has experienced a rapid growth since its foundation: from the initial 5 audios daily uploaded to the later 20,000 videos daily uploaded, Tudou has become the podcast website with the highest daily visits and the largest user group in China only in three years. In March 2012, Youku reached an agreement to acquire Tudou in a stock-for-stock transaction, which leads to the birth of Youku Tudou Inc. Tudou profits from advertising, video charging and advertisements removing charging. Facing the threats from the peers such as LeTV and Tencent Video, Tudou should adopt the effective strategies to solidify its achievements such as improving technical support, the quality of contents and services, strengthening the cooperation with traditional medias, targeting at mobile end, taking advantage of business consolidation and emphasizing brand rebranding.

WeChat is a mobile text and voice messaging communication service developed by Tencent in China, first released in January 2011. It is the largest standalone messaging app by monthly active users. Starting from instant messaging, WeChat has expanded its services to payment and investment. The right entry timing, low price, multi-functionalities and the strong users stickiness are the four factors leading to WeChat's rapid growth. As an all-in-one social media application, WeChat monetizes its social network services by virtue of five ways: In-app purchase, e-commerce, financial services, advertising and enterprise accounts. Being faced with the fierce competition in the instant message market, WeChat has to be prepared.

This chapter introduces how to make a case analysis presentation. A presentation can benefit your ability of analysis, expression and communication. To make a successful presentation, you should organize your presentation, prepare well, use memory props, keep it simple, use quality visual aids and rehearse.

 Exercises & Tasks (练习与任务)

▶ *Exercises*

1. How do you define social media and social commerce?
2. What are the respective business model of Facebook and Tudou? How do you differentiate them?
3. What causes the popularity of WeChat?

▶ *Tasks*

Choose a case of social commerce and prepare a 20-minute presentation which should include:

1. Background introduction;
2. Analyze its advantages or disadvantages or the reasons of its success or failure;
3. Conclusion.

Part IV Supervision and Future

第四部分 监管与未来

Chapter 9 Roles Government Should Play in E-Commerce
第九章 政府在电子商务中应该扮演的角色

 Learning Objectives（学习目标）

After finishing this chapter, you should be able to:
1. Describe the roles that government should play in e-commerce;
2. Explain how government should play its roles in e-commerce;
3. Identify the reasons behind the dispute between Qihoo and Tencent;
4. List the causes of the price war between Jingdong and Suning;
5. Explain what causes Baidu' copyright dilemma;
6. Describe the methods of writing a qualified case report.

 Introduction（内容简介）

　　With the rapid development of e-commerce, market, the invisible hand, can not handle everything any longer. It is time for government to intervene to keep a healthy, orderly and fair environment. What roles should government play in e-commerce? This chapter answers the question.

　　Chapter 9 is composed of 5 sections. The brief introduction to government's roles in e-commerce is made in section 1. Three related cases are provided respectively in section 2, 3, and 4. Section 5 focuses on how to write a case report.

Section 1
Government's Roles in E-Commerce
第一节　电子商务中政府的角色

▶ Key Words

1. incentive *n.* 刺激
2. spur *vt.* 激励
3. in tandem 一前一后的
4. paradigm *n.* 范例
5. conciliator *n.* 调解人
6. nexus *n.* 联结

In June 2015, India government released proposals to adopt several incentives to spur increased adoption of electronic payments, according to draft on June 22. The incentives range from a charge on high value cash transactions to lower transaction fees for electronic payments in tandem with tax benefits. The government wanted to encourage more use of debit cards, credit cards and mobile payments by virtue of the incentives[①]. This is a paradigm that implies the roles of government in e-commerce development.

What roles should government play in e-commerce development? In summary, government should build and keep a fair, open and sustainable environment for online exchanges, which can be achieved by the mature legal, ethical, tax and security systems.

▶ The Roles That Government Should Play in E-Commerce

1. Supporter. At the early stage of an emerging industry's evolvement, government should become a supporter who provides the necessary aids for the industry and the firms such as creating a favorable policy environment for e-commerce, becoming a leading-edge user of e-commerce and its applications in its operations, and a provider to citizens of e-government services to encourage its mass use[②]. Actually, Chinese government has been making efforts to it. In addition to the industrial polices and regulations issued, Chinese government promised further measures to boost e-commerce as it pins its hopes on the sector as a new growth engine for the economy in June 2015. The State Council released a guideline on June 20, 2015 saying the customs administrator will streamline customs procedures for e-commerce exports and imports to make the processes simpler and quicker,

---

① PYMNTS, India's Government to Spur E-commerce with Tax Breaks, Other Incentives, PYMNT. com, 2015-06-23.

② Hamad, What Is the Role of Government in the Development of E-commerce in Developing Countries?, http.//learne-commerece. blogspot. jp/2010/10/what-is-role-of-government-in. html, 2010-10-31.

while the quality supervision authorities will allow collective declaration, examination and release of goods. The government will keep export taxes low while formulating import tax policies with the aim of increasing domestic consumption, promoting fair competition and strengthening import tax management. It will also encourage domestic banks and institutions to launch cross-border electronic payment businesses and advance pilot overseas payments in foreign currencies①.

2. Supervisor. To create a suitable environment for the development of e-commerce, domestically and internationally, government should not only facilitate e-commerce and access to the new technologies, not impeding their development, but also acknowledge the right and the need for government to regulate. Government therefore is constantly faced with the difficult task of striking the right balance between regulation and laissez-faire. By legislating and issuing laws, regulations and policies, government should supervise the e-commerce enterprises and regulate their activities so as to build Internet users trust and confidence in the powerful and relatively new means of conducting business by addressing key issues such as privacy, data security and authentication.

3. Conciliator. Due to the limited resources, the conflicts among the e-commerce players (e.g. the dispute between QQ and 360) are unavoidable. Particularly, due to the immature market system, the disputes occur constantly. How to alleviate the conflict and solve the problems at the lowest cost is challenging government's capability as a negotiator. Government should not only keep neutral so as to make the objective judgments but also communicate with the parties effectively.

▶ How Does Government Play Its Roles in E-Commerce?

No doubt, all the online businesses must comply with the existing laws and regulations that govern the operations of businesses. However, it is not easy to make the appropriate laws and regulations because of the complexity of the Internet which includes:

1. Internet extends a company's reach beyond traditional boundaries, differing from the territorial borders in the physical world that the range of culture and reach of applicable laws of the online business is ambiguous.

2. Internet increases speed and efficiency of business communications, which requires a securer environment.

3. Internet creates a space where sellers and buyers are allowed to make products or services exchanges, which requires a mature legal system to solve the disputes between the different parities of exchange and protect them.

---

① Xinhua, State Council Guideline Promises Further E-commerce Support, english.gov.cn, 2015-06-21.

Facing the complicated environment of the Internet, government should be prudent and active when implementing its tasks in e-commerce. There are some experiences from the U.S. which government can learn. In the United States, the Federal Trade Commission (FTC) and PCI (Payment Card Industry) Security Standards Council are the primary agencies that regulate e-commerce activities and provides security standards. The two organizations issue some e-commerce regulations including protecting consumer privacy, handling customer data, collecting taxes and complying with online advertising regulations:

1. Protecting customer's privacy online

Online privacy is a big issue as many e-commerce sites collect and retain personal information about customers. Some of the personal data obtained would include a customer's name, address, email address, and possibly their credit card and other types of financial information. It is the responsibility of an e-commerce site owner to ensure the personally identifiable information being protected, and when a website collects personal data it should be required to comply with privacy laws. E-commerce site owners should provide a privacy policy and post it on the e-commerce website. This policy should clearly identify what kinds of personal information it will collect from users visiting the website, who it will share the information collected with, and how it will use and store that information.

2. Online advertising compliance

E-commerce site owners must know about the applicable laws for online advertising. Like traditional advertising for brick-and-mortar stores, online retailers must also comply with regulations when advertising online. The FTC regulations for advertising are designed to protect consumers and to prevent deceptive and unfair acts or practices.

3. Collecting taxes online

According to the U.S.A. law, if a business has a physical presence in a state (e.g. a store or office), then it is required by law to collect state and local sales tax from customers. However, if the business doesn't have a "physical presence", then collecting tax on purchases is not required. For e-commerce site owners, one thing they have to research is how their states classifies a physical presence. In legal terms, this is called a "nexus" and each state defines nexus differently.

4. Handling customer financial data

In the U.S., as an e-commerce site owner needs to know about is the PCI DSS standard, which is short for Payment Card Industry (PCI) Data Security Standard (DSS). All organizations, including online retailers, must follow this standard when storing, processing and transmitting credit card data. There are a number of security initiatives in this standard, such as using a firewall between a wireless network and the cardholder data environment, making use the latest security and authentication, and using a network intrusion detection system①.

5. Protecting Intellectual Property (IP)

In the context of e-commerce, IP examples include digital images, digital files, web sites, and online business models. IP laws protect the rights of the property owner (e. g. author, designer). A company can use three devices to protect its IP: patents, copyrights, and trademarks. Patents provide the holder the exclusive right to prevent others from manufacturing, using, or selling the invention. A patent is granted for a period of twenty years; a copyright provides the author exclusive rights over his or her creation. Copyrights protect expressions, not the idea itself. In order to feature a copyrighted product on a website, one must have the permission of the owner; a trademark can be a logo, picture, image, musical phrase, and so on. A trademark is established through usage, not by invention or authorship②.

6. Handling online fraud

For the politics system is composed by central government and local government, "The Local Government Fraud Strategy" can be used for reference. With the supports from central government, local government will be better able to protect itself from fraud and provide a more effective fraud response. To achieve this ambition, this strategy sets out a new approach for tackling fraud in local government underpinned by three principles③:

1) Acknowledge. Acknowledging and understanding fraud risks and committing support and resource to tackling fraud in order to maintain a robust anti-fraud response.

2) Prevent. Preventing and detecting more fraud by making better use of information and technology, enhancing fraud control and processes and developing a more effective anti-fraud culture.

3) Pursue. Punishing fraudsters and recovering losses by prioritizing the use of civil sanctions, developing capability and capacity to investigate fraudsters and developing a more collaborative and supportive law enforcement response.

---

① Vangie Beal, 4 E-commerce Regulations to Need to Know, http://www. E-commerce-guide. com/solutions/building/article. php/3910211/4-E-commerce-Regulations-to-Need-to-Know. htm, 2010-10-27.
② Sandeep Krishnamurthy, *E-commerce Management*: *Text and Cases*, 北京大学出版社, 2003 年.
③ CIPFA, The Local Government Counter Fraud and Corruption Strategy, https://www. cipfa. org/~/media/files/services/ccfc/fighting% 20fraud% 20and% 20corruption% 20locally% 20the% 20strategy% 202016% 2019. pdf, 2016.

Section 2
Battles Between Qihoo and Tencent[①]
第二节 奇虎与腾讯之争

Key Words

1. dispute *n.* 争端
2. escalate *vt./vi.* 逐渐上升
3. allege *vt.* 宣称
4. plaintiff *n.* 原告
5. intervention *n.* 干预
6. oligarch *n.* 寡头
7. bulls management 多头管理
8. in the green tree 占主动地位

Case

Background Introduction

The dispute occurred between two Chinese IT companies—Tencent and Qihoo 360 (abbreviation: Qihoo) in November 2010. The dispute attracted many attention because it happened between two famous companies and escalated even involved their users. As we know, Tencent owns the largest instant message platform QQ while Qihoo is famous for its popular security software—360 Safeguard. Since the two companies seem not closely related, why did the dispute burst between them?

In 2006, Tencent launched QQ doctor (renamed as QQ Computer Housekeeper later), a security software which protects users' QQ account from being thieved. QQ doctor quickly gained 40% of the Chinese market overnight since it bundled with QQ. Tencent' move threatened 360 safeguard directly. Therefore, it is not shocking that the conflict occurred between the two companies.

Timelines of The Dispute[②]

A timeline can help us to understand the dispute (Figure 9-1).

During the Mid-Autumn Festival 2010, Tencent automatically updated its "QQ Software Management" and "QQ Doctor" to "QQ Computer Manager" which covers the main functionalities (e.g. Trojan cleaning, software management) of "360 Security Guards" created by Qihoo. With the large user base, "QQ Computer Manager" is expected to threaten "360 Security Guards", the star product which Qihoo has been proud of.

---

① The battles between the two firms lasted for several years and the case only focuses on the dispute in 2010.
② Susan Ning, Ding Liang and Angie Ng., The QQ / 360 Disputes—Who, What, Where, When and Preliminary Antitrust Analysis, ChinaLawinSight.com, 2010-11-12.

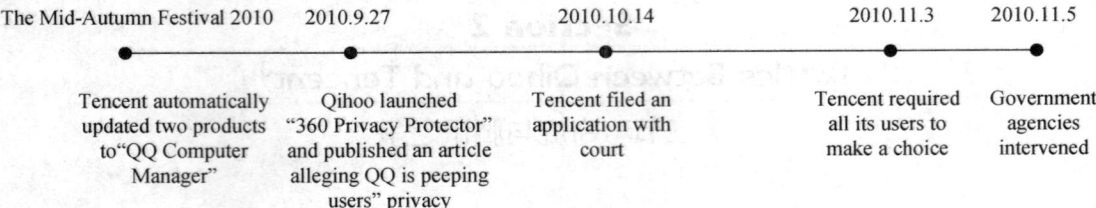

Figure 9-1 Timeline of the Dispute

On 27th September 2010, Qihoo launched a software called "360 Privacy Protector" as a reaction to Tencent's move. The product was alleged to aim to shield a user from software which illegally extracts or retains a user's personal data, or in other words, to protect a user's privacy. Beside, Qihoo published an article on their website entitled "360 Privacy Protector 1.1 Beta—new function—privacy clean up function". In this article, Qihoo alleged that its 360 Privacy Protector software recently detected that "certain instant messaging software" was found to be "peeping" at the private files and data of users, without first obtaining the approval of those users. The article itself did not name which instant messaging software Qihoo was referring to. However a screenshot in the article bored the logo of the Tencent QQ instant messaging software.

On 14th October 2010, Tencent filed an application with the Beijing Chaoyang District People's Court (the Court), alleging that three companies including Qihoo have fabricated or spread false facts about Tencent QQ's instant messaging software resulting in the Tencent QQ's business reputation or "commodity fame" being damaged. In its complaint, Tencent requested that the Court injuncts Qihoo from fabricating or spreading false facts about Tencent QQ's instant messaging software; that Qihoo apologize to Tencent for the conduct described above; and that Qihoo pay damages of 4 million yuan.

On 3rd November 2010, the Court accepted this case. And on the same day, Tencent issued a newsletter to all its users entitled "A letter to all users of QQ". Through this newsletter, Tencent informed all users that they have made the "difficult" decision of making the use of QQ instant messaging service incompatible with the use of 360 privacy or anti-virus software. In other words, QQ users who choose to use 360 privacy or anti-virus software will no longer be able to use QQ instant messaging in the same instance. Tencent explained that this was mainly because they were not confident that they could continue to protect their user's privacy (including data such as chats and passwords), if they continued to use the 360 line of security software. In its newsletter, Tencent also requested users to use its "QQ Computer Housekeeper" or other antivirus or security software in place of the 360 line of security software. From that day, users of QQ reported that they weren't able to use the 360 line of security software and QQ at the same time.

On 5th November, 2010, Several Chinese government departments including the

Ministry of Industry and Information Technology and the Ministry of Public Security intervened. On November 21, 2010, the Ministry of Industry and Information Technology required Qihoo and Tencent to halt the dispute immediately, ensure the usage of the related software, comply with the laws and regulations and make apologies to the public within 5 work days. And users reported soon that they were allowed to use QQ and 360 software concurrently again.

Who Is the Final Winner of the Dispute?

After the dispute was over, people couldn't help asking: who on earth wins the war: Qihoo? Tencent? Or other stakeholders?

1. Tencent. As one of the two parties in the spat as well as an IT giant in China, Tencent drew much attention for the issue. Corresponding to the attention, it had to undertake the tangible and intangible losses. The first as well as the direct loss is its stock. Since the spat, Tencent had experienced the biggest drop in more than two months. Tencent fell 3.1% to HK $181.30 (US $23.39) on November 2, 2010, knocking more than $1.37 billion off Tencent's market value①. The second loss is intangible but even more serious—possibly losing users. Owning the largest instant message platform, Tencent forced users to choose one of two—QQ or 360, which triggered dissatisfaction among many Internet users and they criticized the move as "immoral and irresponsible". As a result, some users may leave to other platforms. Additionally, the case of unfair competition lasted for about 4 years and it costed Tencent a lot though it won the lawsuit.

2. Qihoo. As a famous security software provider, Qihoo did not benefit from the dispute either. Firstly, the market share of its new product—360 browser fell from 19.9% on October 27 to 3% on November 9, 2010②. Besides, it also faced the dilemma that some users uninstalled its security software during the war. The losses are not limited to the two: The court's first instance favored Tencent's arguments and the Guangdong Higher People's Court decided that the 360 Company had engaged in unfair competition. Subsequently, 360 Company appealed to the Supreme Court. In March 2014, the Supreme People's Court made a judgment affirming the initial judgment, deciding that 360's QQ Guard engaged in unfair competition against Tencent. Not only did Qihoo lose the suitcase, but also it paid for the dispute a lot: time, resources, money and the public image.

3. Users. Both the users of the two companies are innocent. Before the dispute, they could enjoy a convenient communication on QQ as well as the protection from 360

---

① Tencent Stock A Fatality of War, *China Daily*, 2010-11-05.
② Chen Limin and Tuo Yannan, Compromise in Sight in Tencent-Qihoo 360 spat, *China Daily*, 2010-11-11.

safeguard. However, they were involved in an unprecedented spat and forced to make a choice between the two products by a so-called "a difficult decision". According to the statistics, about 20 million QQ users were affected by the war[244].

4. Other stakeholders. The only one benefiting from the dispute may be the rivals of Tecent and Qihoo. For example, Kingsoft and Kaspersky, two paid anti-virus software providers, announced they offered their products free for one year to grab shares in China's Internet security market, of which 360 claimed to control a share of more than 70%. The move led to 18% increase of Kingsoft's stock price in HongKong.

Obviously, no one but the opponents of Tencent and Qihoo benefit from the dispute. Particularly, for the two parties of the spat—Tencent and Qihoo, it is a "lose-lose" war.

Behind the Dispute

The dispute between the two famous IT companies attracts lots of attention. Meanwhile, it also incurs the query from the public. Several Chinese government departments, including the Ministry of Industry and Information Technology and the Ministry of Public Security did not interfere until the late stage of the dispute. Why does the administration let it be rather than make the necessary administrative intervention as soon as possible? Is that because of the concern of over-intervention? Or lack of the relevant administrative functions? Why does the dispute evolve into an issue of unfair competition? The causes behind the dispute are worth of probing:

1. Lack of legislation suitable for the new market. Generally, in the case of monopoly, it is necessary as well as complex to define relevant market[①] because it involves substitutable demand and supply analysis of alternatives, sometimes even has the hypothetical monopolist test. particularly, the dispute between Tencent and Qihoo involves a new market—Internet, which makes it even more complex. The dynamic development and the network externality of Internet market makes it even more difficult to define a dominant market position[②]. On the one hand, the existing "Anti Unfair Competition Legislation" lags behind the fast growth of the Internet due to the simple and rough articles, which makes it not suitable for the new market any more. On the other hand, there has not been a new law against unfair competition on the Internet. As a result, it is difficult to make a jurisdiction and some enterprises probably leverage the "grey area" of laws. The dispute between Tencent and Qihoo should be partially attributed to it.

---

① In competition law, a relevant market is a market in which a particular product or service is sold. It is the intersection of a relevant product market and a relevant geographic market (https://en.wikipedia.org/wiki/Relevant_market).

② WeiWei Hu and Yimeei Guo, Anti-monopoly Analysis of Tencent QQ versus 360 Dispute, The Proceedings of 2011 International Symposium on Advances in Applied Economics, *Business and Development*, August, 2011.

2. The punishment is not strict enough. For some Internet companies owing the annual revenue of several hundred million Yuan(RMB), the penal sum is even no more than several hundred thousand Yuan(RMB) accounting a few percentage of the revenue. The low violation cost to some extent provokes even more unfair competition and law breach. In the dispute of intellectual property rights, the reason why infringers are emboldened to engage in acts of infringement is that, in judicial practice, the courts always rule a low amount of compensation as punishment. In such proceedings, in the event that the profits earned by the infringer or losses suffered by the party infringed can not be determined, the court shall apply the provision of the legal amount of compensation. However, in practice, due to the difficulties of proving the profits or losses in question, the court would award the damages of 500,000 yuan OR 1,000,000 yuan. In this case, Tencent provided adequate evidence proving the extent of losses suffered, but the evidence was not be fully dismissed by virtue of the cause-and-effect relationship afforded. The Supreme Court, however, decided that the Guard, publicized by the appellant, had already caused greater losses than the legal amount of compensation, and thus, upon the evidence, increased the payable damages up to the maximum compensation of 5,000,000 yuan. Maybe it is not a large amount of money for these two companies, but such a decision is a revelation to intellectual property rights holders and courts. In the event that the plaintiff can not prove the specific losses suffered, focusing on proving that the losses are far higher than legal amount of compensation will be a good strategy in the interests of obtaining higher compensation. It is good for intellectual property rights holders in protecting their legal interests. Just as the words in a judgment: "free competition and free innovation shall be constructed as the border of protecting others' lawful rights and interests, and a healthy development of the internet requires an orderly market environment and the explicit market competition rules as a guarantee."①

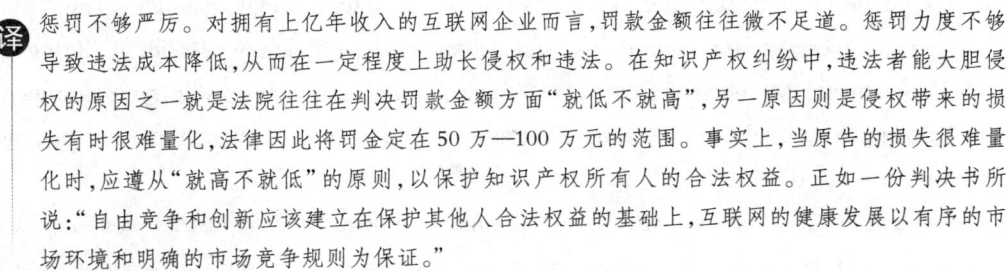

惩罚不够严厉。对拥有上亿年收入的互联网企业而言,罚款金额往往微不足道。惩罚力度不够导致违法成本降低,从而在一定程度上助长侵权和违法。在知识产权纠纷中,违法者能大胆侵权的原因之一就是法院往往在判决罚款金额方面"就低不就高",另一原因则是侵权带来的损失有时很难量化,法律因此将罚金定在 50 万—100 万元的范围。事实上,当原告的损失很难量化时,应遵从"就高不就低"的原则,以保护知识产权所有人的合法权益。正如一份判决书所说:"自由竞争和创新应该建立在保护其他人合法权益的基础上,互联网的健康发展以有序的市场环境和明确的市场竞争规则为保证。"

3. The less effective market supervision. Many economists agree that market entry, competition and exit should be ruled by market—the invisible hand. This point benefits the

---

① Ytybest, Outcome of Unfair Competition Dispute between Tencent QQ and Qihoo 360, http://www.chinaiplawyer.com/china-supreme-court-determined-unfair-competition-dispute-tencent-qq-qihoo-360/, 2014-03-07.

growth of an emerging industry. However, along with the market's evolving into the mature stage, administrative intervention should be adopted since the problems such as online fraud can not be solved by market itself. During the two decades of Chinese Internet development, local government greatly depended on the self-adjustment and self-supervision of the market. It facilitates the fast growth of the industry to some extent. However, the legal problems related to the Internet have not been resolved well due to lack of effective market supervision. The immature industry, the existence of oligarch and the lag of legislation make it difficult to rule and govern the market[①].

4. The existence of oligopoly. Along with the development the Internet technologies, the Internet oligarchs owning the technical advantages are emerging. Tencent is regarded as an oligarch due to its biggest market share of the instant message market and the huge user group of 600 million. Thanks to the technical advantages and the solid user base, the Internet oligarchs are usually in the green tree during the interactions with the partners and customers. They are able to easily gain the price advantages, charge the users unfairly, intrude users' privacy and even impose the unreasonable restrictions on the users. The users are supposed to own the right to choose the Internet products freely. Unfortunately, as long as the oligopoly exists, the users probably accept the unfair restrictions due to their dependence on the products or services. For example, in the dispute between Tencent and Qihoo, users were forced to make a choice: uninstalling 360 software or halting using QQ even though they knew it was not fair. Therefore, it is imperative to issue a law or regulation specified to the unfair competition or oligopoly on the Internet so as to protect the consumers from the market power abusement.

5. The "bulls management" impairs the effects of supervision. Several government departments, including the Ministry of Industry and Information Technology and the Ministry of Public Security are involved in the settlement of the dispute. Obviously, more than one government department are in charge of the Internet-related issues. The "bulls management" increases transaction cost and decreases the efficiency. Besides, during the legal enforcement, Ministry of Commerce, State Administration For Industry & Commerce and National Department and Reform Commission are involved, which makes the legal enforcement more difficult.

6. Lack of legal awareness. Due the immature legal and industrial system, most Chinese Internet enterprises lack the legal consciousness. Some companies adopt, utilize and copy others' works without the permission or payment. It not only leads to the lawsuits between the local competitors but also causes the conflicts between local companies and

---

① 沈洁莹:"论我国互联网行业不正当竞争行为的行政监管——以腾讯QQ和奇虎360之战为例",《电子政务》,2011年3月.

foreign companies.

7. Lack of product differentiation. The dispute between Tencent and Qihoo originated Tencent's action in 2010 spring festival that it released a security tool aiming at the users in medium and small cities. The tool acquired 40% market share, threatening the popular security software—360. Actually, a radical factor incurring the dispute is the product homogenization. Chinese firms are inclined to imitate and even copy the well-sold products to gain the marginal profits because of the extremely low costs. However, a product is unable to distinguish itself in the competition, it is difficult for the firm to attract and keep the customers. Price war and coming out swinging are usually utilized in the competition. As a result, the unfair competition probably harms the players. The dispute is a typical case in which neither Tencent nor Qihoo benefits from the dispute. Instead, both the corporate image of the two famous firms are damaged①.

The case of Tencent vs. Qihoo implies government's intervention is necessary during the evolvement of an emerging industry since market system and ethics are unable to regulate everything. Just as what Sergio Marchi said, the role of government is three-fold: endorsing e-commerce as a tool for increased competitiveness, creating the right domestic and international environment for the use and development of e-commerce and cooperating with other governments, and redefining the public-private partnership by bringing together governments, the business community and civil society②.

Case Analysis

本案例讲述的是2010年发生在奇虎360(以下简称奇虎)与腾讯之间的争端。两家公司之间的这场争端当时引发巨大反响原因在于：第一,腾讯和奇虎都是在中国品牌知名度很高的互联网企业,前者因为推出即时通信工具QQ迅速成为中国社交媒体的翘楚,后者则因为开发出360软件系列成功抢滩中国的安全软件市场；第二,两家企业的争端迅速波及用户,腾讯甚至要求其在QQ和360软件之间二选一,引起用户不满；第三,这场争端从一开始的网络口水战上升到法律诉讼,最后以工信部等几家主管部委介入而暂告一个段落。

引发这场持续了将近2个月的争端的导火线是：腾讯推出的"QQ电脑管家"由于功能与360软件产品类似,直接威胁到当时用户覆盖率已达75%的奇虎。360发布直接针对QQ的"隐私保护器"工具作为回击,并引发双方接下来的争斗,甚至诉诸法律。腾讯和奇虎在这场风波中两败俱伤,不仅要面对股价下跌、客户流失、市场份额降低等直接损失,还得面对为此投入的大量资源以及企业形象受损等间接损失；QQ和360的

---

① 谢春晖："网络产品滥用市场支配地位的法律调整——由腾讯、360案引发的思考",《法制与经济旬刊》, 2012年。
② Sergio Marchi, E-commerce and the Role of Governments (Speaking Notes), World Services Congress, 2001.

用户是这场争端中的无辜者,他们曾被逼迫在两家产品中"二选一";金山和卡巴斯基等杀毒软件才是这场争端的真正获益者,他们也趁机进行促销,希望以此拉拢客户。由此可见,企业非正当竞争的结果往往是"鹬蚌相争渔翁得利"。消费者可能成为受益者(如:降价),也可能成为无辜受害者,但即使是后者,企业也不应该忘记,在互联网年代消费者"用脚投票"变得更加便利,如果触犯其利益,企业将为此付出更长远的代价。

剖析这场争端背后的原因,可以发现内外因素皆有。从企业的内因来看,产品同质化和缺少法律认知是主要因素。事实上,腾讯和奇虎的这场争端早在2010年春节就初见端倪,腾讯推出界面及功能酷似360的QQ医生,试图进军对方主导的安全软件市场,但由于360的快速反应加上产品不成熟而作罢,也使双方的争端拖到当年9月才真正爆发。因此,从头到尾,双方冲突的核心仍然是产品。由于产品同质化,意味着其被取代性增加,企业不得不采取其他手段拉拢消费者,占领市场。降价是解决这类问题的常见措施,腾讯和奇虎则采取了更为激烈的手段甚至诉诸法律。另外,企业缺少法律意识是第二个内因。腾讯在此过程中曾经发表公开信宣称,将在装有360软件的电脑上停止运行QQ软件,倡导必须卸载360软件才可登录QQ,并称此为"一个非常艰难的决定"。此举一出,舆论哗然,用户更是不满,认为该公司实际上是在变相逼迫用户"二选一"。这种以停用产品要挟用户站队,损害其利益的行为实际上已经游走在法律禁区的边缘。而奇虎发布"隐私保护器",宣称其能实时监测曝光QQ偷窥用户隐私,删除QQ广告且同时推广360产品的行为也属不正当竞争。事实上,中国互联网企业在快速增长的过程中由于缺少法律意识,时常出现未经允许收集用户数据,屏蔽对手广告等非法行为,这些行为如果不纠正就可能造成更严重的后果。从外因来看,立法的严重滞后是导致这场争端的重要原因。中国互联网产业兴起于上世纪90年代中期,在经历了2000年的互联网泡沫破灭之后,迎来了高速发展。然而,与这种高速成长极不匹配的是立法体系的严重滞后。以电子商务为例,迄今为止仍然没有一部完整的《电子商务法》出台。回到这场争端,界定"不正当竞争"本就比较复杂,现存的《反不正当竞争法》已经无法适应互联网市场的需求,而新的法律法规又迟迟没有出台,这就可能导致一些企业钻空子,利用法律上的"灰色地带"谋取利益。另外,对于不正当竞争行为的法律制裁力度不够。一方面不正当竞争所造成的损失很难准确量化,加上法庭在裁决时有可能从轻判处赔偿金额,导致企业的违法成本降低。除此之外,缺乏有效的市场监管机制是第三个原因。互联网在中国发展不过二十年时间,尚属新兴产业。早期对该行业的规范主要依靠市场这只"看不见的手"来完成,一批互联网企业也是依靠在监管机制尚不完善的环境中"野蛮生长"而发展起来。然而随着行业规模的迅速扩大,仅仅依靠市场的自我调节机制显然已经不够,这就要求政府发挥监管作用,规范企业行为。事实上,腾讯与奇虎争端的后期,工信部等主管部委的介入正是这种监管职能的体现。但是,从案例中也可以发现,介入后期监管的部委不止一家,说明存在"多头管理"的问题,如果各部委之间的责任不能明确,很有可能出现"踢皮球"的现象,影响监管效果。

在"跨界"现象愈演愈烈的今天,企业尤其是那些规模庞大的平台型企业可以借助互联网优势和网络效应将其业务触角伸向任何可能的领域,并在进行平台拓展的过程中实现"赢家通吃"。未来,企业所面对的竞争对手不仅来自同行,还有可能来自看似不相关的行业,如果不未雨绸缪,那么最终将被那些互联网上"看不见的对手"击败。另外,这种跨界扩张的结果将是行业寡头的出现,如果没有完善的法律法规对其行为进行约束,腾讯和奇虎发生在 8 年前的那场闹剧将频繁上演,带来的后果不仅是企业和客户利益受损,还有市场秩序的混乱。因此,腾讯和奇虎之争无论对于互联网业者还是对于市场监管者都有积极的警醒作用,它呼唤政府尽快完善相关的法律环境,保证互联网行业的健康持续发展。

Section 3
What Does Price War Bring to Jingdong and Suning?
第三节 价格战为京东和苏宁带来了什么?

I Key Words

1. wage *vt./vi.* 发动,开展
2. tumble *vt./n.* 跌倒
3. slam *vt./vi.* 抨击
4. stunt *n.* 噱头
5. mire *vt/vi, n.* 使陷入泥潭
6. predatory *adj.* 掠夺性的
7. topple *vt.* 推倒
8. retaliatory *adj.* 报复性的
9. cede *vt.* 放弃或割让(领土)

II Case

Background Introduction[①]

Price war refers to commercial competition characterized by the repeated cutting of prices below those of competitors. One competitor will lower its price, then others will lower their prices to match. If one of them reduces their price again, a new round of reductions starts[②].

Realizing the huge potential of e-commerce (particularly mobile commerce), more and more home appliance retailers have tapped the e-commerce market. Unavoidably, the online price wars have been escalating more fiercely in the Chinese market. Price wars occur in China almost each year. The price war occurring in the summer 2012 is one of the

---

① Yang Lina, E-commerce Price Wars Escalate in China, Xinhuanet, 2012-08-13.
② en.wikipedia.org/wiki/Price_war

most remarkable not only because the two parties are Chinese online retailing giants—Suning and Jingdong, but also it involves other famous e-tailers like Dangdang, Gome and Tmall.

Started by Suning in April 2012, the first round of the price war involved major Business-to-Customer (B2C) retailers including Gome, Dangdang, Tmall and Jingdong. At that time, the price war had not attracted much attention since the discount was not high and many people only regarded it as a regular marketing strategy. Nobody knew, at that time, it was actually the prelusion of the coming price war.

Jingdong waged the second round on its founding anniversary when the price war began officially. On August 14, Liu Qiangdong, chairman and founder of Jingdong, announced that his company would sell all major electric home appliances at cheaper prices than his rivals Gome and Suning. "Our home appliances will be priced 10% lower than those of Gome and Sunning", Liu wrote in a post on Sina Weibo, while promising faster delivery services. Meanwhile, Liu announced that his company would hire and station 5,000 price observers, all with tailored uniforms, at the outlets of Suning and Gome to ensure that its commodities achieve the required 10% price differential.

Shortly afterwards, Li Bin, vice executive of Suning, threw down the gauntlets by promising, also in a Weibo post, that all items sold by Suning would be cheaper than those on Jingdong. Meanwhile, Suning announced to allocate 1 billion yuan in August on the occasion of its third anniversary to further compete on price. From then on, the third round of the price battle was on the trigger. The average price cut was around 30% during the sales promotion period. The discounts were so attractive that even Suning's workers were awaiting to cash in on the opportunity. Moreover, Suning initiated its Beijing Strategy to unify the prices of its online and offline products. The tactic was seen by industry insiders as a targeted general offensive on its long-time rival Beijing-based Jingdong. The tactic was further extended from Beijing to Shanghai, Guangzhou, Shenzhen, Chongqing and other major Chinese cities. As a counterattack, Jingdong opened a "price war channel" on its website with the page covered in vibrant red.

Outcome of the Price War

Obviously Suning and Jingdong spent a pretty penny in waging a price war so as to drive off some incompetent competitors and gain a larger market share in e-commerce. Did the war achieve the goal? The outcome of the price war can tell the answer:

1. The big discount attracted the attention of shoppers. Attracting much attention is one of the direct benefits of the price war because it benefits the purchase conversion. Right after the discount announcement, many consumers flooded into the online or offline stores for shopping. Jingdong's large home appliances sales exceeded 200 million yuan

only between 9 a. m. and 1 p. m. on August 15, despite the critics that slammed the announcement as a publicity stunt, without the offer of a real discount. Though there was no data on Suning's harvest from the price war, industry analysts estimated that the big discount did attract numerous consumers to visit Suning's website, which increased sales and benefited Suning's brand online.

2. High expenses on the price war. Statistics shows that major e-commerce companies spent as high as 7 billion yuan on the price war. Generally, a price war would not stop until some businesses are marginalized due to huge losses. After rounds of tit-to-tat price battles among the online companies, some escaped narrowly from death while others went to the dogs. Although the promotions or tactics raised sales volume, the price cuts squeezed the limited profit margin, making many companies hogging the limelight at the expense of profits. According to the statistics, Jingdong's gross margin is only 7%–8% annually, while the U. S. online retailer Amazon's gross margin is above 20%. The price war is thus believed to bring bigger losses to those more adventurous online companies.

3. Tumble of stock price caused by the price war. Usually, the stock price reacts to a price war quickly and directly. The involved retailers like Suning and Gome saw their stock prices tumbled on August 15. Shares of the Hong Kong-listed GOME plummeted more than 8% to 0.66 HK dollar as of 11:30 a. m., while the Shenzhen-listed Suning dipped over 3% to 5.68 yuan during the morning trading session①.

4. Consumers' concerns about the price war. Online shoppers who saw the similar price-cutting races felt skeptical about the offer, despite scooping up a fair number of bargains. In a survey conducted on Sina Weibo, Chinese most popular microblogging site, 90.7% of 42,003 respondents said the price war was simply a promotional stunt②. And some consumers thought that prices on the websites wobbled somewhat, but only a few items owned by these retailers had a distinct discount. Some consumers complained that some retailers increased part of product prices before the price war, which caused no benefits for the consumers.

In the short term, price wars are good for buyers, who can take advantage of lower prices. Often they are not good for the companies involved because the lower prices reduce profit margins and can threaten their survival. Meanwhile, excessively low prices may dampen the enthusiasm of suppliers and create problems in securing sufficient stocks, which may lead to a delay in giving the customers their discounted goods. In the medium to long term, price wars can be good for the dominant firms in the industry. Typically, the

---

① Home Appliance Retailers' Shares Slump over Price War, http://news.xinhuanet.com/english/china/2012-08/15/c_131786696.htm, 2012-08-15.

② Online Price War Worries Some Consumers, http://www.globaltimes.cn/content/727526.shtml, 2012-08-17.

smaller, more marginal, firms can not compete and must close. The remaining firms absorb the market share of those that have closed. The real losers then, are the marginal firms and their investors. In the long term, the consumer may lose too. With fewer firms in the industry, prices tend to increase, sometimes higher than those before the price war starts[①].

It is obvious that the players did not benefit a lot from the price war compared to their expenses. Why do they stick to it or even wage it every year? Seeking the reasons behind the price war can help to answer the question.

Behind the Price War

The price war between Jingdong and Suning is neither the first nor the unique one. Actually, price war between Chinese retailers occur constantly. Another price war impressing people occurred in color TV industry and was triggered by the big price dropping offered by Changhong, a famous TV brand in 1990s. Why do price wars occur in China occasionally? The primary reasons that price wars occur are:

1. Product homogeneity. Concerning the high cost of innovation, many Chinese enterprises are unwilling to investment in it. Instead, as long as there is a new product sold well, they are inclined to imitate or even copy it directly. On the other hand, the immature legal system enables the low cost of imitation. Consequently, most enterprises are willing to become "the follower" rather than "the first mover". As a result, the homogenous products occupy the market. Because there is little to choose between brands, price is the main competitive factor. The home appliances market is a typical example of product homogeneity. Lack of innovation has mired Chinese online retailers in the repeated cost-driven price wars.

2. Penetration pricing. Penetration pricing is a pricing strategy where the price of a product is initially set low to rapidly reach a wide fraction of the market and initiate word of mouth. The strategy works on the expectation that customers will switch to the new brand because of the lower price. If a merchant is trying to enter an established market, it may offer lower prices than existing brands. Penetration pricing is most commonly associated with marketing objectives of enlarging market share and exploiting economies of scale or experience[②]. Actually, Jingdong and Suning attempted to acquire more market share through lowering prices and recover the higher price after the market share was gained.

3. Oligopoly. If the industry structure is oligopolistic, the players will closely monitor

---

① Xinhua, Online Retailers Declare Cut-throat Price War, China. org. cn, 2012-08-15.
② https://en.wikipedia.org/wiki/Penetration_pricing

each other's prices and be prepared to respond to any price cuts. Their reactions to others' prices can be explained by "Game Theory". Let's suppose Jingdong and Suning promise to price 10% lower than their competitor and both firms credibly commit to this. Doing so requires that the firms suffer an even greater cost by not following the policy than following it. Applying game theory involves finding each player's "best response" to the other player. Game theory implies that if both firms credibly commit to this policy, they will end up nearly giving away their merchandise. It is speculated that the firms' intentions are to drive the others from the market and the game inexorably leads each firm to undercut the others' prices. The game can only end when all but one of the firms gives up and exits the market. Otherwise, they all continue to suffer losses. In practice, there is a question: will the two firms really continue to honor lower prices when they are practically giving away their products? Actually, cracks appeared in the price war. According to Etao, a web portal for online retailers, Jingdong only slashed prices on 6% of its major home appliances①.

 寡头垄断。如果一个行业的结构是寡头垄断的,那么企业会密切关注彼此的价格并随时准备针对对手的降价予以反击。这种反应策略被称为"博弈"。假设京东和苏宁均承诺价格比其他竞争者低10%,且两家企业都遵守承诺。当然,这一行为的前提是不遵守降价承诺比遵守承诺的成本更高。应用博弈论可以计算出各家企业对于竞争对手降价行为的最佳反应策略。博弈论表明如果两家企业都严格遵守承诺,那么(相互博弈循环下去)他们最后只能以几乎"白送"的方式售出商品。经过推导可以发现,企业试图通过降价将对手赶出市场,而各方的博弈却最终导致竞相降价。这种博弈会持续下去直到其中一家企业停止降价并退出市场以后终止。在现实中,两家企业真的会持续降价直至最后几乎白送产品吗? 事实上,这场价格战并非如此。根据线上零售门户网站易淘的统计,在这场价格战中,京东主要家电产品的降价幅度仅为6%。

4. Predatory pricing. A merchant with a healthy bank balance may deliberately price new or existing products in an attempt to topple existing merchants in that market. Some analysts agree that one purpose of lowering prices greatly is forcing the small and medium competitors to exit the market.

5. Pressures from competitors. A competitor might target on a product and attempt to gain market share by selling its alternative at a lower price. Suning ranked as China's top electronics and appliances retailers in terms of sales in 2011. But with the emergence of the e-platform offered by Jingdong, the traditional dominating forces were facing increasing pressures and trying to catch up by building their own websites, while the money-burning Jingdong had mulled ways to attract more off-line buyers to its website. Due to investment in e-commerce, Suning's net profits dropped nearly 30% in the first half of 2012.

---

① Brain Viard, Invisible Hand Revealed: Games Firms Play, available at http://knowledge.ckgsb.edu.cn/2012/10/10/invisible-hand-revealed/invisible-hand-revealed-games-firms-play/, 2012-10-10.

Meanwhile, Jingdong, which had successfully gained a consumer base for its low prices, suffered a loss of 1.3 billion yuan in 2011 with its gross profit margin as low as 5.5%. With the two giants all aiming big, the fight seems inevitable①.

How to Fight a Price War②?

Along with the even fiercer competitions among Chinese e-commerce players, there is probably a new round of price war in the future. Since the price war is unavoidable in a period, here are some strategies to fight a price war:

1. Diagnosis

The process emphasizes understanding the opportunities for pricing actions based on current market trends and responding to competitors' actions based on the players and their resources. Good diagnosis involves analyzing four key areas in the theater of operations: customer issues such as price sensitivity and the customer segments that may emerge if prices change; company issues such as a business's cost structures, capabilities, and strategic positioning; competitor issues such as a rival's cost structures, capabilities, and strategic positioning; and contributor issues, or the other players in the industry whose self-interest or profiles may affect the outcome of a price war.

2. Responding with high quality

A firm should focus on quality rather than price because the superior quality keeps your customer for a long time while low price can not. Besides, the quality superiority enables premium price, which helps a firm to profit and beat the rivals without joining a price war. For example, the Ritz-Carlton adopted some non-price actions to attract and keep customers such as greeting arriving flights with music, discount coupons, bath menu and a model room when it suffered the economic depression in Southeast Asia in 1997. When luxury hotels started cutting their prices, their ability to offer "luxury" accoutrements dropped. However, the Ritz kept its rates above 200 ringgit (about $52 U.S.) and was able to pay for low-cost services such as providing the embroidered pillowcases. Most importantly, the Ritz avoided any damage to its brand equity. The non-price strategies proved effective: It had no more empty rooms than its competitors in 1999 fall; its monthly gross operating profit on revenue of 2.2 million ringgit was about 400,000 ringgit—a return of about 18%.

3. Using selective pricing actions

Employing complex options such as multiple-part pricing, quantity discounts, time-of-

---

① Xinhua, Online Retailers Declare Cut-throat Price War, China.org.cn, 2012-08-15.
② Akshay R. RaoMark E. BergenScott Davis, How to Fight a Price War, *Harvard Business Review*, March-April 2000.

use pricing, bundling and so on lets price warriors selectively cut rates for only those segments of the population that are under competitive threat. For example, McDonald changed customers' choices successfully when it faced Taco Bell's 59-cent taco strategy in the 1980s. By bundling burgers, fries and drinks into "value meals", McDonald reframed the price war from "tacos versus burgers" to "lunch versus lunch." Similarly, smart managers use quantity discounts or loyalty programs to insulate themselves from a price war. They avoid across-the-board price cuts, and they limit price reductions to areas in which they are vulnerable. In this way, managers can localize a price war to a limited theater of operation—and cut down the opportunities for the war to spill into other markets.

4. Fighting it out

Although direct, retaliatory price cuts should be a last resort, it is sometimes simply impossible to avoid a price war. For instance, when a competitor threatens the firm's core business, a retaliatory price cut can be used to signify your intention to fight long and hard. Similarly, when the firm can identify a large and growing segment of price-sensitive customers, when it has a cost advantage, when its pockets are deeper than competitors' pockets, when it can achieve economies of scale by expanding the market, or when a rival can be neutralized or eliminated because of high barriers to market entry and reentry, then engaging in price competition may be smart. If simple retaliatory price cuts are the chosen means of defense in a price war, then implement them quickly and unambiguously so competitors know that their sales gains from a price cut will be short-lived and monetarily unattractive. A slow response may prompt competitors to make additional price cuts in the future.

5. Retreat

On rare occasions, discretion is the better part of valor. Consequently, some businesses choose not to fight price wars; instead, they'll cede some market share rather than prolong a costly battle. For example, 3M and DuPont are both companies that focus on developing innovations as part of their core strategy—and both have proved willing to cede share rather than participate in an unprofitable price war. In fact, 3M took pride in the fact that roughly 40% of its revenue comes from new products. And in cases where it retreated from pricing battles rather than standing its ground, the company seems to have come out ahead.

Case Analysis

价格战作为一种竞争策略,对于中国的消费者而言并不陌生。几乎每年在中国的市场尤其是零售市场都会上演一次次价格战。商家为什么对此策略情有独钟？价格战背后真正的原因是什么？对本案例的分析可以帮助我们寻找答案。

家电零售行业的价格战屡见不鲜,早期比较轰动的价格战可以追溯至上世纪90年代由著名彩电企业长虹掀起的那场价格大战。2012年爆发的这场价格战仍然与家电零售有关,只不过竞争的双方变成了京东与苏宁,战场也从线下蔓延至线上。中国的零售企业为何对价格战乐此不疲?背后的原因值得我们深入剖析:

首先,产品同质化严重。由于研发创新的成本很高,很多企业尤其是中小企业不愿意为此投入。相反,一旦市场上出现热销的新产品,其他企业会采取低成本跟随策略,甚至仿冒。由于国内知识产权保护体系尚不健全,企业的创新热情受到打击,最终导致恶性循环:企业更愿意做市场跟随者,而非原创者。为了在同质化竞争中占得先机,降价是企业采取的简单而直接的办法。本案例中苏宁和京东的价格战就是这一问题的集中体现。其次,企业本身的竞争和营销策略所致。对某些企业而言,价格战本身就是一种竞争策略,通过价格战将实力不济的竞争对手挤出市场,从而趁机扩大自己的市场份额。这种策略从苏宁和京东的这场价格战中也可以窥见一二。另外,企业采用低价有时也是渗透式定价策略的需要,即最初采取低价以获得较高的销售量及市场占有率,进而产生显著的成本经济效益。再次,寡头垄断的结果。市场寡头会密切注意对手的定价策略,并通过调整价格作出反应。博弈的各方都基于利润最大化的原则选择"最佳反应策略",如一方降价,那么另一方会通过利润函数确定最优定价。博弈的结果就是各方竞相降价直到其中一方停止降价甚至退出市场为止。案例中京东和苏宁在价格战中你来我往的几个回合降价正是这种动态博弈的体现。可见,价格战的原因既可能是企业因为竞争策略和营销策略主动出击,也可能是其对于产品同质化和对手策略的被动反应。

价格战的短期效果比较明显:提高销量,迅速占领市场同时扩大品牌知名度。但从长期来看,其结果往往是两败俱伤:企业为了赢得价格战耗费大量的人力、物力和财力,投资回报并不一定理想;一旦卷入价格战,可能引起股价波动。这场价格战中,苏宁和国美的股价都受到了不同程度的影响。就连一般认为价格战的获益者——消费者也未必能从中真正受惠。在京东和苏宁的这场价格战中,不少消费者抱怨商家的降价力度并不如预期大,甚至有些商家先涨价再降价,有欺骗嫌疑。互联网所带来的更多的产品选择和更透明的信息让消费者变得更加理性和成熟,他们已经从原来一味强调低价向看重产品和服务品质转变。在这样的环境下,企业需要更理性地思考价格战的投资回报和对品牌的长远影响。

Section 4
Baidu's Copyright Dilemma
第四节 百度的版权困境

Ⅰ Key Words

1. dilemma *n.* 困境
2. infringement *n.* 侵犯
3. lobbyist *n.* 游说
4. litigation *n.* 诉讼
5. rampant *adj.* 猖獗的
6. genuine *adj.* 真实的
7. IPR (Intellectual Property Rights) *n.* 知识产权

Ⅱ Case

Background

Baidu, founded in 2000, is a Chinese web services company headquartered in Beijing. As China's top search engine, Baidu offers many online search services for websites, audio files, images and videos.

Baidu offers 57 search and community services including Baidu Baike and a searchable, keyword-based discussion forum. In December 2007, Baidu became the first Chinese company to be included in the NASDAQ-100 index①.

Over more than ten years, Baidu has developed into the most well-known search engine in Chinese. For many people in China, when they attempt to find answers to some questions on the Internet, the first name jumping off their heads is Baidu. According to the statistics, by September 2013, Baidu search had accounted for 72.1% of market share in China, ranking No. 1②. Compared to the competitors overseas, Baidu search has accounted for 7.52% of market share in global search engine market, ranking No. 4③.

In addition to the initial text search, Baidu also diversifies its services by providing multimedia, image files, videos and so on. For example, Baidu offers multimedia content including MP3 music, and movies which popularizes so much in China that Baidu is the first choice of multimedia for many Chinese netizens. The diversification strategy adds value to its services. However, it is the diversified services that push Baidu into a dilemma of copyright.

---

① http://www.chinadaily.com.cn/m/beijing/zhongguancun/2011-12/30/content_14028946.htm
② 易观公布9月搜索市场数据:百度份额稳步回升,新浪科技,2013-11-20。
③ 6月全球搜索引擎市场:百度被Bing取代 排名跌至第四,IDC评述网,2015-07-03。

Baidu's Copyright Lawsuits

Since its foundation, Baidu has experienced three copyright lawsuits which label it an infringer.

1. The first lawsuit

The first copyright lawsuit attracting people's attention is that global music labels accused of facilitating copyright infringement with its song download search service. In 2008, labels Universal Music, Sony BMG Music Entertainment Hong Kong and Warner Music Hong Kong accused Baidu of "deep linking" users to hundreds of thousands of illegal copies of songs hosted on other web sites. The music industry lobbyist IFPI (International Federation of the Phonographic Industry) filed the suit on behalf of the music companies.

Baidu was required to remove all direct links to music on third-party web sites violating artist and label copyrights. However, Baidu refused to remove the links to infringing tracks because they drove up advertising revenue. Baidu alleged that the multimedia search feature was mainly used in searches for Chinese pop music. While such works were copyrighted under Chinese law, Baidu claimed on its legal disclaimer that linking to these files did not break Chinese law[①].

Baidu started with a popular music search feature called "MP3 Search" and its comprehensive lists of popular Chinese music, Baidu 500, based on download numbers. Baidu locates file formats such as MP3, WMA and SWF and allows its users to search for specific music formats without making the distinction between pirated music and user-generated content.

The lawsuit, brought in 2008 at the Beijing No. 1 Intermediate People's Court who ruled Baidu did not infringe as long as all music was downloaded from web servers of third-party sites.

2. The second lawsuit

In 2012, Baidu suffered a copyright lawsuit again. One of the most-read writers in China—Han Han and two other writers sued Baidu over its online library, Wenku, claiming the site offered their works for free without permission. In March 2011, more than 40 writers, including Han, signed a letter saying the online library provided their works for free download without their permission. Four months later, Han and several others established the Writers' Union to appeal to Baidu, aiming to protect their online copyright.

---

① Elaine Chow, Record Labels Hit Replay in Baidu Copyright Lawsuit, http://www.law360.com/articles/46127/record-labels-hit-replay-in-baidu-copyright-lawsuit, 2008-02-05.

Han, who sued after three of his books appeared on Wenku, asked 760,000 yuan for compensation, as well as an apology posted on the company's homepage and the closure of the online library.

As a result, Han Han won the copyright infringement lawsuit against search engine Baidu. The ruling stated that Baidu was at fault because it waited for the authors to contact its staff about their work, instead of taking measures to prevent piracy by users. The trio received a total of just 145,000 yuan ($23,000) in damages, far lower than they were asking[①].

3. The third lawsuit

The copyright lawsuit replayed in 2013. A group of Chinese media companies accused Baidu of piracy, filing litigation that signals the maturation of an online-video industry where illegal copying once was rampant.

The plaintiffs filed suit in Chinese courts against the country's dominant Internet-search company and a smaller site, seeking a total of 300 million yuan, or around $50 million, in damages.

The accusations targeted four services run by Baidu on desktop computers and smartphones that allow users to get access to Western and Chinese television shows and movies that are licensed to other companies. The group said that in some instances, Baidu linked to sites that host pirated content. Baidu argued that it promoted legal content, set an automatic system to filter illegal content and maintained a team that works 24 hours a day to process complaints. Other Chinese companies that complained about Baidu include social-media and online-video company Tencent Holdings Ltd. and Dalian Wanda Group Corp.

The litigation shows how radically China's online video industry has changed over the past decade. Over the past few years, Chinese online video sites—once vast repositories for pirated content—have paid millions of dollars to license Western television shows and movies. The companies then make money on advertisements embedded in the videos, which can attract hundreds of millions of views. Some popular programs, such as the TV show "The Big Bang Theory", can be streamed free legally less than a week after they have aired in the U.S. The model has been a success, but it also has put Chinese online-video companies such as Sohu.com, a plaintiff in the case, on the front lines of copyright enforcement. Many such sites have been forced to send legal notices to sites pirating licensed content[②]. The Baidu site features pirated content is thought "threatening the model of licensing content". It probably leads to the huge loss of American companies, the

---

① Cao Yin, Writers Win Copyright Lawsuit against Baidu, China Daily, 2012-09-18.
② Paul Mozur, China's Baidu Faces Suits over Video Piracy Online-Video and Film Companies Seek $50 Million from Internet-Search Firm, WSJ, 2013-11-13.

original author of the content, in the China market.

4. Copyright violator—Baidu's label?

After experiencing a series of lawsuits and complaints, Baidu was labeled one of China's top two violators of copyrighted video content in 2013 by the National Copyright Administration of China (NCAC). It was subsequently fined 250,000 yuan ($41,225), the highest penalty a copyright violator can be required to pay under statutes.

The NCAC began its investigation into Baidu's and QVOD's alleged infringements in November 2013, after leading legitimate online video providers—including Youku Tudou, Sohu Video, Tencent Video and LeTV, along with the MPA—formed an alliance and jointly filed suit for infringement, seeking damages of up to 300 million yuan from Baidu and QVOD, a Shenzhen-based technology firm. In a related ruling in early December 2013, Baidu was found guilty of copyright infringement and ordered to pay 491,000 yuan in damages to Youku Tudou[①].

Behind The Lawsuits

Why has Baidu, as the largest search engine in China, been suffering the embarrassments? What are the reasons behind Baidu's dilemma? Actually, Baidu is not the unique e-commerce firm in China who suffers the copyright lawsuits. Analyzing the factors leading to the IP piracy like Baidu's case is beneficial for Chinese e-commerce firms to protect IP better.

1. Financial benefit is an important driving force. In China, people are familiar with sort of cheap knock-offs—shanzhai which is the imitation and piracy of name brands. Pirated Hollywood and Chinese films are sold cheap on street corners across the country, not to mention inside smaller, private shopping centers; Illegal video games are pervasive in Internet bars; Illegal DVDs are simply sold right out in the open. Though Chinese government adopts some measures to regulate the market (e.g. fines), the situation has not been alleviated greatly. One radical reason is the financial benefits for the parties of exchange. For the buyers or users who download the multimedia content or purchase the Shanzhai products, the low-price even free products are highly attractive. Since the buyers can gain the products similar with the genuine at much lower cost or even free and enjoy the admiration or compliment from other people why do they choose the genuine they probably can not afford? That's why few really care whether software is a knock-off, or if the playstation is being hacked to allow for a pirated version. For the sellers, as long as there are demands which may bring the profits, they are willing to take the risk even

---

① Patrick Brzeski, Chinese Search Giant Baidu Fined for Copyright Infringement, http://www.hollywoodreporter.com/news/chinese-search-giant-baidu-fined-668155, 2014-01-01.

though they know it is unethical or illegal. For example, many Chinese think illegal software is the smart choice because it's cheaper. Computer sales people have incentive to reinforce this perception because they can increase sales margins by replacing genuine with copies instead.

2. Local protectionism stimulates copyright piracy. China's central government supports IPR (Intellectual property rights) protection. The main problem lies in local protectionism. Even the orders from the central government can not be enforced properly because part of local officials consider it less important. Why don't these officials attach sufficient importance to IP protection? It is partially attributed to the situation that IPR has not been attached importance to yet. For example, the protects for innovation are not enough. Some officials still emphasize economic growth more than intellectual property. Until IP infringement is regarded as an immediate threat to local economic success, or advanced as a vital regional interest, local government would not crack down on IP infringement. Therefore, IP protection will always be an uphill struggle in China and for companies doing business there since intellectual rights remain a theoretical notion at best.

译 地方保护主义助长了侵权行为。中央政府支持知识产权保护,主要问题在于地方保护主义。由于某些地方官员对此并不重视,法律法规在有些地方无法执行。例如,在某些官员仍然强调经济增长重于知识产权保护的情况下,创新无法得到有效保护。只有当知识产权纠纷威胁到当地经济发展的时候,地方政府才会采取措施。因此,对企业而言,保护知识产权仍然是一场艰难的斗争。

3. The immature legal system provides chances for the violators. IPRs have been acknowledged and protected in China since 1979. Protection of intellectual property law has also been established by government legislation, administrative regulations, and decrees in the areas of trademark, copyright and patent. This has led to the creation of a comprehensive legal framework to protect both local and foreign intellectual property. However, the existing legal system is not perfect enough and the loopholes in laws and regulations enable IP infringement. As a result, copyright violations are common in China and intellectual property violations are committed by prominent members of the industries.

1) The existing copyright laws in China is not as strict as those in the United States. For example, American courts hand down criminal penalties even when piracy isn't commercially motivated. China, by contrast, doesn't criminalize copyright infringement that isn't for profit. So if you copy a DVD and distribute it to all your friends, you can't go to jail. It means you can disseminate multimedia content through the Internet without the author's permission as long as you do not make money from it[①].

---

① Christopher Beam, How Strict Are Chinese Copyright Laws?, http://www.slate.com/articles/news_and_politics/explainer/2009/10/bootleg_nation.html, 2009-10-22.

2) Enforcement is weak at least in part because of the country's size. It's difficult to implement anti-piracy laws across such a vast territory, especially in rural areas with limited police resources. Trade restrictions and censorship, meanwhile, spur the growth of China's black market. China limits the amount of copyrighted materials that can cross its borders, driving movie fans to the streets to look for pirated DVDs.

3) Sanction is not tough enough, which makes the cost of violation is low. For example, one usually adopted action against infringers is administrative adjudication which supplies the penalties like administrative fines (in instances where fines are 20,000 yuan or more for an individual defendant or 100,000 yuan or more for an enterprise, the defendant has the right to request a formal hearing), warnings and injunctions prohibiting the production and distribution of infringing products[1]. That is why many experts and lawyers think the compensation in Baidu's second lawsuit should have been higher. As a result, some people would like to take a risk for the possible profits. Even though other actions against infringers like civil litigation and criminal prosecution are chosen, the effectiveness may be decreased due to the difficult enforcement mentioned above.

How to Solve the Dilemma?[2][3]

Since the reasons behind Baidu's case has been explored, it is time to look for the effective solutions to avoid the dilemma. Actually, it is a task which needs the participation of enterprises, government and users.

1. Enterprises should always attach high importance to Intellectual Property. Most content is protected by copyright, and unless it is being used in a manner protected by "fair use", it needs to be licensed before it can be distributed by anyone but the copyright holder.

2. Enterprises should ensure the "fair use" of the works. Article 22 of China's Copyright Law lists the fair use of a copyrighted work, which includes personal use, "appropriate" quotation in order to introduce, republishing or rebroadcasting of another media entity's story and so on. For example, offering pirated MP3 files on the Internet clearly is not a "fair use" and that is why Baidu was accused. If a company is planning on using third-party content in a manner that raises fair use questions, it's a good idea to consult a copyright attorney.

---

[1] Sergio Marchi, E-commerce and the Role of Governments (Speaking Notes), World Services Congress, 2001.

[2] John Villasenor, How to Reduce Copyright Lawsuits and Make the Internet a Better Place to Share Content, https://www.forbes.com/sites/johnvillasenor/2013/07/13/how-to-reduce-copyright-lawsuits-and-make-the-internet-a-better-place-to-share-content/#4057d494417d, 2013-07-13.

[3] Harry Yang, Enforcement the Main Problem of Intellectual Property Protection in China, China IP Publication, http://www.chinaipmagazine.com/en/journal-personality-show.asp?id=355

3. Enterprises should provide some basic intellectual property awareness training for employees. It is necessary to provide the training including not only copyright but also patents, trademarks, and trade secrets since few employees accept the training at the universities. Besides, compared to the cost of defend against a copyright infringement lawsuit, it costs very little to provide employees with an hour or two of training to help them keep copyright issues in mind when harvesting content from the web.

4. Government should improve the existing administrative abilities. Compared to the countries with mature IP legislation like U.S.A., Chinese administrative abilities are far away from enough. The related capacities, knowledge and approaches are needed to be trained. Cooperating with the first movers and learn from them is an effective way.

5. Chinese officials and Chinese enforcement agencies should supply a good support system. "Enforcement of laws must be strict" has been one of the basic principles of Chinese legal policy. However, it is difficult to enforce the laws in practice due to the geographic, economic and cultural environment. Therefore, more resources should be spent in support system like IP complaint centers.

6. Education of IP is necessary. Nowadays everyone in China has more opportunities to get access to the international markets. As a result, it is even easier to republish, rebroadcast the works with out the permission of the originators. People do this not only because of the financial benefits of it but also because of lack of legal awareness. Therefore, Chinese government needs to communicate to the Chinese people that IP enforcement is not something brought in from outside to control Chinese society and to keep Chinese society from progressing.

Case Analysis

本案例聚焦知名的中文搜索引擎——百度曾面临的版权困境。文中百度曾三次面临版权纠纷,分别涉及音乐、文学以及视频的发布。我们需要关注的重点并非法律纠纷本身而是导致这几起纠纷的原因以及减少互联网版权纠纷的解决方法。

百度面临的版权纠纷不止一次,而它也不是中国唯一一家遭遇知识产权尴尬的互联网企业。为什么互联网企业容易触及知识产权雷区?为什么这些现象屡禁不止?归根结底有两个原因:经济利益的诱惑以及违法成本太低。互联网的快速发展使人们获取和传播信息更加便利,成本也更低。一部分人开始利用这一优势进行信息的非法复制和传播以谋取商业利益。例如,我们经常能在街头看到的廉价的 DVD 光碟、书籍,互联网上可以随时免费观看的视频等。即使政府严厉打击,这些违法的"山寨品"仍然屡禁不止,除了因为我国幅员辽阔,再加上互联网没有空间限制的特征,造成打击力度有限以外,经济利益是导致这些非法交易的根本原因:对买家而言,可以以极低的成本甚至免费获得信息的使用权是极具诱惑力的。例如,只花几块钱就可以买一部好莱坞大片的盗版光碟或者免费搜索到该影片的网络资源一睹为快,买家还有什么动力花几十块钱进影院观看正版原片呢?而对于卖家而言,有需求就有利润,加上复制这些音像制品的成本极低,他们宁愿铤而走险。另一个原因是由于不成熟的法律体系以及地方保护主义的存在导致在中国侵犯知识产权的违法成本仍然很低。与美国不同,中国对侵犯知识产权的惩处力度较轻,通常是采取罚款、赔偿金的做法(例如:百度的侵权案就是以赔偿金告终,法庭对其的惩处力度也被认为不够严厉),当事人往往不会有牢狱之灾,导致不法业者有恃无恐。

要减少互联网侵权事件的发生,让企业避免百度的版权尴尬,需要企业、政府以及消费者的共同参与。企业应该对知识产权高度重视,明确他人作品"恰当使用"的界限,并对员工进行专利权、商标权等有关知识产权的法律培训,使其明确利用互联网传播他人作品的规则,降低违法风险。政府则应该完善现有的法律体系,加强执法力度,提升执法能力,并对消费者进行知识产权保护的普及教育,以建设更加公平、有序的互联网环境。

Section 5
Case Reports
第五节　如何写案例分析报告

▶ Types of Report

The case reports mentioned here refer to the formal type of written case report that is polished and stands alone, although it may represent an individual or a group effort. The distinguishing features of this type of report, as opposed to case class discussion or an exam, are the rigorous analysis and attention to presentation. The challenge of case reports is to convey effectively your complete analysis and specific recommendations in written form[1].

▶ Suggestions for Effective Case Reports[2]

To finish an effective case report, you should:

1. Understand your goals. Before you begin your case report, you should be clear about your goals by considering what the purpose of the case report is and whether there are any special requirements.

---

[1][2] Louise A. Mauffette, James A. Erskine, Michiel R. Leenders, *Learning with Cases (Fourth Edition)*, Ivey Publishing, 2008.

2. Review the evaluation criteria. Generally, your teacher provides a complete evaluation criteria which can be used as a reference in your report writing. Case reports are usually evaluated according to the following criteria: clear identification of the issues, soundness and accuracy of analysis, legitimacy, range and evaluation of alternatives, appropriateness and specificity of recommendations, including action and implementation plans, consistency of logic and the quality of the written presentation.

3. Plan your report carefully. A good planning is crucial for your case report. You should determine in advance what to put where and how much to include has major pay-offs. Such planning will not only facilitate the writing of the report but also result in better grades.

▶ Case Report Checklist[①]

A formal case report is generally organized into sections with headings. These are usually numbered as in the example below:

1. Letter of transmittal (not always required)—Title page. Include student names and student IDs;

2. Executive summary. If appropriate—should be written last to focus on key points/findings;

3. Table of contents;

4. Introduction or case background—Body of the analysis. Current situation analysis and pertinent background including a synopsis of the relevant information from the case analysis tool short form;

5. Alternative solutions Conclusion/recommendations—Implementation plan (if requested).

1) Decision criteria;

2) Assumptions;

3) Data analysis (analysis in appendix and summary info in body);

4) Preferred alternative with rationale;

5) Justification/predicted outcome;

6) It is important that all speculation or creative ideas should be founded upon some marketing rationale and a solid understanding of the metrics related to the target market and anticipated financial changes/impact;

7) Be sure to discuss with your teammates or professor if you have any problem with the report.

6. References list. You should find the resource from business journals, periodicals,

---

① CRICOS, Centre for Teaching and Learning Quick Guide, scu. edu. au/teachinglearning/download. php? doc_id = 12775, 2014-12-01.

and textual references as well as any online research. Make sure you support your ideas with facts and figures. And it would be better if you use your own words and ideas based on research rather than copy and paste other's words from the internet;

7. Appendix. All charts, financials, visuals, and other related items can be placed here and referenced in the report.

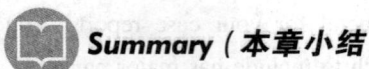

Summary (本章小结)

Online exchanges involve different entities such as consumers, merchants, intermediaries and government. Among the parties, government is a special entity because it not only joins in the product or service transactions (e.g. G2B) as one of the exchange parties but also regulates the exchanges as a supervisor. Putting G2B and G2C aside, what roles should government play in e-commerce development? In summary, government should play the roles of supporter, supervisor and conciliator so as to build and keep a fair, open and sustainable environment for online exchanges. In practice, it involves protecting customer's privacy online, online advertising compliance, collecting taxes online and handling customer financial data.

In November 2010, a dispute occurred between two Chinese IT companies, Tencent and Qihoo. Hundreds of millions of Chinese netizens were involved and forced to choose a side, either to uninstall QQ or Qihoo's privacy guard. The dispute should be attributed to external factors (e.g. lack of legislation suitable for the new market, the less effective market supervision, the punishment is not strict enough, the existence of oligopoly, the "bulls management" impairs the effects of supervision) and internal factors (e.g. lack of legal awareness and lack of product differentiation). The dispute implies that government's intervention is necessary during the evolution of an emerging industry since the market system and ethics are unable to regulate everything. According to Sergio Marchi, the role of government is three-fold: endorsing e-commerce as a tool for increased competitiveness, creating the right domestic and international environment for the use and development of e-commerce and cooperating with other governments, and redefining the public-private partnership by bringing together governments, the business community and civil society.

The price war between Suning and Jingdong occurred in 2012. The main online stores including Suning, Jingdong, Tmall and Dangdang cut the prices one after another during the sales promotion period. The price war initiated by Suning is thought as a strategy driving off some incompetent competitors so as to gain a larger market share in e-commerce. The price cut strategy works effectively in attracting numerous website visitors and improving the brand awareness. However, the price cut squeezes the already limited profit margin, making many companies hog the limelight at the expense of profits. Therefore, for the time being, a price war plays an important role in the e-commerce market, but in the long run, quality of products or services will be the major factor to win customers.

Baidu, the largest Chinese search engine, has experienced a series of copyright lawsuits which involve music download, writing works download and online-video shows since 2008. After experiencing a series of lawsuits and complaints, Baidu was labeled one of China's top two violators of copyrighted video content in 2013 by the National Copyright Administration of China (NCAC). Baidu is neither the unique nor the first Internet firm suffering the dilemma of copyright. The case of Baidu implies the problems with Chinese Intellectual Protection (IP) protection. Financial benefits, local protectionism and the immature legal system are the three factors indulging the rampant copyright infringement. To solve the problems, enterprises should attach high importance to Intellectual Property, ensure the "fair use" of the works and provide some basic intellectual property awareness training for employees. Additionally, Chinese officials and Chinese enforcement agencies should attach high importance to IP problems, strengthen the communications with people, improve the existing administrative abilities and supply a good support system. It will take a long time for Chinese government to establish a healthy and sustainable environment for e-commerce.

Case reports refer to the formal type of written case report that is polished and stands alone. The challenge of case reports is to convey effectively your complete analysis and specific recommendations in written form. To finish your case reports effectively, you should understand your goals, review the evaluation criteria and plan your report carefully. Besides, a case report checklist can aid you to complete your case report efficiently.

Exercises & Tasks (练习与任务)

Exercises

1. How do you describe the roles that government should play in e-commerce?
2. What causes the battles between Tencent and Qihoo?
3. What are the reasons behind the price wars between Suning and Jingdong?
4. Do you have any suggestion for Chinese Intellectual Property protection?

Tasks

Choose a case of roles government should play in e-commerce and prepare a 20-minute presentation which should include:

1. Background introduction to the case;
2. Analyze the causes of the issue;
3. Conclusion (e.g. rationale suggestions or solutions).

Chapter 10 Where Is E-Commerce Going? 电子商务去向何方?

 Learning Objectives(学习目标)

After finishing this chapter, you should be able to:
1. Describe the possible characteristics of e-commerce in the future;
2. Explain the success factors of Alipay and its impacts on Chinese finance industry;
3. Define long tail and understand how Lvmama benefit from long tail;
4. Illuminate uber effect;
5. Grasp comparison analysis.

 Introduction(内容简介)

The rapid growth of e-commerce in the past decades brings a new question: what is the future of e-commerce? The new terms like mobile Internet and long tail are embedded into e-commerce and generating new values. This chapter explains the phenomenon by virtue of three cases.

Chapter 10 is composed of 5 sections. The brief introduction to the future of e-commerce is made in section 1. Three related cases are provided respectively in section 2, 3, and 4. Section 5 focuses on an important case analysis method—comparative analysis.

Section 1
Future of E-Commerce
第一节 电子商务的未来

Key Words

1. forge *vt.* 锻造
2. tactile *adj.* 有触觉的
3. dedicated *adj.* 专注的
4. prerequisite *n.* 先决条件
5. outnumber *vt.* 超过

What does e-commerce in the future look like? What kind of new things will be involved in e-commerce? How will e-commerce penetrate into our lives further?... Answering the questions respectively from the commercial and technical perspective enables us to comb the development trends of e-commerce in the future.

1. Closer integration of the sources online and offline. E-commerce has greatly changed the traditional business models and the way people shop since its emergence. People has benefited from its high efficiency, convenience and personalization so much that some asserted that there is no need for the traditional physical stores. However, those e-commerce giants have refuted the points with their activities of "click + mortar". For example, Amazon opened its first brick and mortar extension—a bookstore in Seattle in 2015. By early 2016, about 20 online companies in the U.S. had launched a physical presence to better market their wares, forge closer customer relations, and boost online traffic and sales. The trend also reflects the broader industry imperative around "omni-channel" retailing, where online merchants begin to open brick and mortar storefronts due to the rising operating cost and the fiercer competition. By opening physical stores, they aim to increase awareness and draw customers in a realm where the retail options aren't infinite or influenced by an all-powerful gatekeeper. And for purveyors of tactile and personal products like clothing, eyewear and jewelry, selling stuff in person has an obvious appeal. Rather than focus on pure online play, merchants aim to provide customers with a seamless experience whether shopping online via desktop or mobile device or at a traditional retail store①.

2. Focusing on long tail. In statistics, a long tail of some distributions of numbers is the portion of the distribution having a large number of occurrences far from the "head" or

---

① Mark Walsh, The Future of E-commerce: Bricks and Mortar, https://www.theguardian.com/business/2016/jan/30/future-of-E-commerce-bricks-and-mortar, 2016-01-30.

central part of the distribution (Figure 10-1). In business, long tail is a phrase coined by Chris Anderson, in 2004. Anderson argues that products in low demand or have low sales volume can collectively make up a market share that rivals or exceeds the relatively few current bestsellers and blockbusters, but only if the store or distribution channel is large enough①. Traditional retail economics dictates that stores only stock the likely hits, because shelf space is expensive. But online retailers can stock virtually everything, and the number of available niche products outnumbers the hits by several orders of magnitude. Those millions of niches are the Long Tail. This represents an enormous opportunity for merchants to specialize in a niche, communicate the essence of their store through core items customers expect to find, then expand expectations with captivating discoveries and irresistible enticements. Long tail creates a new survival space for the merchants, especially for the small and medium sized merchants in the difficult e-commerce environment. Since they can not compete with the branded and first-moving giants like Amazon, the merchants can focus on the minor products or customers and exploit the niche market which has been neglected by most competitors. They probably find a new market—Lvmama in this chapter is a successful example. Moreover, the long tail will drive a new economy. The situation that large suppliers dominate the market will change in the future.

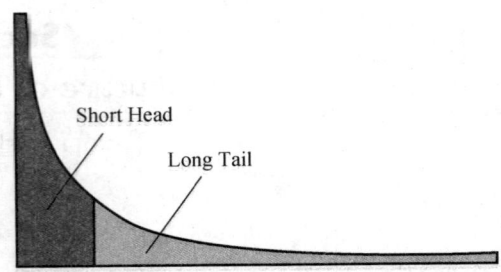

Figure 10-1 Probability Distribution

3. Platform or ecological cycle. A platform refers to a physical or virtual space which facilitates the exchange parties to make deals. A platform has at least two sides—seller side and buyer side. It usually does not sell products directly to the customers, instead, it gains revenues by charging trade commissions (on the transactions). The success of the well-known platforms like eBay not only attracts much attention but also enables platform a promising business model. On the one hand, the traditional e-commerce retailers like Amazon have transited to platform to create values by virtue of the network effects; on the other hand, the existing platforms like Alibaba have expanded its boundary and evolved into a multi-sided platform or a comprehensive ecological cycle which covers more businesses and explores more profiting sources. The future competition in e-commerce will be dominated by the races among the platforms.

4. Growth of mobile commerce. With the rapid growth of mobile internet and the popularity of mobile devices like smartphones and pads, e-commerce based on mobile

---

① https://www.investopedia.com/terms/l/long-tail.asp

internet, or mobile commerce is rising. The new business model enables the e-commerce transactions more efficient and convenient for both sellers and buyers. The trading process from information access, purchase decision making to online payment can be finished on mobile devices. Initially, mobile commerce was rather limited to the businesses that had well-established websites and power-packed smartphones with good web connectivity features. Gradually, mobile commerce has penetrated into both online websites and offline physical stores. For example, the shoppers are allowed to buy the books in Amazon physical store by scanning their smartphones. Another example is from China: consumers don't have to have cash or bank cards with them when shopping offline, instead, they can have a smartphone and pay by scanning the barcode of Alipay or Wechat. The fast penetration of mobile commerce requires new business processes, security strategies and customer services.

5. Rising applications of new technologies in e-commerce. The applications of the new technologies like big data, cloud computing and artificial intelligence in e-commerce industry are increasing. The changing demands of customers and the even fiercer competition are driving the e-commerce merchants to apply the new technologies to their businesses so as to generate more values. For example, Jingdong, Chinese well-known 3C products retailers made its first attempt of delivery by drone in 2016. Though new problems may occur with these applications, people still have an optimistic prospection for these new technologies.

6. Increased customer care. A successful e-commerce merchant in the future will focus on creating experiences, which includes:

1) Personalization and appealing to the consumer. Though e-commerce platforms can present consumers with a wide variety of offerings (e. g. online coupons, exclusive items, express shipping), there still lacks the focus on building personalized relationships with shoppers and providing the interactive experience that comes with in-store shopping. Actually, consumers desire the seamless shopping experience: the same personal experience shopping online as they do shopping in-store and the same convenience and speed of shopping in-store as they do shopping online. Companies such as BaubleBar and TrunkClub have succeeded in making the shopping experience more personal, more social and more interesting by focusing on building customer relationships. At BaubleBar, customers have access to stylists via video chat while TrunkClub's business model centers on employees' building and maintains ongoing client relationships, catering to every individual differently.

2) Product-discovery sites and recommendation engines. Due to the overloaded information, it is even harder for consumers to make the purchase decisions. To solve the problem, successful retailers have begun to incorporate a "guided discovery" process that targets specific items for a consumer based on user suggestions that help narrow down the purchase decision. Many retailers are seeing greater success by creating this custom

guidance for each customer, helping shoppers spend less time browsing and more time locating exactly what they need. Birchbox, for example, has built its platform entirely on discovery, delivering beauty and grooming products directly to the consumer tailored around personalized preferences.

3) Emotion-driven shopping experiences. How to attact and keep your customers in the fierce market competition? High-quality products or services are necessary but not enough. Actually, some retailers have gone beyond selling a product and told a story to establish a firm brand identity and to build a one-to-one relationship with their customers. It is becoming a trend. The ability for users to share their dream shopping lists with friends is just one way of creating a more personalized, online community. These wish lists are an extremely simple way for users to see what friends and family are shopping for, allowing them to save the products they find and share them with others to get exactly what they want, or know exactly what others are looking for①.

Section 2
AliPay vs. WeChat Pay—Mobile Payment Influencing Financial Services
第二节 支付宝与微信支付——影响金融服务的移动支付

Key Words

1. escrow *n.* 第三方担保
2. barcode *n.* 条形码
3. QR code 二维码
4. indispensible *adj.* 不可缺少的
5. acquaintance *n.* 熟人

Case

Background Introduction

1. Alipay②

Alipay is a third-party online payment platform launched in China in 2004 by Alibaba Group. As the largest digital payment platform in China, it is being operated by Alibaba

---

① Jack Lowinger, The Future of E-commerce Will Focus on Creating Experiences, www.entrepreneur.com/article/241065, 2014-12-19.
② We focus on the mobile services of Alipay in this case.

affiliate Ant Financial now. As a payment gateway, Alipay allows consumers to pay with bank cards by bonding the bank cards with their Alipay accounts or pay by Alipay balance by transferring money from checking accounts to their Alipay accounts. In January 2013, Alipay launched Alipay Wallet mobile app which allows consumers to purchase goods and services in shops using their smart phones. It is also the first step for Alipay to move toward mobile ends. Nowdays, Alipay operates with more than 180 financial institutions including Visa and Mastercard to provide payment services for Taobao, Tmall as well as other Chinese businesses. Internationally, more than 300 worldwide merchants accepts Alipay as a payment tool in the transactions with the consumers in China. It currently supports transactions in 25 currencies[①].

2. WeChat Pay

WeChat Pay is a digital wallet service incorporated into WeChat launched by Tencent in August 2013. It allows users to perform mobile payments and send money between contacts. Users can acquire a balance by linking their WeChat account to their debit card, or by receiving money from other users. Users who link their credit card can make payments to vendors. Besides, Chinese users can be connected with overseas vendors by WeChat Pay. When Chinese costumers buy goods in foreign country, they can follow vendors' Official Account to pay their transactions. WeChat Pay can be used for digital payments, as well as payments from participating vendors. It provides airlines, logistics, insurance, games, B2C business and other industries with online payment solutions. Currently, WeChat Pay supports transactions in 10 currencies. For unsupported currencies, transactions can be made in U.S. dollar.

Comparative Analysis

1. Business model. Essentially, both Alipay and WeChat Pay adopt the platform model. Just like other platforms (e.g. Alibaba), they attract the two-side groups to make exchanges on them so as to maximize the payoffs. They are the payment platforms which connect payers(buyers) and payees(sellers) and facilitate the exchanges between the two groups. A remarkable advantage of the business model lies in that a platform can facilitate network effects as long as the amount of group members reaches the critical mass. In another word, when more payers choose to finish the payment with Alipay or WeChat Pay, more payees would like to accept the payment tool and vice versa.

2. Payment methods

1) Alipay

As the leading payment system in China, Alipay provides four payment methods to

---

① https://intl.alipay.com/open/solution.htm

satisfy customers' need:

• Barcode Payment. The merchant scans the customer's Alipay barcode or QR code to collect money and the transaction amount will be paid to the merchant's bank card within the agreed period.

• Merchant QR Code Payment. The customer scans the merchant's Alipay QR code, enters the payment amount and makes the payment.

• Transaction QR Code Payment. The customer scans the merchant's Alipay QR code, confirms the payment amount and makes the payment.

• In-App Payment. When users make payment in an app (e.g. Taobao), Alipay will be authorized to process the payment. Once the transaction is done, the page will redirect to the other app.

Particularly, Alipay designs the online escrow system which not only solves the problems of trust between sellers and buyers but also enables it the undisputed leader in China's online payment. A remarkable characteristic of e-commerce transaction is the virtuality. On the one hand, virtuality increases the risk of online transactions for both sellers and buyers since they can not communicate with each other face to face; on the other hand, the creditability system had not been established in China before the launch of Alipay and the two parties of transactions did not trust each other: The sellers were afraid of failing to get the money after sending the products while the buyers were worried that they were unable to get the qualified products after completing payment and their bankcards could be utilized online illegally by others. Lack of trust between sellers and buyers calls for a system ensuring both the technology security and the creditability security in the online transactions. Alipay fills in the gaps in time because it builds a bridge between sellers and buyers through the escrow system: When paying online, buyers are allowed to store money into their Alipay account for most seven days. Alipay then reminds sellers of the products delivery. Once buyers receive the products and feel satisfied with the products and services, they make the confirmation in their Alipay account. The money is then transferred to sellers' bank account. If there are disputes between sellers and buyers, Alipay provides the necessary negotiation and arbitrations (Figure 10-2). The mechanism works so well that it is still used on the mobile Internet.

2) WeChat Pay

Like Alipay, WeChat Pay also offers multiple payment methods to enable the convenient and fast payment. Basically, four payment methods support users to finish payment at anytime anywhere:

• Quick Pay. Vendors scan the QR Code shown by customers on the Quick Pay page to finish transactions quickly.

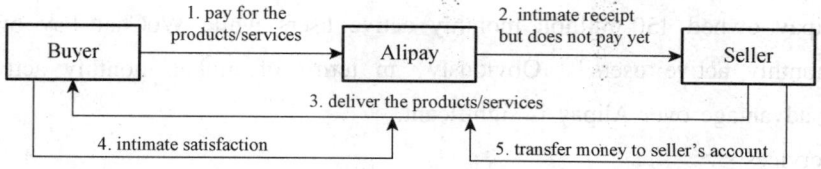

Figure 10-2 The Escrow Mechanism of Aliapy①

• QR Code Payment. Vendors creates different QR codes for different goods. After users scan these codes, they can see related product information and transaction guides on their phone.

• In-App Web-based Payment. Vendors push product messages to their followers via Official Account. With WeChat Pay enabled, their followers can purchase products on the shopping page.

• In-App Payment. Vendors can integrate WeChat Pay SDK into their apps. When users make payment in an app, WeChat will be authorized to process the payment. Once the transaction is done, the page will redirect to the app.

3. Positioning

Alipay has sold itself as a professional payment solution since it was launched. Nobody in China would dispute this claim after it developed into a leading payment system. Alipay's integration with a variety of financial services has been renowned—from insurance to credit rating.

In contrast, WeChat Pay positions its wallet as one of "loose change". This contrast with Alipay's positioning as a money manager. With this positioning, WeChat Pay has captured a large share of the payment market in China②.

4. Target customers and market share

Depending on their respective platforms—Taobao, Alibaba and WeChat, Alipay and WeChat Pay initially targeted on the platform users: the former focused on the users of Taobao and Alibaba while the latter focused on the users of WeChat. Along with the growth of the platforms, the two payment systems have moved across the boundary of platforms and aimed at all the users online and offline.

Alipay and WeChat Pay are dominating online payment market in China: As of the second quarter 2017, Alipay held 54.5% of market share and WeChat Pay got a 39.8% share③. Besides, the two mobile payment giants both have numerous active users: In

---

① KZ., Alipay: Wining the Payments Game in China, https://rctom.hbs.org/submission/alipay-wining-the-payments-game-in-china/, 2016-11-18.

② WeChat Pay for Pennies, Alipay for Big Bucks, https://www.aseantoday.com/2017/09/wechat-pay-for-pennies-alipay-for-big-bucks/, 2017-09-08.

③ 殷怡, 艾瑞:移动支付市场二季度微信支付份额下降, 一财网, 2017-10-15。

2016, Alipay owned 450 million monthly active users while WeChat Pay owned 806 million monthly active users[①]. Obviously, in terms of global monthly active users, WeChat's advantage over Alipay is significant.

5. Services

Alipay and WeChat Pay devote to offering diversified services to attract and keep users. Their services are similar though there are some differences (Table 10-1).

Table 10-1   Service Comparison between Alipay and WeChat Pay[②]

	Alipay	WeChat Pay
Devices supported	All smart phones, tablets and computers	All smart phones
Financial management options	Transactions include: • money transfer • bill sharing • bill payments • e-commerce payments • mobile balance top-up • bank account balance checks • hotel booking • ticket purchasing • investment in wealth management funds • Taxi ordering • consumer credit services	Transactions include: • money transfer • bill sharing • bill payments • e-commerce payments • mobile balance top-up • bank account balance checks • hotel booking • ticket purchasing • investment in wealth management funds • Taxi ordering • consumer credit services
Currencies supported	25 currencies	10 currencies
Transaction charges	• Withdrawing or transferring cash to a bank account: 0.1% per transaction once 20,000 yuan limit passed • Transferring to an Alipay account: free for Alipay app; 0.1% per transaction for PC end, charging from 0.5 Yuan to 10 Yuan.	Withdrawing cash to a bank account: 0.1% per transaction over 1000 yuan

6. Application scenarios

Though Alipay and WeChat pay have the similar services, they emphasize different application scenarios:

1) Pay for big bucks vs. pay for pennies. Alipay has been encouraging saving and investment. In addition to the account balance, users are encouraged to invest with

---

① Alipay vs. WeChat Pay—Who Is Winning the Battle?, https://www.aseantoday.com/2017/02/alipay-vs-wechat-pay-who-is-winning-the-battle/, 2017-02-28.

② http://www.chinadaily.com.cn/m/beijing/zhongguancun/2011-12/30/content_14028946.htm

Yu'ebao since it offers higher interest rates compared to banks. There was no payment limit until July 2016 when PBOC issued a new regulation to limit paying with the balances of third-party payment systems to 200,000 yuan per year. Compared to it, WeChat Pay has been focusing on the petty consumption. Particularly, WeChat launched its "red packet" scheme in 2014 enabling WeChat users to send petty money to family and friends as gifts. As a result, Chinese consumers tend to see WeChat Pay as an application for transactions rather than for money saving. Though WeChat does offer a "wealth" function for users to store their savings, it is less impressive when it comes to non-payment financial services.

2) Payments between strangers vs. payments between acquaintance. Alipay originated from a payment system which supports the payments triggered by online shopping, bill payment and so on. Most of the payments occur between strangers like sellers and buyers in e-commerce. Compared to it, WeChat Pay is an embedded function of the socialization platform. The payments with WeChat like money transferring and issuing red packet usually occur between acquaintances.

7. Supportive platforms behind. The success of both two payment systems should be primarily attributed to their respective platform behind. Alipay has its own platforms behind—Alibaba and Taobao, the former is a B2B platform while the latter is a C2C platform. No matter what business is conducted online, payment is indispensible. Alipay therefore is involved in the transactions on both platforms, which enables it a large customer base. Along with the growth of the two platforms, Alipay expands its businesses to more fields. As result, its user base and customer stickiness are also improved. Compared to Alipay, WeChat Pay lost the advantage of first-mover. Fortunately, it also has a powerful platform behind—Wechat, the leading socialization platform in China. With the popularization of WeChat, WeChat Pay has penetrated into people's lives. Particularly, with the launch of "red packet" in 2014, WeChat Pay has gained significant traction and become Alipay's formidable competitor. Nowadays, both Alipay and Wechat Pay have crossed the boundary of the platforms they depend on and penetrated into the exchanges conducted online and offline.

Conclusion

Alipay and WeChat Pay, as the two online payment giants in China adopt similar business model and provide users similar services though their target customers, market share and application scenarios are different. These two applications are fighting a fierce battle to maintain their positions and get people to use their application rather than that of their respective competitor. Meanwhile, they are influencing the traditional financial services:

1. Changing people's payment method

Due to lack of multiple payment methods, Chinese consumers had to pay the life expenses such as utilities—water, electricity, and Internet bill by cash. They had to go to the branches of banks or service providers, wait in the long line and pay by cash. The process is very time-consuming and irritating for them. The launch of Alipay and WeChat Pay changes the situation: Today, people can seat at home, log on their Alipay or WeChat Pay account by PC or smart phones to transfer money directly to a specific account of utilities. The process can be done within a few minutes. They even don't set out to deliberately overhaul the financial habits since the new mobile applications make life so easy. Besides, by virtue of the two payment systems, customers can go directly to its app and website to save money in their Alipay or WeChat Pay accounts and make payments with the fund in the accounts or bonded bank card. Particularly, funds are held in escrow and are released when the goods arrive in satisfactory fashion. With Alipay, people can pay not only for online purchase but also for other life expenses.

2. Changing people's investment way

In addition to online payment, people keep savings in their Alipay Yu'ebao or Tencent Wealth account, where money accrues higher interest than it does in a traditional bank account. They stop pulling out money and putting it into banks and instead keep all cash flow in the fund management accounts.

3. Enabling a easier life

Since the two payment apps were launched, many people have begun to leave their physical wallets at home and lived their lives only equipped with Alipay and WeChat Pay. By virtue of the two payment systems, a user is able to call and pay for a taxi, split the cost of lunch with friends, go shopping and purchase a beverage from a vending machine. The apps work with sound wave technology so that users don't even have to be connected to the Internet to make in-store payments.

4. Reshaping Chinese finance

China's banks have been staying in the "comfortable zone" for a long time due to the high profits from net interest and their monopoly in the financial industry. With the emergence of the new players like Alipay and WeChat Pay, people do not have to depend on the banks as much as before since some financial services like payment and investment can be done through the new tools. According to Accenture, competition from Alipay and the likes could reduce traditional bank revenues by one third by 2020 as one quarter of banks' revenues are generated from processing payments[①]. With customers' draining

---

① Laure Li, Are WePay and Alipay Going to Kill Banks? https://walkthechat.com/are-wepay-and-alipay-going-to-kill-banks/, 2015-07-26.

away, the banks have to make changes and develop their banking service, like online banking and mobile banking payment to attract and keep customers①.

Case Analysis

本案例不仅分析了我们非常熟悉的两种移动支付工具：支付宝和微信支付，而且通过多维度的对比，完整地展示了比较分析法在案例分析中的应用，并在此基础上总结出移动支付工具的出现将对中国的传统金融服务产生哪些影响。

为了使分析的对象具有可比性，本案例选择支付宝移动端（手机支付宝）和微信支付进行比较分析。就发展背景而言，2004年推出的支付宝显然具有先发优势，多年来在中国第三方支付市场份额上遥遥领先也说明了这一点。然而，如果仅就移动支付而言，手机支付宝和微信支付进入市场的时间几乎同步，均在2013年。两者均采取了双边平台商业模式，即构建一个平台，将付款方和收款方联系在一起，实现两者间的资源交换，并由此实现自身利益最大化。这种模式的一大优势就是一旦平台客户数量达到临界值，就很容易形成网络效应，从而引发平台的爆发式增长。事实上，手机支付宝和微信支付自推出以来的快速增长也说明了这一点。两种支付工具提供的服务大同小异，都包括了转账、缴费、购物、提现以及理财等与民生有关的金融服务，只不过手机支付宝在服务涉及的设备种类和币种方面更具多样性，这与支付宝早期的市场积累有关。从支付方式看，手机支付宝和微信支付也比较类似，都包括条形码、二维码以及APP嵌入式支付。但支付宝早期针对网上交易设计的现金担保支付允许买家先将货款转入支付宝账户，待收货满意后再由支付宝将货款转入卖家账户，这种机制无论对中国第三方支付体系的构建还是对中国电子商务的发展都具有举足轻重的作用。也是因为如此，今天这种机制仍然在手机支付宝的电商APP嵌入式支付中发挥重要作用，这是微信支付所不具备的。两个支付系统都是依赖背后的平台发展起来的：支付宝借助阿里巴巴和淘宝实现了增长，微信支付则依靠微信迅速占领市场。两个支付系统虽源于平台，却不囿于平台，而是向平台之外的其他领域渗透，实现了多领域和多渠道的发展。

由于各自背后平台的性质不同，两种支付系统从诞生之日其就存在差异：首先，在市场定位上，支付宝诞生的初衷是解决电商交易中的支付问题，因此它一直是以支付解决方案的定位存在的；相比之下，微信支付作为社交平台的嵌入功能，则更多地扮演"现金管理"的角色。其次，支付宝的目标客户群是活跃在阿里巴巴和淘宝网上的用户，微信支付则是面向微信用户提供相应的服务。再次，从支付场景上看，支付宝早期多应用于电子商务这种双方不见面的虚拟交易，因此其移动端服务也多是用于陌生人之间的交易；微信作为一款社交应用软件，其支付功能更多地被人们用于和家人朋友之间的交易，尤其是2014年微信红包推出以后，熟人之间收发红包

---

① E-Payment: Digital Finance Revolution-Alipay, https://managementoftechnologyjohnshopkins.wordpress.com/2015/05/03/mobile-technology-digital-finance-revolution-alipay/, 2015-05-13.

更成为潮流,加上微信友好的聊天界面让交易更具亲和力。同时,从交易金额来看,手机支付宝更多地用于大额交易(如:支付、转账等),而微信支付则更多用于小额支付。

作为中国最具影响力的两种移动支付工具,手机支付宝和微信支付之间的竞争一直很激烈,而两者的出现也对中国金融服务产生了巨大影响:它们令支付变得更加方便、高效且打破了时空限制。人们可以借助手机支付宝或微信支付轻松完成以前费时费力才能完成的支付、缴费、信用卡还款等任务;改变了人们的投资理念和投资方式,余额宝和理财通实现了低门槛、灵活而便利的理财方式;同时,两种支付系统的应用拓展令人们可以借助手机轻松完成预订酒店、呼叫出租等多样化的生活需求。更重要的是,以手机支付宝和微信支付为代表的移动支付工具的出现给传统金融机构(如:银行)带来了巨大冲击,它们对银行原有的支付、存款和理财客户的争夺迫使其通过创新与合作提升服务质量,最终带来的是整个中国金融行业服务水平的提升以及良性发展。

Section 3
Lvmama—Seizing the Long Tail of Online Travel Services
第三节 驴妈妈——抓住网上旅游服务的长尾

Key Words

1. embroil *vt.* 使卷入
2. shareware *n.* 共享软件
3. leverage *vt.* 利用杠杆作用
4. converse *vi.* 谈话
5. niche market 利基市场,即小众市场

Case

Introduction to Lvmama

Lvmama, founded in 2008, is a business-to-consumer (B2C) based e-tourism website, as well as a platform for DIY tour advisory and booking in China. The site offers DIY tour service, discount tickets, free walker service and hotel booking service. Most of the offerings are based in Asia.

In June 2015, Lvmama received 500 million yuan in series e-funding from Jinjiang International Group which is one of China's largest tourism conglomerates, best known for owning and managing over 1,600 hotels. The funding came after an 300 million yuan

($49 million) series D funding from GX Capital in October 2014[①].

With the booming of Chinese tourism, the competition is becoming even fiercer. High demands on service quality, fast-developing technologies, and flourishing Internet marketing have brought both opportunities and challenges. As a late entrant of online tourism, how does Lvmama outstand in the competition and find a suitable way differing from the first-movers like Ctrip? The answer is the long tail.

How Does Lvmama Seize the Long Tail of Online Travel Services

1. Business model

As a B2C tourism website, Lvmama positions itself as a DIY travel services provider which focuses on the later part of B2B2C value chain. Essentially, Lvmama plays a role of OTA (Online Travel Agent). Tourism in China is typically split between group tours and private DIY businesses. Considering cost and profit, most OTAs prefer group tours—the short head. Unlike them, Lvmama focuses on DIY businesses—the long tail of online travel services. Based on the long tail, Lvmama chooses the different operating and profiting model.

1) Operating model

As an OTA, Lvmama is supposed to connect resorts and individual tourists. Resorts incline to the group tours and they are not willing to provide low-price tickets for individual tourists due to the low margin on the one hand. Individual tourists are price sensitive on the other hand. How to fill in the gap between the two sides—supply and demand? Lvmama applies the theory of long tail to its operating model successfully. According to Chris Anderson, the products that are in low demand or have low sales volume can collectively make up a market share that rivals or exceeds the relatively few current bestsellers and blockbusters, but only if the store or distribution channel is large enough. In another word, it is possible that Lvmama profits from individual tourists (long tail) as long as the volume of the group is large enough. Based on the theory, Lvmama negotiates with the resorts to acquire the low-price tickets on the one hand and attracts numerous individual tourists to the resorts by virtue of the effective marketing strategies on the other hand. As a result, the resorts make profit from the individual tourists due to the economy of scale while the individual tourists enjoy the low-cost trips.

2) Profiting model

Lvmama designs its profiting model based on the long tail, which enables the revenues from the stakeholders of the long tail—individual tourists and travel service suppliers.

---

① Paul Bischoff, Lvmama Scores $80M Funding to Get a Leg up in China's Crowded Tourism Market, https://www.techinasia.com/lvmama-series-e-funding/, 2015-06-01.

Firstly, the price difference is a primary as well as stable profit source. Lvmama buys the tickets from the resorts at a low price and sells them to the customers at a higher price. The price difference between buying and selling enables Lvmama's margin. Though the tickets are sold to the customers (at a higher price), they are still cheaper than those sold offline or on other websites. The low-price tickets not only enable Lvmama to profit but help it to attract more customers. "One Person, One Ticket, Also At A Discount"—the slogan implies Lvmama's operational philosophy: enabling ordinary tourists to enjoy a low-price and DIY trip like group tour. That is why more and more individual tourists prefer Lvmama.

Secondly, the affiliation fee is another profit source. Lvmama has been exploiting the cooperation with domestic resorts. As long as a resort joins in the membership, it owns the privileges including tickets booking online and the related e-commerce supports. Particularly, it can reach the tremendous customer group directly, which enables the high efficiency of customer acquisition. Due to the privileges, many resorts are willing to pay for the membership, which brings new revenue.

Thirdly, the adverting service is also a profit source. Like many other OTAs, Lvmama provides the online advertising services for the travel service suppliers and charges them the service fees.

Finally, the smart phone apps are becoming another important profit source. Realizing the huge potentials of mobile commerce, Lvmama develops two useful apps—Lvmama Travel and E-Resorts Access. The former allows consumers to choose and purchase the travel services while the latter enables the resorts to push the real-time information (e.g. heavy traffic) to Lvmama's interface, which helps the tourists to schedule and design their trips. The frequent downloading of the two apps also brings Lvmama revenues.

2. Marketing strategies[1][2]

To capture and take advantage of the long tail of online travel services effectively, Lvmama adopts the appropriate marketing strategies:

1) Personalization. Personalization means matching of services, products, and advertising content to individual consumers. Lvmama's target group is the young individual tourists who prefer innovative, efficient and personalized services instead of group tour. To satisfy consumers' personalized need, Lvmama adopts some effective methods: firstly, the e-ticket meets consumers' demands for efficiency and low-cost. E-ticket means the tourists don't have to wait in the line to buy the physical tickets. Instead, they only order the tickets online and enter the resort by showing the confirmation text messages with QR

---

① 石章强,张洪梅:"驴妈妈:个性化与低成本如何兼得?"《经理人》,2012 年 (1): pp.110–111。
② 祁长宵:"看"驴妈妈"如何杀出旅游电商重围",《旅游纵览月刊》,2014 年 10 月。

code, which saves the cost of logistics and improve the efficiency of travel services. Secondly, Lvmama develops a mobile app—E-resorts Access which combines the backend of resorts infrastructure and Lvmama website and allows the resorts to push the real-time information (e. g. facilities maintenance) to Lvmama's interface so that the tourists can gain access to it instantly and plan or schedule their trips. Thirdly, Lvmama designs and recommends the personalized travel services. For instance, according to an individual tourist's need, Lvmama supplies the optional travel plans including schedule, route, hotels and so on.

2) Word-of-mouth marketing. Viewing the first movers' high expenses of marketing, Lvmama decided to take good advantage of word-of-mouth marketing to build its brand strength. Word-of-mouth marketing has been accepted by many merchants due to its efficient dissemination and low cost. Blog and microblog are the effective channels. Lvmama registered (on the famous) blog and microblog platforms such as Sina and actively found as well as communicated with the opinion leaders on them so as to propagate the resorts and the website. The opinion leaders' points or comments were diffused quickly and even incurred a new fashion. Realizing that the college students prefer DIY tour, Lvmama launched a campaign of "Lvmama Travel Website Promotion Ambassador on Campus" which recruits the college students and provids them training, traveling and internship. The campaign not only attracted many young persons but also improved Lvmama's penetration in college students by virtue of word-of-mouth dissemination. By 2011, the campaign had covered all the colleges in Shanghai.

3) Precision marketing. Precision marketing is directed at existing customers to encourage brand loyalty and spur buying behavior. Precision marketing relies heavily on market segmentation, a technique for breaking the market down into smaller, more specific blocks of customers with unique need. When Lvmama entered the online travel industry in 2008, the existing OTAs such as Ctrip had dominated the market and the competition had become white hot. Lvmama found the problems with the market: Firstly, the homogenization of online travel services such as flight tickets reservation led to the even fiercer competition. Secondly, the volume of group tours exceeded much that of DIY tours while the demands for DIY services were rising. Consumers called for a professional DIY tours provider to satisfy their personalized demands. Thirdly, the high price of resorts tickets caused the complaints and the loss of individual tourists. Considering these problems, Lvmama chose an appropriate market segment—DIY tours and positioned itself as a DIY travel services provider focusing on tour advisory and booking. Based on the segment, Lvmama began its businesses from the resort tickets selling. The service not only provides the consumers the low-price tickets but also brings a large individual tourists group to the resorts. As a new incomer, Lvmama can succeed not by battling competitors

directly but rather aiming at the long tail of the market and implementing precision marketing.

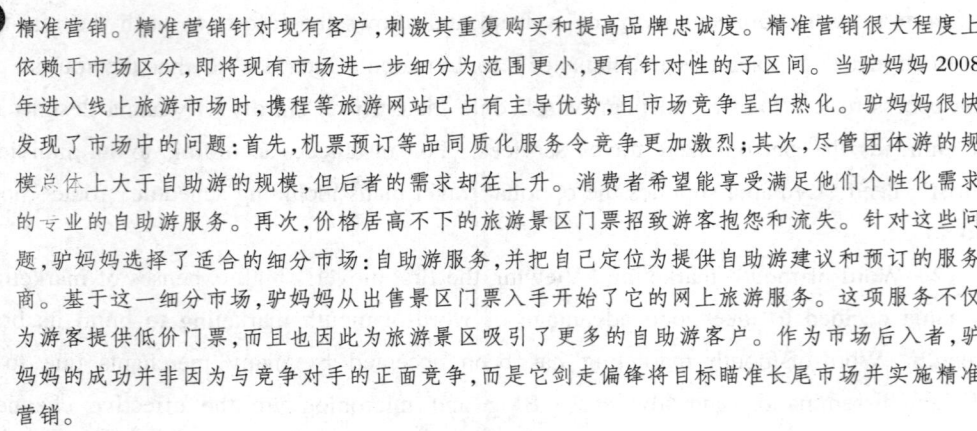
精准营销。精准营销针对现有客户，刺激其重复购买和提高品牌忠诚度。精准营销很大程度上依赖于市场区分，即将现有市场进一步细分为范围更小、更有针对性的子区间。当驴妈妈2008年进入线上旅游市场时，携程等旅游网站已占有主导优势，且市场竞争呈白热化。驴妈妈很快发现了市场中的问题：首先，机票预订等品同质化服务令竞争更加激烈；其次，尽管团体游的规模总体上大于自助游的规模，但后者的需求却在上升。消费者希望能享受满足他们个性化需求的专业的自助游服务。再次，价格居高不下的旅游景区门票招致游客抱怨和流失。针对这些问题，驴妈妈选择了适合的细分市场：自助游服务，并把自己定位为提供自助游建议和预订的服务商。基于这一细分市场，驴妈妈从出售景区门票入手开始了它的网上旅游服务。这项服务不仅为游客提供低价门票，而且也因此为旅游景区吸引了更多的自助游客户。作为市场后入者，驴妈妈的成功并非因为与竞争对手的正面竞争，而是它剑走偏锋将目标瞄准长尾市场并实施精准营销。

4) Differentiation. As a frequently-used marketing strategy, differentiation refers to the process of distinguishing a product or service from others, to make it more attractive to a particular target market. Actually, the strategy of aiming at the niche market rather than the mainstream market is a differentiation. In addition to focusing on the long tail—DIY tours, Lvmama avoids the businesses of flight tickets and hotels booking since they have been highly overlapped. The businesses offered by Lvmama are specified to the DIY tours. For example, the hotel-booking business only focuses on the hotels around the resorts. Thus, the direct competition with the dominant websites can be avoided. Besides, Lvmama is good at analyzing the industrial situation and makes the proper decision. Due to the fierce competition, many online tour websites join in the price war and decrease the prices blindly to plunder the lower-end market share. Lvmama does not follow the strategy. Instead, it aims at the upper-end market. In 2013, Lvmama launched "Feilvwan Club" aiming at the integrated travel services and communications for the upper-end members. The measures distinguish Lvmama from its competitors successfully and establish a unique brand image.

Possible Challenges Faced by Lvmama

Though Lvmama outstands from the online travel service market, the possible challenges for it can not be ignored:

1. Price competition. Though Lvmama does not follow the low-price strategies blindly, the price competition from its peers such as Tuniu may make Lvmama embroiled in an ongoing race-to-the-bottom price war. It's not only an extremely crowded market, but also the one that's growing at a rapid clip. In May 2015, Tuniu received a $500 million injection from the investors such as Jingdong, China's second-biggest e-commerce

company. And the injection enables Jingdong to become Tuniu's second biggest shareholder. In addition to the competitors including heavily funded rivals like Tuniu, Ly. com, 17U, and Yikuaiqu, Lvmama has to compete with China's online travel giants like Qunar and Ctrip, which are backed by domestic web giants Baidu and Tencent respectively. Meanwhile, Alibaba's growing number of travel merchants setting up shop on its Tmall and Taobao Marketplaces are also the potential threats[①].

2. The higher requirements of personalization. Differing from mass tourism firms, Lvmama aims at the long tail of customers—individual tourists. Due to the less universal information and diverse need of each tourist, navigating in the long tail can be confusing and intimidating. It is even more difficult for Lvmama to meet customers' need. Therefore, a challenge is how to realize the more elaborate personalization. To reach farther of the long tail, Lvmama has to build the confidence of the new customers through transparency by virtue of the more precise personalization.

3. Leveraging the long tail with social media. To increase the brand awareness, Lvmama may have to leverage the long tail with social media tools including blogs (or microblogs), discussion forums, user rating and review sites, podcasts (audio and video) and collaborative websites (such as wiki). However, an ineffective social media presence usually provides minimal benefit, as consumers have limited patience when searching through a multiplicity of small websites. The time and money costs of establishing and maintaining the social media presence can be too demanding for Lvmama that has less overhead and lacks the necessary technological skills required[②].

4. Consolidating the cooperation with the resorts. With the entry of new OTAs, Lvmama faces more pressures both from the upstream value chain—the resorts and the downstream value chain—the customers. In addition to acquiring more customers, Lvmama has to consolidate the cooperation with the resorts. Obviously, when more OTAs attempt to build their partnership with the resorts, the resorts gain more power in negotiation, which may lead to the rising transaction cost and the lost partnership. Thus, how to broaden and deepen the coordination with the resorts is a new challenge for Lvmama. When exploring the new partnership and consolidating the existing suppliers, two factors should be taken into account: 1) Resort size. Like a private company, the numeric size of a resort may be measured in the number of visitors to it, the number of employees, and revenues gained from tourists' expenditure in the resort; 2) Resort reputation. The reputation of a resort may be better considered in terms of the renown

---

① Paul Bischoff, Lvmama Scores $80M Funding to Get A Leg up in China's Crowded Tourism Market, https://www.techinasia.com/lvmama-series-e-funding/, 2015-06-01.

② Alan A. Lew, Long Tail Tourism: New Geographies for Marketing Niche Tourism Products, *Journal of Travel & Tourism Marketing*, 2008, Vol. 25(3-4).

of the resort or its attractions. Smaller resorts can benefit from the fame of the larger regions they are located within, while larger resorts and regions can build upon the fame of single attraction. A combination of well-known attractions can be quite powerful for a resort place or region, and can move it out of the tourism long tail and into its short head.

The Long Tail concept essentially defines an Internet-based marketing approach for small and medium-sized companies like Lvmama to enable them to compete in a global marketplace. The rise of DIY tours in the past few years has given rise to individual tourists, who have become the backbone of the long tail in online travel industry. Long tail has been widely acclaimed by tourism bloggers and consultants as the best model for the expanding specialty tourism economy. However, it does not guarantee the success in the niche market. Traditional business considerations and values such as hard work and devotion to one's business are still essential requirements[①].

Case Analysis

提起网上旅游服务，驴妈妈远不如携程或者去哪儿的知名度这么高。这家成立于2008年的网站既没有先发优势，也没有雄厚的资金实力，却能在竞争激烈的网上旅游市场站的一席之地，它的秘诀就是：抓住长尾。

长尾作为一种竞争策略，其核心思想就是：避开竞争激烈且几近饱和的主流市场（红海），转而专注于相对小众但潜力巨大的利基市场（蓝海）并从中发掘价值，实现利益最大化。然而，有效地抓住长尾却并非易事，驴妈妈的案例可以给我们启示。首先，驴妈妈设计了能有效整合旅游供应链上下游资源的运营模式。一方面，它与供应链上游的旅游服务商（如：旅游景点）逐一沟通，以获得成本较低的服务价格，另一方面，它大力进行宣传推广以吸引下游的消费者使用网站的服务。可以看出，驴妈妈扮演的角色与携程等旅游网站一样是旅游分销商，即通过议价，从旅游服务商处以低价获取旅游服务，然后再将其转卖给下游消费者并从中获利。然而，它与一般旅游网站最大的不同就在于：它并未将业务重点聚焦于利润更高的团体游以及商务游，而是将目标对准了个人自助旅游，即旅游市场中的"长尾"。根据安德森的理论，长尾市场所带来的利润并不亚于人们传统观念中所热衷的"短头"市场。然而，要把握如此具有吸引力的长尾市场却并非易事，因为长尾市场通常小众而分散，对企业而言意味着更高的风险和成本。为了实现盈利，驴妈妈广开财路，采取了多样化的盈利模式，通过赚取价差，收取加盟费、收取广告服务费以及开发移动应用等多种方式获取收入。不仅如此，驴妈妈还推出了组合营销策略，通过个性化、精准化以及差异化营销确保营销效果。合理的运营和盈利模式，恰当的营销策略让驴妈妈成功地抓住了网上旅游市场的"长尾"，实现了价值。

---

① Mauffette-leenders, L. A., Erskine, J. A., Leenders, M. R., *Learning with Cases* (*Fourth Edition*), Ivey Publishing, 2008.

实施长尾策略的企业很多,但成功的却寥寥无几。因此,剖析驴妈妈长尾策略成功的原因是本案例分析的第二个重点。首先,差异化的产品和服务是驴妈妈长尾策略成功的关键。既不同于一站式服务的携程网,也不同于搜索引擎式的去哪儿网,驴妈妈专门为自助游顾客量身打造包括景点门票、酒店预订以及旅游度假套餐等服务,在众多竞争对手中独树一帜,给顾客留下了深刻的印象;其次,驴妈妈为实施长尾策略选择了正确的起点。抓住市场的长尾应该从哪里入手？这是很多企业在实施该策略时所面临的主要问题。驴妈妈经过市场调查发现,旅游景区门票的市场仍是空白:自助游的旅客因为无法享受团体票优惠,不得不为门票支付更高的成本,这是旅游景点一直以来为人所诟病的重要原因。在敏锐地意识到这一市场需求之后,驴妈妈从景点门票切入,利用自身的议价优势采购低价门票,以比市场价更低的价格转卖给消费者,并提出"一个人、一张票也打折"的口号,迅速吸引了消费者。除此之外,驴妈妈通过对市场的准确分析,预测中国的旅游市场将向个性化自助游转变,并抓住这一时机一击而中;再次,创业者的经验起到了重要作用。驴妈妈的创立者洪清华在创建该网站之前已经有过两次创业经历,而且都是面向旅游市场,从而具备了旅游服务规划、设计、咨询、营销和运营等方面的丰富经验,为驴妈妈的成功奠定了基础。由此可见,对于初创企业而言,创业团队对市场的理解和把握,实现产品和服务的差异化以及准确选择切入点是驴妈妈成功实施长尾策略的原因。

Section 4
The Uber Effect—Impacts of Mobile Apps
第四节 优步效应——移动应用的影响

I Key Words

1. gratuity *n.* 小费
2. fleet *n.* 车队
3. carpool *vt./vi.* 拼车
4. rollout *n.* 首次展示
5. inclement *adj.* 险恶的,气候严酷的
6. plummet *vi.* （价格等）骤然下降
7. taxi medallion 车牌照
8. startup *n.* 初创公司

II Case

About Uber

Uber, founded in 2009, is a peer-to-peer ridesharing, taxi cab, food delivery, and transportation network company headquartered in San Francisco, California, with operations in 633 cities worldwide①. The company develops, markets and operates the Uber mobile application (app), which allows consumers with smart phones to submit a trip request which is then routed to Uber drivers who use their own cars. As of May 2018, Uber was worth an estimated $62 billion and its chief executives indicated that it might go public in 2019②.

Since its foundation, Uber has experienced a quick expansion: The company expanded into a new city each month starting in May 2011, including New York City, Chicago and Washington, D.C. Paris was the first city outside of the U.S. where Uber's service began operating in December 2011 prior to the international LeWeb Internet conference. Following a soft launch of the Uber app in the Sanlitun shopping district in March 2014, an official launch was held in Beijing, China, in mid-July 2014. The company's service expanded to other cities in China rapidly. In August 2016, Uber China, the regional subsidiary of Uber, merged with Didi Chuxing—its biggest and most formidable rival in China in a $35 billion megamerger③.

Uber's Business Model

1. Uber's serving model④

1) Pricing and payments. Uber uses a dynamic pricing model and its pricing is similar to that of metered taxis, although all hiring and payment is handled exclusively through Uber and not with the driver personally. Prices vary based on projected time and distance as well as the time of day and the supply and demand for rides at the time the ride is requested. At the end of the ride, payment is made based on the rider's pre-selected preferences, which could be credit card, Google Pay, Apple Pay, cash or some local payment methods. After the ride is over, the rider is given the option to provide a gratuity to the driver, which is also billed to the rider's payment method.

2) Surge pricing. Uber uses an automated algorithm to increase prices to "surge" price levels. It means when the demand for taxi rises, or the number of users looking for a ride increases and there aren't enough cars on the road, prices go up and riders can either wait or pay more for the ride. The increased amount to be paid by the riders depends on the surge factor in the area. The pricing mechanism responds rapidly to the changes of supply and demand in the market and attracts more drivers during times of increased rider

---

① https://en.wikipedia.org/wiki/Uber_(company)#Uber_app_software_and_services
② Dana Olsen, 2019 Could Bring Two of the Biggest VC-backed IPOs of the Decade, https://pitchbook.com/news/articles/2019-could-bring-two-of-the-biggest-vc-backed-ipos-of-the-decade, 2018-05-31.
③ Matt Weinberger, Uber to Merge with Chinese Rival Didi in $35 Billion Deal, http://www.businessinsider.com/uber-china-merges-with-didi-chuxing-2016-7, 2016-08-01.
④ CRICOS, Centre for Teaching and Learning Quick Guide, scu.edu.au/teachinglearning/download.php?doc_id=12775, 2014-12-01.

demand. Though the surge pricing is flexible, it often causes passengers to become dissatified and invites criticism when it happens as a result of holidays, inclement weather, or natural disasters.

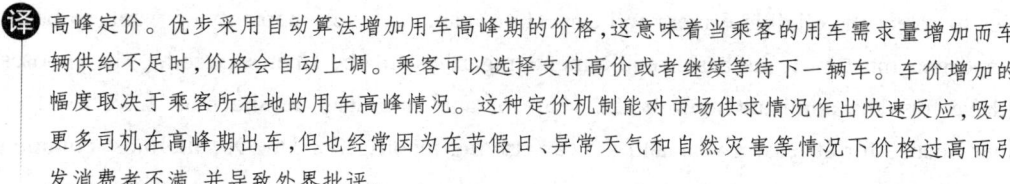
高峰定价。优步采用自动算法增加用车高峰期的价格,这意味着当乘客的用车需求量增加而车辆供给不足时,价格会自动上调。乘客可以选择支付高价或者继续等待下一辆车。车价增加的幅度取决于乘客所在地的用车高峰情况。这种定价机制能对市场供求情况作出快速反应,吸引更多司机在高峰期出车,但也经常因为在节假日、异常天气和自然灾害等情况下价格过高而引发消费者不满,并导致外界批评。

3) Rating score. With the rating system in Uber app, riders and drivers can rate each other based on their satisfaction. A low rating might diminish the availability and convenience of the service to a user. The rating system can ensure the service quality to some extent.

2. Uber's profiting model[①]

Uber takes 20% of total cost of ride and rest of the money is kept by driver. Due to the threats from the rivals like Ola, a mobile app for personal transportation in India, Uber is in heavy need of drivers to increase the fleet and even gives away 2k or 3k to each driver per day if they complete 10 trip in a day.

Though Uber did not make profit initially it does not influence its business value since the investors know they need to spend some to gain a lot later on. Obviously, Uber adopts the business model of two-sided platform. The most important thing for a platform-based startup is user base, traffic to the app and brand awareness. Initially, to increase the client and brand value Uber has been giving many offers to increase the amount of drivers and cars. Once the amount of user groups reaches a critical mass, the network effect can be triggered which may result in the dramatic growth of the businesses. Analogically, Uber will stop all this discount and extra payment to driver as long as it successfully establishes its brand strength and becomes a habit for people to use it. Besides, as client base increases, the valuation of the company goes up and more money comes at very high value. So when the company sells its small stake it earns many folds because of high valuation.

SWOT Analysis of Uber[②]

Strengths

1. High brand awareness. Due to its rapid expansion worldwide, Uber has built its brand strength successfully. For many consumers, Uber is the first priority when they have

---

① Chirag Shah, How does Uber earn their profits?, http://www.quora.com/How-does-Uber-earn-their-profits
② Jim Makos, SWOT analysis for UBER, http://pestleanalysis.com/swot-analysis-for-uber/, 2015-03-11.

the riding demand, which enables a solid customer base.

2. High standard of service, verifying drivers and cars. Uber makes the detailed and strict standard of drivers and cars for all its services like UberX, Uber Black and so on in order to select the eligible drivers and cars. For example, every person who wants to be an Uber driver must meet the basic requirements regardless of the Uber service he/she chooses to drive for: the applicant must be 21 years of age or older; he/she must have a U. S. driver license for at least a year and a clean driving record. For UberX, the most common service for requesting a ride to be picked up as well as a low cost option (cheaper than a taxi), the car must have 4 full, independently opening doors and pass the Uber car inspection. The detailed and strict requirements ensure the quality of Uber's services.

3. Unlimited fleet of vehicles. Due to the regular taxi service regulations and operation cost, the traditional taxi companies usually have a limit fleet of vehicles, which constraints its expansion. Uber, as a two-sided platform of matching transportation need, does not need to own its fleet, instead, it attracts drivers having vehicles and passengers on board and facilitates their interactions. As a result, the Uber has an unlimited fleet of vehicles, which is an obvious advantage over the traditional taxi companies.

4. Operational cost is relatively low. For the traditional taxi companies, recruitment, training and salary are the heavy load for their operation. Due to its business model, Uber does not hire drivers. Instead, it provides a platform for all the drivers to seek for potential passengers and gains commission. This model helps Uber not only save cost but also avoid the responsibilities toward employees. Besides, Uber is an online company which saves the cost of physical stores.

5. Supporting multiple payment methods. Uber app supports multiple payment methods like ApplePay, cash and so on. Particularly, cashless payment system not only enables the convenient and efficient payment, but also enables Uber to track and choose highly rated drivers to make sure the service quality. Another remarkable benefit lies in that data generated by the payment system helps Uber to capture customers' need accurately to provide the personalized services.

6. Dual rating system boosting trust and safety. After each transaction, the driver and the passenger can rate each other based on the performance during the process of service. The mechanism provides not only the supervision on the transaction, but also the reference for the future users.

7. Flexbile work system for drivers. Unlike the employees in the traditional taxi companies, Uber's drivers have the flexible work hours and can even choose to be a part-time employee. Drivers can also reject unwanted clients. The benefits attracts lots of eligible drivers to join in Uber.

8. Lower prices compared to traditional taxi operators. According to a data scientist in

the U. K, Uber's fares can be cheaper than taking a regular taxi. That's especially true for longer trips that cost more than $35. Generally, Uber is the more economical choice outside of large cities①.

Weaknesses

1. It is difficult to improve users' loyalty. Keeping the customers is a big challenge for all the platforms. For example, most users choose Uber due to its low price and convenience. There lacks the real connection between Uber and its users. Besides, due to the multi-homing characteristic of platform, users' incentive to remain with Uber is low. That is, once there emerges a new rival with even lower price, the users can leave if Uber can not find an effective way to improve customers' loyalty.

2. The privacy concerns. Uber records almost all the trip information of customers like where a customer gets the taxi from and where he/she goes with Uber. The information may cause privacy problems. Not only consumers, Uber's drivers also possibly suffer the privacy intrusion like the data breach in 2014.

3. Surge pricing. The surge pricing system which Uber has been proud of also brings problems to the ride-hailing app. Surge pricing is automated and meant to attract more drivers to areas of high demand but it does not exactly strengthens Uber's community-building image. For example, during New Year's Eve 2011, prices were as high as seven times normal rates, causing outrage.

Opportunities

1. Passengers' dissatisfaction with traditional cab services. Passengers have complaint the traditional taxi services for a long time due to its high prices and long waiting time. Besides, the services quality can not be ensured due to the taxi monopoly. Some passengers even experienced the service like "we'll get to you when, and treat you how, we please". As a result, people call for the new ride service with lower price, higher convenience and flexibility, which provides an opportunity for Uber.

2. The huge potential of ride-hailing service in some countries and regions. Uber can exploit new and big markets in countries like India where taxi services are inconvenient and expensive. It can also tap growing markets in suburban areas where taxi services are not available.

3. The rising valuation of Uber which might appeal more investors. As a result, Uber will have more money to operate like improving service quality and spending more on propagation.

4. Emergence of cheaper electric cars. It will reduce the cost and increase the driver's

---

① Aimee Picchi, Uber vs. Taxi: Which Is Cheaper?, https://www.consumerreports.org/personal-finance/uber-vs-taxi-which-is-cheaper/, 2016-06-10.

profit margin and in turn solve the problems of losing drivers. The biggest savings will be in fuel. A gallon of regular gas today costs an average of $2.70, while residential electricity costs only average $0.11 per kilowatt hour①.

Threats

1. The business model is imitated. After witnessing Uber's success, many entrepreneur began to imitate the business model based on a two-sided platform. The competitors like DiDi Chuxing and Ola emerged sequentially and even surpassed it. For example, DiDi Chuxing was thought to take over the world after it purchased Uber China in 2016. Besides, after viewing the trend of more people moving to cities and abandoning their cars, the traditional car companies like Ford and General Motors even have leaned into the "mobility" trend to see where it would take them. For example, Ford spun off its own Limted Liability Company and General Motors launched a car-sharing company②.

2. Drivers' rising dissatisfaction. To main its customer-centric approach, Uber charges a very low price which leads to the low-profit margin for drivers. According to a survey in early 2017, less than half of Uber drivers said they were satisfied with their experience. Uber drivers averaged $15.68 per hour, while Lyft drivers made an average of $17.50③. Though Uber said it was creating thousands of flexible jobs, it was still critized due to the temporary, unstable, and benefits-free employment. Meanwhile, the increasing competition probably ultimately decreases prices. This will discourage drivers from joining in the startup and lead to the loss of passengers. As a result, Uber's revenues will decline.

3. The legal bans from different countries and regions. Some national or regional regulations still ban Uber from operating, which prevents the local passengers from ordering an Uber on the trip way. By September 2017, about ten countries and regions like Italy, Australia and Vancouver had outright banned the leading taxi app④. Besides, Uber has been fined for skirting regulations many times in the countries like Germany, France and India.

4. The legal and ethical problems with the vehicle sharing. In May 2015, a local Uber driver was arrested and accused of sexually assaulting a passenger in Vaughan,

---

① Jamie Page Deaton, Are Electric Cars Cheaper to Run? https://auto.howstuffworks.com/are-electric-cars-cheaper-to-run.htm

② Andrew J. Hawkins, Why Car Companies Are Trying to Imitate Uber and Lyft, https://www.theverge.com/2017/1/18/14230040/ford-gm-maven-mobility-uber-lyft-ces-detroit-2017, 2017-01-18.

③ Laura Sydell, Survey Finds Lyft Drivers Happier Than Uber, Though Pay Has Declined, https://www.npr.org/sections/alltechconsidered/2017/01/21/510479642/survey-finds-lyft-drivers-happier-than-uber-though-pay-has-declined, 2017-01-21.

④ Anna Rhodes, Uber: Which Countries Have Banned the Controversial App, http://www.independent.co.uk/travel/news-and-advice/uber-ban-countries-where-world-taxi-app-europe-taxi-us-states-china-asia-legal-a7707436.html, 2017-09-22.

Canada. A driver in New Delhi of India was charged with raping a female rider in December 2015. In early 2017, there were reports of sexual harassment and a lawsuit over allegedly stolen autonomous vehicle technology, which caused Uber' losing 200,000 passengers in only one weekend①. Besides, as new markets and drivers are joining, fraud and scandals are also increasing. For a business model based on trusting strangers, violent crime is a deal-breaker.

The Uber effect

Since Uber's launch, several other companies have copied its business model, a trend that has come to be referred to as "Uberification". Uber has penetrated into people's lives and social economy. Its impacts on passengers, drivers, taxi industry and even economy are becoming more significant. How will the mobile app and its business model change people's life and economy?

1. For taxi industry

The utilization of Uber has led to the taxi medallion prices' plummeting in some cities. For example, in 2013, after hitting an all-time high of $1.3 million in April, the price of a taxi medallion fell by nearly a quarter of its value to roughly $840,000②. People attribute the dropping price of yellow taxi medallion greatly to the growth of the ride-sharing apps like Uber. Since the competition from ride-sharing apps leads to falling price, some people even anticipated that Uber would replace the conventional taxi. Though the core and the majority of people still choose hand-hailing, but for the population that definitely rely solely on smart phones to get around Uber is undoubtedly attractive.

The popularity of Uber makes people's life more convenient and efficient on the one hand and threats the existing industry on the other hand. It is not surprising that the taxi industry tries to stop this progress and any effort to offer more drivers better earning opportunities.

2. For consumers and drivers

As a "ride-sharing" company that operates by sharing consumers' information with drivers through a mobile app, Uber owns two user groups—consumers (demanders) and drivers (suppliers). Therefore, the Uber effect also involves the two groups.

1) For consumers

Uber's app not only efficiently connects ride-seekers to drivers in hundreds of cities but also invokes the imitated apps covering more fields of people's lives. Among the range of what are sometimes called "on-demand mobile services", there are Uber-like apps for

---

① Team Wall Street Survivor, Uber: The Road to a $69 Billion Valuation, http://blog.wallstreetsurvivor.com/2017/07/17/uber-road-69-billion-valuation/, 2017-07-17.

② Emily Caruthers, Is Uber Crushing the Taxi Industry?, https://www.cnbc.com/2015/03/03/is-uber-crushing-the-taxi-industry.html, 2015-03-03.

groceries, babysitters and valet parking①. Though the "It's like Uber for X" imitations have become an eye-rolling cliché, they do enable an easier life.

2) For drivers

First of all, Uber creates opportunities for the individual drivers to gain income, which is the primary factor that Uber attracts so many drivers. By using Uber app, drivers become available for client requests that are designed to come from clients closest to them. An Uber driver can expect: immediate ride requests, instant billing, direct client communication and a supplement to the existing business. According to a new NerdWallet study in 2015, Uber drivers in six major U.S. cities received paid holidays and health care benefits worth an average of $5,500 a year, plus thousands more in mileage reimbursement, if the company provided them with the same benefits as its full-time employees②.

Though benefiting from Uber, the drivers are also at the risk of privacy intrusion. Uber suffered a data breach on May 13, 2014. The size of this breach is significant in that it affects roughly 50,000 drivers across the United States. The data which was accessed, by an unknown third party, contain names and drivers licenses③.

3. For work

On-demand apps like Uber aren't just changing the way consumers buy products and services, they are also fundamentally changing work. Firstly, the on-demand platforms bring not only new opportunities for independent contractors but also the pressures since the platforms force everyone to compete in the open market. For a person who has a rare, valuable, easy to describe skill, he or she can do very well in this economy. Otherwise, the advantages of it are not that clear relative to having a regular job. Secondly, on-demand apps like Uber empowers workers to have more flexibility and freedom—they can choose their own hours, their own rate and choose where and when they work. As a result, the need for "contingent" workers will keep growing. Because freelance workers give companies more flexibility and enable them to respond to upturns and downturns more quickly.

4. For environment

Uber suffers some criticisms due to its possible negative impacts on the environment. Some experts even suggest that administrative should issue more rigorous regulations if

---

① Kate Allen, The Uber Effect—How on-demand Apps Are Changing Our Habits and Our Economy, http://www.thestar.com/news/insight/2015/05/22/the-uber-effect-how-on-demand-apps-are-changing-our-habits-and-our-economy.html, May 2015.

② Jeffrey Chu, Uber Drivers Could Gain Thousands in Pay, Benefits as Full-time Employees, https://www.nerdwallet.com/blog/auto-insurance/uber-drivers-gain-thousands-employee-benefits/, 2015-08-11.

③ Dave Lewis, Uber Suffers Data Breach Affecting 50,000, Forbes, 2015-02-28.

there is evidence that the proliferation of new services provided by Uber leads to chaos on the streets. Despite the criticisms, Uber has long billed itself as a ride-sharing company that can reduce the number of cars on the road. Uber's goal is to replace private car ownership with driverless vehicles that arrive on demand.

Case Analysis

在打车软件风行的时候，优步作为其中的先锋吸引了无数人的目光。从商业模式来看，优步仍然属于典型的双边平台模式：吸引司机和乘客在平台上进行车辆供求的自由匹配并从中获取佣金。这种模式一方面为乘客提供了更加便利廉价的出租车服务，另一方面也为司机提供了更加灵活的工作模式，而优步也通过向司机收取20%的佣金赚取了可观的利润。正因为如此，这家企业才能在成立之后的短短几年之间成长为市值超过60亿美金，覆盖全球600多个城市的知名平台型企业。除了平台机制和佣金模式之外，优步的定价模式也独树一帜：它采取动态定价模式。除了根据行程和时间计费之外，优步会在用车高峰期基于系统自动算法采取"浮动定价"，乘客如果想叫车，可以支付更高的价格或者等待下一辆车。浮动定价对市场供求关系反应更加迅速，也可以吸引更多的司机在高峰期提供服务，以缓解用车紧张的问题。

优步这种基于共享经济的模式自推出以来既收获了关注和赞誉，也备受争议。完整的SWOT分析有助于我们更好地了解这家企业及其商业模式。首先，优步的优势可以归纳为：低成本、便利性以及高质量。优步的双边平台模式吸引乘客和司机在平台上自由进行供求匹配，一方面降低了双方的交易成本；另一方面也让优步无需雇佣全职司机即可拥有"无限扩大"的车队，大大降低了人力资源成本。便利性则表现在行程开始前和结束后：消费者在App中输入用车信息（如：时间地点）即可快速找到系统匹配的司机，并等待接驾；司机也可以随时获取最近的用车需求信息并决定是否接受订单。这种方式不仅解决了以往乘客打车难的问题，也减少了司机的"空车率"。行程结束后，乘客可以选择多种方式支付车费，非常便捷。为了保证服务质量，优步不仅对司机及其车辆有严格的审核制度，而且通过双向评分机制激励司机提高服务质量，也可以规范司机和乘客在行车过程中的行为。其次，优步的劣势也比较明显：平台本身的多属性给优步提高用户忠诚度造成了困难，尤其是在欧乐（印度）、滴滴打车（中国）等打车软件争夺市场的情况下，要提高用户粘性成为其面临的一大挑战。另外，优步引以为傲的"浮动价格"机制因为导致用车高峰期价格过高而令消费者望而却步，也影响了优步"亲民"的品牌形象。同时，平台上的数据安全问题也造成部分用户的担忧。优步必须寻找有效的方法克服这些劣势。幸运的是，消费者长期以来对处于垄断地位的出租车公司的服务质量和模式的不满，移动互联技术的迅速普及，更加节能环保的电动汽车的问世以及投资者对优步的乐观估值都为优步未来的发展提供了良好的机遇。当然，过去几年中发生的乘客被骚扰甚至被侵犯的事件一度将优步推上了风口浪尖，而面对日益激烈的竞争，优步不得不降低车费，结果导致司机流失，加上不少国家相继出台对共享汽车的限制和禁令都可能成为优步未来发展道路上的障碍。

尽管优步面临不少问题，但必须承认，它的出现对整个出租车行业、乘客的打车方式、司机的工作方式以及自然环境都造成了一定的影响。优步仍然在继续扩张，面对自身的劣势和外部的威胁，它需要寻找新的发展路径，以保持竞争力。

Section 5
Case Analysis Methodology—Comparative Analysis
第五节　案例分析方法解析——比较分析法

▶ What Is Comparative Analysis?

The item-by-item comparison of two or more comparable alternatives, processes, products, qualifications, sets of data, systems, or the like is necessary. In accounting, for example, changes in a financial statement's items over several accounting periods may be presented together to detect the emerging trends in the company's operations and results.

Comparative analysis mentioned here is a method used for case study rather than Qualitative Comparative Analysis (QCA) which is used for analyzing data sets by listing and counting all the combinations of variables observed in the data set, and then applying the rules of logical inference to determine which descriptive inferences or implications the data supports. Unlike QCA used for statistics, comparative analysis here is adopted when two or more objectives need to be described and analyzed in case study. It requires choosing two (or more) objectives (e. g. firms) with analogous or opposite situations from different aspects and concluding from the comparison.

▶ Why Comparative Analysis?

The primary reason for comparative analysis is the explanatory interest of gaining a better understanding of features, relationships or processes involved in a case.

The strength of comparative analysis as a research design is its ability to introduce additional explanatory objectives and make the comparison between the objectives, which enables a more comprehensive and deep understanding for the case. It requires the commensurability of concepts across cases (e. g. terms like "environmental regulation" must have consistent meanings so we are not comparing apples and oranges).

How to Make a Comparative Analysis?

Generally, a complete comparative analysis is composed of the following elements[①]:

1. Frame of reference. This is the context within which you place the two objects you plan to compare and contrast. It is the umbrella under which you have grouped them. The frame of reference may consist of a business model, technology, customer group or problem; a group of similar things from which you extract two for special attention. The best frames of reference are constructed from specific sources rather than your own thoughts or observations. Most assignments tell you exactly what the frame of reference should be, and most courses supply sources for constructing it. If you encounter an assignment that fails to provide a frame of reference, you must come up with one on your own. A case analysis without such a context would have no angle on the material, no focus or frame for the writer to propose a meaningful argument.

2. Grounds for comparison. Let's say you're analyzing a case of global food distribution, and you've chosen to compare apples and oranges. Why these particular fruits? Why not pears and bananas? The rationale behind your choice, the grounds for comparison, lets your reader or audience know why your choice is deliberate and meaningful, not random.

3. Comparison. In a compare-and-contrast case, the analysis depends on how the two things you've chosen to compare actually relate to one another. In the most common compare-and-contrast case—one focusing on differences. Whether your analysis focuses primarily on difference or similarity, you need to make the relationship between A and B clear in your analysis. This relationship is at the heart of any compare-and-contrast case.

Besides, there are some guidelines which help you to finish a qualified comparative analysis:

1. Background introduction. You need to provide the basic introduction to the objects to be compared, like the name, foundation, businesses and so on.

2. Comparison. This is the key part of a comparative analysis in which you are required to compare the objects from different aspects. Usually, a beginner may feel confused because it is difficult to choose the aspects for comparison. The followings are the options you can choose in comparison analysis:

1) Enterprise operation;
2) Marketing strategies (e.g. pricing, promotion, ads);
3) Procurement and logistics (supply chain);
4) Technology (such as information system)/products;

[①] Kerry Walk, How to Write a Comparative Analysis, http://writingcenter.fas.harvard.edu/pages/how-write-comparative-analysis, 1998.

5) Financial analysis;
6) Business credit;
7) Other related aspects.

3. Conclusion. This is the last part of the comparative analysis. Some students ignore the part since it is the end and they usually end the part with several short sentences randomly. Actually, conclusion is important because it helps to summarize or emphasize your key points. A good conclusion is able to glorify your case analysis and make a perfect stop sign for your work. What can be involved in conclusion? A summarization, problem solution, suggestion or prediction can be included in you conclusion.

Summary (本章小结)

Undoubtedly, e-commerce has experienced a rapid development since its emergence. Particularly, in the last decade, the new business models and technologies related to e-commerce has boomed and changed the traditional economic and social structure. In the next decade, where is e-commerce going? And how will it influence our lives? This chapter focuses on describing what e-commerce will be like in the future. Along with the applications of new technologies and business models, some new development trends are going to dominate e-commerce including closer integration of the sources online and offline, focusing on long tail, platform or ecological cycle, growth of mobile commerce, rising applications of new technologies in e-commerce and increased customer care.

Alipay, launched in 2004 by Alibaba Group, originated from a third-party online payment platform. After the ten years development, it has evolved into a top digital finance platform covering online financial services such as payment, investment and so on. WeChat Pay is a digital wallet service incorporated into WeChat, a social network platform launched by Tencent in August 2013. It allows users to perform mobile payments and send money between contacts. Though they supply the similar services, their positioning, target customers and market share, application scenario, and supportive platforms behind are different. The emergence of the two payment tools is influencing the traditional financial services by changing people's payment method and investment way, enabling a easier life and reshaping Chinese finance.

Lvmama is a business-to-consumer (B2C) based e-tourism website, as well as a platform for DIY tour advisory and booking in China. As an online travel agent, Lvmama's particularity lies in that it aims at the private DIY businesses (long tail) rather than the group tours (short head). Though Lvmama makes the initial success in seizing the long tail of online travel services, it has to face some challenges including price war, the higher requirements of personalization, leveraging the long tail with social media, balancing between affiliations and relative ownerships, and consolidating the cooperation with the resorts.

As an American international transportation network company, Uber launched a mobile app, which allows consumers with smartphones to submit a trip request which is then routed to Uber drivers who use their own cars. By now, Uber is such a typical example of successful mobile commerce that a trend "Uberification" has emerged. Part of Uber's success can be attributed to its innovation in serving model (e.g. surge pricing) and profiting model (e.g. Uber takes 20% of total cost of ride and rest of the money is kept by driver). As an e-commerce company, Uber still have its own strengths (e.g. high standard of service), weaknesses (e.g. the idea can be easily imitated), opportunities (e.g. new and big markets) and threats (e.g. some legal regulations probably ban Uber from operating). Though some problems exist with Uber, its impacts on consumers, drivers, workers and environment can not be ignored.

This chapter introduces a new case analysis methodology—comparative analysis. Unlike QCA used for statistics, comparative analysis here is adopted when two or more objectives need to be described and analyzed in case study. It requires choosing two (or more) objectives (e.g. firms) with analogous or opposite situations from different aspects and concluding from the comparison. Comparative analysis helps us to gain a better understanding of features, relationships or processes involved in a case. A complete comparative analysis includes three elements: frame of reference, grounds for comparison and comparison. In order to finish your comparative analysis, you can follow the structure of background introduction, comparison and conclusion.

 Exercises & Tasks（练习与任务）

▶ *Exercises*

1. How do you describe e-commerce in the future?
2. Compare Alipay and WeChatPay from different aspects.
3. How does Lvmama seize the long tail of online travel service?
4. How do you describe the Uber effect?

▶ *Tasks*

Make a comparative analysis of two e-commerce enterprises and prepare a 20-minute presentation which should include:

1. Background introduction to the enterprises;
2. Compare the two firms in different aspects like business model, marketing strategies and so on;
3. Conclusion.

图书在版编目(CIP)数据

电子商务案例分析:中文、英文/王丹萍编著. —上海:复旦大学出版社,2018.9
(通用财经类系列)
ISBN 978-7-309-13822-1

Ⅰ.①电… Ⅱ.①王… Ⅲ.①电子商务-案例-分析-高等学校-教材-汉、英 Ⅳ.①F713.36

中国版本图书馆 CIP 数据核字(2018)第 177048 号

电子商务案例分析
王丹萍 编著
责任编辑/戚雅斯

复旦大学出版社有限公司出版发行
上海市国权路 579 号   邮编:200433
网址: fupnet@fudanpress.com   http://www.fudanpress.com
门市零售: 86-21-65642857   团体订购: 86-21-65118853
外埠邮购: 86-21-65109143   出版部电话: 86-21-65642845
常熟市华顺印刷有限公司

开本 787×1092 1/16 印张 21 字数 437 千
2018 年 9 月第 1 版第 1 次印刷

ISBN 978-7-309-13822-1/F·2484
定价: 45.00 元

如有印装质量问题,请向复旦大学出版社有限公司出版部调换。
版权所有   侵权必究